Praise for Richard Ellis's

On Thin Ice

"[Ellis's] thorough discussion of the polar bear in history and literature and his concise description of its physiology serve as a background to a powerful plea for the survival of one of the most imposing animals."
—*St. Louis Post-Dispatch*

"Masterful. . . . Ellis relieves the more painful passages . . . with fascinating details about polar bear biology and behavior."
—*The Courier-Journal* (Louisville)

"Through [Ellis's] eyes, the ice bear becomes more than a sacrificial symbol; it becomes a vital part of the mental and physical landscape we inhabit."
—*Los Angeles Times*

"Ellis is a master. . . . If you're looking for a complete digest of the history of human–polar bear relations, there's nobody better."
—*The New York Times Book Review*

"In *On Thin Ice* Richard Ellis . . . paints a natural history of the icon of the north, the polar bear. Well-versed in the complicated history and politics of whaling, he describes the long tradition of Arctic explorers who proved themselves by taking on the white bear."
—*The Economist*

"Chatty and thoughtful."
—*The National Interest*

"A memorable and important book about a magnificent animal that now seems doomed to die before our very eyes."
—*The Globe and Mail* (Toronto)

"[Ellis's] newest book captivated me. . . . Ellis covers the wide range of the polar bear, which recognizes no national boundaries while searching for food, mates, and shelter at the top of the world, and outlines the difficulties in protecting an animal whose populations straddle parts of five countries. . . . I found it hard to put down."
—Susan Meadows, *Santa Fe New Mexican*

"This is a thoughtful and well-researched book about the beast of the decade: the beast of the new millennium. . . . Ellis does his best to allow the bears to speak for themselves."   —*The Times* (London)

"It's disturbing to learn just how threatened the polar bear is by the effects of global warming and the melting of ice packs. Ellis offers a detailed look at the lifestyle of Earth's largest predator."
—*The Sacramento Bee*

"If Ellis does not have all the answers, he certainly has a clear vision of all the problems."   —*The Anniston Star* (Alabama)

"An extensive portrayal of impressions, interactions and impacts of humans upon the polar bear. . . . Fascinating." —*Winnipeg Free Press*

Richard Ellis

On Thin Ice

Richard Ellis is the author of more than twenty books.
He is also a celebrated marine artist whose paintings
have been exhibited in museums and galleries around the
world. He has written and illustrated articles for numerous magazines, including *Audubon*, *National Geographic*,
Discover, *Smithsonian*, and *Scientific American*. He lives in
New York City.

www.richardellis.info

On Thin Ice

On Thin Ice

THE CHANGING WORLD
OF THE POLAR BEAR

Richard Ellis

VINTAGE BOOKS
A DIVISION OF RANDOM HOUSE, INC.
NEW YORK

Grateful acknowledgment is made to *The Wall Street Journal*
for permission to reprint excerpts from "The Polar Bear
Express" (*The Wall Street Journal*, January 28, 2008),
copyright © 2008 by Dow Jones & Company, Inc. All rights
reserved worldwide. License number 2261430336592. Reprinted
by permission of *The Wall Street Journal*.

The Library of Congress has cataloged the Knopf edition as follows:
Ellis, Richard.
On thin ice : the changing world of the polar bear / by Richard Ellis.
p. cm.
1. Polar bear.   2. Polar bear—Effect of human beings on.
3. Global warming.   4. Global environmental change.   I. Title.
QL737.C27E47 2009
599.786—dc22   2009020017

Vintage ISBN: 978-0-307-45464-5

Author photograph courtesy of the Explorers Club
Book design by Wesley Gott

www.vintagebooks.com

Printed in the United States of America
10   9   8   7   6   5   4   3   2   1

Even as I speak, the very last polar bear may be dying of hunger on account of climate change, on account of us. And I will sure miss the polar bears. Their babies are so warm and cuddly and trusting, just like ours.

—Kurt Vonnegut
Armageddon in Retrospect,
2008

Contents

On Thin Ice

I

Introduction

It was about 6:00 a.m. on July 18, 1994. I was in my little cabin aboard the Russian icebreaker *Kapitan Dranitsyn,* heading for the North Pole. I was a lecturer representing the American Museum of Natural History, to talk to the paying guests about Arctic mammalian wildlife,

The Russian nuclear icebreaker Yamal *leads* Kapitan Dranitsyn *toward the North Pole, July 1994.*

including seals, whales, walruses, and whatever else showed up. François Vuilleumier, the Swiss-born AMNH curator of ornithology, would identify and discuss the various gulls, terns, jaegers, and geese that we encountered en route. Our AMNH group shared the expedition with one from Harvard's Museum of Comparative Zoology, led by the museum's director, Jim McCarthy. An announcement came over the PA system that a "polar bear is close to the ship." As I rushed to get dressed—we were near the North Pole, and running out in a T-shirt and shorts was not an option—I thought about how extraordinary this was. We had already spotted a couple of polar bears, but they were so far away, and white against a backdrop of snow and ice, that it was usually a case of: "There . . . over that little ridge . . . no, not that one, the bluish one with the pile of ice in front of it . . . see that white thing moving . . . that's the bear." I was wearing a parka, snow pants, and boots, and I'd stuffed five rolls of film in my pockets for my Minolta 35mm camera with a 35/300 zoom lens. The cabins on the *Dranitsyn* were stacked below the bridge in the forward superstructure—somebody once described the 434-foot-long icebreaker as "a block of flats on a barge"—so getting to the foredeck required hustling down five flights

From the deck of a ship, polar bears are most often seen at a distance, making their way across the frozen landscape.

Standing on his hind legs, waiting for crewmen to throw him another slice of bread, was a full-grown polar bear.

of stairs. I reached the foredeck level, opened the door, and got smacked in the face by the early-morning Arctic cold.

As I stepped out on deck, I saw nothing but ice, a vast white landscape interrupted only by an occasional flash of pale aquamarine where the ice had broken, cracked, or melted. Where two rafts had come together, pressure ridges formed into crumbled mounds of broken ice that rose above the otherwise colorless, water-level landscape. The sky mirrored the cold, dull monochrome of the icy plain surrounding us. A large group of people were clustered at the forward port rail, obviously looking at something. I pushed my way to the rail and looked down. Standing on the ice on his hind legs, waiting for crewmen to throw him another slice of bread, was a full-grown polar bear.

We had just left Franz Josef Land, an unoccupied archipelago in the northeastern Barents Sea, north of Novaya Zemlya, and 600 miles from the North Pole. In 1872, the Austrian explorers Karl Weyprecht and Julius Payer, seeking the Northeast Passage in the *Admiral Tegetthoff*, became trapped in the pack ice at Novaya Zemlya and drifted for a year, finally finding land in August 1873. (A replica of the *Tegetthoff*, built by

To this day, I cannot figure out how I got this shot. I was looking straight down on the bear from at least twenty feet.

an Austrian film crew and then abandoned, remains on the ice, a skeletal contrast to the rumbling behemoths in which we were heading for the pole.) Weyprecht and Payer had accidentally discovered a previously unknown group of islands, which they named Franz Josef Land after their emperor. After spending a year exploring the islands, they abandoned their ship and journeyed in a small boat for ninety-six days to Novaya Zemlya. Fridtjof Nansen tried to reach the pole in 1893 by drifting in the specially reinforced *Fram*, but when he found himself heading in the wrong direction, he left the ship with Hjalmar Johansen and attempted to reach his goal by sledge. They had to turn back, and spent the winter of 1896 in a stone hut with a walrus-skin roof on Franz Josef Land. During his three-year stay, Nansen became the first man to map this complicated collection of islands. In 1926 Franz Josef Land was annexed by the Soviet Union, and remote weather stations were erected.

When the bear got tired of the bread—or more likely, when the crewmen got tired of throwing it—he resumed his normal all-fours position and began to circle the ship. We were on the foredeck, some thirty feet above the bear, so he paid no attention to us, just walking slowly, swinging his head, and sniffing the ice. As he changed his position, the angle of the light also changed, so our photographs would appear to show any number of different bears walking in any number of different landscapes, but in fact there was only one bear. After about half an hour, he lost interest and wandered off, which gave us a great opportunity to photograph a polar bear from the rear. As we watched

The bear walks away from the photographers. Although there was only one bear that day, different angles of light made it look as if there were a lot of different animals.

the bear depart, we realized that we had just had a rare and wonderful experience: we had seen one of nature's most spectacular predators; we were able to photograph a dangerous wild animal at absolutely no risk. (At other times on this voyage, when we stopped—or were stopped by the ice—and took a walk, we were always accompanied by a Russian sailor with a rifle.)

We were following another icebreaker, the nuclear-powered *Yamal,* which could summon 75,000 horsepower to our puny 24,000, and could therefore break more ice than we could. Unlike the South Pole, which is located in the middle of the Antarctic Continent, the North Pole is actually under water. Antarctica is a huge rocky landmass, covered by an ice sheet that may be as much as three miles thick, but here in the North, there is only water in a corresponding location. The North Polar ice cap accumulates every winter, a direct result of the Arctic Ocean freezing. The ice can be as much as twelve feet thick, and icebreakers do not plow through it, but rather ride up on it, relying on the weight of the steel-strengthened bow to break it—(*Yamal,* for example, displaces 23,000 tons)—thus creating a path which allows the ship to perform the same feat over and over again. There were times when *Yamal* failed to make a path and had to come about to try a different location. In a driving snowstorm, on July 21, three days after we saw the bear, *Yamal* sounded her whistle to announce that she had arrived at 90°00'N: the North Pole. The passengers dressed warmly and disembarked for a picnic. We had borscht, barbecued meats, lots of potatoes, and a generous supply of champagne and vodka for the celebratory toasts. Of course there is no "pole" there, but enterprising crew members had brought along a bright red metal pole with a banner atop it that said NORTH POLE 90 NORTH, and everybody took the opportunity to pose with it for a photograph.

By 1994, according to my calculations, the total number of people that had ever been to the North Pole, including explorers (by land, sea, and snowmobile), icebreaker crews and passengers, and submariners, was around 2,800. The passengers of *Yamal* and *Kapitan Dranitsyn* were therefore in very exalted company, and as we stood around congratulating ourselves for our singular feat of "exploration," a few hardy Russian crew members began enlarging the hole in the ice where the bow of *Yamal* had actually reached the pole. In addition to our shipboard triumph, we were going to be offered another opportunity for exclusive celebrity: we could go for a swim at the North Pole. In 1975, Canadian diver/doctor Joe MacInnis had taken England's Prince Charles on a scuba dive at the North Pole, but that was for TV. Our swim was for personal glory. One at a time, those of us who opted for the plunge removed our outer clothing and stripped down to our skivvies, and a great hawser was tied around our waists to make sure we could be hauled out in case we panicked and got trapped under the ice. I jumped in feet first, yowled from the shock of the ice-cold water, and was yanked out immediately. Russian sailors, who didn't seem to mind the cold and were wearing nothing more than skimpy European bathing suits, were standing by with towels and a much-needed shot of vodka.

In July 1994, the North Polar ice cap was ten feet thick, and our two icebreakers had a hell of a time crunching through to the North Pole. In August 2000, when Jim McCarthy returned on another North Pole cruise (this time aboard *Yamal*), he was amazed to see that where we had encountered a thick and almost impenetrable ice sheet six years earlier, he saw only open water. Malcolm McKenna, an AMNH paleontologist and lecturer, took the photograph that was reproduced on the front page of the *New York Times,* alongside an article ("Age-Old Icecap at North Pole Is Now Liquid, Scientists Find") written by science reporter John Noble Wilford. McCarthy and McKenna then coauthored an article—"Meltdown at the North Pole"—in the December 2000 issue of the science and policy magazine *Environment*. Their article and Wilford's piece in the *Times*, dated August 19, 2000, were among the first "popular" reports to discuss the diminution of the Arctic ice cap.

Upon encountering open water where there used to be thick ice, McCarthy, identified as "the co-leader of a group working for the Intergovernmental Panel on Climate Change," said, "It was totally unexpected . . . I don't know if anybody in history ever got to ninety degrees north to be greeted by water, not ice." McCarthy and McKenna wrote in their article in *Environment*,

François Vuilleumier (left) and James McCarthy at the North Pole, July 21, 1994

During the summer of 2000, the authors traveled, as part of a team of lecturers, aboard a Russian nuclear icebreaker to the North Pole. The lecturers were well-informed regarding recent scientific papers that discussed climate change in the Arctic, but had no expectations that any of this would be visible to casual observers like ourselves. However, a paucity of ice greeted us along our journey—there was open water at the North Pole—and upon the ship's return, those observations quickly made their way into a global web of print and electronic media.

The nuclear icebreaker Yamal *finds open water at the North Pole, July 29, 2000.*

Long before the *Times* article bemoaned the disappearing ice, polar bear scientists like Ian Stirling and Andrew Derocher were warning that climatic warming would affect the bears. In a 1993 article in the journal *Arctic,* they wrote,

> Eventually . . . it is likely that seal populations will decline wherever the quality and availability of breeding habitat are reduced. Rain during the late winter may cause polar bear maternity dens to collapse, causing the death of the occupants. Human-bear problems will increase as the open water period becomes longer and bears fasting and relying on their fat reserves become food stressed . . . Should the Arctic Ocean become seasonally ice-free for a long enough period, it is likely that polar bears would become extirpated from at least the southern portion of their range. If climatic warming occurs, the polar bear is an ideal species through which to monitor the cumulative effects in arctic marine ecosystems because of its position at the top of the arctic marine food chain.

It took a while before this message made it into the popular consciousness. In an interview ("Some Don't Like It Hot") given to the *Harvard Gazette* in March 2001, McCarthy said, "Thinning ice has made it harder for the bears to hunt, leading to weight loss and 10 percent fewer cubs than 20 years ago. We already see effects that the change in climate has engendered, and the projection of some of those effects into the future do not make a pretty scene."

Even though it was obvious to the observers aboard the *Yamal* that there was no ice at the North Pole in August 2000, the open water did not necessarily signify a meltdown of the Arctic ice cap. Wilford wrote, "The North Pole is melting . . . [and] at least for the time being, an ice free patch of ocean about a mile wide has opened at the very top of the world, something that has never before been seen by humans . . . ," but he did not say that there was no ice to be seen. (In fact, the photograph shows the bow of the *Yamal* breaking through the ice, then open water, then more ice ahead of the ship. According to Wilford, "The *Yamal* had to steam six miles away to find ice thick enough for the 100 passengers to get out and be able to say they had stood on the North Pole, or close to it.") What the observers actually saw was a mile-wide lead—a break in the floating sea ice—or a *polynya*—a wider swath of open water in sea ice. It would be several years before climatologists voiced their concerns that the North Pole might not ever be covered by sea ice again, regardless of season.

The articles describing open water at the North Pole also marked the beginning of the denial of global warming as the cause. McCarthy and McKenna wrote,

> There were attempts to cast doubts on our credentials to observe what we saw . . . The negative op-ed columns were authored by people who clearly feared that some readers would see our simple observations as being consistent with the strong scientific case that Earth's climate is changing in ways that can be expected from anthropogenic greenhouse gas-forcing. Those authors prefer to believe that there is no scientific evidence for recent climate change.

II

Europeans "Discover" the Polar Bear (and the Bear Discovers Them)

In *Moby-Dick,* Herman Melville acknowledged his debt to William Scoresby, a Yorkshire whaling captain who wrote *An Account of the Arctic Regions with a History and Description of the Northern Whale Fishery* in 1820. In his chapter on cetology, Melville wrote, "Of the names in this list of whale authors, only one ever saw a living whale, but one of them was a real professional harpooner and whaleman. I mean Captain Scoresby." In his exemplary study, Scoresby not only discussed whales and whaling, but he devoted the first of two volumes to detailed discussions of the wildlife of the Arctic, including whales, dolphins, seals, walruses, and birds. There is an entire chapter about the Polar or Greenland Bear, "the sovereign of the arctic countries. He is powerful and courageous; savage and sagacious; apparently clumsy but not inactive." Scoresby tells us of what must have been one of the earliest European sightings of a polar bear: "Barentz, in the year 1596, killed two bears on Cherie Island, the skin of one of which measured 12 feet, and of the other, 13."

In medieval times, most Europeans thought of bears as being brown or black. A white bear was so unusual that it was considered an appropriate gift for royalty. In Joseph Fischer's *The Discoveries of the Norsemen in America with Special Relation to their Early Cartographical Representation* (1903) we learn that

> White bears were in Greenland what the white elephant is in Siam. In 1056, Isliev, Bishop of Iceland, brought a white bear from Green-

land as an offering to the Emperor of Germany, Henry III. Einar, the Envoy of Greenland, brought a white bear for King Sigurd of Norway, whose help he needed in the appointment of a Bishop of Greenland. The Einar-Saga states that "he presented the King with a bear which he brought with him from Greenland." To the north of Norway there lay a country where white bears and white falcons were quite common. The land of the white bears may also mean Spitzbergen, which was thought to lead to Greenland. But we never hear of hunters going across this intermediate tongue of land to catch bears, and Greenland, inhabited as it was, must be meant, when such stress is laid on white bears being so exclusively a present from Greenland.

The "King's Mirror" (*Konungs skuggsjá* in Icelandic; *Speculum Regale* in Latin; *Kongspeil* in German) was written in Norwegian around the middle of the thirteenth century, probably as a set of lessons for a king's son. It contains the first known description of the ice in Greenland, a summary of contemporaneous beliefs about the aurora borealis, and the most complete inventory of the sea mammals of Greenland and Iceland up to that time. Twenty-nine kinds of whales are listed, including the unidentifiable horse whale, red whale, and pig whale, but most of the cetaceans on the list would be recognizable today. But, as Fischer noted, "we are more interested in the account of the bears":

> They are white, and people think they are native to that country, for they differ very much from the habits of the Norwegian black bears that roam the forests and kill horses, cattle and other beasts to feed upon. But the white bear of Greenland wanders most of the time on the ice of the sea, hunting seals and whales and feeding on them. It is also as skilful a swimmer as any seal or whale.

Also in the thirteenth century King Haakon Haakonsson of Norway gave white bears to two rulers well known for their menageries: Henry III of England and the Holy Roman Emperor Frederick II, ruler of Germany and Italy. Henry, who reigned from 1216 to 1272, kept his in the Tower of London (along with an elephant given to him by the king of France), and Frederick passed his on to Sultan El-Kamil of Damascus in 1234. In his history of the Tower of London menagerie, Daniel Hahn reproduces this letter from King Henry to the bear's keeper, written in 1252:

Greetings. We commend you that for the keeper of our white bear, recently arrived form Norway . . . ye cause to be had one muzzle and one chain to hold that bear without the water, one long, strong cord, to hold the same bear fishing or washing himself in the river Thames.

The King at Windsor.

Wearing a muzzle and on a stout chain, the bear was led out to the bank of the Thames, where it scooped salmon out of the river. (The Thames was a lot cleaner then.) Hahn wrote, "Foreign visitors coming to London for diplomacy or trade in the mid-thirteenth century, approaching by boat as most did, would have seen an extraordinary sight as they reached the Pool of London . . . on the north bank, just yards away—a large polar bear sitting lazily in the sun, casually pawing salmon out of the water." There was a polar bear at the Tower menagerie in 1287, but it was probably a different one. It is unlikely that a captive bear—no matter how much salmon it ate—would have survived its Tower incarceration for thirty-five years.*

Around 1265, two Venetian brothers named Niccolò and Maffeo Polo became the first European merchants to reach the Mongol court of Kublai Khan in China. They returned to Europe in 1269, and set out again for the East two years later, accompanied by Marco, Niccolò's teenage son. Marco Polo (1254–1324) remained in China until 1292, and then returned to Venice, where he joined the Venetian forces fighting Genoa and was taken prisoner. During his two-year incarceration (1296–98), he dictated his memoirs to a Pisan writer named Rustichello, who transcribed Marco's amazing adventures during seventeen years at the Mongol court, including visits to much of Asia and the Arab world, Persia, Japan, Sumatra, the Andaman Islands, and the east coast of Africa as far south as Zanzibar. In his *Travels,* Polo tells of a king called Kanuchi, in whose country "there are big bears, pure white, and more

---

* In his history of the zoological gardens of Great Britain, Clinton Keeling says that "many historians have related this story, but frankly, doubts have to be expressed: (1) It would have to have been an abnormally tractable bear to be restrained in this way while disporting itself in the water; (2) the muzzle would have been extremely incapacitating had the bear been expected to eat its catch; and (3) while the Thames was then largely unpolluted and probably swimming with fish, a polar bear would not have been interested in fish as this species rarely eats this type of food. There is little doubt some (probably young) bear was accustomed to being led around the grounds, but its alleged riverine activities were probably the stuff of legend."

than twenty palms in length, big black foxes, wild asses, and plenty of sables—the same that produce the costly furs of which I have told you." But in a 2007 biography of Marco Polo, Laurence Bergreen says, "In reality, his route home did not take him anywhere near Russia, or any of the other northern lands that suddenly piqued his interest, but his account, a careful summary based on admittedly secondhand information, is memorable for its eloquence and its evocation of a landscape and way of life that other Europeans could scarcely imagine."

Then as now, the white pelt of the polar bear was held to be among the most luxurious of furs, and only the highest-ranking personages could possess them. In his history of the Arctic, Richard Vaughan said that "a sharp-eyed Venetian traveler noticed a white bearskin rug at the foot of the archbishop's throne in Trondheim cathedral in 1432." Subsequently, the white bear continued to appear in the annals of exploration. Zoologist Richard Perry reviewed more of the early sightings of polar bears by Europeans in his book *The World of the Polar Bear,* and informs us that

> Willoughby, who wintered in 1558 near Murmansk, on the north of the Kola Peninsula, appears to have been the first European of the modern era to have mentioned the polar bear, [and] when Burrough was at the St. James Islands south of Novaya Zemlya, in August three years later, he noted, "There were some of their company on shoare which did chase a white beare over the high cliffs into the water, which beare the native sailors that were aboard of us killed in our sight."

The great British explorer John Davis, sailing in 1585 in *Sunshine* in the Canadian Arctic strait that now bears his name, entered Cumberland Sound, and as Clements Markham described it in his *Life of John Davis,*

> The explorers had their first encounters with polar bears under Mount Raleigh. Four were seen from the ship, and the boat was eagerly manned by eager sportsmen. James, who was on shore, loaded his gun with buckshot and a bullet, and hit one in the neck. It took to the water, and was killed by the boat's crew with boar-spears, as well as two others; and a few days afterwards, another bear was secured after a long and exciting encounter.

In Chilly Observations, *an 1889 painting by Charles S. Raleigh, a polar bear views the arrival of whaling ships in the Arctic with an air of resignation and sad-eyed bemusement.*

Willem Barents (1550–1597) served as navigator on a Dutch expedition in search of a northerly route to India, eastward over the northern coast of Russia in 1594. His ship, commanded by Jacob van Heemskerck, reached Novaya Zemlya on the first voyage, but was turned back by the ice. The following year, an eight-vessel fleet set sail again from the Dutch port of Texel, intent upon finding a way to the Orient around the unexplored ice-choked northern coast of the Eurasian continent— the longest east-west coast in the world. Barents, aboard *Greyhound,* was pilot major of the fleet; aboard the other ships were the capable navigators Jacob van Heemskerck, Jan Cornelizoon Rijp, and Gerrit de Veer. But, as Ernest Dodge put it in *Northwest by Sea,* "well-found ships and able, talented men were not enough. The timing was bad and they were unfortunate in the year, for the previous winter had been one of unusual severity in the North." As de Veer recorded,

The 12 of June in the morning, wee saw a white beare, which wee rowed after with our boate, thinking to cast a roape about her necke; but when we were neere her, shee was so great that we durst not doe it, but rowed backe again to our shippe to fetch more men and our armes, and so made to her again with muskets, hargubushes, halbertes, and hatchets, John Cornellysons men comming also with their boate to helpe us. And so beeing well furnished of men and weapons, we rowed with both our boates unto the beare, and fought with her while four glasses were runne out [two hours], for our weapons could doe her little hurt; and amongst the rest of the blowes that we gave her, one of our men stroke her into the backe with an axe, which stucke fast in her backe, and yet she swomme away with it; but wee rowed after her, and at last wee cut her head in sunder with an axe, wherewith she dyed; and then we brought her into John Cornelysons shippe, where wee fleansed her, and found her skinne to be twelve foote long: which done, wee eate some of her flesh; but wee brookt it not well. This island wee called the Beare Island.*

From de Veer we get the first description of a polar bear den. On April 15, 1597, stranded on northeastern Novaya Zemlya, he wrote,

there came a great beare towards us, against whom we began to make defence, but she perceiving that, made away from us, and we went to the place from whence she came to see her den, where we found a great hole made in the ice, about a man's length in depth, the entry thereof being very narrow and within wide; there we thrust in our pikes to feele if there was anything within it, but perceiving it was emptie, one of our men crept into it, but not too farre, for it was fearfull to behold.

They named the island "Bear Island" (*Beeren Eylant* in Dutch); it was renamed Cherie Island by the British, but it is now Bear Island again—*Bjornøya*, in Norwegian. In 1595 Barents's ships tried to make the passage and failed again, but the following year they landed on Bear Island and proceeded on to Spitsbergen before arriving at Novaya Zemlya, where their ship was wrecked by the ice. They built a house from the ship's timbers and spent the winter in almost impossibly inhospitable conditions. Louwrens Hacquebord (1991) wrote that "polar bear meat was tried . . . but the men didn't like the taste of it and

* Gerrit de Veer's journal was originally published in Dutch in 1598, and translated into Elizabethan English in 1609 by William Philip. It was published by the Hakluyt Society in 1853 as *A true Description of three Voyages by the North-East towards Cathay and China, undertaken by the Dutch in the Years 1594, 1595, and 1596, by Gerrit de Veer. Published at Amsterdam in the Year 1598, and in 1609.*

Afbeeldinghe van een wonderlijck ghevecht die wy hadden teghens een wjerden/sellen Beyr/daer wy nae toe roypden inde Zee/meenende hem een strick om den hals te werpen/maer hy sachse so hyeschijck upt dat wy wederom tscherp voeren/ende haedden meer ghweert/ende bedochten hem langen tydt met twee schuyten bolcks/ende hneten meest alle ons ghweert in stucken eer wy hem vermeesteren conden/ ende hier veur werdt dit Eylandt baer omtrent dit gheschiede/het Beyren Eylandt ghenaemt.

"One of our men stroke her into the backe with an axe, which stucke fast in her backe, and yet she swomme away with it; but wee rowed after her, and at last wee cut her head in sunder with an axe." Gerrit de Veer, 1598

it was not eaten again. Later that voyage they ate the liver, which tasted good, but they became sick from vitamin A toxicity."* When spring came, Barents and his crew abandoned their house and set out for the Kola Peninsula, 1,600 miles away. Heemskerck and most of the men survived, but Barents took sick and died after five days in an open boat.

Arriving at the late date of August 19 at Novaya Zemlya, Barents found the ice stretching so far that it looked like a continent and "was most frightful to behold." For nearly a month they made repeated attempts to penetrate the Kara Sea and continue their voyage eastward,

---

* Ever since Barents's men became sick after eating it, people knew that polar bear liver was dangerous to one's health, but they didn't know why. It was not until 1942 that Norwegian scientist Kaare Rodahl, investigating vitamins in the Arctic diet, discovered that the toxic effects of polar bear liver derived from the extraordinarily high concentration of retinol, the animal form of vitamin A. The liver of the bearded seal, also considered poisonous, contains 12,000 to 14,000 international units (IU) of vitamin A per gram; that of the polar bear contains 24,000 to 26,000. A small amount of polar bear liver will probably not cause significant illness, but thirty to ninety grams (one to three ounces) is enough to kill a human being.

but with little success. The local people told them that there was open water farther east, but they couldn't get through the ice. They were also discouraged by what had happened to two crew members who had gone ashore on September 6 to search for rock crystal. Gerrit de Veer recounted their fate:

> a great leane white beare came sodainly stealing out, and caught one of them last by the necke, who not knowing what it was . . . cried out . . . Who is that that pulles me so by the necke? Wherewith the other, that lay not farre from him, lifted up his head to see who it was, and perceiving it to be a monsterous beare, cryed and sayd, Oh mate, it is a beare! and therwith presently rose up and ran away. The beare at the first falling upon the man, bit his head in sunder, and suckt out his blood, wherewith the rest of the men that were on land, being about 20 in number, ran presently thither, either to save the man, or else to drive the beare from the dead body; and having charged their peeces and bent their pikes, set upon her, that still was devouring the man, but perceiving them to come towards her, fiercely and cruelly ran at them, and gat another of them out from the companie, which she tare in peeces, wherewith all the rest ran away.

A landing party was hastily assembled to avenge the death of their shipmates, one of whom was being eaten by the bear as thirty men climbed down onto the ice. A crewman shot the blood-stained bear between the eyes,

> and yet shee held the man fast by the necke, and lifted up her head, with the man in her mouth, but shee began to stagger; wherewith the purser and a Scottishman drew out their cutlasses and stroke at her so hard that their cutlasses burst, and yet she would not leave the man. At last William Geysen went to them, and with all his might stroke the bear upon the snowt with his peece, at which time the beare fell to the ground, making a great noyse, and William Geysen leaping upon her cut her throat.

Whatever they were seeking, as these doughty explorers passed Spitsbergen they could not help but notice that the waters harbored some very large black whales. These were the whales that Scoresby knew as "Greenland whales," "Polar Whales," or, from their scientific name, the "Mysticetus." Those explorers who made it back alive reported that the waters were thick with whales. In the early years of the seventeenth century, whales were hunted for oil and for the baleen plates that hung from the roofs of their mouths and were, in this species, the longest of any whale, as much as fourteen feet long. The baleen, which was tough and flexible—a sort of organic plastic—was cut into strips that were used in the manufacture of skirt hoops, corset stays, buggy whips, and many other elements critical to civilization. (Although baleen is made of keratin, the same as human hair and fingernails, and is not bone at all, the whalemen referred to it as whalebone, or, simply, "bone.") The oil, also a necessary component of civilization, was used for lighting, lubrication, and tanning. As it was the British and the Dutch who tried (and failed) to find the passages to the Orient, so too it was the British and the Dutch who first sent ships into the waters around Spitsbergen in pursuit of whales. Whoever brought back oil and bone was in a position to dominate the commerce of western Europe.

The British ship *Salutation*, under Captain William Goodler, set out on a whaling voyage on May 1, 1630, heading for Greenland. Upon dropping anchor at Bell Sound on Spitsbergen, eight crewmen were sent ashore to hunt the native reindeer to supplement the ship's provisions. After three days, they headed back to the anchorage, only to find that the *Salutation* had given them up for lost and sailed without them. The eight men marooned on Spitsbergen in 1631 were William Fakely, John Wise, Robert Goodfellow, Thomas Ayers, Henry Bett, John Dawes, Richard Kellett, and the diarist Edward Pellham. They were, as Pellham recorded, "overtaken with the Winter, and wee were there forced to stay it out as wee were. Which being an Action so famous all the world over, encouraged mee to publish this of ours." Publish it he did; in 1631, *Gods Power and Providence; Shewed, In the Miraculous Preservation and Deliverance of eight Englishmen, left by mischance in Green-land, Anno 1630, nine months and twelve days* appeared in London bookstalls.

"Thus tormented in mind with our doubts," wrote Pellham, "our feares, and our griefs; and in our bodies, with hunger, cold and wants, that hideous monster of desperation began now to present his ugliest shape upon us; hee now pursued us, hee now laboured to seize upon us." They were freezing, they were starving, their clothes were disintegrating. From the fourteenth of October to the third of February, they didn't see the sun. A female polar bear and a half-grown cub approached their tent—"Shee soone cast her greedy eyes upon us, and with full hopes of devouring us shee made the more haste unto us"— but the men killed her with their lances. For twenty days they fed on the bear, but "the only mischance wee had with her, that upon the eating of her Liver, our very skinnes peeled off." Having eaten of this bear, the castaways were worried that all they had left to eat was some casked venison, which would have rotted by that time beyond edibility. Once again, the bears came to their rescue:

Amidst these our feares, it pleased God to send divers Beares unto our Tent,* some fortie at least as we accounted. Of which number we kill'd seven: That is to say, the second of March one; the fourth, another, and the tenth a wonderfull great Beare, sixe foote high at least. All which we flayed and roasted upon woodden spits (having no better kitchen-furniture than that, and a frying-pan we found in the Tent). They were as good savory meate as any beefe could be. Having thus gotten good store of such foode, wee kepte not our selves now to such straight allowance as before; but eate frequently two or three meales a-day, which began to increase strength and abilitie of body in us.

On May 25, 1631, there came into the sound "two ships of Hull," one of which was the *Salutation* that had marooned them nine months earlier. One can only imagine the delight of the men when they saw it was the very ship and captain that had abandoned them. They were saved, but more to the point, they had been saved by the bears.

At the time the Englishmen were marooned on Spitsbergen, the Dutch, the English, and the French were vying for control of the rich whaling grounds in the vicinity of the islands. When a French whaleman named Vroliq raided the Dutch warehouses at Kvalrossbukta

---

* The "tent" was actually a building that had been specially built for wintering over. According to Dutch archaeologist/historian Louwrens Hacquebord (1991), the dimensions of the one at Bell Sound were twenty-four by fifteen meters (seventy-eight by fifty feet), and it had plank walls and a tile roof. Inside the larger building, the winterers built a smaller one, insulated it with bricks, double planked it, and filled the space between the planks with sand.

("Walrus Bay") on Jan Mayen Island in 1632 and stole much of the oil and bone from the warehouses, the Dutch decided to protect their interests by sending a crew to Spitsbergen to spend the winter in that island's icy, windy darkness. The "Miraculous Preservation and Deliverance" of the Englishmen on Spitsbergen encouraged the Dutch to put a crew ashore in the fall to protect the station at Smeerenburg and prepare for the arrival of the whale ships the following spring. Accordingly, six sailors—Jan Kunst, Alef Willemz, Kersten Andriesz, Maerten Jacobsz, Adrien Rutten Goud, and Marcus Pouwelsz—and the commander, Jacob van der Brugge, were sent ashore on August 30, 1633, to wait out the winter and greet the whalers when they returned. Van der Brugge kept a meticulous journal, which was published in Amsterdam in 1634, translated into English by J. A. J. de Villiers, and issued by the Hakluyt Society in 1854. During September, life was fairly comfortable, but by October, the weather began to turn: "The 1st of October," wrote van der Brugge, "the wind N.W., with fog, frost and incessant drift-snow, so that in the squally wind outside the tent it was difficult to breathe."

Horrible weather, lack of sunlight, and poor living conditions contributed to the discomfort of the Dutchmen, but their existence was made even more stressful by the bears. Polar bears (*ijsberen* in Dutch) seemed to be much more numerous in Spitsbergen in the seventeenth century than they are now, and they were certainly more curious, because they paid almost daily visits to the sailors during the months from December to April, which visits almost always ended up badly for the bears. At first, the men saw only tracks in the snow, but on December 11,

the barking of the dogs made us aware of a bear being near our tent. This, after much shooting and many thrusts of our lances, we killed at some distance behind our tent. The darkness and unevenness of the snow, made it very dangerous and difficult for us, and nearly all our lances were bent, broken into pieces, and rendered unserviceable.

From then on, the bears visited the camp regularly. December 27:

About mid-day, one of our company wished to make water; and opening the shutter before the loophole . . . saw a bear before the

tent-door, which came and sniffed at said hole; whereupon I got up
and took a gun in my hand, shooting the bear in such a way that the
wad lay burning on his skin. He ran away, roaring, westwards of our
tent, whereupon we went in pursuit of him with our dog, but getting
outside the tent, we found the snow so soft that we sank into it above
our knees, and had to give up the chase.

January 7:

Shortly afterwards, we saw two bears coming down upon us from the
back, being followed, so it seemed, by two others, because they had
long been growling at one another. As soon as they were within
range, one of them was shot by Jan Kunst through the loop-hole,
with two bullets in the body. He remained lying on his side, whereupon five of us immediately ran out and killed him with lances. The
others at once took to flight, amid great bellowing.

February 7:

This morning I shot a bear in the hind leg, behind our tent, but he
escaped us. In the afternoon, we again gave chase to a bear, who also
escaped us. Then we skinned the two bears killed yesterday. We saw
several more bears upon Deadman's Island. In the evening we saw an
old bear with a cub; I shot the old one, and it was killed with lances
by the other men. The dam giving us enough to do, the cub escaped.

The next day, February 8, three men went to Deadman's Island "in
order to see whether there was anything of profit or for refreshment to
be got; also to see if any of the bears already wounded might not be
found dead." Van der Brugge continues:

On arriving there they saw many bears going in troops, like the cattle
in the Netherlands; but these, on seeing the men, stood up on their
hind-legs, as did also the cubs beside them, which was curious to see.
On our men coming nearer, they fled. They had pitched their camp
behind a hill, and made large, deep pits in the ice and snow. They
found there a carcass or tongue of a whale, which they had clawed up
out of the ice to the length of a man, and had nearly devoured. I and

Polar bears with a ringed seal, which does not seem to mind its captors. Marvelous Wonders of the Polar World, *1885*

the carpenter, having remained in the tent, observed five bears at the same time before our tent. An old one with its cub, as it seemed, coming towards our tent-door, we got our guns ready, and I sent a double charge into the body of the old one. The carpenter, also taking aim, hit the cub; whereupon we immediately ran out with our lances. The old one, seeing that they were being pursued, both came down upon us. The carpenter, making a thrust, caught one of them in the mouth with his lance, which the bear dragged towards him and bent. We then went on either side of him, and lanced him by turns until he fell down dead. Meanwhile the dogs skirmished round the cub, giving it so much to do that it could not come near us to assist its dam; but on seeing us approach, it escaped.

Throughout the long, dark night of the Spitsbergen winter, as the *ijsberen* approached the camp with some regularity, they were shot at from within and without the tent, chased by men and dogs, and stabbed with lances in the snow. There is no question that this bear killing was done in what was conceived as self-defense, but it is also likely that at least some of the bears, who had never before encountered human beings, came around the tent motivated by nothing more aggressive than curiosity. Van der Brugge's journal from December to April indicates that the men killed at least forty-five bears, sighted more than 200, and sometimes saw "ten or twelve together" or even "many bears going in troops." We know that they skinned the dead ones for the pelts—the thick fur made excellent sleeping skins—but there are only a few references to what happened to the rest of the bear. If they didn't eat the bear meat, but just skinned the bear and occasionally collected the fat, it is possible that they left the carcass out in the snow. If they did that, it's not at all surprising that so many bears came round. On March 15, van der Brugge shot a bear, "cut its belly open and got out much fat and lard with its entrails," and on April 19 the men shot a bear "then killed it with lances; it was immediately skinned and the skin and fat put safely away." During their nine months on the island, they ate scurvy grass and sorrel (collectively called "salad") and reindeer venison, and when they shot a fox they "stewed it with plums and raisins," but van der Brugge says nothing about eating the meat of the bears. (Louwrens Hacquebord says that "the Smeerenburg winterers had such a strong aversion to bear meat that they even disliked foxes that fed on bear carrion.") When the Dutch whale ships arrived in May, all the men were alive and healthy, and when Captain Cornelis Croff came to their tent, he was "greatly surprised by our mode of living and good health, the honour of which is due to God alone." Before they boarded the ship for the return voyage, they sent the commander "a piece of our dried reindeer flesh and presented him with a salad."

Jan Mayen is a lonely island in the Arctic Ocean, due north of Scotland, about 300 miles north of Iceland, and the same distance east of Greenland. The island is twenty-five miles long and nine miles wide, and covers 145 square miles. It is the peak of a submarine ridge that culminates in the forbidding 7,470-foot-high Beerenberg volcano that is Norway's only active volcano. The island was first seen in 1607 by Henry Hudson as he was searching for the northeast passage to Asia. By 1614, after Dutch sea captain Jan Jacobsz May claimed the island, whalers discovered the rich whaling grounds in the vicinity, and contested the British for the bowhead whales there. Because they knew the whales to be plentiful in the island's inshore waters, the Noordsche Compagnie sent whalers to Jan Mayen. To avoid a disaster like that visited upon them by the outlaw Vroliq in 1632, they attempted to replicate the experience of the Pellham party of two years earlier, where all the men survived the winter, even though they had been left on the island unintentionally. Accordingly, seven Dutchmen were transported to Jan Mayen in August 1633 and left there to wait out the winter. They didn't make it. They could not collect the critical "salad" that they knew was needed to prevent scurvy, because it rained and snowed so heavily that they could not leave their miserable hut. In a surviving copy of a logbook kept by one of the unfortunate mariners, we learn that they managed to kill a total of five polar bears, but they didn't know that eating undercooked bear meat was almost as dangerous as eating nothing at all. In a 1991 comparison of the outcomes of the various Arctic winterings, Hacquebord noted,

> It is possible that eating bear meat, which was salted and not well cooked, was the real reason for the disaster of the Jan Mayen wintering . . . it is well known that a possible consequence of the consumption of uncooked bear meat is trichinosis. This disease is caused by a larva that has an incubation period of six weeks. Because victims of this disease have great difficulty moving after this period of incubation, their activities decrease markedly. From both of the Jan Mayen journals we may conclude that in the course of the winter the men's activities indeed decreased sharply.

Dutch whaling historian Rob Dijksman concluded his account of the Jan Mayen tragedy with an anonymous seventeenth-century poem:

> But it is a lonely land; a land where wild bears
> And cold north winds reign over ice and snow:
> A land with little daylight where the mournful night
> Is ever present and keeps a mournful watch.

In 1993, Herbert Blankesteijn and Louwrens Hacquebord published "God and the Arctic Survivors: Without modern medicines, windcheaters or ski boots, explorers still managed to survive the Arctic win-

ters of 400 years ago. Who was their unseen ally?" Those expeditions
that had access to scurvy grass *(Cochlearia officinalis)* fared better than
those without, and seamen who ate badly cooked polar bear meat
inevitably got fatigue-inducing trichinosis: "The first mention of
extreme fatigue comes shortly after the first bear was eaten, and long
before they mention scurvy." The authors conclude,

> This brings us to a striking difference between the successful and
> unsuccessful overwinterings: those who survived took religion much
> more seriously . . . prayer and Sunday observance would have pro-
> vided a structure to their stay, as well as a daily routine to help orien-
> tate the men during the Arctic night . . . with faith came hope
> and confidence for the future. By contrast, the journals from Jan
> Mayen and the second winter at Smeerenburg—both unsuccessful
> attempts—make no mention of Christmas, even though other details
> are reported on that date.

So there really wasn't an "unseen ally"—the survivors just believed
there was.

As part of a three-ship convoy, the German whaler *Jonas im Walfisch*
("Jonah in the Whale") set sail for Spitsbergen in April 1671 and arrived
in August. Seaman Frederich Martens kept a diary of the voyage, in
which he recorded the number of whales killed and an attack by a walrus, but *Voyage into Spitzbergen* is largely a description of the land and
the wildlife, to be superseded only by Scoresby's classic work, which
was to appear a century and a half later. Many of the animals he
described were poorly known (many of them were not known at all),
and his accounts may have been the first that anyone had ever read
about creatures such as "the Sea Horse, called by some the Morse" (the
walrus); "the Kirmew" (the Arctic tern); and "the Mallemucke" (the ful-
mar). His description of the "White Bear" is a brilliant summary of
what was known (or believed) about the polar bear in the latter part of
the seventeenth century. Here it is, in its entirety:

> These *bears* are quite otherwise shaped than those that are seen in our
> country; they have a long head like unto a dog, and a long neck, and

they bark like dogs that are hoarse, and all their whole body is much otherways shaped than ours. They are slenderer in the body, and a great deal swifter.

Their skins are brought to us, which are very comfortable to those that travel in the winter; they prepare or dress the skins at *Spitzbergen* after this manner: they heat sawdust, and tread these skins in it, which sucks up the fat, and the skins become to be dry, after the same manner as we use to take out spots of *fat* out of fine linnen or other clothes, when we hold it against the sun: they are of the same bigness as ours, great and small: their hair is long, and as soft as wool: their nose and mouth are black before, and their talons also black. The fat of their feet melted out, is used for pain of the limbs; it is also given to women in travail, to bring away the child; it causes also a plentiful sweat. The said fat is very spongy, and feels very soft; it is best to try it up there presently; I strove to keep it until I should come home, but it grew foul, rancid, and stinking. I believe it would be very good to try it up with orris-root, for then it would remain the longer good and smell well.

The other is like suet when it is tryed up, it becometh thin like train-oyl, or the fat of whales; but this is not to be compared to the other for vertue and goodness, it is only used in lamps, where it does not stink so much as the train-oyl: the skippers melt it out there, and bring it home with them to sell it for train-oyl. Their flesh is whitish and fat, like that of a sheep, but I did not care to try how it tasted, for I was afraid that my hair would turn grey before its time, for the seamen are of opinion, that if they eat of it, it makes their hair grey. They suckle their young with their milk, which is very white and fat, as I observed, when we cut up an old suckling she one. They say our bears have a very *soft* head, but I found the contrary in these at *Spitzbergen*, for we struck them with large and thick cudgels upon their heads, with such blows that would have knock'd down a bullock, and yet they did not matter it at all. When we had a mind to kill them, we were forced to run them through with our launces.

They swim from one sheet of ice to the other, they also dive under water; when they were at one side of our long-boat they did dive, and came up again on the other. They also run upon the land. I did not hear them roar so as ours do, but they only bark.

We could not discern the young ones from the old ones, but only by the two furthermost long teeth, which in the young were hollow within, but those of the old ones were close and solid. If you burn their teeth and powder them, and give them inwardly, it disperseth coagulated blood. The young ones keep constantly close to the old ones; we observed that two young ones and an old one would not leave one another, for if one ran away, it turned back again immediately as soon as it did hear the others, as if it would come to help them. The old one run to the young one, and the young one to the old one, and rather than they would leave one another, they would suffer themselves to be all killed.

They feed upon the carcasses of whales, and near them we killed the most: they also eat men alive when they have an opportunity to master them. They remove or roll away the stones of the burial places, open the coffins, and eat the dead men, which many have seen; and we can also conclude it from hence, because we find the dead mens bones lye by the coffins that are opened. They also eat birds and eggs. We kill them with guns, or any other way we can. We caught three of them, one whereof I drew after the life, on the 18th of *July*.

What becometh of these *bears* and *foxes* in the wintertime I do not know; in the summer they have in some places, for a few months, provision enough, but in the winter, when the rocks and hills are covered with snow, there is but very little to be had for them; yet being it is supposed that the deer stay also there all winter long, I believe that these beasts do the same.

In his 1906 *No Man's Land: A History of Spitsbergen*, lecturer and explorer Sir Martin Conway recounts the celebrated tale of "The Man Under the Bear," said to have occurred in 1668. A bear appeared on the ice floe where the men had been flensing whales, and Captain Jonge Kees took after it in a boat. He drove his lance into the bear's ribs thinking he had administered a death blow, but the bear climbed out of the water and onto another floe, resting his head on his paws. To administer the coup de grâce, the captain "spring onto the ice alone with a throwing-lance in his hand. Suddenly the bear, with one leap of 24 feet, was upon him and had overthrown him and thrown the lance far away. With his feet upon the man's breast the bear was about to tear him to pieces." In a driving snowstorm, one of the men grabbed a boathook, and drove the bear away. The wounded bear climbed onto another ice floe and stood defiantly as Captain Kees threw another lance at him—and missed again. "The bear stood over [the lance] as if daring any one to come and get it . . . At last the brave beast's strength failed and he laid down and died." Kees adopted as his badge the figure of a man lying beneath a bear, and had the incident carved in stone as a bas-relief over the door of his house.

There is also the even more famous story of Nelson and the bear. Horatio Nelson (1758–1805), England's most famous and beloved naval hero, died tragically aboard the flagship *Victory* at the Battle of Trafalgar on October 21, 1805, shot by a sniper as his fleet defeated the French in one of the last great battles of the age of sail. In 1773, the story goes, the fourteen-year-old Nelson was a midshipman aboard HMS *Carcass*, under Captain Skeffington Lutwidge. He was serving on a two-ship expedition led by Constantine Phipps* aboard HMS *Racehorse* seeking a northeast passage to the Pacific. When the vessels found their way barred by the impenetrable ice north of Spitsbergen, Nelson set off with a friend to stalk a polar bear on the ice. His musket misfired, and as he was attacking the bear with the butt end of his weapon, a growing fissure in the ice separated the combatants. A gun fired from the ship scared the bear off, and when he was back on board, Nelson justified his action to a furious Captain Lutwidge by stating that he wished to kill the bear so he could take its skin home to his father. Clarke and McArthur's 1810 *Life of Admiral Lord Nelson* not only includes an elaborate account of Nelson's adventure with the bear but reproduces what purports to be Nelson's exclamation when "he was at this time divided by a chasm in the ice from his shaggy antagonist": "*Never mind,*" exclaimed Horatio, "*do but let me get a blow at this devil with the butt end of my musket, and we shall have him!*"

In a prodigiously researched and detailed article, Huw Lewis-Jones of the Scott Polar Research Institute at Cambridge University digs

---

* An animal acquires its scientific name when the name is first published. In 1774, Constantine Phipps published *A Voyage towards the North Pole,* in which he described the polar bear and gave it the name *Ursus maritimus,* the name it bears today. The description is: "Found in great numbers on the main land of Spitsbergen; and also on the islands and ice fields adjacent. We killed several with our musquets, and the seaman ate of their flesh, though exceeding coarse." The proper scientific name of an animal includes the name of the person who first published the name and the date of the publication, so the full name of the polar bear is *Ursus maritimus* Phipps, 1774.

After his musket misfired, Horatio Nelson clobbered a bear on the ice off Spitsbergen in 1773 (maybe).

deeply into the etiology of the myth, reading almost every biography of Nelson ever written* and locating every picture ever etched, drawn, or painted of Nelson and the bear. Lewis-Jones says that on August 4, the *Carcass* did indeed encounter bears on the ice, but diaries and journals kept contemporaneously by various crew members contain no mention of Nelson's attempt to kill one. "Master James Allen, the only member of the expedition to make any reference to bears on that day," says Lewis-Jones, "wrote in his log that at about six in the morning 'a bear came close to the ship on the ice, but upon people's going towards him he went away.' " When Phipps published the official narrative of the voyage in 1774, the incident was not mentioned, and when Nelson himself was asked to provide a "sketch" for his autobiography in 1779, he said nothing whatsoever of the bear encounter.

Heroes require a succession of heroic deeds to fill in the gaps in their life stories, and within a couple of years of the apotheosis of Viscount

---

* Roger Knight's biography of Nelson, *The Pursuit of Victory,* was published in 2006, a year after Lewis-Jones's article appeared, but Knight also says that "no record exists of Nelson venturing alone on the ice to shoot a bear."

Lord Nelson, the bear encounter began to appear in books and paintings, without a shred of evidence to justify its inclusion. From about 1806 onward, the story appears in virtually every biography of Nelson, but it received even greater play around the middle of the century, when Arctic heroism—or, in some cases, the lack thereof—filled the newspapers. All England was grimly aware of the loss of the ill-fated Franklin expedition, which had set out to find the Northwest Passage in 1845 and subsequently disappeared. Despite numerous relief expeditions sent to find him, Sir John Franklin's fate was not learned until 1859, when a note was found by Francis McClintock in a cairn on King William Island, saying that after Franklin's ships *Erebus* and *Terror* were beset in the ice for a year and a half, the party abandoned the ships and set out on foot. They all died. In 1867, Sir Edwin Landseer, Queen Victoria's favorite artist, painted *Man Proposes, God Disposes,* a gruesome reflection on the failure of the Franklin expedition. The painting shows two ravenous polar bears chewing on what are supposed to be the remains of Franklin's ships; one tears at a sail wrapped around a spar, the other gnaws on a bone of what might or might not be a human.*

Was "Nelson and the Bear" a true story of epic Arctic bravado, or was it a myth created by those who would enhance the reputation of the great Lord Nelson? We will never know for sure, but the story, as Lewis-Jones traces it through British art and literature, seems to incline more toward fable than fact. "The episode with the polar bear," he concludes, "will always be enjoyed as a small part of a colorful narrative that makes up the Nelson story, however fictitious it should prove to be." The fact that the story is probably untrue does not detract from the reputation of either Nelson or the bear. One is reminded of the line in John Ford's 1962 film, *The Man Who Shot Liberty Valance;* when a newspaperman refuses to publish the true story of a celebrated showdown, he says, "When the legend becomes fact, print the legend," suggesting that we are more comfortable with treasured legends than with hard facts.

---

* Standing proudly in London's Trafalgar Square (itself named for the scene of Nelson's last and most famous battle) is *Nelson's Column.* Built between 1840 and 1843, the monument is 151 feet high with an eighteen-foot-tall statue of Horatio Nelson at the top. Landseer was commissioned to sculpt four massive bronze lions when the memorial was originally designed, but he was unable to deliver until 1867, the same year he painted *Man Proposes.*

Sir Edwin Landseer's Man Proposes, God Disposes, *painted in 1867, supposedly depicting the fate of the Franklin expedition.*

In the early years of Canadian exploration, it was not uncommon for travelers in the northern reaches to encounter polar bears. In 1769, Samuel Hearne (1745–1792) left Fort Prince of Wales (now Churchill), on the western shore of Hudson Bay, to investigate reports of copper mines. While he found the mines and traced the Coppermine River to the Arctic Ocean, he returned to report that there was no Northwest Passage at lower latitudes. In *A Journey from Prince of Wales's Fort in Hudson's Bay to the Northern Ocean in the Years 1769, 1770, 1771, and 1772,* Hearne described some of the polar bear's more unusual characteristics:

> The males have a bone in their *penis,* as a dog has, and of course unite in copulation; but the time of their courtship is not exactly known; probably it may be in July or August, for at those times I have often been at the killing of them, when the males were so attached to their mistresses, that after the female was killed, the male would put his two fore-paws over and suffer himself to be shot before he quit her . . . Though such a tremendous animal, they are very shy of coming near a man; but when closely pursued in the water, they frequently attack the boat, seize the oars, and wrest them from the hands of the strongest man, seeming desirous to get on board; but the people on those occasions are always provided with fire-arms and hatchets, to prevent such an unwelcome visit.

In 1784, when David Thompson was fourteen, he left England for an apprenticeship with the Hudson's Bay Company, where his first job was copying the personal papers of Samuel Hearne, who had become governor of Fort Prince of Wales in 1775. It is therefore likely that Thompson transcribed the descriptions of polar bears that appeared in Hearne's *Journey*. As a fur trader and surveyor, first for the Hudson's Bay Company and later for the rival North West Company, Thompson mapped over nearly two and a half million square miles of North America, earning him the sobriquet of "greatest land geographer who ever lived." He died in obscurity in Montreal in 1857, never having completed his book about twenty-eight years in the fur trade, and it was not until 1916 that J. B. Tyrell resurrected Thompson's notes and published them as *David Thompson's Narrative*. During his apprenticeship at Fort Prince of Wales, Thompson saw a lot of polar bears. On one occasion, a she-bear hooked a fallen grouse hunter by one of his snowshoes "and dragged him along for her cubs; sadly frightened, after a short distance he recovered himself, pricked and primed his gun, and sent the load of shot like a ball into her belly; she fell with a growl and left him." Even during those times when man and bear coexisted peacefully, they ended badly for the bear. "The Polar Bear, when taken young, is easily tamed," wrote Thompson, and continued:

In the early part of July, the whaling boat in chase of the Beluga came up with a she-bear and her two cubs; the bear and one of the cubs were killed; the other a male, was kept, brought to the factory, and tamed. At first he had to be carefully protected from the dogs, but he soon increased in size and strength to be a full match for them, and the blows of his forefeet kept them at a distance. This Bruin continued to grow, and his many tricks made him a favourite, especially with the sailors, who often wrestled with him, and his growing strength gave them a Cornish hug . . . On Saturday the sailors had an allowance of rum, and frequently bought some for the week, and on that night, Bruin was sure to find his way into the guard room. One night, having tasted some grog, he came to a sailor with whom he had been accustomed to wrestle, and who was drinking too freely, and was treated by him so liberally that he got drunk, knocked the sailor down and took possession of his bed. At fisty-cuffs he knew the bear would beat him and being determined to have his bed, he shot the bear. This is the fate of almost every Bear that is tamed when grown to their strength.

The son of a whaling captain of the same name, William Scoresby was born in 1789 and went to sea at the age of ten aboard his father's ship *Resolution*. Before he returned to sea, he entered the University of Edinburgh, where he studied chemistry, natural philosophy, and anatomy. At the age of twenty-one, he was made captain of *Resolution*, and began his illustrious whaling career. He sailed the "West Ice"— Greenland and Spitsbergen—for sixteen years, becoming the most successful whaler in history, but he is remembered not only for his deeds, but for his words. In 1820, he wrote one of the most influential books on whaling, *An Account of the Arctic Regions with a History and Description of the Northern Whale-Fishery*. The work is divided into two volumes: the first on the Arctic, with chapters on the polar countries, the sea, the ice, the weather, and the zoology; and the second on the history, theory, and practice of northern whaling. As might be expected, Scoresby's "zoology" is mostly about whales, particularly the species he was hunting, the Greenland whale or Mysticetus, but there are also detailed discussions of the Arctic fox, the walrus, the seals, and *Ursus maritimus*, the polar bear. When Scoresby's volumes were published, those Englishmen not involved with the whaling business probably didn't know very much about Arctic wildlife, so his description of the great white bear was more than a little exciting and educational to the layman. What is surprising is how accurate his descriptions were, even in the light of our current sophistication about animal behavior and zoogeography. He wrote:

Bears occur in Spitsbergen, Nova Zembla, Greenland, and other Arctic countries, throughout the year. In some places they are met in great numbers. By means of the ice, they often affect a landing in Iceland; but as soon as they appear, they are generally attacked by the inhabitants and destroyed. Near the east coast of Greenland, they have been seen on the ice in such quantities, that they were compared to flocks of sheep on a common.

The description of the bear is as accurate today as it was when he wrote it in 1820:

The size of this animal is generally 4 or 5 feet in height, 7 or 8 feet in length, and nearly as much in circumference. Sometimes, however, it occurs much larger . . . Its weight is generally from 600 lb. to above half-a-ton. It is covered with long, yellowish white hair, and is particularly shaggy about the inside of the legs. His paws are 7 inches or more in breadth; his claws 2 inches in length. His canine teeth, exclusive of the portion imbedded in the jaw, are about an inch and a half in length. Having an amazing strength of jaw, he has been known to bite a lance in two, though made of iron half an inch in diameter.

For the most part, the whalers were on ships or in longboats, where the great white bears were not considered threatening, but Scoresby does tell a story about a crew in the Spitsbergen Sea that attacked a bear in the water, which "made such formidable resistance that it was enabled to climb the side of the boat and take possession of it while the intimidated crew fled for safety in the water, supporting themselves by the gunwale and rings of the boat, until, by the assistance of another party from their ship, it was shot as it sat inoffensively in the stern."

Walruses and polar bears inhabit the same icy habitat as Arctic whales, so it stands to reason that at one time or another the whalers would come into contact with all of these large marine mammals. The Englishmen who hunted the Mysticetus during the nineteenth century were whalers, but when they encountered walruses or polar bears, they killed those too. In *Arctic Whalers, Icy Seas*, W. Gillies Ross has collected the stories of these Davis Strait whalers. Here is David Duncan's, written on June 9, 1827:

> This morning I was called out of bed as there was a bear on the floe edge . . . I saw the animal standing about 100 yards from the ship. Before I could get loaded one of the men fired a ball at him. He turned over heels uppermost but immediately got to his feet, gave a loud growl and walked away towards the land. I and two others got up on the ice and pursued him. When he saw us he began to run and soon distanced us. We saw drops of blood at every footstep. We followed him about two miles. He was a rather small animal; his footsteps were about four inches across.

The Scottish whaler *Enterprise* sailed from the port of Fraserburgh on February 7, 1856, heading for the whaling grounds of Greenland and Spitsbergen. The crew of sixty included Dr. Alexander Trotter, who

Whalers attacking (or being attacked by) a herd of ravenous polar bears

kept a journal of the seven-month voyage. The entry for June 3 reads as follows:

> We got 2 bears today. They were swimming in the water. One was young, the other was old. These animals are all white and the largest of them about 9 feet long and 4 feet high. They are in reality formidable looking animals and they are ever on the alert for their prey, eating whale and seal carcasses, birds, and human beings if they can get them. Sometimes they will crouch at the back of a hummock or large lump of ice and watch an opportunity of springing upon a boat's crew: but when they do so they meet their match, speedily receiving a few balls at once, which generally kill them outright or else make them take to their heels. Many anecdotes are told of these bears or bruinies as they are called. Sometimes they will swim for a day or two and come close to a ship's side, sometimes when their leg or lower jaw is broke by a shot they will sit down and plaster it with snow, endeavoring to set it, and sometimes they will watch the seals

and other fish as they pop their heads above water and instantly seize them, and so on—all of which I can readily believe.

On ice, on land, or in the water, early explorers seemed to regard it as their duty to kill polar bears. Some of the bears appeared threatening, but most were going about their business—which sometimes consisted of investigating strange creatures in their heretofore unassailable stronghold. When no word was heard about the fate of Sir John Franklin, who had set out in 1845 to seek the Northwest Passage, the British Admiralty offered £20,000 for information about Franklin, the crew, and the ships *Erebus* and *Terror*. In all, ten expeditions were sent to search for him, some financed by his wife, Lady Jane Franklin. One of those who joined the quest was Elisha Kent Kane (1820–1857), an American doctor from Philadelphia, whose first participation was as senior medical officer aboard the *Advance*, part of an 1850 expedition financed by Henry Grinnell. Kane persuaded Grinnell to back another search, again using the *Advance*. The ship was stopped by the ice off western Greenland, but Kane explored and named Grinnell Land on Ellesmere Island and then proceeded southward to Baffin Bay, where the *Advance* was beset in the ice for twenty-one months and had to be abandoned as the men began to weaken and show symptoms of scurvy. After a ten-week trip of 1,300 miles, Kane led them safely to Danish settlements in Greenland, with the loss of only one man. Upon his return to America, he was awarded a Congressional Gold Medal. A year after the publication of his *Arctic Explorations*, Kane died, at the age of thirty-seven.

In his book (full title: *Arctic Explorations: The Second Grinnell Expedition in Search of Sir John Franklin, in the Years 1853, '54, '55*), Kane recounts a harrowing tale of men lost and starving in the Arctic, dependent upon Inuit villagers (whom he refers to as "Esquimaux") to help them, and eating what they had on board or what they could catch in that most unsupportive and hostile of environments. Kane describes the events of September 29, 1854, when they were still on the ship, stuck in the ice:

A medium sized bear, with a four months cub, was in active warfare with our dogs. They were hanging on her skirts, and she with won-

derful alertness was picking out one victim after another, snatching
him by the nape of the neck and flinging him many feet or rather
yards, by a barely perceptible movement of her head . . .

It seemed as if the controversy was adjourned: and Nannook evidently thought so, for she turned off to our beef barrels, and began in
the most unconcerned fashion to turn them over and nose out their
fatness. She was apparently as devoid of fear as any of the bears in the
stories of old Barentz and the Spitzbergen voyagers.

I lodged a pistol ball in the side of the cub. At once the mother
placed her little one between her hind legs, and, shoving it along,
made her way behind the beef house. Mr. Ohlsen wounded her as she
went in with my Webster rifle; but she scarcely noticed it. She tore
down by single efforts of her forearms the barrels of beef that made
the triple walls of the storehouse, mounted the rubbish, and, snatching a half barrel of herrings, carried it down by her teeth, and was
making off. It was time to close, I thought. Going up within half pistol range, I gave her six buckshot . . . The poor animal was still backing out, yet still fighting, carrying her wounded cub, embarrassed by
the dogs, yet gaining distance from the brig, when Hans and myself
threw in the odds in the shape of a couple of rifle balls. She staggered
in front of her young one, faced us in death-like defiance, and only
sank when pierced by six more bullets.

The bear was a small one; the dressed carcass weighed 300 pounds.
"Bears in this lean condition," wrote Dr. Kane, "are much the most
palatable food. The impregnation of fatty oil throughout the cellular
tissue makes a well-fed bear nearly uneatable." After eating the cub's
liver, Dr. Kane wrote, "I have symptoms of poison in full measure—ver-
tigo, diarrhea, and their concomitants." On November 15, while on a
reconnaissance mission from the ship, Kane was chased by a bear, and,
"I ran as I never expected these scurvy-stiffened knees to run again,
throwing off first one mitten and then its fellow to avoid pursuit. I
gained the brig and the bear my mittens." On January 17, 1855, as Kane's
expedition was nearly out of food, he wrote,

I found an overlooked godsend this morning—a bear's head, put
away for a specimen, but completely frozen. There is no inconsider-

able quantity of meat adhering to it, and I serve it out raw to Brooks, Wilson, and Riley. I do not know that my journal anywhere mentions our habituation to raw meats, nor does it dwell upon their strange adaptation to scorbutic disease. Our journeys have taught us the wisdom of the Esquimaux appetite, and there are few among us who do not relish a slice of raw blubber or a chunk of frozen walrus-beef. The liver of a walrus (awuktanuk) eaten with little slices of his fat—of a verity it is a delicious morsel. Fire would ruin the curt, pithy expression of vitality which belongs to its uncooked juices. Charles Lamb's roast-pig was nothing to awuktanuk. I wonder that raw beef is not eaten at home. Deprived of extraneous fibre, it is neither indigestible nor difficult to masticate. With acids and condiments, it makes a salad which an educated palate cannot help relishing; and as a powerful and condensed heat-making and anti-scorbutic food it has no rival.

Captain Francis McClintock, one of those commissioned by Lady Jane Franklin to look for her missing husband and his ships, found the remains of the expedition on King William Island in 1859. Hailed as a hero when he returned to England, McClintock published *The Voyage of the Fox*, an account of his unfortunately successful quest. Like almost everyone else who ventured into the High Arctic, McClintock had encounters with bears. During the night of October 29, 1857, the *Fox* was locked in the ice of Melville Bay, off the coast of Greenland, when a noisy fracas outside the ship woke everybody:

The alarm of "A bear close-to, fighting with the dogs," was the cause. The luckless beast had approached within 25 yards of the ship ere the quartermaster's eye detected his indistinct outline against the snow, so silently had he crept up that he was within 10 yards of some of the dogs. A shout started them up, and they at once flew round the bear and embarrassed his retreat. In crossing some very thin ice he broke through, and there I found him, surrounded by yelping dogs. Poor fellow! Hobson, Young, and Petersen had each lodged a bullet in him, but those only seem to increase his rage. He succeeded in getting out of the water, when, fearing harm to the numerous bystanders and dogs, or that he might escape, I fired and the bullet passed through his brain. He proved to be a full-grown male, 7 feet 3 inches in length. As we all aided in the capture, it was decided that the skin should be offered to Lady Franklin.

In Alexander Trotter's journal, we can read of the whaleman's attitude toward polar bears. Sighting a bear from the masthead as they were made fast to an ice island, the crew put some beef bones on the fire "in order that their smell might attract him." The bear approached the *Enterprise,* crouching and creeping from one hummock to another,

taking advantage of every cover to get nearer them. On he advanced slowly but surely, smacking his lips and doubtless thinking to himself, "Now I'll have a feast—oh! how savoury these curious creatures smell." Nearer still he came, and then prepared for a rush, when pop, pop went five guns, and he started, crouched, and ran off.

From the whalers' first encounters with the bears of Spitsbergen to the tundra-buggy tourists of Churchill, everyone assumed that polar bears were potentially dangerous man-eaters. There are enough documented instances of attacks to take such an idea seriously, but there are far more encounters in which the big white bears surprised (and frightened) people just by appearing. In most of these instances, the bears were driven off by shouting or shooting, and many times they simply turned and walked away. A dog is much closer in size to the polar bear's usual prey than a man in a parka, and many of the "encounters"—such as McClintock's above—look like the bear was just curious about the dogs rather than planning to climb aboard the ship and eat the men. And even though dogs have been used by Eskimos in polar bear chases for millennia, the bears probably do not associate them with hunting, but rather as possible prey. That all bears do not go after all dogs, however, is revealed in the extraordinary series of photographs by Norbert Rosing in Churchill that show a bear happily playing with a sled dog, which continued every night for a week. If bears sometimes attack people, sometimes don't attack people, sometimes attack dogs, and sometimes play with dogs, it merely demonstrates that they are unpredictable.

They might be few and far between, but there are unequivocal records of polar bears attacking humans. In his 1978 book, *The World of the Polar Bear*, Thor Larsen, a Norwegian specialist, says that he has experienced a dozen attacks from polar bears, but admits they were all provoked. Canadian photographer/naturalist Fred Bruemmer (1989) tells a story of two bears that attacked men in 1983 at an oil-drilling installation in the Beaufort Sea: "One hit and killed the foreman of a seismic camp and loped away easily with the 235-pound body. The other bear climbed aboard a frozen-in crew barge, killed an 18-year-old driller, and carried him off like a dog carries a stick." Attempts to drive the bears off with flare guns had no effect (the men had no rifles), and the horrified crew stood by as the bears ate their victims. In a letter to me, Nikita Ovsyanikov, a Russian researcher who studies the polar bears of Wrangel Island, wrote, "From more than fifteen hundred personal encounters with polar bears, I experienced only three when polar bears attacked and tried to kill me. In all three cases, the attacks were provoked by my wrong actions." Still, the number of "attacks" that have resulted from face-to-face encounters between bears and men must be minuscule when compared to the number of encounters where the bear has *not* attacked.

One of a remarkable series of photographs taken in Churchill by Norbert Rosing of a bear that came every night for a week to play with a chained-up sled dog.

When a mother bear is sedated, the cubs, which are unafraid of humans, will often bond with a researcher. This is Norwegian scientist Thor Larsen on Svalbard.

Another way of looking at the "unpredictable" nature of polar bears is to assume that not every one will respond the same way. As Andrew Derocher wrote, "It would be unwise to believe that what the last 80 bears did will be the same as the next bear you see." Very few animals—but especially not large predators—can be expected to do the same thing every time. Lions might remain lying down as a herd of zebras passes before them, or they might begin to stalk them. Tigers might wander into a village in India and calmly walk out again, or they might grab a villager, drag him into the jungle, and eat him. Similarly, polar bears might stand up on their hind legs to get a better view of a sledge or snowmobile, or turn and run away. They might wade into a pack of sled dogs, swiping at them, or they might play with them. They might also ignore them completely. There are more instances of bears ignoring men in tents than there are of bears poking their noses in—but of course we don't see the bears that do not wander into camp. Some will follow a snowmobile over the ice; others will turn and head off in the opposite direction. At Churchill, a bear known as Ozzie used to rear up next to a tundra buggy and allow people to scratch his ears. Hungry bears behave very differently from well-fed bears; skinny bears do things that fat bears would never do. Individualistic behavior seems to characterize the daily lives of polar bears; but because people are ready to interpret almost any behavior as aggressive, whatever the intentions of the bear, they have believed that "the only good bear is a dead bear."

Canadian American Ernest Thompson Seton (1860–1946) was probably the most famous American naturalist of his time, writing and illustrating more than forty books, almost all about the wildlife of North America. Although he spent a lot of time in Manitoba, he probably never saw a wild polar bear (in his 1929 book, *Lives of Game Animals*, the photographs are of polar bears in a zoo), and relied on published material for his information. In his discussion of the male polar bear, he asked,

> But the Ice-king—what of his way? Is his appeal to eye, or ear, or nose, when the mating May-time thrills his world, and sends him gallivanting? Does he anoint the angle stones on the headlands with his body-scent? Does he gallop at random? Does he sing some loud heroic song like a Lion roar? Or does he follow every trail that his discriminating nose announces as a she-bear's trail?—till he finds her. And if it so be there arrive at the trail's end together two great King-bears of the ice, what then? A mortal combat, a finish fight, or a meek submission to the lady's judgment?

His answer: "Of all this we know nothing. It is recorded only that mating is in midsummer. The Eskimo and Northern Indians say that this mating is a pairing. Polygamy has seemingly died out in the upper classes of the bears."

In *The World of the Polar Bear*, Richard Perry devotes a chapter to "Bears and Men," almost all of which is about the unpredictability of polar bears:

> The long and short of it is that the reactions of any class of polar bear are unpredictable, depending no doubt on whether to this bear a man is merely a new kind of animal which he has not previously encountered and about which he is curious; and to that bear an animal that he has previously encountered and found to be either dangerous or harmless. Some bears are afraid of a single man providing he has dogs

with him, seeking to escape rather than stand and fight; whereas a very large he-bear, following up Frederick Jackson's sledge tracks at a fast trot on the afternoon of April 30, finally charged him while he was standing beside the sledge. Others may ignore the presence of a sledge party, or when followed by its member, merely keep at an adequate distance from them by increasing their pace from time to time, occasionally turning around nonchalantly to gaze at them.

A careful reading of the historical literature reveals very few accounts where an enraged bear charged at a human being. As a matter of fact, there are few stories of bears aggressively charging at dogs or sledges, either. Most frequently, the encounters consist of bears following humans or poking around a camp. The reputation of the polar bear as an unreconstructed man-eater colors every encounter, and even bears minding their own business on the ice or casually strolling into somebody's camp are killed in what is perceived as an absolutely necessary demonstration of "self-defense." Sending a pack of yelping dogs after a bear is very likely to make the bear cross, and if a hunter gets hurt trying to kill a bear with a spear, whose fault is that? She-bears with young cubs are understandably protective, and they might charge or otherwise attempt to stave off a threat, actions that all too easily can be perceived as aggressive. Although protective mothers can sometimes intimidate a big male, the big he-bears, by virtue of their size and fearless nature, are usually oblivious to the puny threats offered by humans. The explorer Vilhjalmur Stefansson, writing of the Beaufort Sea bears, wrote, "Knowing no fear, he comes straight into the camp, walking leisurely because he does not expect the dead seal that he smells to escape him; neither has he in mind any hostility or disposition to attacks, for, through long experience with foxes and gulls, he expects any living thing he meets to make way for him." All the waving, shouting, and flare shooting only serves to pique the bear's interest. In most instances, all the bears did was get too close for the comfort of the people, so they had to be shot.

The whalers shot the bears because they believed them to be dangerous, because they made handy targets, and (occasionally) to collect the cubs for sale, but killing bears for food, self-defense, or commerce is different from killing them for fun. Hunting polar bears was popular with whale men, the occasional "sportsman" who ventured into the Arctic for

The men's clothing, their halberds, and the unusual way the shooter is holding his weapon, suggest a re-creation of a seventeenth-century bear attack. Marvelous Wonders of the Polar World, *1885*

adventure, or maybe even people just along for the ride. In 1880, when he was a twenty-year-old medical student at Edinburgh, Arthur Conan Doyle shipped out as a surgeon aboard the Peterhead whaler *Hope*. For seven months, the future creator of Sherlock Holmes sailed through the northern seas around Greenland and Jan Mayen, watching the wildlife and occasionally falling overboard. There were few whales around by that time—Captain Gray told him that "there were probably no more than 300 left alive in the whole expanse of the Greenland Sea"—but he did manage to describe some of the Arctic's exotic wildlife. In an 1897 article he called "Life on a Greenland Whaler," Conan Doyle delineated his impressions of the polar bear:

Occasionally one sees a white Arctic fox upon the ice, and everywhere are the bears. The floes in the neighborhood of the sealing ground are all criss-crossed with their tracks—poor harmless creatures with the lurch and roll of a deep sea mariner. It is for the sake of the seals that they come out over those hundreds of miles of ice—and they have a very ingenious method of catching them, for they will choose a big ice field with just one blow-hole for seals in the middle of it. Here the bear will squat with its powerful forearms round the hole. Then, when the seal's head pops up, the great paws snap together, and Bruin has got his luncheon.

In his 1917 *Modern Whaling and Bear Hunting*, Scotsman William G. Burn-Murdoch introduces his Arctic exploits also by quoting Scoresby:

"When the bear is found in the water, crossing from one sheet to another, it may generally be attacked with advantage; but when on the shore, or more especially when it is upon a great sheet of ice, covered with snow—on which the bear, supporting itself on the surface, with its extended paws, can travel at twice the speed of a man, who perhaps sinks to the knee at every step—it can seldom be assailed with either safety or success. Most of the fatal accidents that have occurred with bears have been the result of reencounters on the ice, or injudicious attacks made at such disadvantage."

It is Scoresby's treatise that sets the stage for everybody who would write about whales, whaling, or hunting in the Arctic. Here is the Table of Contents for Chapter 25 of Burn-Murdoch's book, which neatly summarizes his adventures with polar bears:

Six Bears in Twenty-four Hours—A Bear's Meal—C. A. Hamilton's Veteran Bear—The Writer and Bear Stalk Each Other—Tips for Animal Painters—Sensation Facing a Bear at Three in the Morning—Bear Flesh as Food—The Colour of the Polar Regions—Method of Pulling a Live Bear on Board—A Bear Eating a Seal

Burn-Murdoch appeared almost as interested in capturing bears as shooting them, for he always had one in a cage on deck or another being towed after the ship. Captivity notwithstanding, however, he and his fellow hunters shot plenty of whales with harpoon guns and plenty of bears with rifles. "Six Bears in Twenty-four Hours" refers to five bears that Burn-Murdoch & Co. shot during one long Arctic day, and one that they captured alive. Burn-Murdoch (who was a piper and enjoyed playing the bagpipes on the ice) wrote, "Now we have a bear alongside, all alive-O!" The captured bear was being towed behind the boat:

> He is tied with a rope and is swimming just like a man, hard astern trying to tow our little whaler from the floe-edge; and roars every now and then in angry disgust, and then upon his hind quarters and dives and swims a few strokes under water, only to be pulled up again on the rope or lasso. He can swim apparently without fatigue for many hours, occasionally taking a dive as deep as the lasso will allow him. We hope to get him to the Edinburgh Zoological Park, where he will be much appreciated, especially by myself and other artists and children and seniors.

When whaling ended in the eastern Arctic around 1860—the area had just about run out of whales—the polar bears that lived around Greenland and Spitsbergen were granted a temporary reprieve. In 1848, an American whaling captain named Thomas Welcome Roys sailed the bark *Superior* north through the Bering Strait and discovered a population of bowheads that theretofore had been known only to the local Inuit. These were of the same species as the Mysticetus, and because oil and baleen were still in great demand (oil for soap, heat, lighting, and lubrication; baleen for corset stays, skirt hoops, umbrella ribs, and fans), Americans went whaling in the remote ice-choked fastness of the Beaufort and Chukchi seas. They hunted whales in the vicinity of islands such as Wrangel, St. Lawrence, and Herschel, also a favorite habitat of the peripatetic polar bears. (One of the ships used in this whaling was the gasoline-powered *Polar Bear*.) Once again, whalers not otherwise occupied with whales took the opportunity to shoot at the local bears.

Eskimos always boil bear meat before eating it (Lentfer 1979). They will eat raw whale meat, raw whale blubber, and raw seal meat, but never uncooked bear meat or liver. On the Danmark Expedition to East Greenland in 1913, the expedition's doctor, Jens Peter Johannes Lindhard, carried out a clinical investigation into the effects of eating bear liver:

nineteen men took part in the meal, and all of them became ill. The sickness manifested itself in the form of sleepiness, general malaise, and headaches. In general the symptoms could be described as a kind of intoxication similar to that caused by eating fresh shark meat. Afterwards the skin started to peel, in some cases only the head, in others over the whole body. (Pedersen 1962)

Toxic liver notwithstanding, there can be times when just eating the meat of a polar bear can be dangerous. Reminiscing about his whaling days in the Arctic, Hartson Bodfish (who later became Captain Bodfish, and continued his whaling career until 1911) told a story about a whaling crew that had killed a bear and had eaten a considerable amount of the meat:

It made them all fearfully ill, in fact they nearly died . . . But the explanation was simply that the bear had been feeding on old carcasses of dead walrus and other things that were poison. Natives eat bear that has been feeding on freshly caught food, and I have eaten it as I have explained. But, of course, when a bear is killed it is not always easy to determine what it has been feeding on, and it doesn't pay to take chances.

Fridtjof Nansen (1861–1930) was a Norwegian explorer and scientist who made the first crossing of the Greenland ice sheet in 1888–89. (He won the Nobel Peace Prize in 1922 for his humanitarian work with Russian refugees dying of starvation after the famine that followed World War I and the Russian Revolution.) His ship *Fram* ("forward") was specially designed to resist the ice by means of a reinforced hull shape that would cause it to be squeezed up on top of the floes rather than crushed between them. In 1893 he traversed the Northeast Passage to the New Siberian Islands, headed north, and deliberately let the *Fram* get frozen in. For a year and a half the ship drifted slowly northwest with the pack. He hoped that the drift would take him to the North Pole, but when the ship began to trend southward, Nansen and Hjalmar Johansen set off on skis. Frozen into the ice, the *Fram* drifted for three years as the crew made meteorological measurements and astronomical observations to determine the direction of their movement.* In *Hunting and Adventure in the Arctic* (1925), Nansen devotes an entire chapter to the natural history of the polar bear, much of his information coming from firsthand observations. He wrote,

> Huge and heavy as it is, it can be remarkably agile when the occasion demands. It can make a spring to seize its prey almost like that of a cat, and it can move over the uneven ice with speed that is almost incredible. It has surpassing strength and its mighty fore-paws are its usual weapon. One single blow from them may dispose of a seal.

With *Fram* locked in the ice, Nansen's crew occupied themselves by hunting polar bears, an activity that they seemed to pursue with alacrity. Two full chapters of Nansen's book—"Bear Hunting" and "Still Beset"—are devoted almost entirely to bear hunting. For the most part, the hunters would walk out onto the rough, frozen plain, sight the bears at a distance, and sneak up on them, but occasionally the animals would come up to the ship. At one point, the men made a bonfire of old bear flesh, liberally fueled with blubber, and kept it burning for several days, in the hope that the bears would be attracted by the smell. "The ruse worked well, for in all, about twenty bears were sighted from the crow's nest during the next few days"—and their sport was assured. Here is one account as Nansen tells it:

> We soon caught sight of the animal and made our way towards it. The ice was rough and difficult to traverse; so we had to take our time and advance in a very roundabout way. At length we mounted a tall hummock, and the bear saw us.

* More than a century after Nansen's historic voyage and ice-pack drift, the international Damocles Project launched *Tara,* a 118-foot-long schooner with the goal of measuring climate change in the Arctic. Using a special aluminum alloy where Nansen had used oak, *Tara* had the same rounded hull shape that would enable the ship to pop up when squeezed in the ice. With a complement of eight scientists and engineers aboard, *Tara* was locked in the pack ice on September 4, 2006, and drifted for sixteen months before being released off northeast Greenland on January 21, 2008. She had survived gigantic winter storms, ice quakes, and, during her enforced incarceration in the ice, visits from eighteen polar bears. "The most important question that the Damocles hopes to answer," wrote Ben Crystall of *Tara,* "is whether the Arctic pack ice will disappear for good, and if so, when. If the ice vanishes, it will take an entire ecosystem with it." (For more information, see http://www.taraexpeditions.org)

Nansen's ship, Fram, *was locked in the ice, so the crewmen occupied themselves by hunting polar bears, an activity that they pursued with alacrity.*

We crouched down, but in order to excite its curiosity we popped our heads up from time to time above the edge of the ice. It began to approach us at once, now under cover of pieces of ice, now across the flat floes. A fine, full-sized animal, it came on towards us with long strides, advancing rapidly although it seemed to be taking things easy.

We waited as long as possible in order to have a good look at it. Now it had already reached a hummock about twenty yards ahead of us. There was its head peering cautiously over the edge. A huge head it was, too, about as big as a good-sized portmanteau. But there was no need to shoot yet, for the animal could not possibly escape now that it had come so close.

The head swayed this way and that, and disappeared again behind the head of the hummock.

We held our rifles for readiness, for one never knew where it would turn up next. Ah! There it came, shambling along one side of the hummock with its chest fully exposed. Our shots rang out simultaneously. A roar—the bear sank to its haunches, bit at the wounds, staggered back a few paces and then rolled over.

What a beautiful sight it looked, as it lay there with its beautiful yellow-white coat against the white snow, the crimson blood dripping from its chest. It seemed so unfair that a little bit of lead should suddenly bring to an end that free life on the boundless expanse of ice.

Even though they were stuck in the ice, the *Fram* was well provisioned, but because Nansen believed that bear meat was healthy, the men ate the meat of many of the bears they shot. He wrote,

> Roasted cub-steak and tasty bear's tongues made a welcome addition to our menu for some time . . . We thought the bear's meat, especially that of the cubs, was excellent, but strange to say many of the sailor-men refused to touch it; obviously in their opinion animals with claws were not fit for human consumption, and there was also the old superstition about their flesh was poisonous.

In 1894, when they were some 400 miles from the North Pole, Nansen and Johansen left the *Fram* with two kayaks, three sledges, and twenty-eight dogs, and before they were forced to turn back they had managed to get to 86° north, farther north than anyone else up to that time. They headed for Franz Josef Land, arrived there three months later, and spent the winter of 1895–96 in a hut they built of stones, moss, and walrus skins. They had eaten the last of the dogs, their flour had mildewed, their chocolate had dissolved, and their pemmican had rotted, so they subsisted almost entirely on walrus blubber and bear meat. From Nansen's journal for Wednesday, July 17, 1895:

> Meanwhile we have lain here—"Longing Camp" as we call it—and let the time slip by. We have eaten bear-meat morning noon and night, and so far from being tired of it, have made the discovery that the breast of cubs is quite a delicacy. It is remarkable that this exclusive meat and fat diet has not caused us the slightest discomfort in any way, and we have no craving for farinaceous food, although we might, perhaps, regard a large cake as the acme of happiness. Every

now and then we cheer ourselves with lime-juice grog, a blood pan-
cake or some stewed whortleberries.

In May of the following year they started off again for Spitsbergen.
After traveling for a month over unknown territory, they happened
upon the British Jackson-Harmsworth expedition (led by Frederick
George Jackson), whose party was wintering on Franz Josef Land.
After the ordeal, Nansen discovered that he had put on twenty-two
pounds.

Frederick Jackson (1860–1938) is best known for his rescue of Nansen
and Johansen on Franz Josef Land in 1896. Completely lost, Nansen
had been sighted by members of Jackson's team at a distance from their
camp at Cape Flora. Here is Jackson's account of the meeting:

> I saw a man on skis with roughly made clothes and an old felt hat on
> his head. He was covered with oil and grease, and black from head to
> foot. I at once concluded from his wearing skis that he was no En-
> glish sailor but that he must be a man from some Norwegian walrus
> sloop who had come to grief, and wintered somewhere on Franz
> Joseph Land, in very rough circumstances. His hair was very long
> and dirty, his complexion appeared to be fair, but dirt prevented me
> from being sure on the point, and his beard was straggly and dirty
> also. We shook hands heartily and I expressed the greatest pleasure at
> seeing him. I inquired if he had a ship? "No," he replied, "my ship is
> not here"—rather sadly I thought—and then he remarked, in reply
> to my question, that he had only one companion who was at the floe
> edge. It then struck me that his features, in spite of the black grease
> and long hair and beard resembled Nansen, whom I had met once in
> London before he started in 1893, and I exclaimed: "Aren't you
> Nansen?" To which he replied, "Yes, I am Nansen." With much
> heartiness I shook him warmly by the hand and said: "By Jove, I'm
> damned glad to see you," and congratulated him on his safe arrival.

On August 7, after two weeks of rest and recuperation (and a little bear
hunting), Nansen and Johansen were aboard Jackson's ship *Windward*
en route to Vardo in northern Norway, arriving there just as *Fram* came

to port, having escaped from the ice north of Spitsbergen. During their time on Franz Josef Land, the eight men of the Jackson-Harmsworth expedition had more than enough opportunities to interact with the only inhabitants of the area that were larger than they were. Then as now, Franz Josef Land was uninhabited by people, the only mammalian occupants of this ice-covered archipelago being walruses, Arctic foxes, and polar bears.

In his 1899 book, *A Thousand Days in the Arctic*, Jackson kept a careful record of everything that happened, including their frequent encounters with polar bears. Their supplies included plenty of canned meat, but because the expedition believed fresh meat was better, they took advantage of the large number of bears that visited their camp:

November 13, 1894—Crowther woke me saying there was a bear near the ship. I tumbled out of my bunk, putting a coat, waistcoat and trousers over my pyjamas. It was brilliant moonlight and quite calm, and I could see the bear at some distance with five or six dogs yapping at him. I ran between him and the bay ice towards which he was retreating, and so headed him. He came at me at a good fast trot and when six paces off I fired and he fell dead . . . He was an unusually large he-bear. He had every intention of "going for" me when I shot him, and I stopped him just in time.

November 14, 1894—I shot a bear at 9 p.m. on the floe. He showed a disposition to clear out, so I lay down on the ice and imitated the movements of a seal, quite taking him in, for he at once came running towards me, and then at ten paces off I fired, finishing him off in two shots with my .450 Express rifle. I was curious to see the look of doubt and misgiving that came into his face as he approached me. On nearer inspection evidently thinking me the oddest seal he had ever seen he began to think better of it, and when I fired was on the point of reversing.

On February 3, 1895, Jackson "adopted" a polar bear cub after shooting its mother as she emerged from a den in the snow. With a noose, he dragged the cub from the den:

Great was the amusement when a white, soft, fluffy thing, hardly larger than a big cat, appeared, and instead of a desperate struggle with a savage beast, it was quietly transferred to my arms, where it nestled contentedly as if they had always been its cradle, and was then wrapped up warmly and placed on the sledge to be driven back to the hut.

In the entry for February 7, Jackson wrote,

The bear cub is a source of great amusement. She cries exactly like a young infant, and in many ways behaves like one, but shows much vice by biting and scratching. She hisses and growls much like her elders of that ilk, and sometimes, when going off to sleep in a contented frame of mind, makes a noise like the propeller of a small steam launch . . . It is an unfeminine little animal, and its conduct generally anything but ladylike, sorry I am to say such things of our foster child. I hope to send her home by the *Windward* to the "Zoo" in London.

Because they acquired the cub at Cape Gertrude, they named her Gertie. Later, while out hunting at Mabel Island, Jackson spotted two bears together, and "my first shot put a bullet through the head of the higher one, a large female, which was looking at me over the back of her husband . . . but a shot from my .303 evidently convinced him that I was not a nice person to become acquainted with." The female was accompanied by two cubs, which the men brought back to camp and named Mabel and Benjy.

The bears of Franz Josef Land seemed unusually numerous; Jackson and his men shot an average of one every eight days.

February 11, 1895—A bear came up to within a couple of yards of the door at noon today, just after all the members of the Expedition had gone out on the usual walk. Burgess was on the point of leaving the hut when he saw him just outside the door, and just had time to slam it. I went out with my .450 double rifle and in a second had put a bullet into him . . . We found him on top of a snow bank, about eight yards from the house on the south-west side. He fell, and lay there for half a minute nearly, when he staggered to his feet and made off, followed by the dogs . . . As he went over the fresh water pond, I gave him one in the left flank, ripping it up and fracturing the left shoulder, but still on he went, bleeding profusely, and scrambled down the steep icy slope towards the flow; he and the dogs getting mixed up into a confused heap on the way down . . . On their separating out a little, I put two more bullets into him and finished him.

Franz Josef Land is in the northeastern Barents Sea, north of Novaya Zemlya, and 600 miles from the North Pole. There are more than 100 islands, mostly covered with ice, with rocks and lichens occasionally poking through. In 1872, the Austrian explorers Weyprecht and Payer, seeking the Northeast Passage in the *Admiral Tegetthoff*, became trapped in the pack ice at Novaya Zemlya and drifted for a year. Polar bears were more than likely to welcome anybody who landed on Franz Josef Land. As Herman Dieck wrote in his 1885 account of the Weyprecht and Payer expedition,

Almost no journey was undertaken without more or less danger from the immense bears which inhabit these regions, and sometimes the creatures approached the vessel itself with great boldness. An incident occurred on the 6th of March, in which a valued member of the expedition nearly lost his life from the boldness of one of these beasts. "We were sitting," writes Lieutenant Payer, "fortunately silent in the cabin, when Koldewey suddenly heard a faint cry for help. We all hurriedly tumbled up the companion-ladder to the deck, when an exclamation from Börgen, 'A bear is carrying me off,' struck painfully on our ears. It was quite dark; we could scarcely see anything, but we made directly for the quarter whence the cry proceeded, armed with poles, weapons, etc., over hummocks and drifts, when an alarm shot which we fired into the air seemed to make some impression, as the bear dropped his prey, and ran forward a few paces. He turned again, however, dragging his victim over the broken-shore ice, close to a field which stretched in a southerly direction. All depended upon our coming up with him before he should reach this field, as he would carry his prey over the open plain with the speed of a horse, and thus escape. We succeeded. The bear turned upon us for a moment, and then, scared by our continuous fire, let fall his prey."

When the Jackson-Harmsworth expedition explored the icy archipelago some years later, they were among the first humans (and dogs)

the bears had ever seen. The bears demonstrated their natural curiosity by snooping around the camp and investigating the dogs. At that time, polar bears were considered extremely dangerous, so Jackson and his men naturally interpreted the bears' proximity as a precursor to aggression, and shot every bear within range. Then they went looking for more bears to kill to stock their larder.*

Except in denning areas such as Churchill and Wrangel Island, where many polar bears can be seen at one time, the white bears generally lead isolated lives, so there is little chance that anyone would be able to establish a concentrated hunt for them. But armed men in the area where the bears were found wouldn't pass up an opportunity to shoot at a bear, and during the eighteenth and nineteenth centuries in Svalbard, Franz Josef Land, and Novaya Zemlya a great many were killed. In his 1988 book, *Polar Bears,* Ian Stirling wrote that "in the winter of 1784–85, a single Russian crew at Magdalena Bay [Svalbard] killed 150 bears, and similar harvests were taken in subsequent winters." Savva Uspenski, a Russian polar bear expert, wrote that from 1890 to 1910 (including Jackson's total), no fewer than 150 bears were killed every year in the archipelago of Franz Josef Land. Around Novaya Zemlya, the main target of the Russian hunters was the walrus, but they shot at bears whenever they spotted them. "Overall," wrote Stirling, "Uspenski estimates that more than 150,000 polar bears have been killed or captured in Eurasia since the beginning of the eighteenth century—quite an impressive record."

Knud Rasmussen, born in 1879 to a Danish missionary and an Inuit mother in Jakobshavn, Greenland, led the "Fifth Thule Expedition," an

---

* Included in Jackson's book is a thirty-page "Game List," identifying every animal that was shot during the expedition, by whom, with what weapon, and at what distance. They shot various birds, such as plovers, kittiwakes, ducks, and guillemots (which they called "looms"), but the most important "game" was the polar bear and the walrus, and the list includes a detailed accounting of the demise of every he-bear, she-bear, he-walrus, and she-walrus. From August 17, 1894, to August 11, 1897, Jackson and his men killed eighty-three polar bears and thirty-seven walruses. After Nansen's rescue (June 16, 1896), he too participated in the bear hunts. The entry for June 24, a she-bear shot by the flagstaff at Cape Flora from forty yards, reads, "Shot by Nansen. Jackson took a number of negatives of her before being fired at and after being wounded. She had thin milk in her teats, but was not pregnant. Hair on belly very thin. Probably had just got rid of cub."

epic journey of ethnographic investigation across the top of North America from Greenland to Siberia. From 1921 to 1924 he and six companions traveled 20,000 miles by dogsled, collected 20,000 artifacts, and compiled thousands of pages of information about Inuit culture and life. Because wildlife was—(and is)—an important part of life of Arctic peoples, Magnus Degerbøl and Peter Freuchen observed the animals in the wild, collected specimens, and published their extensive observations in a 1935 report. They collected and wrote about everything from lemmings and Arctic hares to wolves, foxes, wolverines, walruses, caribou, moose, musk oxen, various seal species, and, of course, polar bears. In the report, Freuchen wrote, "The life of the polar bear is well known from innumerable reports of journeys and observations and I shall therefore merely reproduce a few of the many field notes made on the subject." Many of these involved spotting a bear and shooting it, as in this one from July 28, 1922: "From the shore shot a bear on an ice floe out in Frozen Strait. It lay quietly on the ice, looking curiously up at us as we stood on a point where it was passing. When it was shot it leaped into the air before expiring." Or May 15, 1923: "Shot a lean female bear, not very old, at Pitoqaq on Melville Peninsula. Its stomach was full of blubber and a single lemming." Freuchen also wrote a chapter on the lives of polar bears, in which he included many of his own observations:

One never sees a bear in parts where there are no seals. Of course, in emergencies it has to be content with other animals, and sometimes it will do what it can with a walrus; this animal, however is not easy to kill. A bear cannot overpower it direct, as the walrus is too powerful, and I have once found a bear, a large one, killed by a walrus which had thrust its tusks into its side to their full length. The bear was dead and frozen stiff.

Years on the ice with Inuit gave Freuchen some interesting insights into the behavior of polar bears:

There are too many accounts of its holding up a piece of ice for concealment to doubt that it does so. On the beach the bear can take a slab of ice and carry it a good distance to where it can stalk a sleeping seal . . . In summer the bear catches seals in open water by springing down upon them from icebergs or floes . . . The seal must be hit on the head, where even a light blow will render it unconscious; the bear however, always strikes with such force that the skull is smashed . . . The polar bear seems to be very sagacious. Its calm, collected behavior imparts the impression of well-considered action, and it is not surprising that the Eskimo, to whom a bear is the most noble quarry, considers it a worthy opponent, quite on a level with himself . . . A polar bear must be described as having a raging temper. If one shoots a bear in the leg, for instance, without its knowing that it is being hunted, it will claw at the wound and bite it, as if to punish it for the pain. If two bears are together and one is wounded by gunshot, it at once blames the other and will strike out violently at it, doing the same thing at the next bullet, until a vital part is hit.

Freuchen wrote, "The polar bear is usually hunted with dogs," but that would change when non-natives decided that polar bear hunting would make a good "sport." Where the Inuit would follow the bear's tracks, often for days, later great white hunters often spotted their bears from helicopters or fixed-wing aircraft and then landed to shoot them. Although there were transgressions—and there still are—around 1956 the then Soviet Union prohibited the hunting of polar bears. Trophy hunting for polar bears from airplanes began shortly after World War II, and continued until 1972, when Alaska (which became a state in 1959) outlawed the activity. The U.S. Marine Mammal Protection Act of 1972 transferred jurisdiction from the states to the federal government and prohibited the taking of any marine mammals in Alaska, including polar bears, by anyone other than Alaskan natives. As of Jack Lentfer's 1979 discussion of hunting, Norwegian sealers could kill bears because they interfered with the seal hunt; Spitsbergen trappers could kill bears and sell their hides; and in Greenland (which belongs to Denmark) the local people were allowed to kill bears for subsistence and the personal use of the skins. The same is, and was, true for Canadian Inuit, but sport hunters could purchase a permit to hunt a bear as long as they made use of a dog team and a local guide.

Including a species under the Marine Mammal Protection Act would seem to indicate that it is, in fact, a "marine mammal." There is no question about whales, dolphins, porpoises, and manatees; they are air-breathing mammals that spend their entire lives in the water and die if they come or are brought onto land. But what about the pinnipeds—the seals, sea lions, and walruses? They spend a lot of time in the water, but come onto land or ice to breed and raise their young. They are marine mammals. So too the sea otters, whose common name comes from their lifestyle—they spend most of their time in the sea. But like other otters, they can and do come out on land. So is the polar bear a marine mammal? Its scientific name, *Ursus maritimus,* seems to suggest that it is, but like seals, sea lions, and walruses, polar bears spend most of their time out of the water. If living full-time in the water is the criterion for defining a marine mammal, then the only species that truly qualify are the cetaceans (whales, dolphins, and porpoises) and the sirenians (manatees and dugongs).

But while every book with "marine mammals" in the title includes seals, sea lions, walruses, and, frequently, the sea otter, some do not include the polar bear. The white bear does not appear, for example, in Ken Norris's 1966 *Mammals of the Sea,* and we find no sign of it in R. J. Harrison and Judith King's 1968 *Marine Mammals.* The authoritative (and otherwise comprehensive) six-volume *Handbook of Marine Mammals* (1981–1999) does not include a section on the polar bear, but in the *Encyclopedia of Marine Mammals* (also published by Academic Press), *Ursus maritimus* rates a proper entry. In his 2008 article on the evolution of Arctic marine mammals, C. R. Harington says that the polar bear is one of the "core" marine mammals, and therefore discusses *U. maritimus* at some length. The bear shows up (quite erroneously, I think) in the 1992 *Sierra Club Handbook of Seals and Sirenians;* and in the 2002 Audubon Society *Guide to the Marine Mammals of the World,* the polar bear has the honor of being the first mammal discussed after the introduction. In a 2007 report on Canada's polar bears (Page, Gue, and Moola), the question "terrestrial or marine mammals?" is asked, but not answered.

By its inclusion in many (but not all) marine mammal books, the polar bear would appear to qualify for the title. But does it really? It certainly fails if the criterion is spending all your life in the water, as whales and dolphins do. Breeding on land but feeding in the water, the way pinnipeds do? Well, it doesn't do those things either. As we've seen, polar bears take to the water to get from here to there, or when they're stalking a seal, but most of their lives are spent on land or ice. Female polar bears can spend up to eight months holed up in a den, and males can pass the better part of any year walking around looking for a receptive female or a sleeping seal. Polar bears are excellent swimmers, certainly the best of all the bears, but this on its own doesn't qualify them as marine mammals—Irish water spaniels, Newfoundlands, Portuguese water dogs, Labrador retrievers, and Chesapeake Bay retrievers are also very good swimmers, but nobody thinks of them as marine mammals. All bears can swim—and, in fact, Charles Darwin had read of a bear swimming through the water with its mouth open, catching insects, and from that he came to the rather surprising conclusion that bears could, over time, develop into whales. In the first edition of *The Origin of Species*, he wrote, "I can see no difficulty in a race of bears being rendered, by natural selection, more and more aquatic in their structure and habits, with larger and larger mouths, till a creature was produced as monstrous as a whale." He removed the bear story from later editions, but he seemed to regret having done so, and later wrote that he saw "no special difficulty in the bear's mouth being enlarged to any degree useful to its changing habits."

At one time or another, every polar bear will set foot on land, something no whale, dolphin, porpoise, manatee, or dugong can ever do intentionally—all these marine mammals have flippers instead of feet, of course, so they couldn't set *foot* on land anyway. Pinnipeds also have flippers instead of feet, but unless the criterion for defining a marine mammal is that it spends all its time in the water, seals, sea lions, and walruses are almost always included. Calling the polar bear *Ursus maritimus*, as Constantine Phipps did in 1774, does not automatically make it a "marine bear," but it certainly spends more time in the water than other bear species. Probably the most confusing element in the conundrum is the nature of the "terrain" on which it spends a lot of its life—it is not, in fact, "terrain," which comes from the Latin *terra*, meaning "earth" or "ground," but ice, the solid form of water. So the polar bear spends a lot of time walking on water or swimming in it—which might legitimately qualify it as a true marine mammal.

Whether to consider the polar bear a marine mammal or not is probably a matter best left to nomenclatural taxonomists, if indeed there are such specialists. But no matter what category you put the white bear in—marine mammal, or terrestrial mammal that likes to swim—the only important classification, for the bears, if not the taxonomists, is that the polar bear was included in the Marine Mammal Protection Act of 1972. The act was passed in response to increasing concerns among scientists and the public that significant declines in some species of marine mammals were caused by human activities. The act established a national policy to prevent species and population stocks from declining beyond the point where they ceased to be significant functioning elements of the ecosystems of which they are a part. The Department of Commerce, through the National Marine Fisheries Service, is charged with protecting whales, dolphins, porpoises, seals, and sea lions, while walruses, manatees, sea otters, and polar bears are shielded by the Department of the Interior, through the U.S. Fish & Wildlife Service. Regardless of the agency, however, all marine mammals are protected under the Marine Mammal Protection Act. The "prohibitions" for polar bears read as follows:

Sec. 502 (a) IN GENERAL—It is unlawful for any person who is subject to the jurisdiction of the United States or any person in waters or on lands under the jurisdiction of the United States—

(1) to take any polar bear in violation of the Agreement;

(2) to take any polar bear in violation of the Agreement or any annual taking limit or other restriction on the taking of polar bears that is adopted by the Commission pursuant to the Agreement;

(3) to import, export, possess, transport, sell, receive, acquire, or purchase, exchange, barter, or offer to sell, purchase, exchange, or barter any polar bear, or any part or product of a polar bear, that is taken in violation of paragraph (2);

(4) to import, export, sell, purchase, exchange, barter, or offer to sell, purchase, exchange, or barter, any polar bear gall bile or polar bear gall bladder;

(5) to attempt to commit, solicit another person to commit, or cause to be committed, any offense under this subsection; or

(6) to violate any regulation promulgated by the Secretary to implement any of the prohibitions established in this subsection.

The inclusion of the polar bear in the 1972 Marine Mammal Protection Act would become an integral component of the 2008 controversy regarding its listing as an endangered species.

The brown bear that we know today is probably the same species that spun off the polar bears—large, dark brown animals, though they can vary from a light creamy color to almost black. Brown bears are thickly furred animals, and low temperatures would not be much of a deterrent to their earning a living. But brown bears are omnivores, which means that they are adapted to eat a variety of foods, depending on what is available at a particular time of year. The mighty and formidable grizzly, for example, with its intimidating canine teeth and great hooked claws, eats mainly vegetation such as berries, bulbs, and roots, but it also consumes ants, fish, and mammals large and small. The farther north you get, the sparser becomes the plant life, and when you reach the sea ice, there is none whatsoever. To survive, bears of the North had to learn to eat what was available—mostly seals. But a predator that is very large and dark brown in color might have a problem sneaking up on wary

Spooked by the helicopter, a grizzly runs along the shore of the Beaufort Sea in Alaska.

seals, so the bears that were even a little lighter in color stood a better chance of blending into the landscape. The naked soles of the feet of brown bears are not particularly well adapted to walking on snow and ice, but if some brown bears had even a bit more fur on the soles of their feet, they would have had an advantage over those with naked soles, and might therefore have been more successful in traveling over the frozen wastes. Unlike the claws of grizzlies, which are particularly effective for digging or even tree climbing, those of polar bears are shorter and heavier, useful for hooking seals or scrambling up walls of ice. Where brown bears have a powerful muscular hump on their shoulders, the back of the polar bear is relatively smooth. Both species, however, have enormously powerful forelegs; the grizzly can break the neck of a moose with a single swipe of its arm, and the polar bear can yank a 400-pound seal completely out of the water.

III

The Great Ice Bear

Lord of the Arctic

According to Björn Kurtén, a Finnish paleontologist with a Swedish name—and a first name that means "bear"—there was an even larger polar bear, *Ursus maritimus tyrannus*, before the advent of *Ursus maritimus*. In *Pleistocene Mammals of North America* (1964) he wrote, "The Late Pleistocene Polar Bear *U. maritimus tyrannus*, new subspecies, was markedly larger than the living. As late as in Yolida times, the Polar Bear was on average more *arctos*-like than at present, indicating that evolution within the species has continued in the Postglacial." A fossil of a polar bear was discovered in a most unlikely location: Kew Bridge, near London, England. Kurtén dates this find, which consists only of the right ulna (the forearm bone), as "Late Pleistocene, probably early Würm," which corresponds to the Wisconsinian in North America, and represents the last glaciation, dating from about 100,000 years ago. As described by Kurtén, the fossil is "a bear ulna of gigantic proportions . . . the largest ursine ulna on record," including those of the huge, long-legged cave bears of the Americas, now extinct.

At one time, the polar bear was placed in the genus *Thalarctos* (meaning "sea bear") because of its different morphology and aquatic habits, but it is now in the same genus—*Ursus*—as the black bear *(U. americanus),* brown bear *(U. arctos),* sun bear *(U. malayanus),* and sloth bear *(U. ursinus).* The only bears not in this genus are the spectacled bear of South America, *Tremarctos ornatus,* and the giant panda, *Ailuropoda melanoleuca.* That brown bears and polar bears diverged fairly recently—in geological terms, that is—can be seen in their potential for interbreeding. Usually, when two species (like horses and donkeys) interbreed, the offspring are sterile, but when captive brown bears and polar bears have been interbred, the female offspring have been fertile. At the National Zoo in Washington, D.C., a brown bear and a polar bear produced a fertile "golden bear" offspring, as was discovered by attendants after a romantic liaison that the workers were wise not to try to interrupt. (In 2006 a hunter in Alaska bagged what was almost certainly a wild polar bear–grizzly hybrid, but that story comes later.) Hybrid cubs are usually light at birth and become darker with age, but there are some that have been partially white and partially dark.

The brown bear has a round face and a dished profile; the polar bear has a narrower head with an almost Roman nose. Why would a shorter nose and a dished face be disadvantageous in the polar regions? Well, if you're an eater of berries and grasses, you probably don't have to smell them to find them—you're usually walking on or up to your food, and it's not likely that you're going to have to locate it by smell. But if you're hunting elusive mammals, it helps to be able to smell them from a distance even before you see them (or they see you), so you can adjust your approach accordingly. Because most of the world's polar bears live in areas where hardly any land plants grow, they are restricted almost exclusively to a diet of meat. Originally placed in the category of polar bears that fast until the seal-catching season begins, the bears of Manitoba, who spend the autumn on land, often take that opportunity to eat plant matter of one sort or another. Between 1986 and 1992, Derocher et al. examined the feeding habits of polar bears during the ice-free period in western Hudson Bay, and found that 34 percent of the females and 26 percent of the males had eaten quantities of "terrestrial vegetation," specifically bogberries and crowberries. Polar bears will eat vegetation when they have to, but the energy gained from plant matter is considerably less than that from eating animal fat and flesh.

The polar bear's scientific name is *Ursus maritimus,* but we would call it *Ursa major* if that name hadn't already been taken by a constellation. Polar bears are "super-bears"—bigger, stronger, faster, prettier, and probably smarter than all others. However, it's not at all clear how they climbed to this pinnacle of bear evolution. "Most of what we know about the origins of the polar bear," wrote Ian Stirling, "is the result of years of painstaking examination by the Finnish paleontologist Björn Kurtén." In his 1964 study "The Evolution of the Polar Bear" Kurtén detailed his examination of the few existing fossil polar bear specimens, but admitted that "fossil remains of the polar bear . . . are very scarce. Why this should be so is not altogether clear. In the beach deposits within its present range, for instance Spitzbergen, Polar Bear bones of recent or sub-recent age are certainly quite common." When did a wandering band of brown bears begin to evolve into polar bears? Kurtén answered, "Biometric comparisons of growth patterns of Polar Bear skull . . . may suggest that *Ursus maritimus* branched off from the evolving Brown Bear phylum at a fairly late date, perhaps during the Middle Pleistocene." On the geologic timescale, the Pleistocene epoch is usually dated from 1,808,000 to 11,550 years before the present (BP), and covers the earth's recent period of repeated glaciations, especially in the high latitudes. In *The Evidence of Evolution,* paleontologist Nicholas Hotton described the (hypothetical) process:

> In the north . . . groups of brown bears were forced out or exterminated by bitter cold and shrinking food supplies, and what survivors there were remained as small groups struggling for existence in an ever harsher environment. But since climates, no matter how cold (or hot) are often more tolerable near the sea, it is very possible that some of these surviving brown bears made a desperate stand along

northern seacoasts. Here they became totally isolated by the migration or extinction of others of their kind in the interior. As food became even scarcer and conditions grew steadily worse, it was perhaps inevitable that these coastal bears would, on an increasing scale, turn to the sea for food. Some, of course, were better able to utilize the new marine environment. They were the ones who survived to reproduce, and in doing so transmitted the features that had been proved successful to their offspring.*

In Alaska or Siberia, within the last million years, a population of brown bears separated from the rest of their conspecifics and wandered northward into climes that became progressively colder and colder. During that time, the continents were arranged pretty much the way they are now, but the climate was constantly changing. Ice sheets advanced and receded, altering the conditions in which animals had to live. When the ice advanced, the region was cooled; as the climate warmed and the ice melted, different plants took root, and forests grew where there had previously been only glaciers. Faced with changing environmental conditions, animals can move to a place where conditions are still suitable or they can die off. Inability to adapt is one of the accepted explanations for the otherwise mysterious phenomenon we call extinction. In *Pleistocene Mammals of North America,* Björn Kurtén and Elaine Anderson wrote,

> Extinction, the end of a phyletic line without replacement, has occurred throughout the history of life on earth and is the ultimate destiny of every species. The extinction of the dinosaurs at the end of

---

* Although this is the conventional Darwinian explanation, some evolutionary theorists suggest that the transition from dish-faced, naked-soled brown bears to Roman-nosed, fur-footed white bears was somewhat more complicated, and that there were other factors at work besides random mutations. If only a small group of brown bears wandered north from Siberia, the opportunity for passing along advantageous modifications would be greatly increased by inbreeding. Epigenetics, the study of inherited changes in gene expression that occur without a change in the DNA sequence, demonstrates that genetic modifications can be engineered by environmental conditions—for example, researchers have been able to alter the epigenome of certain mice by changing their diet—so the mutations are not necessarily random. Moreover, it has been shown that genetic modification rarely affects only one gene at a time, so a modification of the genome can produce multiple changes in subsequent generations. Paleontologists Niles Eldredge and Stephen Jay Gould's hypothesis of "punctuated equilibrium" suggests that after long periods of stasis, a suite of modifications can kick in, essentially creating a new species in a relatively short period of time.

the Mesozoic and the "sudden" disappearance of the megafauna at the end of the Wisconsonian are the best-known examples of widespread extinction. Hundreds of causes have been suggested to explain extinction (Van Valen 1969 lists eighty-six reasons for the late Pleistocene alone), yet, for the most part, extinction remains an enigma.

The megafauna that disappeared at the end of the Wisconsonian included the mastodons, mammoths, saber-toothed cats, dire wolves, woolly rhinos, and ground sloths on the North American plains, as well as American camels, lions, horses, and short-faced bears. The Wisconsonian was the last major advance of the continental glaciers in North America, consisting of three glacial maximums (commonly called ice ages) separated by interglacial periods, such as the one we are now living in. The Tioga, the least severe and last of the Wisconsonian group, started about 30,000 years ago, reached its greatest advance 20,000 years ago, and ended with the retreat of the glaciers about 10,000 years before the present. We don't know if it was the arrival of man-the-hunter or climate change (probably a combination of the two) that caused the extinction of the North American megafauna—but we do know that they are all gone. Long before the Wisconsonian, however, that cohort of brown bears had wandered north to begin the process of becoming polar bears.

In his 1990 *White Bear*, Charles Feazel neatly sums up what was required to become a polar bear: "The polar bear's changes, though recent, are profound. Not only has he gone from brown to white, from land to sea, and from omnivore to carnivore, but he has completely reversed the seasons of the bear year. Winter is a time of activity; summer is for fasting, resting, and conserving energy." In a remarkably short time, polar bears developed many of the modifications that enable them to function in one of the harshest climates on earth. Their feet became larger, and their footpads developed hair. They acquired the ability to store large stores of fat under their skin. They became long-distance swimmers. They learned to run faster than most other bears. They learned to depend almost exclusively on a single food source, and then figured out how to catch an animal that spends a lot of time under thick ice.

The idea that a population of brown bears separated from the rest of their conspecifics, wandered northward into climes that became pro-

Comfortable in one of the harshest environments on earth

gressively colder and colder, and then became polar bears is a convenient explanation, but an unlikely one. The DNA of brown bears and polar bears is very similar, but that does not mean that the white bears are descended from the brown ones. The similarity of the DNA of *Homo sapiens* and chimpanzees does not prove that men are descended from apes, but rather that they share a common ancestor. (When Darwin's *Origin of Species* was published in 1859, the vociferous and numerous critics of his theory of evolution claimed that he had said that humans were descended from monkeys, which he certainly did not.) The scant fossil evidence of polar bears may not demonstrate the relatively recent development of *Ursus maritimus,* but rather something more prosaic: an absence of fossil material. Somewhere under the northern ice or permafrost, there may be a "missing link" that would show a transitional phase between the brown bears and the white.

White fur is obvious for an animal that lives amid ice floes and has to resort to stealth to capture its prey, but we don't know why a polar bear's skin is black. The bear's coat consists of two layers—an undercoat of dense woolly hair and an outer coat of long guard hairs, which may be six inches long. The guard hairs are hollow, but probably not enough to contribute to the bear's buoyancy when swimming. When dry, the polar bear's coat is thick and coarse, with 10,000 hairs per square inch, making it one of the densest coats of any animal. (The densest coat belongs to the sea otter, which has no insulating blubber layer, and has as many as 200,000 hairs per square inch.) Polar bear fur does not mat when it is wet, which allows the bear to shake out water before it freezes. Small ears also prevent heat loss, and the Roman nose is equipped with large sinuses that amplify the bear's sense of smell. In short, the polar bear shows every evidence of having evolved from its forest omnivore predecessor to become an apex predator of the Arctic snow and ice. Imagine a lifestyle that requires large carnivores to go for as long as eight months without eating.

That's what pregnant female polar bears do, as the males wander around looking for trouble and something to eat. And in the time that the great northern bears were turning from *Ursus arctos* into *Ursus maritimus*, they became what Alanda Lennox and Allen Goodship (2007) called "the most evolutionarily advanced hibernators, . . . [which can] avoid significant bone loss during hibernation." Twenty-one wild female polar bears were captured before and after hibernation near Churchill, Manitoba, as part of an ongoing research program by the Canadian Wildlife Service in conjunction with Lennox and Goodship of the Royal Veterinary College in Hertfordshire, England. Analysis of blood samples revealed that during hibernation, female bears do not lose any of the strength in their bones; in fact, they actually ratchet up the creation of new bone. (If they could figure out how polar bears are able to do this, scientists might find a way to prevent osteoporosis, a disease in humans—most often seen in older women—characterized by abnormally porous bone that is compressible like a sponge, rather than dense like a brick. Osteoporosis weakens the bone, increasing the risk for fractures.)

The modifications that turned a brown, temperate-zone, land-based bear into a white, semi-aquatic, cold-weather bear appear to be textbook examples of "descent with modification," Darwin's explanation for the origin of a species, but this interpretation leaves a great deal to be desired. It implies that animals evolve toward perfection—or, as is often said about the polar bear, "perfectly adapted to its environment"—and this comes dangerously close to the idea of "intelligent design," postulating a governing force that fits every creature neatly into the niche designed for it. More likely, those lines that didn't develop traits that would enable them to survive and prosper in the new environment died off, leaving only the better-adapted lines. And while many of the polar bear's adaptations appear perfect for a carnivorous life on the ice, they are often limitations—or even handicaps—as well. Being the world's largest terrestrial predator may not be that much of a benefit; polar bears have to be able to find enough food to sustain their huge bodies, and the seals that the bears prefer are not that easy to catch. The polar bear has evolved into the consummate specialist, and rather than sitting comfortably at the top of the Arctic food chain, its continued existence is being threatened by the changing climate. As long as the ice retreats, those bears that do not head inland might become modified in time to spend more time in the water—becoming mammals that are even more marine.

The polar bears of the Arctic have a circumpolar distribution, and wander freely across national borders. They are found in Canada, Norway, Greenland, Russia, and Alaska, remaining on the ice in winter but often coming onto dry land in the summer. The bears have enormous home ranges, and they roam over vast distances in their constant search for food. It has been estimated that an individual polar bear might cover an area equal to 100,000 square miles during its lifetime. An adult female tagged with a satellite transmitter in a radio collar in 1992 traveled from the Alaskan Beaufort Sea to northern Greenland, covering a

Polar bears are at home in the water as well as on land, and are probably marine mammals.

total of 5,256 kilometers (3,538 miles) in four months, and on this "polar route" came within 2° of the North Pole (Durner and Amstrup 1995). In 2001, from the deck of the Russian icebreaker *Yamal*, crewmen spotted a polar bear walking slowly on the ice about 500 meters from the ship. The Global Positioning System (GPS) located the ship at 89°46.5'N, 26°21.1'E, about thirteen miles from the North Pole, the northernmost sighting of a polar bear on record (van Meurs and Splettstoesser 2003).

The size of the home range is extremely dynamic and varies from year to year depending on ice conditions and the location of the seal populations. Polar bears do not defend their home ranges from other bears, and thus it is normal for the ranges of individual bears to overlap. The most accessible—and therefore the best known—of all polar bear populations is the one that arrives in Churchill in the fall and then ventures out onto the ice as Hudson Bay begins to freeze. There are perhaps 1,000 bears in the area of western Hudson Bay. Pack ice that is fractured by wind and currents appears to be the favorite habitat of polar bears, perhaps because seal hunting is most expeditiously pursued in these circumstances.

Male polar bears (sometimes, but not often, called "boars") are considerably larger than females (sometimes called "sows"); in fact, a full-grown male polar bear is among the largest land predators in the world. (The only land carnivore that can rival it in size is a male brown bear of Kodiak or Admiralty Island. Because polar bears have longer bodies, however, one standing on its hind legs is taller than a brown bear.) Male polar bears grow two to three times the size of females, weigh in at 800 to 1,700 pounds, and can measure eight to ten feet from black nose to stubby tail. The largest polar bear ever recorded was a male that weighed 2,209 pounds—more than a ton—and whose stretched skin was twelve feet long.* Adult females can weigh 500 pounds, but just

---

* Gerald Wood's 1982 *Guinness Book of Animal Facts and Feats*—which is, despite its Barnum-like title, a fairly serious work of investigative scholarship—confirms this weight in the entry titled "Greatest Weight Recorded for a Polar Bear in the Wild." Wood writes that it was a "white colossus shot by Arthur Dubs of Medford, Oregon, at the polar entrance to Kotzebue Sound NW Alaska in 1960. In April 1962, the 11 foot 1½ in. tall mounted animal was put on display at the Seattle World's Fair, but the present whereabouts of this exhibit are unknown." Wood cites no authority for this record, but "Arthur R. Dubs" is listed as producer/director of 1970s documentary films, mostly about Alaska, with titles like *Vanishing Wilderness* and *Wilderness Family*, so it is not unlikely that he was shooting bears at Kotzebue in 1960.

before going into a maternity den they might weigh twice that. The size discrepancy between males and females places polar bears among the most sexually dimorphic terrestrial mammals in the world; only in elephant seals is the size ratio of males to females greater.

The teeth of polar bears are similar to other carnivores'—that is, the cheek teeth (carnassials) have evolved a sharp-edged surface suitable for shearing off bite-size chunks of meat and blubber. Also, the canine teeth, used for seizing and holding prey, are enormous, and longer, sharper, and wider apart than in brown bears. Indeed, the polar bear is classified as an obligate carnivore, meaning it eats only meat. Polar bears do not chew their food; they bite off a chunk of meat and swallow it. At birth, the skin of a polar bear is pink, and the neonate is covered with a fine sparse coat (Kenney et al. 2005). It takes several months for the skin of its body, nose, and those parts of the feet that are exposed to turn black. (The skin of brown bears is brown.) "Allen's Rule" holds that the farther north an animal is found, the smaller its extremities, to prevent the escape of body heat. Thus, the ears and tails of polar bears are much smaller than those protuberances on brown bears.

Like Moby-Dick, polar bears aren't really white, except perhaps when they leave their birth den for the first time. As they grow, their fur begins to darken. Eventually it becomes a yellowish-cream color, for which the word "ivory" is sometimes used, but some bears are definitely yellow and some are grayish. Quite often the bear's face is stained dark by the blood of the animal it has been eating, but the white bears are fussy about hygiene and appearance, and clean themselves often, by licking their paws or rolling in the snow. (Frequent baths in ice water also help.) There are polar bears that are more yellow than white, which would make it difficult to sneak up on a seal in the snow, but if seals see in color—and most mammals do—it wouldn't be that hard to spot even a slightly yellowish bear against the blue-white snow. Sometimes, however, things aren't what they appear to be in this white-on-white landscape. When Elisha Kent Kane's ship was stuck in the ice in 1854, he looked over the traps he and his men had set and thought he saw a bear in the distance: "I resolved to crawl to the edge of the ice-foot," he wrote, "and peer under my hands in the dark shadow of the hummock ridges. I did so. One look: nothing. A second: no bear after all. A third: what is that long rounded shade? Stained ice? Yes, stained ice. The stained ice gave a gross menagerie roar and charged on the instant for my position." Kane had no weapon, so he turned and ran back to the ship, throwing off his mittens as he went to distract the bear.

It is difficult to compare the sense of smell in different animals, but we know that dogs rely heavily on their ability to track their prey by scent, and the entire sport of foxhunting on horseback is based on the ability of hounds to find and follow the trail of a fox that may have traveled that way hours or even days earlier. People have long capitalized on the dog's sense of smell by using them to sniff out explosives, drugs, missing children, and buried survivors of avalanches and earthquakes. Researchers are now attempting to harness the olfactory powers of canines for use in the field of medicine, to warn of epileptic seizures, low blood sugar, and heart attacks. Canine scent trackers like bloodhounds are believed to have a sense of smell that is much more sensitive than that of humans, and a polar bear's is better than the bloodhound's. Depending upon wind direction and other environmental variables, it is likely that a polar bear will smell sled dogs long before the dogs can smell the bear.

Bears rely on their sense of smell to find food, locate mates, detect and avoid danger in the form of other bears and humans, and identify their cubs. In their book *Bears* (the cover of which uses one of my photographs shot from the *Kapitan Dranitsyn*), Dagmar Fertl and Michelle Reddy wrote, "By far, the bear's best sense is smell—some people even call them 'noses with legs.'" Although the region of the bear's brain devoted to the sense of smell is average in size, the area of nasal mucous membrane in a bear's head is a hundred times larger than in a human's, and there may be as many as a billion receptor cells that transmit olfactory information to the bear's brain. Bears and many other mammals have something called Jacobson's organ (also known as the vomeronasal organ) in the roof of the mouth, which further enhances their olfactory senses and may even enable them to "smell" electrostatic disturbances in the air that occur within storm systems. The longer muzzle of the polar bear contains more sinus spaces than the shorter snout of the brown bear, strongly suggesting a keener sense of smell. (That is not to say that the brown bear has a poor sense of smell; it's just that the polar bear's is better.) Polar bears are often seen rising on their hind legs to smell the air. They can smell seals through two feet of ice, and a decaying whale carcass twenty miles away; a male bear can track a female for weeks by following her scent trail. An old Indian saying may best describe the

A polar bear is a "walking nose" in a white fur coat.

olfactory awareness of bears: "A pine needle fell in the forest. The eagle saw it. The deer heard it. The bear smelled it."

The sensitivity of a bear's nasal passages makes it particularly vulnerable to irritants such as pepper spray, often advertised as a way of stopping a bear attack. Also known as OC spray (from oleoresin capsicum—*Capsicum* is the hot peppers' scientific name), pepper spray is a chemical compound made from dried peppers that can irritate the eyes and nasal passages and is used in crowd and riot control, personal self-defense, and defense against dogs and bears. It works on bears, according to a 2008 study by Smith et al., who wrote, "Red pepper spray stopped bears' undesirable behavior 92% of the time when used on brown bears, 90% for black bears, and 100% for polar bears." In a letter to me, Nikita Ovsyanikov wrote that in the three bear attacks he has experienced, "all three times, I could manage to stop the bear by sharp and right reaction and help of pepper spray."

The neck of a polar bear is longer than that of a brown bear, and its head is proportionately smaller. All bears can stand upright on their hind legs, a technique they use to see over greater distances. And all bears walk in a *plantigrade* manner—that is, on the soles of their feet with their heels hitting the ground first, just like humans. Polar bears swing their front paws outward with each lumbering step, then turn them inward, so they land slightly pigeon-toed. Richard Perry described the walking style of the polar bear: "The whalermen also referred to the polar bear as the Farmer, in recognition of his somewhat agricultural gait, with heavy hindquarters—elephantine in their bluffness—higher then low shoulders, and the lean head poised on the long, powerful neck, humped with muscle, ever swaying from side to side with the movement of his bandy forelegs." This bandy-legged, pigeon-toed walk in polar bear cubs is one of their many endearing qualities, and it often transfers to adults. Even when you know how dangerous the polar bear can be, its thick white coat, black button eyes, and shambling walk combine to make it appear harmless.

Nobody doubts that a polar bear charging a seal can cover a lot of ground very quickly—but how quickly? Many researchers give twenty-five miles per hour as the bear's maximum speed, but in *Lords of the Arctic*, Richard Davids says that a polar bear "was reliably clocked along

A bear stands atop an old whale carcass.

the road to the Churchill airport at thirty-five miles an hour." Davids then quotes biologist Mitchell Taylor, who has studied polar bears from Wrangel Island to Svalbard: "Thirty-five miles an hour is not unusual, and some bears may go considerably faster . . . Fastest of all are the subadults of good size but not fat; they are nicknamed 'runners' by biologists."* In *Polar Animals*, his 1962 account of six years spent in East Greenland, Alwin Pedersen wrote, "I have seen bears moving so fast on the fresh-polished ice that no dog could catch them, and they are absolutely unequalled in deep snow, where, with their long limbs and great paws, they can move faster than any other animals." As with so many of their advantageous modifications, polar bears can move through snow and on ice fast enough to catch what they need to catch. But Andrew Derocher writes, "I have clocked them and never above 35 mph. Not even close. If a greyhound can do 43 mph, does it make sense that a bear can do 35 mph? No."

Even though they might be capable of short bursts of speed, most moving polar bears are walking, and not particularly fast, either. When trotting—an unusual activity for a polar bear—they move both right and both left legs together, like a harness horse "pacing." They are remarkably good climbers; their powerful shoulder muscles and sharp claws enable them to scale nearly vertical walls of ice. When not actively hunting, migrating, or searching for a mate, however, polar bears spend a lot of time not moving at all. They will wait immobile for hours at a seal's breathing hole, or flop down wherever they happen to be—on snow, ice, or dry land—and have a nap.

Polar bears are world-class sleepers. They can sleep almost anywhere, at almost any time. They will curl up for a nap in a blizzard or lie down in the late-autumn sunshine of Churchill for a snooze. For a polar bear, there is no such thing as an uncomfortable or inappropriate bed. They have been seen sleeping sitting up, and sprawled out on their backs in the snow. A polar bear will go to sleep in a snowstorm and wake up

---

* The cheetah, usually considered the fastest land mammal, can run seventy miles per hour, but so can the American pronghorn antelope. Other antelopes can reach fifty mph. A thoroughbred race horse has been clocked at forty-five mph; the American quarter horse, bred for speed over short distances, can reach fifty mph in a sprint. (All quarter-horse races are sprints.) A racing greyhound can reach forty-three mph, as can a coyote. The fastest humans (as clocked for the one-hundred-yard dash) can reach twenty-two mph, which means that a polar bear could catch the fastest human sprinter—if there were ever a bears vs. humans track meet (and the winner got to eat the loser).

completely covered in snow except for its black nose. When Klondike and Snow, two orphaned bear cubs at the Denver Zoo, were given book-sized blocks of ice to play with, they promptly put their heads on these "pillows" and went to sleep.

Anyone who has seen enough polar bears can easily distinguish adult he-bears from she-bears: the boars are huge and powerful looking, with an air of swaggering, hulking majesty. Their heads are broad and massive, contrasted with the narrower heads of the females, and their eyes are relatively smaller than those of the doe-eyed she-bears. Everything about them reeks of power. By the age of fifteen, a wild male bear will have a broad, triangular head, often scarred from fights with other bears. In the wild, polar bears rarely live more than twenty-five years, but in zoos, where they do not have to work very hard for a living, they have been known to reach thirty or more. (Debby, a female at the Assiniboine Park Zoo in Manitoba, was born in Russia in 1966, and died in 2008.)

An adult polar bear is immensely strong, able to kill a 500-pound seal with one blow of its powerful forepaw. "On Wrangel," wrote Nikita Ovsyanikov, "I once tracked a bear that had dragged the 660-pound carcass of a young walrus 495 feet across a gravel spit, then 990 feet through the ice and slush of a lagoon, and finally 165 feet up a 20-degree tundra slope." When Canadian anthropologist Milton Freeman was conducting fieldwork at Grise Fiord on Ellesmere Island, he heard about three belugas that had been trapped by an iceberg in a small area of water and then killed by polar bears. Freeman did not witness the carnage, but he visited the site shortly after the event and was able to tell from the carcasses and the bear tracks that an adult female beluga had been dragged from the water for about twenty feet. From the remains of the beluga, Freeman was able to calculate its weight at about 2,000 pounds, and that of the bear about 285—meaning that the bear had dragged something that weighed seven times as much as it did. In addition to their muscle power, polar bears are armed with formidable claws and teeth. When the *Advance* was stuck in the ice in 1854, bears found Kane's final food cache and completely destroyed it, despite its having been protected with heavy rocks that the men could only move with capstan levers:

Debby, the longest-lived polar bear on record, died in November 2008 at the age of forty-two.

The pemmican was covered with blocks of stone which it had required the labor of three men to adjust; but the extraordinary strength of the bear had enabled him to force aside the heaviest rocks, and his pawing had broken the iron casks which held our pemmican literally into chips. Not a morsel of pemmican remained except in the iron cases, which being round with conical ends, defied both claws and teeth. They had rolled and pawed them in every direction, tossing them around like footballs, although over 80 pounds in weight. An alcohol-case, strongly iron-bound, was dashed into small fragments and a tin can of liquor mashed and twisted almost into a ball. The claws of the beasts had perforated the metal, and torn it up as with a cold chisel.

Although they can "play-fight" for hours—Downs Matthews says that while waiting for Hudson Bay to freeze, they have nothing else to do—during the breeding season adult males sometimes fight in earnest. In a more intense version of ritualized play-fighting, the adult males are trying to win, or least drive their opponent away from a female, who is usually standing by quietly. During the bout, they rise up on their hind legs like furry sumo wrestlers, and using all the weapons at their disposal, they punch, bite, claw, and try to bowl their opponent over. They rarely fight to the death; evenly matched bears will fight until one quits. A well-armed bear can do great damage to another one, and most of the older males exhibit scars from old wounds. During fights, bears growl, bawl, and roar, so unless the viewer is too far away to hear it, battles between polar bears can be very noisy. When an older male approaches a young female with cubs, she (correctly) assumes that he would kill and eat the cubs if he could, so she takes the initiative, and with mouth open and teeth bared she yowls at him that she will defend her cubs by any means necessary. A big he-bear may be three times the size of the female, but in the face of such maternal valor, he is forced to rethink his intentions, and often lowers his head and walks away. Her brave intimidation technique doesn't always work, and there have been instances where half-eaten cubs have been found on the blood-stained ice.

Separated by great distances, it is difficult enough for male bears to find mates in the Arctic vastness, but somehow they are able to track potentially receptive females and follow them unerringly, sometimes for days. Of courtship, Ovsyanikov wrote,

A mated pair walks together. The animals touch each other often and lick each other's faces. They play on the ice, rolling and leaping in the snow. Mating during one season, however, may not be restricted to a single partner; one male may copulate with more than one female (polygamy), and the same is true for females (polyandry.) Almost nothing is known about the strength of the social bonds between sexual partners. Until now, there has been only one piece of evidence that the same partners may get together again in subsequent years. One spring in Svalbard, a female marked with a transmitter mated with a marked male. Three years later they were seen together again at the female's next estrous cycle.

Mating usually takes place on the ice from March to June, and the newly impregnated female then hunts steadily to put on enough fat to support her through the denning, birthing, and early lactation processes. Only pregnant polar bears sleep for months at a time. Other bears will enter a shelter and rest for a short period of time, but the future mothers are the only ones who remain there for the duration of

An old he-bear, identifiable by his size and scars, rests in Churchill before heading out onto the ice.

their pregnancy and beyond. Unlike many other mammals, however, the polar bear's body temperature lowers just slightly. A bear's high body temperature is important, as it keeps the temperature in the den above freezing when the cubs are born. The bear passes neither fecal nor urea waste during hibernation, but has developed a unique process of recycling the urea into usable proteins. Urea buildup would kill most animals within two weeks.

Through a remarkable process called delayed implantation, the fertilized ovum divides a few times and then floats free within the uterus for about six months with its development arrested. Sometime in the early fall, the embryo will attach itself to the uterine wall and resume its development. (Delayed implantation clearly serves an important survival need for the mother. Should she not have put on enough fat reserves before the time to den arrives, the embryo will not implant; it will then be reabsorbed by her body, and she will continue her winter hunting out on the pack ice.) Dens are usually dug in snowbanks, but the bears of Churchill in Hudson Bay occasionally dig their dens in the earth above the permafrost level. The cubs—usually two, occasionally three, and very rarely four—are born between late November and early January. Like all newborn bears, polar bear cubs are small and undeveloped, and weigh about a pound. Their eyes are closed, and open only after a month. When the cubs weigh about fifteen to twenty pounds, the mother breaks out of the den and takes her babies out on the ice to learn to hunt seals. During the first few months, the female nurses the cubs (usually while sitting on her haunches), but when they are three or four months old, she teaches them how to hunt. Cubs stay with their mothers for a couple of years, or until they are large enough to fend for themselves.

Zoologist C. Richard Harington, whom Stirling calls "the original polar bear biologist for the Canadian Wildlife Service," wrote (in 1968) that there are three categories of dens: natural shelters, temporary dens, and maternity dens. A natural shelter can be any cave, rock formation, snow pile, or iceberg that affords the bear shelter from the wind. Temporary dens, said Harington, "are generally excavated by single bears, such as adult males, non-pregnant females, and immatures . . . bears may occupy these dens for periods of a day or two up to 3 or 4 months." Temporary dens vary from a single-room structure with a long entrance tunnel to a small shallow pocket gouged in the snow. The bears use these temporary dens as a sort of base camp, where they take refuge to escape bad weather or rest up between feeding sorties. Pregnant females dig their dens with the intention of remaining inside them for as much as six months. "For polar bears," wrote Ramsay and Stirling (1990), "maternity dens may serve primarily as thermal refugia where the tiny, undeveloped cubs can survive until they have grown sufficiently to survive the arctic winter." Ovsyanikov (1998) describes the emergence of polar bears on Wrangel Island:

> Polar bears emerge from their dens when spring comes to the Arctic. The first signs that a female is ready to come out are a few small pieces of snow visible on the otherwise unblemished wind-blown slope. The female pushes their pieces out of the entrance's snow cover to make an air hole. She may make the small initial opening to monitor outside conditions or to gradually accustom her cubs to the cold. For a few days no further changes indicate the bear family's presence.

Then, all of a sudden, blocks of snow are pushed out from behind, and a black nose appears in the entrance. The nose tests the air for a few minutes. Only then will the female show herself.

Maternity dens may be dug anywhere, on snow-covered hillsides or even in the frozen peat banks of Churchill, but for the most part they are situated in snowbanks, close enough to the sea ice that upon emerging, the female can begin hunting almost immediately. Often the dens face in a southerly direction to take advantage of solar radiation. Snow density is an important factor in choosing a den site: too densely packed, and it is difficult to excavate; too soft, and the den collapses. Blown snow is porous enough to allow oxygen to pass through, but if too much snow accumulates over a den, the female may emerge to scrape some of it away. When Harington poked a thermometer through the roof of a couple of occupied dens, he found that the temperature inside was anywhere from eighteen to thirty-seven degrees warmer than the outside air. The warmth comes from the body heat of the mother and the insulating properties of snow. In many cases, female polar bears display a fidelity to certain denning areas, returning year after year to the same general area, if not to the same den.

In 1967, mammalogist J. Kenneth Doutt wrote that "a review of the literature has failed to reveal any published description of polar bear dens, except in a paper by C. R. Harington [above]. There may be others that I have overlooked, but these excerpts from my field notes of 1935 seem worth recording." In James Bay (the southern extension of Hudson Bay), Doutt encountered a hunter on two small treeless islands, North and South Twin. On South Twin, the man had killed a male polar bear, a female, and a cub; he had then gone over to North Twin and killed three more bears. In the high gravel ridges of South Twin, Doutt found "literally hundreds of disintegrating bear dens. There were so many, in fact, that in places they actually overlapped." Some of the dens were very old, but others were quite recent. Because the resident bear population had been eliminated, Doutt crawled into one den, which he found "quite large, and permeated with a smell of stale urine. The den was entered through a passage way that was about 4 ft. wide and 7 ft. long. The end of this passageway opened into a hemisphere about 5 ft. in diameter, and a little over 4 ft. high." Doutt concluded, "From my observations I am convinced that polar bears had been denning on South Twin Island for hundreds of years, and it would seem that they were much more numerous in the past than in 1935."*

Ramsay and Stirling (1990) observed that "approximately 100–150 adult female polar bears with their new-born cubs emerge from their over-winter dens and walk to the sea ice of Hudson Bay." For the most part, the dens consist of a single chamber, but, wrote Stirling, "some females become architecturally creative and dig two- or even three-room complexes." Harington diagrams a three-chamber den on Southampton Island, Northwest Territories, with an entrance tunnel, an upper room, a lower room, and several alcoves, probably dug by the cubs. The dens are solo efforts, but when suitable locations are found by many she-bears, there are regions—such as the western shore of Hudson Bay and Wrangel Island—where many maternity dens can be found close together.

Even knowing that polar bears are dangerous, it is hard to keep that in mind when watching the cubs at play. "High on a Wrangel Island slope," Downs Matthews saw triplet cubs playing in the snow:

One sat on his haunches and careened downhill like a small toboggan. Scampering back to the top, he slid down again. With his mother watching benignly, he slid down a third time and a fourth. While scientists caution against assigning human emotions to wild animals, even the most objective of observers would find it difficult to interpret the cub's gleeful look and big grin as anything other than pleasure. His siblings, meanwhile, were taking turns leaping onto each other and rolling over and over in the snow.

With polar bears, it isn't only the kids that play. In the 2007 National Geographic movie *Arctic Tale*, two adult bears are obviously having a

* Digging dens in gravel banks isn't the only thing that is unusual about the polar bears of James Bay. In a study of the summer and autumn feeding habits of these bears, Richard Russell (1975) found that they ate more birds—particularly ducks and geese—than polar bears elsewhere, but they also ate seals, seaweed, grasses, and berries. According to Stirling (1988), "The most southerly dwelling polar bears in the world live all year round in James Bay in Canada, at latitudes as far south as Calgary, Alberta, or London, England. [Also northern Newfoundland.] There, and in Hudson Bay to the north, the ice melts completely in summer. There is no ice anywhere else to migrate to so the bears simply spend the summer along the coastline, or on various of the islands, waiting for winter to return."

great time as they slide and tumble on a slick patch of ice. Young adult males often engage in play-fighting, in which two bears, usually males, rear up on their hind legs and wrestle each other, obviously trying to throw the opponent off balance. They will even bite each other, but it is a play-bite, with no real harm intended. They will spar for a while, then flop down in the snow for a rest. (Matthews described three bears, two young males and an old boar, who went at it, on and off, for four days.) Some observers say it is training for the real fights, but Fred Bruemmer says that "watching the wrestling bears for so many years, I feel they do it partly for fun, a bit of high-spirited roughhousing carefully controlled by well-observed rules."

While, as mentioned above, the soles of the other bear species are naked, polar bears' soles are thickly furred between the pads to provide purchase on slippery ice and to keep them warm. The part of the black pad that is exposed is roughly nubbled to add to its grip on the ice. Because so much of their year is lived on ice, bears have to learn how to walk on sometimes treacherous footing. Their broad paws—all four of them—distribute their weight widely, and an 800-pound bear can walk on ice that would break under the weight of a 150-pound man. They

To distribute their weight over the widest area, polar bears will adopt a spread-eagle walk on fragile ice. If this doesn't work, they will crawl on their bellies.

sometimes assume a very wide stance, spreading their legs so far apart that they are practically crawling. If all else fails, they do crawl, lying on their stomachs and pulling themselves along with their claws.

The front paws of polar bears are considerably larger than the hind ones; they use these broad, paddle-like paws for swimming, trailing their hind limbs behind for use as rudders. The forepaw of a big male polar bear may be thirteen inches long and nine inches wide. The toes on their huge forefeet are webbed. They are powerful swimmers, and can swim for miles without stopping to rest, maintaining an average swimming speed of approximately six miles an hour. There have been reports of polar bears found swimming a hundred miles from the nearest land or fast ice. They are excellent divers, and can remain submerged for up to two minutes and attain a depth of fifteen feet. While underwater, their eyes remain open so they can see possible prey. (Deeper and longer divers like seals and sea lions can close their nostrils, but polar bears cannot.) Like many other diving mammals, such as sea lions and manatees, polar bears have a nictitating membrane (a "third eyelid"), which may be useful underwater but may also be helpful on land or ice in filtering ultraviolet glare and preventing snow blindness.

It is not quite true that bears, even pregnant females, as noted above, hibernate, because hibernation, as strictly defined, means a slowing down of metabolic functions, including heart rate and breathing, and a substantial reduction in body temperature. (The true hibernators include some rodents, bats, and insectivores.) Most bears just sleep for a long time when food is scarce, depending on their stored fat reserves, accumulated by gorging on high-energy foods before denning up. When a black bear emerges from its den, it may have lost as much as 45 percent of its body weight. Polar bears, however, have developed a completely different strategy to deal with periods of food scarcity, particularly in the late summer and early autumn before they venture out onto the ice. They remain awake and alert, but simply stop eating. This condition, known as "walking hibernation" or "walking torpor," can last as long as the food shortage persists. In some cases, pregnant females do not eat for eight months, during which period they must support themselves as well as nurse their young so the cubs can grow large enough to survive the Arctic environment. As Stirling (1988) wrote, "This seems to indicate that the polar bear has advanced to the point where it can

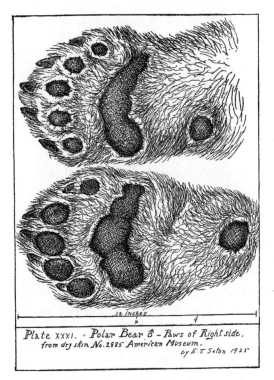

Plate XXXI. - *Polar Bear* ♂ - *Paws of Right side*.
from dry skin No. 2885 American Museum.
by E.T. Seton 1925

Ernest Thompson Seton's drawing of the heavily furred soles of a polar bear's feet (the forefoot is at the top), from Lives of Game Animals, *1929*

turn the mechanism on or off at will in relation to the availability or scarcity of food." The ability to fast for eight months is just one of the many remarkable adaptations made by the polar bear to survive in one of the harshest climates on earth.

All adult polar bears, male and female, have the ability to store large amounts of fat during periods when food is plentiful. In Hudson Bay, where the ice melts completely by mid-July and does not form again until November, all the bears in that population must fast for four months on their stored fat. Fat deposits provide insulation from the cold and add buoyancy while swimming. According to Nikita Ovsyanikov,

A thick layer of fat under the skin covers nearly all of the bear's body, including its head and the undersides of its paws. On the bear's rump, this layer of fat may be 5 inches thick. Polar bears also have layers of fat up to 1.6 inches thick between their muscles, and particularly plump individuals may even have fat deposits around their internal organs . . . The total weight of the fat on an adult polar bear may exceed 220 pounds, or 40 percent of the animal's total weight.

This kind of insulation is needed to swim for miles in icy water or walk around day after day in an Arctic blizzard. Typically, adult bears will eat only the fat of their kill, whereas younger bears, with more protein required for growth, will eat some of the meat as well. Derocher (2005) wrote that "the blubber of seals is preferentially stripped from the carcass to maximize energy intake. A single meal can comprise over 10% of a bear's body mass, and in one case the meal weighed 70 kg [154 pounds]."

Polar bears are mammals, and as such have to maintain a constant body temperature. The fat stores and thick fur coat provide the necessary insulation to keep their bodies at a temperature of 98.6°, the same as yours. Because of their thick two-layer fur, polar bears overheat easily, and after any form of exertion, like running or playing, they have to rest to cool down. It rarely gets too warm in the Arctic—although, of course, that may be changing—but a temperature of 70°F or more is uncomfortable for polar bears in the wild, and they often cool themselves by taking a swim. Polar bears in captivity do not eat the same fat-rich diet as their wild cousins, and therefore do not accumulate thick layers of fat. But they can't take off their heavy fur coats either, and can become seriously overheated in a zoo that is in a tropical or even a warm climate.

In *Hunters of the Northern Ice,* anthropologist Richard Nelson noted that "it is remarkable that the polar bear has been able to perfect an adaptation to the sea-ice environment. Certainly this is one of the most unusual habitats in which a terrestrial mammal has been able to live. One of the most interesting aspects is the polar bears' ability to locate and kill the animals on which they prey." The preferred prey is the ringed seal (*Pusa hispida*), which is one of the smallest of the earless seals, rarely reaching four and a half feet in length. Their English common name refers to the random pattern of light-colored circular "rings" on the dark background of their coat. Throughout their circumpolar range, ringed seals are hunted by Inuit, who use the meat, blubber, and skins, and by polar bears, who stalk them, often from a distance, and then eat them. Polar bears have also been observed leaping out of the water to surprise seals resting on an ice floe. Young seals, at up to 50 percent fat by weight, are probably easier to catch, because they are vulnerable and less experienced. A dark-colored seal on the ice is easy to see, even from a great distance, and the bear's sense of smell is so acute that it is said to be able to smell a seal from more than a mile away. After a slow and patient stalk, the bear charges at the seal on the ice, grabbing it before it can dive back into the water. The bears will also wait—sometimes for hours—for the seal to poke its head out of a breathing hole in the ice—then, with a swipe of a heavy-clawed paw, will yank the seal out of the water and kill it. Not every time, however. Seals are wary, and bears often fail to catch them. It has been estimated that bears succeed one out of every twenty tries. Here Peter Freuchen describes the bears' seal-hunting technique:

> In winter, before the seals come out on the ice, the bear catches them at the breathing holes. As a rule a breathing hole is no bigger than a florin at the top, but the bear scratches it open with its claws and then sits patiently until it becomes so large that it can get its paw down into it. Then when a seal comes up, the bear hits it a mighty blow on the head and kills it instantly. Here we gain a good idea of the strength of the polar bear for it is able to haul a seal up through a hole

Ringed seal on the ice

which has not been widened to more than the size of a good-sized dinner plate. It can be seen that the bear has taken a grip with its teeth and claws and drawn up the seal with such force that its shoulders and ribs are crushed, and its intestines pressed out through the abdomen.*

Sometimes the bear cannot rely on brute force, but has to resort to guile. Pedersen described a successful—and most unusual—seal hunt that he watched in East Greenland:

A young ringed seal, about half-grown, was basking in the sun at the edge of a small ice-floe. The bear had seen it from the edge of the fast ice. He stood up for a moment to scent the air and to examine the position of the seal, and then he entered the water in a rather strange way. Approaching the water's edge backward, he gripped the ice with his front paws, and then put first one hind-leg then the other into the water. Finally, he let go his grip on the ice, and let himself sink until only his muzzle remained above the surface. This seemed a very clumsy method, but he succeeded in this way in getting into the sea with the least noise . . . He swam towards the seal with the tip of his nose making only a very slight ripple on the surface of the water. When he was ten yards from the ice-floe he lifted his head cautiously, just enough for me to see his ears, and then dived. Suddenly the thin skin of ice which had formed round the floe shattered into pieces, and the head of the bear appeared exactly underneath the seal, which was completely taken by surprise. Before it could make the slightest movement the bear brought his paw on to its head and killed it with a single stroke.

The ringed seal and the bearded seal *(Erignathus barbatus)* share the polar bear's habitat, and both species are high on the bear's regular menu. Bearded seals are named for their long and plentiful whiskers (technically known as *vibrissae*), which give the animal its common name in English. After the walrus, the bearded seal is the largest Arctic pinniped, reaching a length of twelve feet and a maximum weight of

* Derocher: "Freuchen is clearly making this up. Ringed seals claw open the holes and use them to haul themselves out on the ice. In order for the seals to climb out, the holes have to be seal-sized . . . A seal pulled out through a seal-sized hole would not be crushed."

Ice floes are the natural habitat of the bearded seal.

more than 900 pounds. Ringed seals, among the smallest of all pinnipeds, do not weigh much more than 150 pounds, so a bearded seal
would make a much more desirable prey item for a hunting bear.
(When it is weaned, a bearded seal pup weighs more than an adult
ringed seal.) Although ringed seals probably make up the bulk of the
polar bear's diet, the weight discrepancy suggests that bearded seals
contribute more than is usually recognized.

Polar bears also have been known to catch sea birds as they sit on the
water, and there is a documented case of a polar bear "feeding inten-
sively in the little auk colony on Rubini Rock, Hooker Island, Franz
Josef Land." Also known as dovekies, little auks *(Alle alle)* are chubby
little birds that flit rapidly in and out of their huge, noisy colonies. At
Rubini Rock in 1992, Polish ornithologist Lech Stempniewicz observed
as many as twenty-two polar bears "overturning the boulders, some of
which weighed several hundred kilos, that covered the nests . . . and
then eating the eggs, chicks and adult birds." Several years later, Stempniewicz observed a polar bear "stalking and chasing adult flightless barnacle geese at sea, and plundering the nests of a glaucous gull colony in
Hornsund, southwest Spitsbergen." The geese, unable to fly because
they were molting, ran and flapped along the surface and successfully
escaped the swimming bear. The bear continued to swim along the
shoreline, and encountered a nest of breeding gulls. As the bear was

climbing out of the water, the panicked chicks jumped in, and the bear gobbled them up. "These observations," wrote Stempniewicz (2008) "are the first documented instances of a polar bear hunting for barnacle geese and glaucous gulls and provide additional evidence of the use of terrestrial prey by polar bears during the season of minimal ice extent."

Polar bears are often characterized as loners, trudging day and night over the frozen ice plains, searching for a mate or something to eat. While there is no such thing as a herd of polar bears, there are times when it is expeditious for the bears to forsake their solitary existence and join a community banquet. If a whale carcass washes up on the beach, dozens of hungry bears might gather to eat their fill. The whales of the Bering Sea are likely to be bowheads or gray whales, but at Churchill on Hudson Bay, the only other place in the Arctic where one might see large numbers of bears simultaneously, the local whales are belugas. Nikita Ovsyanikov once counted 100 polar bears concentrated like a herd around a gray whale carcass on Wrangel Island. The carcass had washed up on a shoal near the beach, forcing the bears to jump into the water to get a meal. Ovsyanikov has also seen as many as fourteen polar bears eating shoulder to shoulder at a single walrus carcass. Though one bear may "own" a whale or walrus carcass, he will not object to sharing with others, particularly if a supplicant follows proper protocol. Proper begging behavior includes a submissive, low-to-the-ground approach, followed by a slow circle around the carcass and nose touching with the bear in charge. In Ovsyanikov's 1996 book, *Living With the White Bear,* he wrote, "At Cape Blossom [Wrangel Island], I was privileged to live and work in an area where, in certain months, polar bears are the most numerous animals around . . . Every year I witnessed high concentrations of polar bears on the shore. In 1990, 140 animals were gathered in the observation area at one time. In 1991 there were 37. There were 12 in 1992 and 39 in 1993."

Every mammal that shares the Arctic with the polar bear—including other polar bears—can be considered fair game at one time or another. "The eighteenth century trader-explorer-hunter Captain George Cartwright came upon more than a dozen polar bears scooping salmon out of a south Labrador river in the fashion of the great Alaskan brown bears," wrote Fred Bruemmer in 1972. The bears prefer seals, but will occasionally catch and eat walruses, and when the ice melts in the sum-

Caribou, which are members of the deer family, ought to be able to outrun a polar bear on dry land.

mer and the bears are forced onto land, they will hunt herbivores that never venture onto the ice. Ryan Brook and Evan Richardson (2002) reported instances where bears were seen to prey on reindeer on Svalbard, musk oxen on Bathurst Island, and caribou in Manitoba, three miles from Hudson Bay. (In Canada *Rangifer tarandus* is known as the caribou; in Europe it is the reindeer.) Brook and Richardson observed "a subadult polar bear of unknown sex approaching a group of about 120 grazing caribou . . . the bear generally kept its head down, below shoulder level, stopping every five seconds to face the caribou as it approached." The caribou saw the approaching bear but were not visibly disturbed by its presence. When the bear was within about sixty feet of the herd, it charged, but the herd easily outran it. A bear would have obtained more than sufficient nutrition from a caribou, but a long chase would probably expend more energy than it could expect to realize. (Lunn and Stirling [1985] predicted that a bear chasing snow geese "would not receive a net gain in energy unless it caught a goose within 12 seconds.") The nutritional requirements of the ice bear are well suited to the capture of seals and (occasionally) walruses, where the walking in search of prey does not necessarily require a great expenditure of energy. Polar bears are competent swimmers, but, as we will see, seals are better, and can usually escape in the water.

Polar bear predation on caribou is rare enough to warrant an article in a scientific journal, but the primary predator of the caribou in the Arctic is the gray wolf *(Canis lupus)*. In 1983, Malcolm Ramsay and Ian Stirling came across evidence of a pack of wolves, in the large denning area south of Churchill, that had learned to kill polar bear cubs when they were on the way to the sea from their maternity dens. Reconstructing the attack from tracks in the snow, they determined that

the bears had been walking northeast across tundra and had crossed over a frozen river bordered by 3-m high banks. Within 75 m of the river, two wolves had intercepted the family to the southeast. The mother bear had moved northward while the two cubs ran parallel to her track . . . At first both wolves followed the mother, then one turned and ran at the cubs, attacked the female cub and lifted it off the ground. The wolf carrying the cub then moved eastward away from the mother. Approximately 15 m beyond where the cub had been grabbed, the mother bear veered and ran toward the wolf and captured cub. Approximately 7 m after turning, the bear suddenly stopped and ran back to the unharmed cub . . . The dead cub was completely eaten, only bits of fur and blood remained.

Most of the time, however, it is the bear that is the aggressor.

Polar bears are competent swimmers, but not particularly fast. More marathoners than sprinters, they can swim for days without stopping, by paddling with their great forepaws and trailing their hind legs behind. All seals are lithe and maneuverable swimmers, and it is unlikely that a bear could catch a seal in open water. There are reports of bears jumping from the ice into the water when a swimming seal passes too close to the ice edge, but this doesn't seem to happen very often. Seals sometimes sleep on the surface of the water, a situation that would enable the bear to pounce if the seal drifted too close. Mythology surrounds the bear's ice-hunting techniques. Some people say that the bear covers its black nose when it is creeping up on a seal so the seal sees only the white of the bear on the white of the ice. It has been said that most polar bears are left-handed and favor that paw for swiping at seals.

There are (usually unsubstantiated) stories of bears picking up chunks of ice and throwing them at, or dropping them on, seals or walruses; others have heard about (but not seen) bears that use chunks of ice to smash through iced-over breathing holes. As far as we know, none of these stories are true. Also relegated to the category of myth is the story that the hollow hairs of the polar bear's coat are "fiber-optic," capturing energy by conducting ultraviolet light to the black skin. This idea was tested—and disproved—by physicist Daniel Koon in 1998. In the journal *Applied Optics* Koon described his examination of hairs collected from a polar bear from the Rochester (New York) Zoo. Less than .001 percent of the red light and less than a trillionth of the transmitted violet light traveled the length of an inch-long hair. Even less light made it from the tip to the base of the hair. Too bad; it made for a nice story.

Highest on the bear's menu are the ringed seals, bearded seals, harp seals, hooded seals, and then walruses, small whales, large whales (as carrion), occasional birds, and some vegetation. The only mammal that

Arctic foxes follow polar bears as they hunt on the ice.

doesn't normally fall victim to the bear is the ubiquitous Arctic fox, a sort of miniature polar bear with an all-white coat (in winter), furry soles, short ears, and the ability to survive temperatures as low as -60°F. Where the tail of a polar bear is short and stubby, the fox has a long, fluffy brush that it wraps over its head when trying to keep warm in a snow burrow. In summer, *Alopex lagopus* has a gray or bluish coat, but in winter it becomes as white as a polar bear and is often seen scampering around bear kills, trying to snatch a morsel of meat. The little white fox does not provide a warning system for the bear (what would it warn the bear *against*?), and feeds on scraps of the bear's kills, so the benefit from the relationship accrues to the fox. Although a fox will occasionally trail a bear to feed on the predator's scraps, the bear may lunge at or slap at a pesky fox. During the spring season on the ice, when both the bear and the fox are hunting ringed seal pups, the relationship could be considered more competitive than symbiotic.

In their 1989 observations of the interactions of polar bears and small whales, Thomas Smith and Becky Sjare wrote that "because of the low density of polar bears and the large densities of uninhabited coastlines where they hunt [in the Canadian High Arctic], there are few documented instances of bears killing whales." The beluga *(Delphinapterus leucas)* and the narwhal *(Monodon monoceros)* are small whales that are found in the same Arctic regions as polar bears, but like all cetaceans, they never come out of the water. Bears are obviously not as well adapted to the water as whales, but Smith and Sjare witnessed bears stalking belugas in shallow water and making two successful kills of subadult whales in shallow water. This is unusual, and in most of the instances where a bear has been seen feeding on whale carcasses, the bear probably came upon a stranded whale that had died. The same holds true for bowhead whales; there is no way a bear could attack a bowhead, but a sixty-ton carcass could feed many bears for weeks or even months.

On July 31, 1594, as Willem Barents tried to round the northernmost point of Novaya Zemlya, his ship *Mercury* was stopped by the ice, and could not go any farther. As Barents turned back (he would try again to get through the next year, and again the year after that), he encountered some small islands that he named for his prince, William of Orange.

Off the Orange Islands (*Eylandt van Oraengien* in Dutch; now *Oranskiye ostrova* in Russian), Barents spotted a herd of some 200 walruses that Gerrit de Veer, Barents's shipmate and the chronicler of the voyage, described as follows:

> The sea horse is a wonderful strong monster of the sea, much bigger than an ox, which keepes continually in the sea, having a skin like a sea-calf or scale, with very short hair, mouthed like a lyon, and many times they lie upon the ice; they are hardly killed unless you strike them just upon the forehead; it hath foure feet but no eares, and commonly it hath one or two young ones at a time . . . They have two teeth sticking out of their mouthes, one on each side, each being about half an elle long, and are esteemed to bee as good as any ivorie or elophants teeth, especially in Muscovia, Tarataria, and there abouts where they are known, for they are as white, hard, and even as ivory.
>
> These sea-horses that lay basking themselves upon the land, our men, supposing that they could not defend themselves being out of the water, went on shore to assaile them, and fought with them, to get their teeth that are so rich, but they brake all their hatchets, curtle-axes, and pikes in pieces, and could not kill one of them, but strucke some of their teeth out of their mouthes, which they took with them; and when they could get nothing against them by fighting, they agreed to goe aboard the ship and fetch some of their great ordinance to shoot at them therewith, but it began to blow so hard that it rent the ice into great pieces, so that they were forced not to do it.

There are two subspecies of walrus, the Atlantic and the Pacific, inhabitants of the moving pack ice and rocky islands of the eastern and western Arctic. (The Atlantic walruses are somewhat smaller than their Pacific counterparts.) They have no visible ear flaps, so they are not eared seals (Otariids), and they can rotate their hind limbs forward, so they are not classified with the earless seals (Phocids). *Odobenus rosmarus* is, in a phrase, sui generis. Walruses are compulsively gregarious, and often cluster together in huge herds, sometimes numbering in the thousands. The largest bulls can weigh more than two tons, while the daintier females rarely reach a ton. The ivory tusks of walruses make for

Walruses are not seals and not sea lions. They are sui generis.

an easy way of differentiating males from females: the tusks of females are smaller and thinner, and often splay slightly outward; the tusks of a big bull walrus are much heavier, point straight down, and may be three feet in length. Feeding underwater, they employ powerful suction to suck clams out of their shells. Although early observers thought that the tusks were used to dig clams from the bottom, their primary function seems to be to serve as sort of "sled-runners" as the walrus glides along the bottom inhaling mollusks. They also serve as secondary sexual characteristics—the most powerful males have the largest tusks—and they can help a walrus pull itself up onto an ice floe. The tusks also make formidable weapons.

When American whalers entered the Bering Sea in the latter part of the nineteenth century, they found great herds of walruses packed together on the ice or the shore, and shot them for their ivory. As Gavin Maxwell wrote in his 1967 *Seals of the World*,

> The professional, commercially-motivated walrus hunters of the eighteenth century employed methods similar to those of the Eskimo, using harpoons and lances, but these hunters worked from boats. They also killed walruses on land, usually at night, using dogs to break up the herd into smaller groups. The dogs and the darkness caused great confusion in the herd, and hunters entered the scene with sharp spears . . . Although they probably envisaged walrus-

hunting as a side-line, during the years 1868 to 1873, the whalers took
at least 60,000 walruses per year, yielding 50,000 barrels of oil.

On board the steam whaler *Belvedere* in the western Arctic in 1880,
Hartson Bodfish described a walrus hunt:

> Finding no whales, we started to hunt walrus, a regular feature of this
> kind of voyage when whales were scarce. Hundreds of walrus would
> haul out on a floe, and many smaller groups. It was the custom to row
> or paddle up to the floe with a whaleboat, and the officer in charge, or
> some good shot, would start shooting those nearest the edge of the
> ice. When several had been killed, the men would land behind the
> dead animals, and the shooting would continue from there until all
> were killed or the flock became gallied and went overboard. A Sharps
> 45–70, the regular buffalo gun, was the weapon used. When one got
> too hot to handle it was dropped overboard with a lanyard to cool. I
> believe that Captain Owen killed 250 walrus on the first cake of ice.

Historian John Bockstoce devoted an entire chapter of his comprehensive *History of Whaling in the Western Arctic* to "Walrusing." (If
"whaling," why not "walrusing"? Hunting elephant seals was called
"elephanting.") Bockstoce observed that when the whalers realized they
were running out of whales, they turned their attention to the walruses.
Here he describes the walrusing:

> If the weather was clear, the ship would often stay three miles away
> while the whaleboat towed the walrus boat toward the animals. The
> approach was always made from downwind because the walrus has a
> good sense of smell. Although a walrus's eyesight is poor, the walrus
> boat was usually painted a light color and the men wore white cloth
> shirts and trousers over their clothes to avoid spooking the herd. If
> they happened to see any polar bears while they were on their way to
> the herds they would try to kill them. The scent of a bear would
> frighten the walruses, quickly driving them off the ice and into the
> water.

Throughout the historical and scientific literature, there are conflicting reports about what happens when a polar bear meets a walrus.

There are many descriptions of bear attacks on walruses—usually, but not always, small ones. In a 1998 report on the polar bears and walruses of Wrangel Island, M. S. Stishov wrote, "The main reason for the polar bear concentration appears to be the possibility of feeding on dead walruses on the beach after the other animals have returned to the water. If there are not enough dead animals, then active hunting of walrus calves takes place. Polar bears do not hunt adult walruses." In *Wildlife of the Polar Regions,* Carleton and M. G. Ray wrote that

> walruses panic when approached on the ice by humans or bears, and in their rush to the water, a calf is often the last one in. A polar bear will actually charge a walrus group, seemingly so that it will panic. It may be lucky enough to grasp a youngster by the rear flippers before it enters the water. After killing the little walrus, the bear makes an incision behind the head and proceeds to eat away the blubber and the flesh so that, eventually, the skin of the walrus is turned inside out and all that is left is the bones.

(In a 1979 *National Geographic* article Carleton Ray included a photograph of an empty walrus skin, which he said was "turned completely inside out, like a coat sleeve.")

There are many reports of bears *not* attacking walruses, such as one from a 1971 Russian publication about the walruses of the North Pacific, in which V. I. Krylov wrote that some believe that "walruses are killed by predators such as killer whales and polar bears, but not one case of walrus pups or immature animals being killed by attack of predators was observed, although attacks of bears on the walrus herds were repeatedly observed. The gregarious life mode of walruses gives reliable protection against predators." In his definitive monograph on the Pacific walrus, Francis Fay (1982) wrote, "I know of no confirmed records of [polar bear] predation on walruses," but he then quoted at length from "three anecdotal accounts by Soviet biologists," in which attacks on walruses are described. During extensive travel by helicopter in the High Canadian Arctic to tag polar bears from 1971 through 1976, Ian Stirling and H. P. L. Kiliaan saw two walruses that had apparently been killed by bears:

One was an adult female, 22+ years old. There was blood on the top of her frozen over haul-out hole, indicating she might have been frozen out when the bear attacked. The other was just under 2 years old. A blood trail indicated that it had been captured on or in a wide channel that went around the circumference of a grounded iceberg. Examination showed that both walruses had large numbers of sharp deep punctures about their heads which could only have been made by bear claws, suggesting that they may have been killed by multiple blows.

A full-grown bull walrus can weigh twice as much as an adult male polar bear, and the skin on the walrus's immense neck and shoulders

Like polar bears, walruses spend a lot of time in ice water.

may be three inches thick. A walrus is also built so close to the ground that it offers few points of access for the bear's teeth or claws. And then there are those tusks. While it is rare that a polar bear will attack a full-grown walrus, there are any number of observations of bears feeding on walrus carcasses. It may be that in the cases where bears cause walruses to panic and stampede into the water, members of the herd are killed or trampled and left on the beach. Nikita Ovsyanikov (1996) tells of an incident where a small plane flew over a herd of some 20,000 walruses and instigated a mass panic in which

> thousands of walruses frightened by what for them was a terrifying noise, made for the sea at once. In their haste to reach the water, they clambered over each other until their bodies were stacked as many as four deep. This would be a terrible weight even for the strongest males to bear, and some of them were simply squashed. The aircraft found its way through the clouds leaving behind 104 dead walruses.

Whether it is bears or low-flying planes that cause the walruses to stampede, the result is the same: an enormous amount of meat on the beach for the bears to eat without having to fight for it. Ovsyanikov reproduces several photographs of the beach at Wrangel Island's Doubtful Spit covered with dead walruses, and in the 2007 National Geographic film *Arctic Tale* (about which more later), shot on a Nunavut island in Foxe Basin, there is a long sequence of a single bear swimming ashore into a stampeding herd of walruses, grabbing an adult female that weighs a good deal more than he does, and killing her. From various sources, the evidence for polar bears attacking walruses (not though always successfully) is indisputable.

A diet of mollusks would seem to preclude any carnivorous intentions on the part of the walrus, but, as Fay reports, "remains of two species of pinnipeds, the ringed seal and the bearded seal, consisting mainly of skin and blubber with some muscles and viscera, have been found with remarkable frequency . . . Probably most of these seals are taken as carrion, although it is conceivable that some are killed by the walruses." And there is at least one report of a walrus "attack" on a bear, which was surely self-defense. In *Wild Life Beyond the North*, Frank Illingworth recounts a tale of bear vs. walrus:

The name "walrus" is derived from the Old Norse hvalross, *which means "whale-horse."*

The bear crept forward with the utmost care, making for the smallest of three animals lying at the edge of the water close to the sleepy eyes of an old bull. As the bear made its final sally the bull turned to the defense of its smaller companion. Exactly what happened next I cannot say. But in a matter of seconds the bear lay bleeding from a mortal wound and the old bull, roaring angrily, lifted itself on its foreflippers and surveyed the scene of the victory before taking to the water. When I examined the bear I found a jagged wound in the neck from which its life blood flowed across the rocks.

Seals, and to a much lesser extent walruses, make up the regular diet of polar bears. But to a hungry bear, a man is obviously a mammal, and since almost everything else it eats is also a mammal, it probably would not hesitate to attack anything that was somewhat furry and smelled edible. If an Inuit hunter managed to wound a bear, either with a harpoon or a rifle, and was careless enough to get too close to the enraged animal, we would probably be able to record another "bear attack." But, as Richard Nelson wrote, "well-fed bears are particularly unlikely to bother with man, because they are afraid or because humans are regarded as a second-rate meal." A bear that has been wounded will not necessarily charge at its assailant; it is just as likely to run away. In 1990, Ovsyanikov was on Wrangel Island, reading in his cabin for one of his long stays. The first night, he and the cameraman found their cabin surrounded by polar bears, peering in the windows, snuffing, and scratching the walls. Ovsyanikov felt compelled to go outside and close the shutters, shooing away bears in the process. The next day, Ovsyanikov went for a walk among the bears, carrying only a stick for protection, and acting confident and aggressive. The bears stood quietly and looked at him. In his book *Polar Bears,* he wrote, "From my experience, the polar bear is such a calm and curious creature that there can be nothing exciting about hunting it."*

But there was one bear that Ovsyanikov could not bluff so easily. An old male nicknamed "Grandfather" approached them as they were filming a walrus rookery, and when Ovsyanikov stood up to intimidate the bear,

Grandfather continued to advance, ignoring me. By now I was getting used to commanding more respect from the bears. My uneasiness grew, and it became clear that this was no time to be taking pictures . . . I suddenly realized that my hard-won feeling of superiority was evaporating more quickly than I would have expected only a few short minutes ago . . . I walked slowly toward the cabin. The male gave no sign that he had noticed me. In fact the way he totally ignored me was somehow offensive.

The bear got closer: "He showed no signs of aggression, no fear, no excitement, no emotions at all. He behaved like a giant who has noticed an insect in his path and has decided to take a closer look. He was definitely not like the other bears." From the safety of the porch

---

* Randy Green, whose company, International Wildlife Adventures, pioneered polar bear tours in Churchill, says that most times you can bluff a bear. Green said he learned the technique from a Russian scientist who spends summers on Wrangel Island. "If the bear starts to charge, just open your parka and run at it . . . it works . . . when you open your parka, that increases your size two or three times, and you seem more threatening" (Young 2008).

Ovsyanikov threw a stone at the bear and hit him on the hip. Unfamiliar with flying stones, the bear turned to see what was behind him. Ovsyanikov threw another rock: "And then this giant once again behaved in a manner I had completely failed to anticipate—he suddenly got terribly frightened," turned away, and ran back to the coastal ridge.*

During the 1933 Cambridge expedition to Scoresby Sound, Alwin Pedersen had left his sledge on foot, looking for a way through the broken terrain. He was unarmed, because he thought it would be only a brief excursion. In *Polar Animals,* he tells what happened:

I had reached the foot of a glacier and was looking for a route when suddenly, I saw a bear. It did not appear to have seen me, and so I immediately tried to hide between two blocks of ice at the foot of the steep wall of the glacier. To do this I had to remove my skis; I sank in up to my knees in the snow and was quite immobilized. The bear was ambling along quite peacefully, and it still did not appear to have noticed me. When it reached the tracks made by my skis it stopped and sniffed the air. Then for a moment it gazed far away on to the ice. It turned its head and at the same time saw me. The distance between us was exactly five paces. I did not move a muscle. The bear remained watching me for about a minute. I was still quite motionless, but I swear I could hear my heart beating. Then the animal moved off and continued its journey as though I did not exist. I have no doubt that if I had moved at the critical moment, or shouted for help, it would have come at me and the situation would have been very tricky.

---

* I have already quoted from Nikita Ovsyanikov's two books eleven times. Although they are fairly small books, *Polar Bears* and *Living With the White Bear* are among the best books ever written about *Ursus maritimus.* Ovsyanikov lived and worked among the bears of Wrangel and Herald islands for many years, and has recorded more than 500 face-to-face encounters with them. He has reported any number of unique behaviors of bears (and walruses), often in contradiction to the conventional wisdom. Although I am tempted to quote Ovsyanikov even more, that would present obvious problems of copyright infringement. The best I can do is recommend his books to readers of this one, in the hope that between us we can present a more complete picture of the lives of the great white bears.

Charles Jonkel, PhD, began his studies of bears in 1959, the first year the dart gun became available commercially.* In a 1970 discussion of the behavior of captured polar bears, he wrote,

Captured polar bears are, surprisingly enough, as tractable as black bears when approached by man. I have captured 92 polar bears in foot snares and only occasionally have any growled, charged, or even raised from reclining or sitting position if I approached slowly. A bear would usually watch warily, turning slowly to face me as I approached the trap.

Of the polar bears of Churchill, he wrote,

The Churchill settlements contain about 4000 people, and, considering that as many as 20 bears can be found at any one time in and around these settlements, it is unusual that there have not been more attacks. My recapture studies of polar bears indicate that the same bears return to this area each year; the return of these "conditioned" bears may explain their compatibility with man.

Or, it may be that polar bears are not particularly interested in people, either as potential meals, as adversaries, or as rivals for dominance in the bear's territory.

On Christmas Day, 2007, a young tiger escaped from its enclosure at the San Francisco Zoo, killed one man, and mauled two others. Tigers have always been regarded as aggressive, so while the escape was unexpected—the cat had to clear a thirty-foot moat and scale a fourteen-foot-high wall—the attack was not. "Man-eating" tigers are known

* Chuck Jonkel began by studying black bears—the subject of his 1967 doctoral dissertation at the University of British Columbia was "The Ecology, Population Dynamics, and Management of the Black Bear in the Spruce-fir Forest of Northwestern Montana"— moved on to polar bears, and later concentrated on grizzlies. He is now president of the Great Bear Foundation, based in Missoula, Montana, which is dedicated to the conservation of bears and bear habitats worldwide. In 2001, Dorothy Hinshaw Patent wrote *A Polar Bear Biologist at Work,* a children's book about Jonkel's work. When Jonkel was about to begin his study of the polar bears of Churchill, everybody told him how dangerous they were. "Luckily for me," he said, "those people were wrong. Polar bears are actually quite a bit easier to work with than grizzly bears or black bears. They don't get upset by people. Sometimes they even fall asleep while you're watching."

throughout India, and it is, after all, the ferocious nature of tigers that makes them such important elements of circus acts. When Roy Horn of the Vegas act Siegfried and Roy was attacked on stage and nearly killed, it was considered an unequivocal manifestation of the tiger's reputation as an untamable wild animal. Even though there have been people who foolishly entered a polar bear's enclosure in a zoo and were then killed by the bears, it is difficult to imagine one escaping from its enclosure, going on a rampage, and killing people. It's easier to envision the bear finding its cage door unlocked and wandering out just to see what was going on. Polar bears roamed the streets of Churchill for years before the garbage dumps were moved out of town, and there were hardly any "attacks." Still, on January 4, 2008, nine days after the San Francisco tiger incident, the San Jose *Mercury News* reported that San Francisco Zoo officials decided to "bolster" the polar bear exhibit, fearing that if a tiger could jump a thirty-foot moat and kill people, a polar bear probably could too.*

Even for those who regard the polar bear's reputation as a "man-eater" to be greatly exaggerated, there have been unfortunate instances where the bear was probably trying to kill the person in order to eat him. On September 3, 2003, at Kimmirut, Nunavut, Inuit guide Kootoo Shaw was sleeping in his tent when a young male polar bear, weighing about 350 pounds, tore it open. Shaw ran out of the tent but tripped on a rock, and the bear pounced on him, biting his head, clawing at his neck, and jumping on his chest with its front paws, thereby breaking his ribs. Kelsey Eliasson, a guide from Churchill, recounted the details on his Web site, Polar Bear Alley: "The latest urban legend/email forward is the polar bear attack images of the scarred man and the dead polar bear. I have seen about six different explanations of these, most commonly that it was a camper in the Yukon, but this is the real one." The images, which first appeared on the Internet in 2004, include a shot of Shaw's heavily scarred back, another of most of his scalp ripped away,

---

* It was the mere *possibility* of an attack that led to the shooting of a polar bear in the vicinity of the Nunavut capital of Iqaluit in June 2008. Thirty-seven students of a local school were having a picnic in Sylvia Grinnell Territorial Park when a park employee spotted a polar bear rooting through the contents of a nearby garbage can. Conservation officers decided that the bear was too close to too many children, so they shot the bear. Officer Johnny Nowdlak skinned the bear and doled out the meat to nearby residents (CBC, June 25, 2008).

and two pictures of the dead bear, which was shot by Shaw's companions before it could do any more damage. The injured guide was transported to Kimmirut by boat, and then flown to Iqaluit, where 300 stitches were required to reattach his scalp and sew up the "multiple bites and slashes" on his back, arms, and feet.

While attacks by polar bears may be rare, attacks by grizzlies are not. Too much of the intermingled history of brown bears and men involves the aggressive nature of the bear that was once known as *Ursus horribilis*. A couple of recent incidents will serve to point out the great difference in the behavior of the big brown bear and the big white one.

The most elaborately documented grizzly attack was the one on Timothy Treadwell and his girlfriend, Amie Huguenard, in October 2003 in Katmai National Park on the Alaska Peninsula. For thirteen consecutive summers, Treadwell lived among and filmed the grizzlies of Katmai, and believed he had a special rapport with the bears. Under the pretext of studying and protecting them, he befriended them—or thought he did. Treadwell and Huguenard were camped in a tent when they were killed and eaten by a bear. Werner Herzog's 2005 documentary *Grizzly Man* incorporates a lot of the footage that Treadwell shot of the bears and himself over the years—but not of the fatal attack. (The lens cap was on his video camera during the attack, so the death of Treadwell and Huguenard is documented by sound only. Mercifully, the audio of the killing is not included in the film.) Apparently believing that because he loved the bears they would not harm him, Treadwell showed himself to be so ignorant of the nature of wild animals—especially grizzly bears—that it cost him his life. In a couple of other recent attacks the victim escaped, but in one, the bear killed its trainer.

On April 22, 2008, as Marc Johnson was jogging near his home on Alaska's Kenai Peninsula, he came across a brown bear sow and her two cubs. He did something that wildlife officials say no one should ever do: he ran. The sow caught him, knocked him down, slashed his head, arm, and backside, and then took off (Halpin 2008). The following day, a captive 700-pound grizzly in California killed a man named Stephan Miller. At Predators in Action, the compound at Big Bear Lake maintained by Randy Miller and his cousin Stephan to supply "wild" animals for movies and television, Stephan and two other handlers were putting "Rocky" through what was described as a "normal training routine," when the bear bit him on the neck, killing him almost instantly.

Rocky, who had been trained by Randy Miller to simulate attacks on people, was driven away from the body with pepper spray, and caged immediately. As of the date of the posting of this news item, California Fish & Game officials had not decided whether or not to put the bear down (Larocco 2008). Some two weeks later, on May 3, Brent Case was doing forest survey work east of Bella Coola, British Columbia, when he was attacked from the rear. The bear threw him to the ground, and when Case tried to crawl under a log, the bear pulled him out by the arm and chomped on the back of his head. According to the news report by Becky Rynor, "The bear jumped up and down on him several times then wandered off. In spite of severe gashes on his head and upper arm, bites to his elbow and knee and bleeding profusely, he managed to drive his pickup truck about 25 kilometers out of the bush to the nearest town." Three grizzly attacks in two weeks. Stephan Miller was bitten on the throat and killed, but the captive bear obviously wasn't trying to eat him. In the case of the hapless jogger, he surprised a sow with cubs, and she probably attacked to protect her offspring. It is difficult to interpret the Bella Coola incident as anything but an attack by a bad-tempered bear; after mauling Mr. Case, the bear just walked away.

The time usually allocated for the evolution of the polar bear is around a million years, and while that is but an eyeblink in evolutionary history, it is really quite a long spell. In comparison, the biped known as *Homo sapiens* has been around for only about 400,000 years, and the entire history of "civilization," from the first known communities in the valley of the Euphrates to the tiger attack in San Francisco, has occurred within the last 7,000 years. (In April 2008, German geologist Klaus Schmidt uncovered evidence of a primitive settlement in Turkey that predates the first known cities of Mesopotamia by 5,550 years, dramatically changing the history of civilization.) Until humans ventured into its icy kingdom, the polar bear was the unchallenged monarch, and as such may not have developed any sense of the feeling we know as fear. What could possibly frighten a polar bear? Every other Arctic land animal is smaller; only the walrus exceeds the bear in size, and the bears avoid contact with the formidably toothed "whale-horses" except in times of extreme hunger.

After self-preservation—which includes eating—the predominant instinct of the polar bear seems to be curiosity. In the past, as long as there was nothing that could harm it, the bear was free to investigate anything new and different, from dogsleds to walking men, villages to tents, snowmobiles to nuclear submarines. As Peter Freuchen (1935) wrote, "On the whole, a bear's curiosity must be said to exceed its bellicosity, and the many tales of bears advancing to attack people are doubtless in many cases simply the outcome of their curiosity driving them to investigate what it is that they have seen." In *Shadow of the Bear*, Brian Payton said, "Polar bears are famous for their curiosity, which—owing to their power and size—they are able to indulge with abandon. Because any unusual feature in the tundra might yield something good to eat, it is always worth investigating." Many of the early encounters with polar bears consisted of a bear getting too close to a man, a ship, an igloo, a tent, or a cabin, and rather than assuming that the bear was just curious, the men believed that the bear was about to kill and eat them, and defended themselves accordingly.

There have been and will continue to be times, however, when the line between curiosity and bellicosity becomes so faint as to be almost invisible. In February 2006, a 700-pound polar bear wandered into the Inuit village of Ivujivik, on the eastern shore of Hudson Bay, at the northernmost tip of Quebec. When Ivujivik resident Lydia Angiyou saw the bear, it was a few feet from her seven-year-old son, Jesse. As the boy ran away, Lydia ran at the bear shouting, but when she got close enough, the bear reared up and whacked her on the head with its forepaw. As she fell to the ground, the bear hit her again. She thought the bear was going to pounce on her "like he does to a seal," and she fainted. When she came to, the bear was standing over her, and a villager fired a shot into the air to drive the bear away. The bear turned and went after the villager, who then shot and killed it. As told by Katherine Wilton in the *Montreal Gazette* (January 17, 2008), Lydia Angiyou was awarded Canada's Medal of Bravery for her actions.

The polar bear is one of the strongest of all terrestrial predators, capable, as we have seen above, of dragging a half-ton beluga a quarter of a mile, or yanking a 500-pound seal out of its hole with one swipe. The bear's immense strength and dangerously sharp claws and teeth are perfect for capturing seals, but this armament also makes it a formida-

Eskimo soapstone carving of a bear dragging the half-eaten carcass of a seal

ble adversary to humans. Such a characterization is largely responsible for the bear's reputation for malice toward man, but in truth, it may not be the dangerous man-eater that all those explorers, hunters, and Eskimos believed it was. There have been circumstances where a provoked or hungry bear has attacked a person, and these events cannot be explained away by "curiosity." But chasing a she-bear with cubs at her side or loosing a pack of howling dogs will definitely provoke the bear, and will probably result in some sort of confrontation. Except for seals, which escape by taking to the water, every other natural prey of the polar bear (and its ursine ancestors) tries to run away. An animal running away probably triggers an instinctive desire to give chase, so a man who decides to run from a bear may be inviting an attack. (Walking away or lying down may not be such good ideas either.)

Cooking fires generating the odor of roasting meat or fat can attract a bear from miles away, and stimulated by the smell, an otherwise recalcitrant bear might march boldly into camp to see what he can find to eat. Except when feeding on a whale or walrus carcass, there is no time when a polar bear's food comes easily. It may miss nineteen out of twenty seals that it hunts on the ice, and there may be long stretches during which it finds no seals at all. A thousand-pound carnivore needs plenty of calories to survive, and while they prefer seals, hungry bears will try to eat anything, including motor oil, frozen and canned food, leather boots, and even the people who packed those supplies in what they thought were bear-proof containers.

Ursus maritimus has blended into its environment as few other animals have ever done. It has perfected unique abilities to live year-round in subfreezing temperatures; to find food buried under solid ice; to swim for miles in cold water; to find a mate over trackless frozen plains; to give birth to two cubs in a snow cave after fasting for eight months. Having honed their lifestyle over time, polar bears reigned supreme over their isolated Arctic homeland—until human interlopers arrived and changed everything. Feeling threatened by the bears, early Arctic explorers shot or speared them. They killed them and made the bear's outer covering their own outer covering. They killed and ate them when they were hungry. They killed them for "sport." They brought in huge, noisy machines to drill for oil in the bear's habitat and threatened that habitat with pernicious oil spills. They contrived to heat up the environment so that the bears' life-supporting ice would melt and dissolve itself into an uncomfortably warming ocean.

The polar bear is much less dangerous to man than man is to the bear.

IV

Polar Bear Nations

The Antarctic Continent belongs to no country, but under the Antarctic Treaty of 1961, it was designated an international preserve, which established freedom of scientific investigation and banned military activity on that continent. (This was the first arms control agreement established during the Cold War.) The original signatories were the twelve countries that were active in Antarctica during the International Geophysical Year (IGY) of 1957–58 and were willing to accept a U.S. invitation to the conference at which the treaty was negotiated. These countries were Argentina, Australia, Belgium, Chile, France, Japan, India, New Zealand, Norway, South Africa, the Soviet Union, the United Kingdom, and the United States.

In contrast, there is no Arctic continent, so administrative control of the regions north of the Arctic Circle falls to the nations whose boundaries incorporate Arctic Ocean coastlines. (Three countries—Russia, Norway, and the U.S.—have positions in both the Arctic and the Antarctic.) Within each nation's boundaries there are polar bears quietly minding their own business, unaware of politics, treaties, or the perils of anthropogenic global warming. Under international law, no country owns the North Pole, and the five surrounding Arctic states—Russia, the U.S., Canada, Norway, and Denmark (via Greenland)—are limited to a 200-mile economic zone around their coasts. But in August 2007, Russian president Vladimir Putin asserted his nation's ownership of 460,000 square miles—an area larger than France, Germany, and Italy combined—of Arctic territory (and its huge reserves of oil and gas), after a mini submarine had planted the Russian flag under two and a half miles of water at the North Pole. Russian scientists claim that the Lomonosov Ridge, an underwater mountain range crossing the polar region, is an extension of its territory. (Russia is already the world's largest country, spanning eleven time zones and stretching from Europe to the Pacific Ocean.) The brazen land grab raised the hackles of Russia's neighbors, who also have their eyes on the vast mineral deposits that could lie under the Arctic area. "This isn't the fifteenth century," said Peter MacKay, Canada's foreign minister. "You can't go around the world, plant a flag, and say, 'We're claiming this territory.'" (American astronauts planted a flag on the moon, but that didn't make it U.S. territory.)

Except for those in zoos, there are no polar bears in the Southern Hemisphere and no penguins in the Northern, but the two polar regions differ in more than wildlife. Antarctica is mostly a continent with some outlying islands, while "The Arctic" incorporates the Arctic Ocean and those countries that border on it: Canada, the United States (Alaska), Denmark (Greenland), Norway (Spitsbergen), and Russia. In 1973, those "polar bear nations" ratified the multilateral Agreement on the Conservation of Polar Bears.

At first it was assumed that the world's polar bears constituted a single homogeneous population, but tracking and satellite monitoring have shown that there are distinct groups distributed throughout the Arctic. Generally, the polar bears of Spitsbergen do not mingle with those of Russia, but there was always the possibility that a roaming bear might avail itself of a "polar route," go over the top, and change its affiliation. A wandering bear would not join a group, but simply continue its lonely trek on the ice. Advances in satellite technology over the past thirty years have enabled researchers to follow individual bears over time and locate dens under the snow by using infrared thermal sensing equipment; the researchers themselves can take advantage of new developments in communications and transportation. But even with the new technology, a significant proportion of polar bear research is conducted by scientists in helicopters, who can only wish they were as well prepared for the ice as the animals they are studying. In the past, it was the very harshness of the bears' environment that protected them; there are very few people hardy enough to live where the bears live. But now, people who live nowhere near the Arctic have unintentionally engineered a potential catastrophe for the eponymous occupants of the polar bear nation. The very climate that protected them in the past is deteriorating to the point where the bears are endangered.

Wrangel Island, now an important part of the Russian polar bear nation, was first identified in 1764, when a Cossack sergeant named Andreyev claimed to have sighted it. North of eastern Siberia, it was named for Russian admiral Ferdinand Petrovich von Wrangel (1796–1870), who had searched in vain for what he thought would be an undiscovered Arctic landmass, but never actually saw the island. While on an expedition seeking the missing British explorer Sir John Franklin, Captain Henry Kellett of the Royal Navy probably sighted the island in 1849, but it was officially "discovered" in 1867 by Thomas W. Long, captain of the New London whaler *Nile*, who proposed that it be named Wrangel Land. (The passage between the island and the mainland is now known as Long Strait.) In 1879, American explorer George Washington De Long thought he could reach the North Pole by sailing north along what he believed to be the large landmass of Wrangel Land, and then sledging to the pole. In the *Jeannette* he passed north of Wrangel Island, proving that it was actually an island and not part of the northern landmass, but his ship was trapped and drifted for twenty-two months before she was crushed in the pack ice. During their escape in small boats, many of the crew died, including De Long. (It was the wreckage of the *Jeannette*, eventually washing ashore in Greenland, that prompted Fridtjof Nansen to try to drift to the pole in the *Fram* in 1893–96.) The first known landing on Wrangel Island took place on August 12, 1881, by a party from the U.S. research vessel *Corwin*, who claimed the island for the United States. This expedition, under the command of Calvin L. Hooper, was seeking the *Jeannette* and two missing whalers in addition to conducting general exploration. Aboard the *Corwin* were the naturalist John Muir, who published the first description of Wrangel Island, and Edward W. Nelson, an American naturalist and ethnologist who had been sent by the U.S. National Museum (now the Smithsonian) to study the weather and the natural history of the High Arctic.

As the *Corwin* left Herald Island in August 1881, it approached what Muir called "Wrangell Land," and the men found what they believed (correctly) to be pieces of the *Jeannette*, but, as Muir wrote, "the grand excitement of the day, apart from the untrodden shore we were seeking, was caused by three polar bears, magnificent fellows, fat and hearty, rejoicing in their strength out here in the bosom of the icy wilderness." Muir, the consummate naturalist, described in detail the bears' "commanding view of the ship, an object they no doubt saw for the first time in their lives . . . They watched, motionless, for some time, throwing forward their long necks and black-tipped noses as if to catch and pass judgment on the scent of the big, smoking, black monster that was approaching them." As the ship came within fifty yards of them, the bears turned and trotted off,

> then broke in to a panicky, walloping gallop . . . until they reached the far side of the ice field and plunged into the water with a splash that sent spray ten feet into the air. Then they swam, making all haste to a larger floe . . . But the steamer gave chase and headed them off, and all were shot without the least chance of escape, and without their being able to offer the slightest resistance.

Muir was deeply upset by what he described as "as easy a butchery as shooting cows in a barnyard from the roof of the barn," and wrote that

> the Eskimos hunt and kill them for food, going out to meet them on the ice with spears and dogs . . . But how civilized people, seeking for heavens and angels and millenniums, and the reign of universal peace and love, can enjoy this red, brutal amusement, is not so easily accounted for. Such soft, fuzzy sentimental aspirations, and the frame of mind that can reap giggling, jolly pleasure from the blood and agony and death of these fine animals, and their humanlike groans, are too devilish for anything but hell.

For many years, John Muir was alone in his condemnation of the reckless, senseless slaughter of any and all polar bears that were spotted by Arctic explorers. Almost a century would pass before people would understand that the bears had as much right as they did—probably more, since it was their homeland—to live unthreatened on the ice.

Vilhjalmur Stefansson (born November 3, 1879, of Icelandic parents) was a Canadian ethnologist and explorer who discovered many previously unknown native tribes and territory. His first Arctic expedition was in 1906–07, on a trip led by the Danish explorer Ejnar Mikkelsen.

In 1908, he returned to the Arctic and traveled to Herschel Island, Cape Parry, and the south side of Victoria Island. En route he encountered the Copper Inuit (a previously unknown group), who made their tools of copper. Stefansson stayed with the Copper Inuit until 1912. He then commanded the ill-starred Canadian Arctic expedition of 1913–18, whose main objective was to explore the Beaufort Sea. With the ships *North Star* and *Mary Sachs* serving as support vessels, parties of Europeans and Eskimos ranged over the ice to perform surveying tasks. When the *Karluk,* the expedition's principal ship, was trapped in the ice, Stefansson and a few men took off. The *Karluk* drifted along the coast of Alaska, finally ending up at Wrangel Island, where it was locked in the ice for nine months and then crushed. The survivors were rescued after Captain Robert Bartlett walked across the frozen Chukchi Sea to Siberia to summon help.

Meanwhile, Stefansson and seventeen men remained on the ice for five years, living in igloos like Eskimos and eating what they killed or caught. The final leg of their journey consisted of a 400-mile drift on an ice floe that took them to Alaska. By 1921, Stefansson believed that Wrangel could be a potential refueling stop for transpolar flights, so he tried to colonize the island again, but decided this time not to go himself, sending five settlers instead in an attempt to claim the island for Canada. The settlers consisted of an American, three Canadians, and the sole survivor of this disastrous affair, Ada Blackjack, the Eskimo cook and seamstress, who was rescued two years after the last man died of scurvy. Stefansson then "sold" the island to a Nome, Alaska, merchant, who planned to turn it into a reindeer farm. On August 19, 1924, Red Army troops stormed ashore, and raised the hammer and sickle, putting an end to the foreign "colonization" of Wrangel Island. It is now a *zapovednik,* a Russian nature preserve.

Native peoples in the Canadian Arctic, Greenland, Alaska, and Russia have hunted polar bears as long as there have been men on the ice and bears to hunt. The white coat, huge size, and fierce reputation of the polar bear make it a highly desirable big-game trophy, and the introduction of small planes and helicopters has made it possible for "hunters" to be put down on the ice for a shot at a bear or even to shoot at it from the air. This kind of activity is illegal everywhere, but unscrupulous hunters and guides still do it. It is also illegal to bring a polar bear skin into the United States, Russia, or Canada, but this law is often circumvented. The number of bears had been in decline for many years due to severe overhunting by all the northern nations. During the 1960s the world population of polar bears was so low—some thought that there were no more than 10,000 bears left—scientists feared that the species was headed for extinction.* The 1976 agreement among the polar bear nations banned all hunting except by natives, who were required to hunt in the traditional manner. The elimination of sport hunting allowed the world's polar bear population to bounce back, and when Thor Larsen wrote "We've Saved the Ice Bear" for *International Wildlife* in 1984, the population was believed to be "holding steady" at around 25,000. Larsen concluded his article (and moderated his titular euphoria) with a warning that was prescient and optimistic, but soon to be proven wrong:

> We cannot rest on our laurels, however. The North Pole is changing rapidly. The industrialized world needs the oil and minerals that can be found there, and the Arctic ecosystem is fragile and vulnerable to interference. Even with the hunting of bears drastically curtailed, other disturbances could have the same negative effects. An airport, helicopter base, or oil rig in a major denning area for polar bears will prevent new cubs from being born or surviving. Fortunately, many nations understand this and have set aside large reserves where transport, drilling and other human activities are banned.

In a May 15, 2008, article about the decision by the U.S. government to list the polar bear as "threatened" under the Endangered Species Act, *Toronto Globe & Mail* environment reporter Martin Mittelstaedt wrote, "An estimated 20,000 to 25,000 polar bears roam the Far North, among 19 relatively distinct populations," which he delineated as follows:

---

* "The two greatest problems in polar bear research and management," wrote Richard Harington in 1968, "are establishment of confident population estimates and major patterns of population movement." Before the introduction of the technology that permitted even an approximation of a proper circumpolar census of polar bears—helicopter and airplane spotting; capturing bears and outfitting them with radio collars and satellite tracking them—estimating the number of polar bears living at any one time was guesswork at best. In his 1968 report on denning habits, Harington took an educated guess: "The world population is about 10,000, of which 6,000 live in Canada. In 1964, the total world kill was about 1,300. The Canadian kill has approached 600."

Arctic Basin:	UNKNOWN
Chukchi Sea:	2,000
Southern Beaufort Sea:	1,500*
Northern Beaufort Sea:	1,200*
Viscount Melville Sea:	215*
Norwegian Bay:	190*
Kane Basin:	164*
Lancaster Sound:	2,541*
McClintock Channel:	284*
Gulf of Boothia:	1,523*
Foxe Basin:	2,197*
Western Hudson Bay:	935*
Southern Hudson Bay:	1,000*
Baffin Bay:	2,074*
Davis Strait:	1,650*
East Greenland:	2,000
Barents Sea:	3,000
Kara Sea:	UNKNOWN
Laptev Sea:	800 to 1,200

Mittelstaedt's numbers, which came from the 2007 IUCN/SSC Polar Bear Specialist Group Report, add up to 24,673, but do not include the "unknown" Arctic Basin population or that of the Russian Kara Sea. (The figures also appear in Rachel Courtland's May 22 *Nature* article, "Polar Bear Numbers Set to Fall.") Some populations, such as Western Hudson Bay (Churchill) are remarkably precise, while others, such as the Barents and Laptev seas, are rough guesses. Of the nineteen polar bear populations, thirteen—those marked with an asterisk in the list— live, in whole or in part, in Canada. Courtland wrote,

> Projecting the fate of a creature that ranges over more than 25° of latitude is difficult. The IUCN Polar Bear Specialist Group has identified 19 distinct populations that live in markedly different habitats . . . For instance, bears that spend the majority of their time on ice may have to migrate long distances to maintain their life lifestyle, an additional stress if food is scarce . . . The southernmost populations around Hudson Bay may already be experiencing the effects of climate change. Recent studies have shown that such bears

Norwegian scientists photograph a sedated bear at Churchill.

are losing valuable hunting time in the spring, when the animals take most of the year's energy by fattening up on nesting ringed seals. West of Hudson Bay, young bears are less likely to survive after earlier sea-ice breakups, a process that now occurs roughly three weeks earlier than it did 30 years ago.

ICELAND

While its name alone might seem to qualify it for membership in the polar bear nations, Iceland does not, in fact, belong. It is touched at its very northernmost extensions by the Arctic Circle, and is a mere 185 miles from eastern Greenland, but because the ice conditions conducive to the breeding of seals do not usually occur off Iceland, polar bears have shown little inclination to visit this large volcanic island, much of which is covered by the Vatnajökull Glacier, the largest in Europe. In the past, however, when the ice moved closer, the bears often came with it. As University of Manitoba historian Tryggvi Oleson wrote in his 1950 article, "Polar Bears in the Middle Ages,"

> The earliest known instance of the exportation of polar bears from Iceland and their importation into northern Europe dates from the last years of the ninth century (c. 880). Igimundr the Old captured two bear cubs which had come ashore with their mother from the ice floes of Iceland. When he went abroad he took the cubs with him and presented them to King Harold the Fairhaired of Norway.

Oleson—who used original Icelandic texts as his sources—continued: "In 1279, when the winter in Iceland was very severe and the ice lay off large parts of the coast causing everywhere the death of men and animals, an annalist writes that God sent white bears and seals to alleviate the famine." The driftwood brought by the ice was used for fuel, and the bears and seals were eaten. But polar bears were also valued for their pelts: "The priests used them as rugs on which to stand in cold weather, and penitents who stood barefoot before the church door were often given a bear rug on which to stand in inclement weather. In the thirteenth and fourteenth century, every church seemed to own one or more of these rugs."

In 1906, when he compiled "Icelandic Beast and Bird Lore," Stefansson wrote,

> The most powerful animal with which the Icelander is directly acquainted is the polar bear. The bear is not really an animal, but a man under the spell of sorcery. This may be known from the fact that the young of the bear, when born, are not bears, but human children. The mother, however, immediately touches them with her paw, whereupon they turn into cubs and remain bears ever after.

He also said that "the great ice floes that sometimes drift down upon the country bring numbers of these animals within swimming distance of the shore." While a branch of the Gulf Stream (the Irminger Current) warms Icelandic waters, the East Greenland Current often brings rafts of polar ice to Iceland, often in the form of huge icebergs that have broken free of Greenland's glaciers. For most of the twentieth century, this phenomenon was rare, but in 1968, the polar ice off Iceland was more extensive than at any time since 1888. Again in 1979, floating ice appeared off northern Iceland, completely surrounding the little island of Grimsey, which lies on the Arctic Circle. In the past, polar bears have hitched a ride on the floating ice, and fetched up in Iceland. In "Curse of the Drift Ice," his 2003 article in *Iceland Geographic,* Thor Jakobsson wrote that "in 1802, two bears came ashore in the Standir region of the West Fjords . . . In 1874, a number of polar bears came to Iceland; three were killed in the Hornstradir region of the West Fjords while three bears came ashore at Mjóifjörur in the East Fjords." The last record of a polar bear in Icelandic waters was in 1993. "Iceland Fears Bears That Go With the Floe" was the clever title of an April 2, 2007, London *Telegraph* article by Gethin Chamberlain, in which we read that

> thick pack ice, the likes of which has not been seen for decades, stretched into the western fjords as temperatures plummeted and a bitter wind blew in from Greenland. The ice has proved a headache for fishermen, who have been unable to put to sea, but it is what comes with pack ice that has caused the most concern—polar bears . . . When chunks break off, as appears to have happened last week, the bears become stranded, drifting wherever the ice takes them.

So in early June 2008, the ice (or the lack thereof) brought a single polar bear to a mountain road near Skagafjördur on Iceland's northern coast. A farmer spotted the 500-pound male walking along the road, and called the police. Environment Minister Thorunn Sveinbjarnardóttir had planned to tranquilize the bear and return it to Greenland, some 200 miles away, but because the proper tranquilizer could not be found in Iceland, they decided to shoot the bear instead. A video of the bear wandering across black lava fields and then being shot caused a public outcry, and the minister said that they would try to avoid shooting the next polar bear that landed in the country. Even if the bear had not been killed, it would have been difficult to figure out how (or why) it came to Iceland, but it might have left Greenland because it was unable to find food there. Two weeks later, a twelve-year-old girl spotted another polar bear on a farm near the town of Saudarkrokur, also on the Skagafjördur. This time, the chief veterinarian of the Copenhagen

Ice lake, striped ice, and black lava at the Vatnajökull Glacier, Iceland

Zoo was flown in to help, but they couldn't get close enough to the bear to anesthetize it, and when it started running toward an inhabited area, they shot it. "It was a security problem," said one of the Icelandic policemen. About three weeks after the first sighting, a woman out for a walk claimed to have spotted another bear. Hrefna Björg Gudmunds-dóttir reported her sighting to the police, but when the constables searched the area, they found only sheep tracks. Icelanders in the vicinity of Skagafjördur keep on the lookout for polar bears; it is not unlikely that the polar bear invasion will continue—and it may even intensify.

ALASKA

Until the Russians sold Alaska to the United States in 1867 for $7.2 million (about two cents an acre), there were no polar bears in the U.S., but with the addition of 600,000 square miles of territory that included shorelines on the Bering and Beaufort seas, many white bears instantly became American citizens. Some people derided the Alaska purchase as useless, calling it "Seward's Folly" (after William H. Seward, President Andrew Johnson's secretary of state, who engineered the sale),

"Seward's Icebox," "Icebergia," and "Andrew Johnson's Polar Bear Garden," because it was believed foolhardy to spend so much money on a remote region which promised no return. In addition to the oil, gold, and furs, America found itself landlord to populations of bowhead whales, walruses, seals, and polar bears. Two populations of the bears occur in Alaska: the southern Beaufort Sea (about 1,500 animals) group, shared with Canada; and the Alaska-Chukotka (Chukchi Sea) group (approximately 2,000 bears), shared with Russia. Some denning occurs along the north Alaska coast, especially in the 1.5-million-acre Coastal Plain area at the northern edge of the Arctic National Wildlife Refuge. Bordered on the north by the Beaufort Sea, on the east by the U.S.-Canadian border, and on the west by the Canning River, it is ideal country for polar bears.

Edward W. Nelson, who sailed aboard the *Corwin* in 1881, published his findings in the *Report upon Natural History Collections Made in Alaska between the Years 1877–1881* in 1887. In *The Eskimo about Bering Strait* (1900) he wrote:

A number of Eskimo on the Alaskan coast show frightful scars obtained in contests with [bears] in winter. One man, who came on board the *Corwin,* had the entire skin and flesh torn from one side of his head and face including the eye and ear, yet had escaped and recovered. One incident was related to me which occurred near Point Hope during the winter of 1880–81. Men went out from Point Hope during one of the long winter nights to attend to their seal nets, which were set through holes in the ice. While at work near each other, one of the men heard a bear approaching over the frosty snow, and having no weapon but a small knife, and the bear being between him and the shore, he threw himself upon his back on the ice and waited. The bear came up and for a few moments smelled about the man from head to foot, and finally pressed his cold nose against the man's lips and nose and sniffed several times; each time the terrified Eskimo held his breath until, as he afterwards said, his lungs nearly burst. The bear suddenly heard the other man at work, and listening for a moment he started towards him at a gallop, while the man he left sprang to his feet and ran for his life for the village and reached it safely. At midday, when the sun had risen a little above the horizon, a large party went out to the spot and found the bear finishing his feast upon the other hunter and soon dispatched him. Cases similar to this occur occasionally all along the coast where the bear is found in winter.

Nelson also wrote a 1916 *National Geographic* article entitled "The Larger North American Mammals." In the description of the polar bear, he repeated his observations made aboard the *Corwin*, and added, "One large old male climbed to the top of an uplifted ice-pan and, after looking about lay down on one side, and, giving a push with one hind foot, slid down head foremost 30 or 40 feet, striking the water with a great splash. He then climbed out and walked sedately away."

In 1946, when Frank Dufresne published *Alaska's Animals & Fishes,* the polar bear was little known, except to Eskimos, visitors to zoos, and Arctic historians who mostly reported its predations on people. Dufresne wrote, "When the animal is suffering pangs of hunger, the sight or smell of an Eskimo hunter may bring a careful stalk, followed by a swift rushing attack. Not in anger is this assault made, but for the

Bob Hines's illustration from Alaska's Animals & Fishes. *Many illustrators and museums used a ribbon seal as the bear's prey because it was more colorful than a ringed seal.*

sole purpose of providing Nanook with a meal!" Because he obviously subscribed to the notion that the great white bear was a man-eater, he seemed genuinely surprised that the bear would not attack in anger. He also believed that the bear was protected by its environment:

> Because the land regions it chooses to visit are sparsely inhabited by humans, this monarch of the ice has not been over-hunted. Except to furnish food for the Eskimos who seem to prize its rank tasting flesh, few polar bears are taken. The coarsely furred pelts have little use other than decoration. As a result there is no great incentive for hunting the polar bear, and its numbers show little fluctuation in recent years.

In earlier, simpler times, Eskimos hunted polar bears with dogsleds and spears, and "white hunters" shot at them with rifles. (There were, of course, no airplanes to bring the hunters to where the bears were, because there were no landing strips in these remote areas.) There was no concern for "endangered species," and there were no pesky regulations to stop anybody from shooting anything he wanted. In his 1947 *Mammals of North America,* biologist Victor Calahane mused on polar bears:

> At times and in certain places, polar bears are so numerous as to be a substantial source of food for the Eskimos. Their hides make excellent mukluks, other small articles of clothing, and sleeping robes. Their teeth and claws are favorite ornaments and are frequently strung for necklaces. In the days of big houses, when the Arctic was being explored, Americans paid as much as one thousand dollars for one of the enormous white pelts to be used as a rug or wall hanging. Now that small apartments are more popular, the skin of the ice bear is worth about forty dollars. An average of sixty-five pelts are exported each year from Alaska. Somewhat fewer are traded in Canada.

Until the mid-1950s, the only people hunting polar bears in Alaska were Eskimos, and their average take of 120 a year did not have much of an impact on the population. Around that time, in what was still the territory of Alaska, non-natives invented sport hunting from airplanes. No dogsleds, no trudging over ice and snow: just spot the bear from the air, land within rifle range, and shoot it. The only restriction was money: a hunter had to pay $3,000 or more to have a pilot fly him out over the ice. Soon hunters were taking some 300 bears a year in this disgracefully unsportsmanlike manner. On August, 8, 1965, the *New York Times* published this editorial, entitled "Memo to the Hunter":

The white polar bear is one of the world's biggest, most adaptable and extraordinary animals. He is also rapidly becoming one of the rarest.

The polar bear is a victim of a peculiar—and peculiarly repulsive—expression of man's egotism. Wealthy men have taken to hunting bears in Alaska from airplanes. Two planes are used to herd the bear to an ice floe suitable for a landing. While one plane lands and the hunter gets set, the other plane maneuvers the bemused animal into the hunter's gun sights. More than 300 polar bears, a new record, were killed in this fashion last winter in Alaska.

This kind of hunt is about as sporting as machine-gunning a cow. Its only purpose is to obtain the bear's fur as a trophy for the floor or wall of someone's den. The carcass is left for the predators.

Norway and Alaska are the only places that actively encourage this degraded "sport" as a tourist promotion. Russians do not hunt polar bears for sport and Canada forbids it by law, except by Eskimos for whom bear meat is a delicacy in their traditional diet.

The polar bear maintains a higher standard than some humans. He kills only for food, never for pleasure. Although eight to ten feet long and weighing more than a thousand pounds, he can run on ice too thin to support a man and can swim the iciest waters. He is an animal with great style, playful yet powerful, heavy yet swift, and strikingly independent. "There's no such thing as a pack of polar bears," one writer has noted.

A conference on the fate of the polar bear is to be held at the University of Alaska in September. But a conference is scarcely necessary to point up the desirability of a ban by Alaska and Norway on senseless killing by trophy hunters. This splendid animal deserves a better fate than slaughter by pseudo-sportsmen.

When Alaska became the forty-ninth state in 1959, a polar bear management program was initiated, but it did little to protect the bears, so in 1966, the state proposed to limit permits to 350, and prohibited helicopter hunting, in which the hunter shot the bear from a hovering helicopter. In 1972, polar bear hunting with airplanes was also banned, and in that year, the Marine Mammal Protection Act was passed. The MMPA prohibited hunting by anyone except Alaska natives.

In a 1983 study, Jack Lentfer of Alaska Fish and Game marked a number of bears and then noted where they were seen or recaptured. ("Capturing" a bear consisted of tranquilizing it from a helicopter, marking it with an ear tag and a lip tattoo, and painting numbers on the fur that can be seen from the air.) Lentfer observed that there was a significant interchange between the polar bears of Alaska's North Slope and those of the mainland coast of northern Canada, along the coast of the Beaufort Sea. Lentfer found little or no interchange between Alaska's bears and those of the rest of Canada, Greenland, or Svalbard, suggesting that the bears of Alaska "tend to occur in the same general area in the late winter and early spring each year."

A couple of years later, Steven Amstrup, Ian Stirling, and Lentfer published a study called "Past and Present Status of Polar Bears in Alaska," in which they observed that

> the discovery of the world's tenth largest oil field at Prudhoe Bay, land disposals resulting from the Alaskan Claims Settlement Act of 1971, which was spawned by that discovery, and concomitant increases in wealth have resulted in dramatic changes in population of humans in Alaska . . . Industrial activities may threaten the security of polar bears directly and indirectly. The most important indirect threat is increased hunting. The influx of cash, as a result of oil and gas development, into previously cash-poor areas will continue to improve the harvest of polar bears. Hunting is the most significant cause of polar bear mortality.*

---

* Exactly the same thing happened with bowhead whales. Before the 1968 discovery of oil at Prudhoe Bay, whaling captains in Inuit coastal villages were chosen upon the basis of seniority and experience. Local workers on the Alaska Pipeline (completed in 1977) made enough money to buy and outfit a whaling boat and appoint themselves captain. In 1975, whalers from the villages of Barrow, Point Hope, and Wainwright killed (or struck and lost) a total of forty-three whales. By the following season, the total was up to ninety-one, and by 1977, it had jumped to 108 (Ellis 1991).

Eight hundred and eighty bears (out of an estimated total population of 2,000) were tagged from 1967 to 1983, and sixty-four of these were fitted with radio collars. Some were tracked for more than a year. There was a slight decline in the total population at the end of the trophy-hunting period in 1972. Because sport hunters seek the largest males, 75 percent of the polar bear "harvest" was male. Moreover, Amstrup, Stirling, and Lentfer wrote, "the harvest of polar bears has a long history, and polar bears must be recognized as a valuable renewable resource." Airborne hunters could observe several bears in a brief time period, and were highly selective of the animals they harvested. This, the authors believed, was a good thing, because "the Beaufort Sea population can sustain little if any increase in mortalities of females." As of now, the inhabitants of fourteen Alaskan villages hunt polar bears, but the number varies by village and by year. Even today, polar bears provide the villagers with meat and raw materials for handicrafts, such as boots, mittens, and pants. For the Inupiat and Yupik cultures on either side of the Bering Strait, polar bear hunting is a source of pride, prestige, accomplishment, and, for some, economic necessity.

The MMPA prohibits taking and importing marine mammals unless a permit is issued for the purposes of public display, native subsistence, scientific research, or sustaining a depleted species. Polar bears in Alaska can be hunted only by Alaska natives, but revisions added to the MMPA in 1994 allow U.S. citizens to import polar bear "trophies" acquired in Canadian hunts. As long as the hunter can prove he shot the bear from an approved population in Canada, he is allowed to bring his trophies into the U.S. From 2002 to 2005, a total of 298 requests were made by U.S. citizens to import sport-hunted polar bear trophies from Canada. Of these, 252—a staggering 85 percent—were issued. As we know, there have been many (so far unsuccessful) legislative attempts to allow drilling for oil in the Arctic National Wildlife Refuge (ANWR), and if this were to occur, the bears would be disturbed and threatened by exploration and drilling, which might drive the bears from their traditional denning areas. An oil spill or the rupture of a pipeline would be a disaster for them.

For the 2007 "Green" issue, *Vanity Fair* included a story of Knut, the baby polar bear born in the Berlin Zoo; on the cover, actor Leonardo DiCaprio was pictured with the bear cub on an ice floe. In the May 2008 "Green" issue, polar bears were again featured, but they didn't get the cover this time—Madonna did. In that issue, Michael Shnayerson's article "The Edge of Extinction" incorporates a visit to Kaktovik, "the one place, and the one place only, to see polar bears in America," and a well-reasoned account of the conflict between those who would protect the bears by listing them as an endangered species and those who are dedicated to opening up the Chukchi region to oil exploration. Arguing for the defense (of the bears), Shnayerson quotes Ian Stirling:

> You observe an animal that's not only beautiful and impressive in its size, but you get a sense of how exquisitely polar bears have adapted to survive in one of the most rigorous environments in the world. We often think of them as living in a harsh environment, but to a bear, it's not harsh at all. It's home, and a comfortable home at that.

Randall Luthi, the head of the Minerals Management Service, the agency that auctioned off the oil leases, said that before the lease sale, which occurred on February 6, 2008, many steps had been taken to protect the polar bear and its habitat: "Through these reviews, we assessed the direct, indirect, and cumulative effects of the lease sale on marine mammals, including polar bears." In fact, "the direct, indirect, and cumulative effects of the lease sale" on polar bears would be enormous, but protecting the bears at the expense of the oil companies would be unthinkable. When Interior Secretary Dirk Kempthorne was asked to appear before a U.S. Senate Committee on Environment and Public Works to explain why the polar bear remained unlisted, he declined.

Biologists were baffled when a young female polar bear showed up in the village of Fort Yukon, Alaska, 250 miles inland, evidently having crossed the entire Brooks Range from the ice of the Beaufort Sea. Quoted in an article in the *Fairbanks Daily News-Miner* (Mowry 2008), biologist Steven Amstrup said that finding the bear this far south was "highly unusual," and that "this is the time of year that polar bears are on the sea ice foraging." On March 31, 2008, the bear was spotted feeding on a lynx carcass (if this is true, it would add a totally unexpected prey species to the polar bear's diet) outside a cabin, and hunters Zeb Cadzow and Paul Herbert tracked it into the brush near the Porcupine River. They said the bear charged them, and Cadzow, who hunts with an AR-15 assault rifle, said, "I shot from the hip seven or eight times, if I had gotten it to my shoulder, the bear would have been on top of me." As noted above, under the terms of the Marine Mammal Protection Act, native hunters may legally shoot polar bears for subsistence, but because Fort Yukon is not a coastal village, shooting must be in defense of life or property. That the bear—which seemed to be in good shape—charged the hunters was the only justification for shooting her. (Bear hunting with an assault rifle raises other questions.)

But when a mother and two cubs were seen prowling around the Northwest Territories town of Déline, also 250 miles from the coast, RCMP officers—"Mounties"—had no choice but to shoot the bears when they appeared to be threatening some tied-up dogs. Although the sightings were hundreds of miles apart (Fort Yukon is far to the west of Déline), it was the second time in less than a week that polar bears were seen that far inland. In an April 4 article in the *Edmonton Journal,* Ed Struzik asked Andrew Derocher what he thought about these anomalous sightings. "Weird," said Derocher. "I'm not sure what's going on, but we do know that last summer, the ice in the Beaufort Sea retreated a lot further north than it usually does. My guess is that they got separated from the ice and spent the winter on land." It is only coincidence that Fort Yukon and Déline are both on the Arctic Circle, but we assume that polar bears don't read maps anyway, and that their appearance so far from the coast is a clear sign—perhaps even the beginning of a trend—that the bears' natural habitat and habits are being upset by the retreat of the ice.

It's August 2008, and five biologists have come to Teshekpuk Lake on the shore of the Beaufort Sea to study shorebirds on the declining shoreline. (As the ground warms and sloughs off into the sea, there is less and less territory for breeding birds.) Teshekpuk is part of a vast network of lagoons, deep lakes, wet meadows, and river deltas that characterize much of the Arctic coastal plain. According to the Wildlife Conservation Society, which sponsored the study, an adult polar bear, which should have been out on the sea ice by that time, appeared on the shore. The scientists had had "bear safety training," but they were not sure what to do about a polar bear landing in the middle of their study. The region is on the North Slope of Alaska, not far from the bear's regular habitat, but because the ice was gone, the bear had headed inland. Although the bear never came near them, they were worried that they would have to maintain a round-the-clock vigil—just in case—so they called for a plane to fly them out. Wandering bears are

A bear comes ashore at Teshekpuk Lake, Alaska.

not the only problem around Teshekpuk. There have been recent efforts to open the entire North Slope wetlands to oil drilling. The Bush administration tried to sell the area as part of an oil and gas lease sale held on September 27, 2006, but the federal courts ruled that the plan was illegal, and the critical wildlife habitat around Teshekpuk was removed from the sale.

RUSSIA

Polar bears in Russia are found along the northern coast of the Eurasian continent, a stretch of nearly 4,000 miles where the seas are frozen for half the year. For centuries, this formidable coastline defeated anyone who sought a northeast passage, blocking the way with endless, impenetrable fields of ice. Willem Barents failed to make it across every time; in the final effort his ships made it to Bear Island, and then to Spitsbergen (both of which he was credited with discovering), but when they finally got to Novaya Zemlya their ship was wrecked by the ice and they were forced to overwinter in the frigid climate of northernmost Eurasia. In their retreat in the spring of 1596, they made it to the Kola

Peninsula, but Barents died after five days in an open boat. The Barents Sea, bounded by the archipelago of Franz Josef Land in the north, the Norwegian and Russian mainland to the south, and Novaya Zemlya to the east, covers more than half a million square miles. The Barents Sea off Norway, and all the indents of the Arctic Ocean along the northern Russian coastline—the Kara Sea, the Laptev Sea, the East Siberian Sea, and even the Chukchi Sea, which debouches through the Bering Strait—are ideal habitats for seals, walruses, and polar bears. The low salinities and high latitudes of these Arctic marginal seas mean that they are often the first to freeze as winter approaches and can remain frozen well into the brief Arctic summer, particularly in the east.

The islands of the Russian Arctic are located wholly within the Arctic Circle, stretching from the Arctic coast of European Russia in the west to the northern coasts of central and far-eastern Siberia in the east. The largest of these islands is Novaya Zemlya—actually two islands separated by the narrow Matochkin Strait. (*Novaya Zemlya* means "New Land" in Russian.) As of the 2002 census, the island's human population was 2,716, almost all of whom reside in Belushya Guba, the administrative center of Novaya Zemlya District. Other island groups are Severnaya Zemlya (North Land); Novosibiriskye Ostrova (New Siberian Islands); Ostrov Herald (Herald Island); and Ostrova Vrangeyai (Wrangel Island). Nikita Ovsyanikov describes the view of Wrangel:

A cold wind is blowing streams of snow over the frozen Arctic Ocean. Tiny powdery crystals sparkle in the sun and fill the air, obscuring the icy landscape and the yellowish figure of a bear slowly making its way between the ice hummocks. No other living creature can be seen for miles in this chaotic jumble of pressure ridges, flat ice fields, and the occasional dark strips of open water that cut across the endless white expanse.

For more than thirty years, Nikita Ovsyanikov has worked on Wrangel Island, where the polar bear density is among the highest in the world. Wrangel and Herald islands were once part of the frozen ice field that formed in winter, but now they might be cut off, giving the bears the option of swimming to and from the islands. The islands house the largest number of polar bear dens in the Russian Arctic, with

between 350 and 500 dens on the two islands, or 80 percent of the
Chukotka region breeding population. Some areas support six to twelve
bears per square kilometer. The bears of the Chukchi Sea inhabit the
eastern part of the East Siberian Sea, all the way to the Beaufort Sea off
Alaska's North Slope. This population has been estimated to number
between 2,000 and 5,000 animals, and might even be increasing. Most
of the females of this international community den on Wrangel and
Herald islands, but there are also many dens on the mainland of
Chukotka.

Headline in the Russian newspaper *Izvestia,* December 15, 2006:
"Hungry Polar Bear Sieges Russians for 2 Days." A group of meteorol-
ogists and gamekeepers spent two days in the attic of their weather station in Chukotka, as a bear broke into the lower floors. The *Izvestia*
report continued:

> The hungry bear broke into the weather station, tore apart two dogs
> and went in to find food in the house. The inhabitants hid in the
> attic, where they sat two days. They waited until they got permission
> to shoot the animal, which was given by the environmental ministry
> in Moscow. The newspaper reported that about 170 polar bears,
> which are a protected species, have been stranded along Russia's Arc-
> tic shore during unseasonably warm temperatures. Every year the ice
> forms later. For example, right now the ice is not thick enough to
> support the polar bear and the animal is being forced to look for food
> where people are.

The polar bear population north of the coast of central Siberia is the
least studied and poorest known, probably because this region is difficult to reach for most of the year. Denning areas are on the islands of
Severnaya Zemlya and the northern coast of the Taimyr Peninsula,
where there might be anywhere from 800 to 1,200 bears, and the Franz
Josef Land/Novaya Zemlya population may number as many as 3,500
bears, while in Svalbard—not part of the Russian Arctic—there may be
1,700 to 2,000 (Ovsyanikov 1998). For the most part, the Russian bears
have been protected by government restrictions, but despite the nationwide ban on hunting and the 1973 International Polar Bear Agreement,
the polar bears of the Russian Arctic are still not safe. Poachers were the
problem when Russia banned polar bear hunting, and poachers are the

problem today. As with many other regulations the government has tried to impose on the people who live in remote corners of this huge country, anti-poaching laws are more than a little difficult to enforce. A polar bear skin can sell for as much as $4,500, and hunters are not about to let that kind of money walk away.* In an interview she gave to Radio Free Europe on January 18, 2007, Margaret Williams, leader for the World Wildlife Fund's Bering Sea and Kamchatka Program, said, "The stakes are high and fines and prison sentences are relatively small. A couple of years ago, our group found 55 polar bear skins available on Russian websites" (Corwin 2007). Under Russian law, villagers are allowed to shoot a polar bear in self-defense, and the number of bears that threaten or attack people in Russia is surprisingly high. In Russia as elsewhere in the Arctic, warmer winters have led to less sea ice and a shortened hunting season for the bears, driving them farther inland and increasing their contact with humans.

In April 2007, Williams went to Chukotka with several Russian and American colleagues. They traveled more than 700 miles across the roadless, snow-covered Chukotka Peninsula to reach the small village of Vankarem, north of the Arctic Circle on the Chukchi Sea. The expedition was part of an ambitious effort to protect and study polar bears and address an increasing problem caused by climate change: conflict between polar bears and humans.

From Williams's journal, posted on the WWF Web site (www.wwf blogs.org/polarbears):

I am here to start an expedition my colleague Viktor Nikiforov, Director of regional programs from WWF–Russia, and I have organized. [Viktor] is a "Jack of all trades" in conservation, with over 20 years of experience in the Arctic. With us is a group of polar bear biologists from the Russian Institute of Nature Conservation, the Chukotka Research Institute for Fisheries and Oceanography, and the US Fish and Wildlife Service in Alaska. Also joining us are a

---

* Although they live in different parts of Russia, there is a parallel between polar bears and "Siberian" tigers (now known as Amur tigers, after the Amur River in the Russian Far East). Both of these great carnivores are hunted, mostly illegally, for their spectacular—and therefore extremely valuable—fur coats, which are mostly turned into coats or rugs. Aboriginal peoples occasionally use tiger or leopard skins in ceremonial dress, and while some women wear leopard-skin (or leopard-patterned) articles of clothing, men never do.

senior advisor to the Governor of Chukotka, and a journalist, photographer and interpreter from *The New York Times*.

We are here as part of an ambitious effort to protect and study
polar bears in the face of numerous challenges—foremost being the
tremendous change in polar bears' sea ice habitat. On our trip we will
visit with members of an Arctic community with whom WWF has
developed a pilot "bear patrol" program. We will hold a seminar on
human-bear conflict management, and complete the planning and
documentation for a protected area on the Arctic coast . . .

During the meeting, I am again impressed by Sergey [a member
of the expedition, and one of the overseers of the new bilateral polar
bear treaty]. He reminds people that when the polar bear hunt is
legalized for indigenous residents of Chukotka as part of the US-
Russia polar bear treaty, it's not going to be possible for everyone to
hunt them, or even every village. They may have to take turns, or
there may be times when hunting won't be an option at all. His message is that the hunt is going to be something special and it will be
managed very carefully.

The reporter on Williams's WWF Chukotka expedition was Steven
Lee Myers of the *New York Times*. He wrote an article entitled "Russia
Tries to Save Polar Bears with Legal Hunt," which appeared on April
16, 2007. In recent years, the people of Chukotka—Siberian Yupik,
Koryaks, Chuvans, and some Russian settlers—have poached the bears
for meat, which is consumed locally, and for the pelt, which can fetch
thousands of dollars on the black market. Although Russia officially
banned polar bear hunting in 1956, the changing climate has brought
the bears into greater contact with people, and now the country is preparing to allow hunters of Chukotka to kill a number of bears for the
first time in fifty years. The residents of the town of Vankarem are being
allowed to hunt polar bears that have been moving into the region.
Polar bears have attacked and killed three people since 2003, which
may add revenge to the list of reasons to hunt the bears. The idea is to
allow the Chukchi people to hunt in an attempt to cut down poach-
ing. Myers wrote, "If hunters are allowed to take at least some bears
legally, the reasoning goes, they might be less tempted to break the law."
This seems more than a little specious in a region where bear hunting
was once a way of life and, more significant, in a country where corrup-

tion and ignoring environmental strictures is the rule rather than the exception.

Nevertheless, on October 3, 2007, the United States and Russia ratified a bilateral agreement for the long-term conservation of shared polar bear populations in Alaska and Chukotka. The treaty unifies joint management programs that affect this shared population of bears, calling for the active involvement of native people and their organizations in future management. It will also enhance such long-term joint efforts as conservation of ecosystems and important habitats, harvest allocations based on sustainability, collection of biological information, and increased consultation and cooperation with state, local, and private interests. The treaty fulfills the spirit and intent of the 1973 multilateral Agreement on the Conservation of Polar Bears among the United States, Russia, Norway, Denmark (for Greenland), and Canada by allowing a sustainable harvest by Alaska and Chukotka natives but prohibiting the harvest of females with cubs or of cubs less than one year old. It also bans the use of aircraft and large motorized vehicles in the taking of polar bears and enhances the conservation of specific habitats such as feeding, congregating, and denning areas.

In March 2008, Moscow newspapers reported that illegal trade in polar bear skins was on the rise. Monitoring Internet offers of pelts for sale, Viktor Nikiforov, polar bear scientist for the World Wildlife Fund–Russia, noted that the number of skins offered increased sharply from 2003 to 2008, and that the price of a single skin had swelled to $6,000 during that five-year period. The poaching sites were identified as the Taimyr Peninsula on Siberia's Arctic coast, and Chukotka in the Russian Far East. On March 25, the Russian Information Agency (RIA Novosti) announced that the WWF–Russia is starting an operation dedicated to protecting the bears of Chukotka from poachers.

As with every other population of polar bears, those of the Russian Arctic are threatened by humans; but those humans are usually comfortably far from the northern coasts. They can be found in every city, factory, and highway where greenhouse gases are generated, heating the atmosphere and melting the summer sea ice. As the level of the world's oceans rises, there is a concurrent increase in coastal erosion—the actual loss of the coastline itself. Melting permafrost (soil at or below the freezing point of water for two or more years) causes the ice to slide seaward over the frozen soil, a process known as thermal abrasion. Virtually all 4,000 miles of the northern coast of Russia is in retreat, in some places at a rate approaching twenty feet per year. For obvious reasons, there are few human settlements along this coast, but from the Beloye More (the White Sea) in the west to Wrangel and Herald islands in the far east, the Russian polar bears, once the undisputed rulers of this ice-bound world, are in serious trouble.

SVALBARD

Spitsbergen is an island group (also known as Svalbard) that consists of Spitsbergen, the largest island, North East Land (Nordaustlandet), Edge Island (Edgeøya), Barents Island (Barentsøya), Prince Charles Foreland (Prinz Karls Forland), and many smaller islands. Kong Karls Land is separated from the main island group, as is White Island (Kvitøya) and, far to the south, Bear Island (Bjornøya). Nearly 60 percent of Spitsbergen is covered by glaciers; most of North East Land has a thick ice cover, and White Island, sixty miles to the east, gets its name because it is almost completely covered with ice. All the islands are far to the north of the Arctic Circle; Spitsbergen is the northernmost inhabited region of Europe. The administrative capital is Longyearbyen, named for J. M. Longyear (1850–1922), an American businessman who visited Spitsbergen on holiday in 1901 and later formed the Arctic Coal Company, whose mining camp became the permanent settlement known as Longyear City—*Longyearbyen* in Norwegian.

At Spitsbergen's latitude, spanning 81° north to 76° north, sea ice begins to form in September, and by November most of the islands are iced in. (Or at least they used to be.) In his 1820 discussion of the polar ice, Scoresby wrote, "With each returning spring, the north polar ice presents the following general outline. Filling the bays of Hudson and Baffin, as well as the straits of Hudson and that part of Davis, it exhibits an irregular waving, but generally continuous line from Newfoundland or Labrador, to Nova Zembla." The islands of Spitsbergen fall well within this region, and by the end of winter large areas were completely surrounded by ice and the fjords were frozen.

Because of Dutch and British whaling, Spitsbergen was the scene of some of the earliest contacts between Europeans and polar bears. In *Purchas His Pilgrimes* (published in 1625) Jonas Poole, pilot of the *Ami-*

tie, who led the third expedition to Spitsbergen in 1610, describes an encounter with the "Beares" of Spitsbergen:

> When we were within a mile of the other side, one of my compan-
> ions said he saw a Beare whereupon we looked up and saw three great
> ones. Whereupon I made a stand and gave each of my companions
> some *Aqua vitae,* and a little Bread, and told them that wee must not
> in any case become fearefull, because the nature of them is such, that
> whosoever seems fearefull, or offereth to runne away, they will seize
> upon him. In this time I made my musket readie, and the Beares see-
> ing us to come towards them, stood upon their feet, and two of them
> went towards the Sea. The third stood still champing and foaming,
> as though hee would have eaten us. When I was within shot of him,
> he beganne to follow his fellowes, still looking behind him with his
> former gesture. In the meane while I got ground of him, and three
> men following mee with their weapons. In the end the angry devil
> turned backe, and came directly toward mee; I let him come within
> two Pikes lengths and gave him such a welcome, that he fell downe
> stone dead.

During their brief visit, the crew of the *Amitie* killed five cubs and twenty-seven adult bears. From the outset, Europeans seemed to regard it as their duty to kill polar bears. The hulking ghostlike predators were certainly a threat, but they also interfered with the intentions of the whalers and settlers to dominate these icy, snow-covered islands. Mostly, in the early years, the polar bears of Spitsbergen were killed simply because they were there; later, they were killed for commerce of one kind or another. Sealers, who killed seals for their pelts, shot the bears because they believed that they were saving the seals for them-selves. Odd Lønø (1920–2007), who had worked as a trapper on Sval-bard before writing his PhD dissertation on polar bears, published "The Polar Bear in the Svalbard Area" in 1970, in which he detailed the hunting methods and kill statistics from the end of the eighteenth century to 1968. (He said, "Statistics covering Norwegian polar bear catches from earliest times do not exist.") From 1909 to 1944, the sealers killed a total of 7,704 bears. For that same thirty-five-year period, the total for trappers, who killed the bears for their hides and to collect liv-ing cubs to sell to zoos, was 2,530. For the most part, the bears were shot, either out in the open or from carefully constructed blinds. Waiting for a polar bear to happen by was largely ineffectual, so the hunters devised all sorts of hidden "spring-guns" that could be tripped by a bear pulling on a bait, usually seal blubber but occasionally a slab of bacon. Poison was also used, and even though the Norwegian government made its use illegal in 1927 it was still being employed well into the 1930s. "Another way of catching polar bears is by driving after them with a dog-team," wrote Lønø, but "this method has been very seldom used in Svalbard."

First the Dutch sent whalers to these remote islands, and by 1611 the British did the same, followed by French, German, Norwegian, Swedish, and Danish ships. The rivalry for bowhead whales was fierce, and after several failed attempts to have crews winter there to be ready to hunt as soon as the ice began to break up, the Dutch established Smeerenburg (Dutch for "blubber-town") on tiny Amsterdamøya. (*Øya* means "island" in Norwegian, so *Amsterdamøya* is Amsterdam Island.) Jacob van der Brugge's party survived the winter in 1633, so the Dutch returned to Smeerenburg every spring after that, but nobody stayed on through the winter. The station consisted of a small village with try-works and other facilities for processing whale oil and baleen. After Longyear, American, British, Swedish, Russian, and Norwegian companies started coal mining on Spitsbergen. Norway's sovereignty was recognized by the Svalbard Treaty of 1920, with the proviso that there would be limited military use of Svalbard and that the other nations retained the rights to their settlements. In 1924, Norway officially took over the territory.

There were never many people on Spitsbergen—the population of Longyearbyen fluctuates around 3,000—but there were always plenty of bears. Known as the Barents Sea population, these bears occupy the area from Spitsbergen in the west to the Russian archipelagos of Franz Josef Land and Novaya Zemlya in the east. On these frozen plains, the bears respect no political or biological boundaries; some of them wander as far west as eastern Greenland, or as far east as the Kara Sea. The Barents Sea population is believed to contain more than 3,000 bears (one bear for every person), approximately half of which live on or around the islands of Svalbard. The predominant denning areas are Kong Karls Land, Hopen, Edgeøya, and Nordaustlandet. In 1980, there

Buck reindeer in Svalbard

were twelve dens per square kilometer at Bogen on Kongsøya, and in 1984, 168 bears were observed on that island.

Like polar bears everywhere else, those of Svalbard favor ringed seals as prey, but they will also take bearded and harp seals. Seals have an insulating layer of blubber under the skin, which the polar bears favor. An adult polar bear needs to kill fifty to seventy-five seals a year to meet its energy requirements. Andreas Umbreit (1991) wrote that "reindeer do not appear to be part of their diet. There have been reports of bears passing grazing reindeer without either taking any notice. Hungry bears will rarely indulge in a hunt which shows little promise but costs precious energy." That is probably correct, but polar bears are opportunistic, and are quite capable of changing their techniques when the occasion demands. (Or, as the scientists would say it, they are capable of "behavioral plasticity in response to a novel prey item.") The bears are also scavengers, and will feed on rotting whale carcasses or dead seals if they come across them. On Svalbard, researchers Derocher, Wiig, and Bangjord (2000) observed "seven predation events and six instances of scavenging by polar bears on Svalbard reindeer between 1983 and 1999." Most of these events consisted of the examination of evidence in the snow—tracks, blood, a still-warm reindeer carcass—but on several occasions they actually saw a bear chasing reindeer.

While the polar bears of Nunavut, Greenland, or northern Alaska have to be tracked by hunters, those of Spitsbergen occasionally initiate contact. In Spitsbergen, polar bears were "harvested" heavily, primarily for fur, from the early 1900s until 1973, when the International Agreement on the Conservation of Polar Bears came into effect. According to an official Svalbard publication (by Aars, Andersen, and Kovacs), "In the 1920s more than 900 bears a year were killed . . . and even after WWII the numbers of bears killed annually were as high as 400–500. During the last 25–30 years before the treaty entered into force, harvesting decreased somewhat but still several hundred polar bears were killed each year."

With hunting officially ended, the bear population of Svalbard increased, nearly doubling from 1973 to 1983 (Larsen 1984). The increase in bears precipitated a corresponding rise in the number of human-bear confrontations. According to a study by Ian Gjertz and Endre Persen, these confrontations can be grouped into three categories: 1) bears destroying human property; 2) bears threatening people, dogs, or property; 3) bears killing or injuring people. During that decade, there were fifty confrontations, eight of which took place at manned field stations, in towns, or at mining camps. The rest occurred in the open field. Four bears were shot in self-defense, and four as precautionary measures. Eleven bears were killed to protect property. "Most confrontations occur in winter," wrote the authors.

December is the peak month, possibly because people are just as surprised every year when the first bears show up. November and December are difficult months for hungry bears because there is usually little ice at this time of year, at least on the Spitsbergen west coast, which is where almost all of Svalbard's human inhabitants live. Bears may therefore come close to settlements either out of curiosity or in search of food.

In his 1991 *Guide to Spitsbergen*, Andreas Umbreit described an attack:

The worst recent serious accident with a polar bear happened at the beginning of September 1987 when neither of the two men involved was armed despite warnings. A bear tried to disturb a rubber dinghy belonging to two scientists. One man tried to drive it away with a flaming torch, but the bear attacked him instead. The second scientist succeeded in distracting the bear from his severely wounded colleague who was able to crawl the few meters back into their hut while the bear turned its attentions to its new victim. The second scientist, now also wounded, managed to get back to the hut. The bear besieged the hut during the next three days. Finally the two men made radio contact with a small Dutch ship, *Plancius,* which was already on its way to pick them up at the end of their stay. From the *Plancius* a helicopter with medical help was requested, which freed the pair and flew them to the hospital in Longyearbyen. The bear was shot; the two scientists were very lucky.

Ian Gjertz (with Sissel Aarvik and Reidar Hindrum) tallied the number of bears killed on Svalbard between 1987 and 1992. A total of twenty-six were shot; of these, tourists and scientists were involved in thirteen incidents. "We believe," wrote the authors, "that many of these incidents could have been avoided had those involved been more experienced with high Arctic conditions." So in the 2005 booklet *Polar Bears in Svalbard,* published by the Norwegian Polar Institute, visitors are told to take these precautions: 1) Never move about in polar bear territory without being well prepared. 2) Avoid confrontations: if you see a polar bear in the distance avoid an encounter by staying out of its path, and never move toward the bear. 3) Be armed. Always have a sufficiently powered weapon at hand when traveling outside the settlements. If an aggressive bear attacks with no sign of being scared away by warning shots, shoot with intent to kill. If forced to shoot a polar bear, aim at the chest or the shoulder.

Probably because of their proximity to human settlements, the polar bears of Svalbard are beset by even more problems than hunting and global warming. "High concentrations of polychlorinated biphenyls (PCBs) in polar bears from Svalbard have increased concern for that population's reproductive health," wrote Haave, Ropstad, Derocher et al. in 2003. "Long-range transport of persistent organic compounds by air and ocean currents from industrialized areas has produced high levels of these pollutants in top predators of the Svalbard area, Barents Sea, and the Kara Sea." Polar bears are at the top of the food chain, consuming prey such as seals that have accumulated pollutants from lower trophic levels. In her 2005 book *Silent Snow: The Slow Poisoning of the Arctic,* Marla Cone wrote,

> Polar bears are exposed to hundreds of contaminants, including DDT, but, for some reason, they are able to metabolize more of them, purging them from their bodies. The exception is PCBs, which build up in their tissues. In Svalbard bears, PCB levels peaked at 80 parts per million (ppm)—which Norwegian scientists consider an alarmingly high amount—and averaged about 30 ppm between 1987 and 1995. To the east, around Russia's Franz Josef Land and Kara Sea, polar bears have even higher PCB levels—twice as much, with an average estimated at 60 ppm in the 1990s. The region's other top predators—Arctic foxes and glaucous gulls—are highly contaminated too.

For the March/April 2006 issue of *Mother Jones,* Cone wrote "On Thin Ice" (good title), in which she wrote,

> Several hundred of the industrialized world's most toxic chemicals, especially PCBs and organochlorine pesticides such as DDT, have

The fearless cub perches on its mother, which has been sedated for study in Svalbard.

transformed Svalbard and much of the Arctic into a giant chemical repository, and polar bears into its unintentional lab rats ... Originating mostly in North America and northern Europe, the pollutants hitchhike to Svalbard, Greenland, and other remote reaches of the Arctic on northbound winds and ocean currents.

Examination of the tissues has shown that the bears are permeated with various chemicals—in addition to PCBs, flame retardants (PBDEs) and a compound used in the manufacture of Teflon—that weaken the bears, suppress their immune cells and antibodies, and alter their sex hormones, thyroid hormones, and even their bone composition. More than one in every hundred females has rudimentary male genitalia. In the *Mother Jones* article, Andrew Derocher asks, "Could you realistically put 200 to 500 foreign substances into an organism and expect them to have absolutely no effect? I would be happier if I could find no evidence of pollution affecting polar bears, but so far, the data suggest otherwise."

CANADA: CHURCHILL

Hudson Bay is a large, shallow, inland sea with an area of 475,000 square miles (1.23 million square kilometers), bounded by Nunavut on the north and west, Manitoba and Ontario on the south, and Quebec on the east. (Hudson Bay and James Bay are contiguous; James Bay is the southern extension of Hudson Bay.) Europeans first arrived in the area in 1619 when a Danish expedition led by Jens Munk wintered where Churchill would later stand. The first permanent settlement was a log fort built at the mouth of the Churchill River in 1717 as a part of the extensive fur-trading network established by the Hudson's Bay Company (HBC). The town is named for John Churchill, first Duke of Marlborough (and an ancestor of Winston Churchill), who was governor of the HBC in the late seventeenth century.

The Hudson's Bay Company is the oldest commercial corporation in North America and one of the oldest in the world. From its longtime headquarters at York Factory, just south of what is now the town of Churchill, it dominated the fur trade throughout much of British-controlled North America for several centuries, sponsoring much of the early exploration of western and northern Canada. Samuel Hearne

The bears wait for Hudson Bay to freeze before going out on the ice.

became governor of the HBC in 1775, and his notes were transcribed by his apprentice David Thompson, who went on to become one of early Canada's most celebrated explorers. Thompson recorded much of the early history of Churchill (known as Fort Prince of Wales when he was there), including many observations of the local people, whom he referred to as "Indians." One day, while out on the "immense extent of alluvial in marsh, morass and numerous ponds of water," Thompson and the Indians passed

twelve to fifteen Polar Bears, lying on the marsh, a short distance from the shore. They were from three to five together, their heads close to each other, and their bodies lying as radii from the center. I inquired of the Indians if the Polar Bears always lay in that form, they said it was the common manner in which they lie. As we passed them, one or two would lift up their heads and look at us, but never rose to molest us. The Indian rule is to walk past them with a steady step without seeming to notice them.

Every year, Hudson Bay goes through a complete cryogenic cycle: the bay begins to freeze in the fall, becomes a solid sheet of ice by mid-winter, and begins to thaw by April. The bay is ice free in August and September, after which it begins to freeze, and the cycle begins anew. "These unusual conditions," wrote Gough and Wolfe in 2001, "have led to a unique ecosystem involving a vast range of species. The system is symbolized by the polar bears at the top of the food chain. Polar bears use the ice as a platform to hunt seals during the winter and spring. They increase in weight sufficiently to survive the summer and fall months on land, where food is scarce." Canada's foremost polar bear researcher is Ian Stirling, of the Canadian Wildlife Service/Environment Canada. Stirling has been studying the bears for more than thirty years, and is the author or coauthor of hundreds of scientific papers, as well as the 1988 book *Polar Bears,* in which he wrote,

> The most famous polar bears in the world live on the western coast of Hudson Bay; some of them come into the town of Churchill, Manitoba, every fall. This annual arrival of polar bears in a community has focused the attention of both science and the public on Churchill's bears. They have been the subject of dozens of television programs and hundreds of newspaper and magazine articles. Untold thousands of photographs have been taken by photographers, both amateur and professional, who visit them every year. Over the years, many people have asked me why the polar bears are there, what they are doing, and whether there is anything special about them. In fact, the polar bears of Churchill are quite remarkable and merit a chapter of their own.*

In that chapter, we learn that it was in the 1960s that the bears began coming to Churchill in larger and larger numbers; and in 1968, when a

---

* In addition to countless articles about the bears of Churchill, there have been several books that have featured this easily visited and even more easily photographed population. Dan Guravich's photographs of the Churchill bears appear not only in Stirling's *Polar Bears,* but also in Downs Matthews's *Polar Bear.* Norbert Rosing traveled to the west coast of Hudson Bay for more than twenty years, and *The World of the Polar Bear* (2006) is the result. Smaller in scale is Kelsey Eliasson's *Polar Bears of Churchill,* an introductory pocket guide to polar bears, written by a man who "currently resides at Camp Nanuq—a cottage 'suburb' about fifteen miles east of Churchill in the midst of some prime polar bear real estate."

Mother and cubs in the snow at Churchill

nineteen-year-old boy, following bear tracks in the snow, surprised a sleeping bear, it leapt up, grabbed him, and carried him in its jaws until would-be rescuers shot the bear. The boy died in the hospital. There were two other occasions when bears killed people in Churchill: In 1984, when the Churchill Hotel burned to the ground, a bear and a man were scavenging in the wreckage, and the bear grabbed the man and took off with him. The bear was shot, and the man died. A couple of years later, north of Churchill, a man known as Pickles shot at a bear with birdshot, and followed it into the brush. Bad idea (Derocher, pers. comm., 2008).

Because the aboriginal people who lived in the area that would later become Churchill saw—and probably even hunted—polar bears, the first person to see one will be forever unrecorded. But because we tend to equate "discovery" with *European* discovery (think of Columbus's "discovery" of America), we would like to know which European adventurer first spotted a white bear on the shores of Hudson Bay. Stirling awards that honor to Jens Munk, who spent the winter of 1619–20 ashore at Hudson Bay. But nine years earlier, Henry Hudson plied the great bay in search of a way out, and while he left no journal of this failed expedition, he surely must have seen the bears. In his biography of Hudson, Llewelyn Powys wrote that on the voyage of the *Discovery* in 1610, Hudson's crew "was diverted by the sight of a polar bear . . . which seemed to be making her way towards the ship; but when she realized she was being watched, she forthwith cast her head between her legges and dived under the ice." Does it matter who saw the first polar bear on the shores of Hudson Bay? Not really; what does matter is that in our own time, the polar bears of Churchill, the most-watched, most-photographed, and most-studied polar bears of all time, have provided researchers with a window into the lives of the bears that would be unobtainable elsewhere.

Preliminary research on Hudson Bay polar bears began with a tagging program initiated in the 1970s by Chuck Jonkel, whose goal was to learn where the bears went and when. Aerial surveys of the denning areas between the Nelson and Churchill rivers showed that some 100 to 150 cubs were born there each spring, making it the largest known denning area in North America. Indeed, the concentration of bears west of Hudson Bay is one of the densest anywhere. Working with other researchers, Stirling has tranquilized, tagged, tattooed, weighed, measured, teeth-checked, blood-tested, and behavior-recorded 80 percent of the adult bears in Churchill. In a CBC interview given on the ice to Eve Savoury in 2004, Stirling said that it's the bear's fat that really tells the story: "We take a subjective sort of fat condition, with three being the average size, and what we basically do is feel along the spine for how much fat is in here. A really big pregnant female with lots of fat would be a five out of five. They are just big tubs of jelly with little stubby legs sticking out." To get through a summer of fasting, the bears have to pack on the fat, but "if the ice breakup gets shortened by two or three weeks, that's a lot of energy they don't get to store in their fat and that's pretty important to them."

As this book goes to press, a Google search for "polar+bears+churchill" serves up 245,000 hits. Many of these are photo albums of bears taken by tourists, but the majority are offers to sign up with some sort of tour that will allow you to visit the bears. There is Tundra Buggy Adventure, Great White Bear Tundra Lodge, Great Canadian Travel Polar Bear Tours,

Polar Bear Adventure, Polar Bear Photo Tour, Churchill Polar Bear
Safari, and dozens more. Designated "The Polar Bear Capital of the
World," the town of Churchill (population 923) offers visitors the opportunity to see more polar bears than anywhere else. Every October, this
remote little village on the shore of Hudson Bay plays host to as many as
1,500 bears, spread out across the tundra west of the town, but occasionally strolling down the streets in search of something to eat. The bears
come to Churchill after a fast of about four months, to await the forming
of the ice thick enough to hold them so they can head out and look for
something to eat. (No wonder tourists are warned to keep away from the
bears; these guys are *hungry.*) When (or if) the ice forms, the bears
leave—almost overnight.

Polar bears are loners, the furthest thing in the world from herd animals. But when they assemble around Churchill in the fall, it is possible
to see a great many at one time. In 1998, Stirling wrote,

> The fall of 1970 still stands out in my mind as one of the great times
> for seeing polar bears along the coast. In early November, I saw
> thirty-six adult males in an area the size of a football field out at Cape
> Churchill. From a distance, they looked like a small herd of caribou.

The three bears alongside a tundra buggy in Churchill

Mother and half-grown cub swimming in the Churchill River

It took me a moment to realize what I was looking at. During the same period, we spent four hours flying in an old slow helicopter, on two overcast days with snow on the ground, and saw 239 polar bears!

As Hudson Bay freezes over, the bears head onto the ice to hunt for seals. In his 1975 study of ringed seals, T. G. Smith estimated the seal population of Hudson Bay at approximately 455,000, more than enough for the peripatetic polar bears of Churchill. (The estimate for the population of ringed seals in James Bay was approximately 61,000.) The ice forms first around the western shore of the bay, and the bears head north and east from Churchill on their annual feeding pilgrimage. The mass departure usually occurs in November, but sometimes the freeze-up occurs later, and there may be bears around until mid-December. (Pregnant females remain in their onshore dens until the cubs are born.) Hudson Bay covers an area almost twice as large as Texas, providing the bears with ample hunting grounds, as long as the ice holds up. The bears of Churchill, James Bay, and Wapusk spread out in the bay during the winter, and return to land by summer, to begin the cycle again. Most Hudson Bay bears spend their entire lives around (or on) this great body of water.

In earlier years, the bears around Churchill found that the town dump was an excellent source of snacks, a situation that made the residents more than a little nervous. Although there were few actual encounters between bears and people, the townsfolk were understandably wary of having hungry, 1,000-pound bears wandering around town, and they took steps to separate the bears from the people. The dump was moved far out of town, and finally, in 2005, it was eliminated altogether. The Department of Public Works replaced the garbage dump—where eerie pictures of dirty bears feeding amid burning garbage had been taken—with a former military cold-storage structure, known as L5. Structurally fortified to keep bears from breaking in, L5 has separate bays for household waste, liquids, dangerous goods, and recyclable materials. The waste materials are packed up and shipped to Thompson, Manitoba. Although they have not succeeded in breaching the defenses of L5, polar bears have been seen prowling around the building, curious to discover just what's being denied them.

A "polar bear jail" was built near the Churchill airport, so bears that were too close to town could be incarcerated until they could be airlifted onto the ice. The jail has been designed to be uncomfortable for the bears. They aren't fed but they do get water and bedding. If they liked it too much, they would probably figure out a way to get captured.

The polar bear jail in Churchill: luckily, the bears can't read

(One bear, nicknamed "Linda," was caught and put in jail so many times that she was eventually transferred to the Albuquerque Zoo.) In virtually every store and restaurant window in Churchill there is a sign that reads POLAR BEARS ARE DANGEROUS. THEY ATTACK WITHOUT WARNING. In Churchill, you can buy polar bear T-shirts, hats, ties, sweaters, books, postcards, statuettes, coffee mugs, and copies of the POLAR BEARS ARE DANGEROUS signs. Basing the idea on a "swamp buggy," designed to navigate Louisiana marshes, Churchill native Len Smith cobbled up the "Tundra Buggy" from an old school bus, a snowplow, a gravel truck, and a front-end loader. The prototype, completed in 1980, was an oversize vehicle with ample viewing windows and huge tires, designed to carry tourists safely over the rocky, often waterlogged terrain of the Churchill tundra in the fall. The bears have now become familiar with the buggies, and either ignore them or come right up to them, which makes for thrilling close-up photography. Bear watchers are urged to keep their hands, cameras, and sandwiches well inside the vehicle.

For tourists, however, the bears of Churchill provide entertainment, photo ops, and maybe even a little biology. Almost everybody has heard

Polar bear out for a stroll in Churchill. Note tundra-buggy tracks.

Uncle Arthur's stories of his death-defying experience as a giant bear tried to climb in the window and eat him, but for the few who are still awaiting the opportunity to fly to Winnipeg and take an overnight train to Churchill, here is James Brooke of the *New York Times:* "Bristling with cameras, tourists roll out daily in tundra buggies, heated, elevated, bear-proof viewing mobiles, or lift off in sleek helicopters with bears painted on the noses." One anonymous buggy rider wrote,

> My favorite moment came when our driver opened the inner door of the tundra buggy, leaving only the steel-bar outer gate in place. A curious bear who had come up to the vehicle, took advantage of an opportunity to see what was inside by sticking his head and paws in through the openings, much to our delight. Although their demeanor reminds one of large, sloppy, friendly dogs—huge white-furred, black-eyed mutts—their charm disguises their power and the potential danger they represent. While we were all awwwwww- and ooooooo-ing, the bear was probably looking at us as potential food.

It probably wasn't—these bears had doubtless seen the buggies many times before and have never tried to eat anybody—but the Churchill experience depends on the perception of polar bears as man-eaters. That is not to say that they're not dangerous, but many of the stories of bear attacks are exaggerations, and many of the "stalking" bears were nothing more than curious. Still, treating a polar bear as a "large, sloppy, friendly dog" might spell trouble for the treater. Even the title of Brooke's piece adds to the de-mythification of the polar bear: "Canada's 'Gentle Giants' Await Vanishing Winter."

Canadian journalist Brian Payton stayed at the "lodge" on the tundra, a sort of "mother ship" (his term) for tourists who want to remain out for a week at a time and board the Tundra Buggies for daily excursions. At one point, Payton is standing on the rear observation platform:

> The bear rises up on his hind legs and reaches all the way to the level of my boots. His claws clink against the metal as his paws spread out and up, trying to reach even farther. We look into each other's eyes, and I become aware that his head is wider than my shoulders . . . The

A mother and her two cubs, recently emerged from their den in Churchill

look of curiosity I've encountered in other bears is missing; it is replaced by frustration and determination. I recognize that I'm being viewed as prey. He begins banging on the side of the platform with both paws and the full weight of his upper body. I feel the floor shift below me . . . I snap a few photos as he excitedly sniffs and snorts. Other bears gather around to watch. He shoves the wall again, and sways his head back and forth. Suddenly, I kick my side of the wall. Stunned, he drops on all fours and takes a few bounding leaps away. From the safety of fifteen yards and the company of his associates, he considers me anew.

To better understand the behavior of the bears on the Churchill tundra, the biologists had to be able to observe them closely on a regular basis, but as Stirling observed, "camping in a tent on the ground, literally in the middle of a herd of polar bears, was an unattractive option," so they had a high steel tower built.

Biologists Paul Latour and Dennis Andriashek began working in the tower in October of 1976. The first night a rip-roaring blizzard screamed out of the northwest and shook the tower back and forth until well into the next day . . . The two men were faced with a classic dilemma. They could stay in the untested tower through the pitch-black night as it swayed back and forth. Or they could risk climbing down the exposed ladder in the storm (no mean feat in itself) and seek refuge on the ground in the willows where they knew the polar bears would also be hiding from the wind.

They stayed in the swaying tower.

But not quite the way Fred Bruemmer stayed in the tower. In October 1980, Bruemmer and John Kroeger moved in for two weeks. In his 1981 *Audubon* magazine article ("Two Weeks in a Polar Bear Prison"), Bruemmer wrote,

> Three bears sleep near our tower. All are young males, weighing between 250 and 400 pounds . . . One bear . . . rises, yawns, stretches luxuriously, and comes slowly to investigate. He rears up directly beneath us, leans with his huge, sharp-clawed, fur-fringed paws against the tower for support, and looks at us with small, deep-brown, slightly slanted eyes. In an odd way, it's a zoo in reverse. We are the captives, and the bears come from time to time to watch our antics.

On October 23, a large old male approached the tower:

> Toward noon a huge, emaciated bear comes to the tower. We call him Cassius; he has that lean and hungry look. He appears both evil and pathetic. Both ears are torn and the left one is nearly missing; his eyes are bleary and bloodshot; his head and face are heavily scarred; his nose, broken in some past encounter, has healed askew, giving him a permanent leer; his fur is ragged and smeared with dirt . . . He shuffles straight to the tower, rears, reaches as high as he can, and tries to hook John off his perch . . . Then he begins to rock the tower rhythmically, whether in frustration or in the hope of dislodging us we will never know. He looks ancient and decrepit but his strength is awesome.

Subsequent observations revealed a great deal about the polar bears of Churchill. For the most part, the bears did very little of anything while waiting for the ice to form; adult and subadult males were inactive around 75 percent of the time. Occasionally the males become quite

Young males play-fighting at Churchill

active, engaging in ritual play-fighting, which involves rearing up on their hind legs and sparring vigorously. A pair of powerful, thousand-pound bears armed with sharp claws and teeth are more than capable of inflicting damage on each other, but they hardly ever do, being content to push and shove in an attempt to throw the opponent off balance. In fact, says Stirling, "we do not fully understand the significance of the male polar bears' ritualized fighting in the autumn. We suppose that it provides the bears with experience in fighting and an opportunity to improve their motor skills and coordination in circumstances where the risk of serious injury is minimized." Whatever the value of play-fighting is for the bears, it is a godsend to photographers, who, if they are in the right tundra vehicle at the right time, can get spectacular shots of the great Arctic predators in action. (Sometimes with an incongruous background of brown earth and shrubs.) In other circumstances, however, when male bears are vying for the favors of a female in estrus, the fights can be deadly serious, and may result in large wounds, sprained limbs, and broken teeth, and even the death of the injured bear.

In a 1998 report, Calvert et al. presented the most recent estimate of the number of polar bears in western Hudson Bay. "Our best estimate of this population," they wrote, "is 1,250–1,300 ± [plus or minus] 274 animals. From a management perspective, it is probably prudent to continue to manage the population on an estimated 1,200 polar bears." Stirling, Lunn, and Iacozza noted that from 1981 to 1998, these bears were growing thinner and there were fewer new cubs. "Over this same period," they wrote,

> the breakup of the ice on western Hudson Bay has been occurring earlier . . . We suggest that the proximate cause of the decline in physical and reproductive parameters of polar bears in western Hudson Bay over the last 19 years has been a trend toward earlier breakup, which has caused the bears to come ashore in progressively poorer condition. The ultimate factor responsible for the earlier breakup in western Hudson Bay appears to be a long-term warming trend in April–June atmospheric conditions.

Cub survival depends on well-fed nursing females and, after weaning, a reliable food supply. As the temperature climbs and the ice breaks up earlier, more of the bears will suffer. There is a direct correlation between the thinning ice in Hudson Bay and the decline of the condition of the bears—which decline will only be exacerbated as the bears move north onto ice that is also thinning.

Bordering Hudson Bay is a vast low-lying plain designated as Wapusk National Park. Established in 1996, Wapusk ("white bear" in the Cree language) encompasses some 11,475 square kilometers, or about 4,450 square miles. The park's marine coastal habitat is characterized by salt marshes, dunes, beaches, and an extensive intertidal zone. The area is rich in wildlife, with large numbers of waterfowl and shorebirds in wetland and coastal areas, and forty-four species of mammals, including the Cape Churchill caribou herd. The range of the western Hudson Bay population of about 935 polar bears extends into Wapusk, and a large percentage of these bears congregate here, south of Cape Churchill. Hungry from a summer of fasting, they wait along the coast for the first opportunity to reach their winter hunting grounds, and by late October, when freshwater floes are pushed by wind and currents against the northern shore of Cape Churchill, they take to the ice. Wapusk contains one of the world's largest polar bear maternity denning areas. There are no roads or visitor facilities to disturb the wildlife in this wilderness park, which was created specifically to preserve the fragile tundra environment and protect the habitat of the bears.

Unfortunately, the habitat itself is threatened, and the number of bears is declining. In a 2005 article about Wapusk in *National Geographic,* John Eliot wrote,

> Hudson Bay polar bears, some of the southernmost in the world, are feeling the heat of global warming. The region is about two degrees (F) warmer in winter than 50 years ago. The bay's ice is breaking up early in July rather than late July . . . The earlier the ice disappears, the less time the bears have to feed on seals. Pregnant females need to gain at least 200 pounds to sustain them through the long fast in their dens, where they may spend eight months. In the past they've been able to kill many seal pups being weaned by their mothers in early July. Now, with the ice melting sooner, the bears can't hunt and must forsake that nutrition. Such deprivation leads to fewer cubs surviving to adulthood.

In northern Ontario there is also Polar Bear Provincial Park, covering 9,300 square miles, with shorelines on Hudson and James bays. Established in 1970, it is the largest of Ontario's provincial parks. Like Wapusk (which is a *national* park), it is accessible only by plane or boat, and travel within the park is restricted in order to preserve the abundant wildlife, which includes woodland caribou, marten, black bear, red and Arctic fox, and moose. In the coastal areas, there are seals and belugas (the walruses are gone), and in the fall, as many as 200 polar bears have been spotted in the park, preparing to head out onto the ice when the bay freezes. Because Polar Bear Park is about 500 miles southeast of Churchill, the bears here are among the southernmost wild polar bears in the world—only the bears of James Bay are found farther south.

The town of Cochrane, Ontario, is located 450 miles north of Toronto, and about 200 miles south of James Bay. At the entrance to the town on Highway 11, the northern route of the Trans-Canada Highway, you will see Chimo, a huge sculpture of a polar bear, the town's mascot. (*Chimo* is an Inuit term meaning "I am friendly," or "welcome.") Cochrane is the home of the Polar Bear Habitat and Heritage Village, which has a snowmobile museum, a general store, a ser-

What's going on here?

vice station, a blacksmith shop, and a farmhouse. It also has four polar bears, adults that have been rescued from substandard zoos or cubs that have lost their mother. The bears can be seen from inside or outside the Viewing Building, but there is also a wading pool, separated from the bears' pool by a glass barrier, which enables visitors to swim with the bears—or at least look as if that's what they're doing. Photographs of children apparently swimming with adult polar bears are surely among the most unusual images in the entire polar bear canon.

In a 2007 study, Regehr, Lunn, Amstrup, and Stirling calculated that the ice breakup in western Hudson Bay occurred approximately three weeks earlier in 2004 than in 1984. During that period, the polar bear population around Churchill declined from 1,194 to 935, and the researchers proposed that "this correlation provides evidence for a causal association between earlier ice breakup (due to climatic warming) and decreased polar bear survival." They continued, "It may also explain why Churchill, like other communities along the western coast of Hudson Bay, has experienced an increase in human–polar bear inter-

White bear in green grass: a young female polar bear spotted in Churchill, July 20, 2008

actions in recent years. Earlier sea ice breakup may have resulted in a larger number of nutritionally stressed polar bears, which are encroaching on human habitation in search of supplemental food." A completely unexpected result of the earlier ice breakup would be the bears coming into town for food that they might not find elsewhere. There is lots of "supplemental food" wandering around the streets of Churchill for "nutritionally stressed bears."

ATLANTIC CANADA AND NEWFOUNDLAND

In the little ship *Matthew* on a 1497 voyage of exploration for King Henry VII of England, John Cabot (originally Giovanni Caboto—he was born in Genoa) became the first "Englishman" to explore the rocky coasts of Labrador and Newfoundland. (It was on this voyage that he reported that codfish were so plentiful that they could be caught simply by lowering a weighted basket into the dense schools.) Although the actual location is unrecorded, somewhere along the way Cabot saw "great plentie of beares in those regions which used to eat fysshe. For plungeing theym selves into the water where they perceve a multitude of these fysshes to lye, they fasten their clawes in their scales, and so drawe them to lande and eate them." Cabot's quote comes from H. P. Biggar's 1903 *The Voyages of the Cabots and the Corte-Reals to North America and Greenland 1497–1503*, and is also found in Fred Bruemmer's *World of the Polar Bear*, where it is followed with: "The Labrador polar bears have vanished. Warming weather in the 19th century and the use of firearms by natives and European settlers first diminished and then destroyed the population. With them ended salmon and char fishing by polar bears, for it seems to have been a specialty known only to the Labrador bears."

In his 1984 book, *Sea of Slaughter*, Canadian author Farley Mowat wrote:

> The earliest account of encounters with white bears is in Jacques Cartier's voyage of 1534. A white bear was found on Funk Island, where it had presumably been living the life of Riley on a diet of great auks. The following day, Cartier's ship overtook a white bear swimming in the open sea and the men killed it. While reconnoitering the Gulf of St. Lawrence a short time later, Cartier found bears on Brion Island in the isolated Magdalen archipelago. Those, too, were almost certainly of the white kind, enjoying the abundance of seals, walrus, and seabirds then inhabiting the Magdalens.

In his book, Mowat documented the wholesale destruction of almost every living creature unfortunate enough to have ever come into contact with human beings on, in, or near the North Atlantic. In the chapter called "White Ghost," he chronicled the fate of the polar bear, just one of the myriad creatures that Canadians and Americans hunted to near extinction. (Some of them—the great auk, for example—were completely eliminated.) Mowat says there are no more polar bears in Newfoundland or the Gulf of St. Lawrence, because they were all killed.

During the late 1930s, the *Journal of Mammalogy* published a series of short articles about polar bears spotted in unexpected locations in eastern Canada. For example, Hartley Jackson (1939) wrote of a polar bear in the Lake St. John District of Quebec that "must have traveled overland nearly 400 miles from James Bay to Ste. Jeanne d'Arc, up rivers and through dense forests to the mouth of the Peribonka River, where it was shot." (Lake St. John—now Lac St. Jean—is about 250 miles northeast of Montreal.) Upon reading that note, George Harrison of Philadelphia wrote in to tell his story (also published in the *Journal*) about a polar bear that had come down the Thunder River in 1938 and had been killed swimming in the St. Lawrence River. In 1942, mammalogists Harrison Lewis and J. Kenneth Doutt published a ten-page report on records of walruses and polar bears in or near the Gulf of St. Lawrence. Each sighting (or anecdotal account) of a polar bear in the region was recorded, and the authors amassed records of thirteen bears spotted between 1920 and 1940. They noted that this region is very sparsely populated, and it is likely that many more bears passed through during this period but were not observed (or killed) by people. The St. Lawrence River debouches into the Gulf of St. Lawrence, immediately west of Newfoundland. Except for Stirling's 1988 comment that "in the heavy ice year of 1973, four bears came ashore along the northeast coast [of Newfoundland] and were subsequently shot," there are few records of polar bears in Atlantic Canada from around 1940 onward—until 2008, that is.

Newfoundland's northern peninsula is separated from the Labrador mainland by the ten-mile-wide Strait of Belle Isle. Sometimes the strait is choked with ice, but when it's not, it's an easy swim for polar bears. On March 27, 2008, there were several sightings on the northern peninsula: one bear entered an empty cabin by breaking a window, another was spotted at a distance, and a mother and two cubs were observed in the area of Coles Pond. The Department of Natural Resources warned the residents of Conche, Quirpon, and Roddickton to store their garbage inside to reduce the chances of a human-bear encounter, and, because "mother polar bears are known to be extremely protective of their cubs, anyone encountering them is advised to stay calm, give the bears space, back away slowly—never run—and avoid direct eye contact with the bears." On Fogo, a little island east of the northern peninsula, Mrs. Ivy Harnett spotted a polar bear fifty feet from her cabin and called for help. Wildlife officers came, tranquilized the bear, and transported it to the other end of the island, three miles away. About a week later, a polar bear was spotted at Newfoundland's Trinity Bay, 120 miles from Quirpon, and another 150 miles from Fogo. It's possible that the Trinity bear was the same animal that had been captured on Fogo, but because there were at least three different bears (one a mother with cubs) seen on the northern peninsula, it is obvious that several bears have at least temporarily migrated to Newfoundland.*

Such as the one seen sitting in the middle of the road to Gander by Shauna Abbott. Gander, remembered as the refueling stop for prop-driven passenger planes in the pre-jet era, is inland, about eighty miles south of Fogo. When Ms. Abbott saw the bear sitting in the road, she slammed on the brakes and stopped a few feet from the bear. Then, according to her account (CBC, April 14), "I put the truck in reverse, and I blew the horn to try and frighten it, and so it stopped, and it just kind of looked at me, and stayed there for a little while and turned around, walked a few steps, and turned around and looked at me again." When the bear finally walked away, Ms. Abbott continued her drive. Polar bears have also been spotted recently on the Labrador mainland, suggesting that the bears of Atlantic Canada are venturing farther south, into regions where they had not been seen for years.

With walruses, ringed seals are the most northerly of all pinnipeds, sharing the circumpolar distribution of their traditional nemesis, the polar bear. Ringed seals are not normally found as far south as Labrador and Newfoundland, but harp seals *(Phoca groenlandica)* and hooded seals *(Cystophora cristata)* are; both species share breeding areas off Newfoundland. According to David Lavigne and Kit Kovacs, the authors of *Harps and Hoods: Ice-Breeding Seals of the Northwest Atlantic,* "predators of the hooded seal are likely to be the same as those of the harp seal—polar bears on whelping patches, Greenland sharks, and perhaps killer whales." It is not unreasonable to assume that the bears, unable to hunt ringed seals on the disappearing ice pack, have begun to head south in search of other kinds of seals or whatever else they can find to eat.

---

* The Canadian province of "Newfoundland and Labrador" consists of the Labrador Peninsula and the island of Newfoundland. Labrador's area (including associated small islands) is about 104,000 square miles, approximately the size of Colorado. After Baffin, Victoria, and Ellesmere (all in the Northwest Territories), Newfoundland, at 42,000 square miles, is the fourth largest island in Canada. Around the year 999, Vikings led by Leif Eriksson landed on Newfoundland at a place that they named Vinland, for the wild grapes growing there. Their landing, at the tip of the northern peninsula, is now called L'Anse aux Meadows, and was the first European landing in North America.

CANADA: NUNAVUT

As of April 1, 1999, some 40 percent of Canada's northern wilderness was administratively separated from the Northwest Territories, and amalgamated into a new territory known as Nunavut—the Inuit word for "our land." The creation of Nunavut was the first major change to Canada's map since the incorporation of the new province of New-foundland in 1949. Constituting one-fifth of all Canada, Nunavut consists mostly of empty, ice-covered islands, and is divided by the Arctic Circle. The capital is Iqaluit (formerly Frobisher Bay) on Baffin Island; other major communities include the regional centers of Rankin Inlet and Cambridge Bay. Nunavut also incorporates Ellesmere Island to the north, as well as the eastern and southern portions of Victoria Island in the west. Nunavut is the largest and least populated of the provinces and territories of Canada. In its 770,000 square miles—an area larger than Mexico—Nunavut's population is 29,000. (Mexico has 108 million.)

In Nunavut, the Netsilik Eskimos live in a harsh, unforgiving climate; based on their primary food item, they are called "people of the seal." They call themselves *Netsilingmiut*, and their homeland is *Taloyoak* ("large caribou blind" in Inuktitut, referring to a stone blind traditionally used to corral and harvest caribou). On April 1, 1999, the region that contains Taloyoak became part of Nunavut. (Taloyoak is also the name of the Netsilik's main village on the Boothia Peninsula.) In his 1970 study of the Netsilik, anthropologist Asen Balikci wrote, "Certainly this is one of the most desolate environments on earth, particularly inappropriate for human occupation, yet the Netsilik survived here, their success in adapting to the extreme rigors of the Arctic climate made possible by the abundance of certain animals which they used for food, fuel, clothing and tool materials." The most important of these animals were seals, caribou, musk oxen, and fish, but the Netsilik also hunted polar bears. As Balikci wrote,

> Occasionally traveling or hunting Netsilik came across polar bears or their tracks. These bears were almost always pursued, and ferocious battles followed. First they let loose the dogs, who rushed madly at the bear, attacking it from all sides. The bear clawed viciously at the

dogs, but they were quick enough to avoid his attacks and were able to keep the bear at bay until the arrival of the hunters . . . Generally the Eskimos carried with them a special barbless harpoon head, specifically designed for polar bear hunting . . . It was a dangerous fight, and often the hunters suffered many scars and wounds, but the Netsilik never withdrew from a bear hunt. Bear meat was highly valued and was shared by all the hunters, while the man who delivered the fatal thrust kept the skin.

The polar bear was deeply embedded in Netsilik taboos and rituals. As Balikci put it, they believed that "the soul of the bear was particularly dangerous and powerful, and numerous exacting observances were necessary to counter any revengeful intentions its soul might have had at the end of a hunt." As with human souls after death, the hunter had to pay homage to the animal he had killed by observing a number of religious taboos. "A failure in any of these observances could turn an animal soul into a crooked spirit, a bloodthirsty monster." The Netsilik lived in perpetual fear of wandering animal ghosts, since they depended for survival on regularly killing game animals and believed that "the soul of a slain bear remained on the hunter's spear for four or five days, and they performed elaborate rituals to avoid the soul's turning into an evil spirit."

Eskimo print showing two of the most important mammals in Nunavut

Even today, dogs play an important role in polar bear hunting. When Canadian anthropologist George Wenzel observed a hunt originating in the small settlement of Kuganayuk, Resolute Bay, NWT, that took place in May 1983, it consisted of sixteen people, including seven children, all transported on five snowmobiles and one team of twelve dogs pulling a sledge. Following the trail of two bears, the hunting party sighted one in the distance, and released one of the dogs "considered to be a particularly good hunter," to harass the bear. Two snowmobiles were deployed directly toward the bear, and "the effect of two fast-approaching snowmobiles and a chase dog was immediately evident: the bear began to run." It was herded back toward the hunters by the snowmobiles, and the dog continued to harass the bear, nipping at its flanks every time the bear's back was turned. The rest of the dogs were released "in case the bear should again begin to run," but it stood its ground until the lead hunter walked to within thirty feet of the bear and shot it. When Wenzel told the hunters that the bear had been foolish to allow the snowmobiles to get so close before it started to run, he was told not to speak in such a manner, because "the polar bear was fully as intelligent as a human being and that it understood when it was being ridiculed or belittled."

Although Nunavut has a few semi-urban centers, such as Iqaluit, Kuujjuaraq, Rankin Inlet, and Cambridge Bay, most of the vast archipelago consists of ice-covered, uninhabited islands. Uninhabited by people, that is. The light-colored caribou subspecies known as the Peary caribou *(Rangifer tarandus pearyi)* lives here, and is preyed upon by the white Arctic wolf *(Canis lupus arctos)*. Nunavut is also a prime habitat for polar bears, walruses, and seals; of the thirteen semidiscrete polar bear populations that live in Canada, almost all are wholly or partially in the Nunavut territory. To the Nunavut Inuit, *nanuq* has special significance: it is the archetypal symbol of the majesty of the Arctic, and is proudly displayed on the government logo and license plates. The polar bear may be a revered symbol, but on a more pragmatic level, it has long been a traditional object of Inuit hunting.

Most Inuit live outside of the urban centers, and subsist on what they catch. As a signatory of the 1973 Agreement on the Conservation of Polar Bears (ACPB), Canada was responsible for the bears within its jurisdiction, and 60 percent of all the world's polar bears live in that vast country. But, as Wenzel wrote in his 2005 discussion of the Nunavut and the polar bear, "Canada also recognized that it had an obligation to balance the agreement's conservation goals with the socioeconomic and cultural needs of its Inuit citizens. Among the indigenous people living in the five signing nations, only Canadian and Greenland Inuit were provided with subsistence access to bears. The annual quota of about 500 included the right by Inuit to assign part of the allocation for use by non-Inuit sport hunters." Since 1970 Canadian provinces and territories have permitted recreational polar bear hunting, as long as the hunter is accompanied by local guides and dogsled teams. Until Nunavut was created by Canadian fiat in 1999, each of the thirty settlements in the NWT was allocated a polar bear quota. By 1980, the price of polar bear skins sold in Europe had skyrocketed, and Inuit subsistence hunters, for whom money had previously meant little, suddenly found that by killing two or three bears, they could earn $4,000 to $6,000 a year. Change was in the cold Arctic air.

When *Boston Globe* reporter Randall Shirley boarded the cruise ship *Lyubov Orlova* at Iqaluit in 2007, he became part of Nunavut's newest industry: polar bear watching. It might better be designated "polar bear seeking," because cruising the ice-filled waters of Frobisher Bay and Hudson Strait does not guarantee bear sightings. The *Orlova* is a Russian ship, leased by Cruise North Expeditions, an Inuit corporation founded to take advantage of tourist interest in the High Arctic and the ice bear's popularity. Cruise North's Web site (www.cruisenorth expeditions.com) explains what they're doing:

> Our expeditions offer exceptional opportunities to encounter a wide variety of birds and animals in their natural habitats. The sightings are sometimes unpredictable, and can be sudden and dramatic. There's the collective screech of a half-million thick-billed murres nesting on the cliffs, the silent gliding of white beluga whales, and the humorous cacophony of a walrus colony. Seals poke their heads from the water, and polar bears measuring 10 feet in length—the undisputed monarchs of the Arctic—patrol the ice floes and their favorite beaches.

Passengers on the twelve-day voyage can also experience the spectacular scenery of the Arctic, but as Shirley found out, "My informal poll of the passengers reveals that on a scale of 1 to 10, a polar bear sighting is required for the cruise to be a 10." Shirley's group had only two bear sightings—a lone male and a female with two cubs—but the cruise was considered a great success. Cruise North charges around $5,000 per person, and although it does not include airfare to Montreal, it does include the flight to Iqaluit. It's a lot cheaper than a $20,000 Antarctic cruise, where one might have to spend fifteen hours in a plane to reach Ushuaia, and then three days at sea getting to the Antarctic Peninsula—where the main attraction is a bunch of chubby little birds in tuxedos.*

CANADA: NORTHWEST TERRITORIES

Before the 1980s, few of the NWT settlements were reachable by airplane. When the sealskin market collapsed, the Canadian government looked to tourism—for which read: hunting and fishing—as a possible source of income and enhanced economic development. Airstrips were built. "The present situation in Nunavut," wrote George Wenzel, "is that polar bear sport hunting offers the opportunity for individual Inuit and their communities to obtain considerably larger sums of scarce money than is possible through more traditional (the sale of furs) or 'green' (non consumptive ecotourism) means." Communities began to train guides for sport hunters, and Clyde River and Resolute Bay (in the Baffin region), as well as Taloyoak, on the Arctic coast, emerged as the destinations of choice for sport hunters. Clyde River has an annual quota of twenty-one bears; Resolute has thirty-five. Taloyoak had twenty, but was shut down after the U.S. Fish & Wildlife Service imposed MMPA sanctions on the sport hunt there, believing that the bears of the McClintock Channel area had been overexploited.

Of the polar bear nations, Canada has the most land area north of the Arctic Circle that is habitable by humans. (Greenland also has a

* In July 2008, I joined the crew of the *Lyubov Orlova* at Churchill as a lecturer. Because it was much too early in the year for the bears to assemble, I was fully prepared to tell the passengers not to expect to see any bears until the ship sailed much farther north. I never got the chance. On the ride from the airport to the ship, people on the right side of the bus were astonished—as was I—to see a young polar bear ambling down the greensward that separated our road from the adjacent one. If a bear in Churchill in July wasn't weird enough, the sight of a wild, snow-white bear in the middle of lush, belly-high grass will surely be ranked among the most unusual sightings of the species outside of a zoo.

substantial northern landmass, but most of the island is covered by a thick ice sheet, and most villages and settlements are on the coast.) The Churchill region supports a large population of polar bears, and there are more people close to them there than anywhere else, especially tourists who travel to Churchill expressly to see the bears. Before the creation of Nunavut in 1999, Stenhouse, Lee, and Poole studied those instances between 1976 and 1986 in which polar bears were killed in the Northwest Territories as a result of "conflicts with humans," including bears that wandered into settlements or villages, bears that came too close to Inuit camps on the ice, and bears that approached research camps. In the decade under consideration, there were 265 recorded kills, and Stenhouse et al. wrote, "With proper training, equipment and experience, people will be better able to deal with problem polar bears, thereby reducing the number of unplanned bear mortalities. The realization and appreciation that polar bears are part of the arctic ecosystem may enable humans and bears to cohabit this environment successfully."

Because polar bears are not the circumpolar nomads they were once thought to be, and actually show a certain fidelity to home ranges, thirteen populations were designated throughout Canada and adjacent regions in Alaska and Greenland. In their 1995 analysis of these populations, Mitchell Taylor and John Lee did not claim that the groups are genetically isolated, nor did they say that the geographic boundaries are absolute; and furthermore, they recognized that "immigration and emigration do occur," but for management purposes—to calculate how many bears are where—the thirteen-part division is useful. In his 1998 book, Ian Stirling estimated that there were a minimum of 20,000 polar bears in the world, but he then said that "it could be as high as 40,000. Personally, I am inclined to the upper end of that range." Taylor and Lee (1995) wrote that "extrapolation of the mean density observed in Canada to the total 'polar bear habitat' in the circumpolar basin suggests a world population of approximately 28,000 animals." Of these, say Taylor and Lee, "there are about 12,700 polar bears in the thirteen populations that are within or shared with Canada." It is important to know the number of polar bears because, say the authors, "the impact of toxic chemicals, global warming, oil spills, and harvest cannot be evaluated without understanding polar bear movements and fidelity to local areas."

In 2006, Marcus Dyck of the Nunavut Arctic College in Iqaluit said that "wherever humans venture into the polar bear's habitat, confrontations arise that can lead to the death of 'problem' bears and death and injuries to humans. Such confrontations include bears entering communities, camps, or industrial sites, destruction or damage of human property, raiding food caches, attacking dogs and humans, and endangering public safety." Furthermore, he wrote, "The potential for polar bear–human interactions is increasing in northern Canada. Increases in the population (Inuit and non-Inuit), economic development, through natural resource exploration and development, and interest in the Arctic as a tourist destination can contribute to the likelihood of human–bear interactions." These "interactions" often result in polar bears being killed in defense of life or property—"DLP bears." Dyck found that there were a total of 618 killed in defense of life or property from 1970 to 2000, most of which were male bears over six years of age that were too close to native camps. He wrote,

> There will always be polar bear DLP kills in the Arctic. However, learning more about the circumstances leading to them and knowing where these incidents are more likely to occur can help to minimize the outcome . . . Nunavut is a new territory offering many economic opportunities, especially in the field of exploration or tourism. Educating the public about the proper use of proven bear deterrents and the continuation of a bear safety program could minimize the number of bears that become part of statistics.

In addition to DLP kills, the Inuit of Nunavut also hunt polar bears, which has resulted in a conflict between old values and new realities. The bears are pursued for meat, which goes to Inuit families, friends, and elders, and for the hide, from which they make pants or parkas. Accompanying the traditional dog teams are snowmobiles with plastic tarps securing wooden food boxes, synthetic equipment bags, and nylon ropes. Rather than the bear spear of old, each man now has a high-caliber rifle. Once hunted year-round, the bears are now a "species of special concern" because of overharvesting, which rose with the introduction of snowmobiles, and global warming. The Nunavut Wildlife Management Board sets a yearly hunting quota; it was 403 for 2005, though only 385 bears were killed. Most of the quota went to the Inuit, but sixty-nine were shot by foreign sport hunters, who pay $30,000 or more for the privilege.

Since becoming a territory Nunavut has been immersed in polar bear problems. The shrinking ice has driven more hungry bears into some Arctic communities, threatening the human inhabitants and encouraging some residents to call for more, not less, bear hunting. The practice serves as one of the few sources of outside income for the people of Nunavut, and the Inuit understandably do not want hunting curtailed. Nunavut accounts for some 80 percent of all Canadian kills, but this will change when the United States declares the polar bear an endangered species: at that point, the import of polar bear parts—skins or rugs, for example—into America will be prohibited. Moreover, the Canadian government, under their Species at Risk Act (SARA), is also considering nationwide protection for polar bears because of the acknowledged shrinking of the Arctic ice cap, which it feels constitutes even more of a threat to the bears than Inuit or sport hunting.

Some scientists believe that the changing sea ice is already causing the polar bear numbers to drop, but the Nunavut Inuit, who can earn a lot of money leading hunters to trophy-sized bears, maintain that the population is healthy and may even be growing. The hunters agree with them. I received a letter from one of the companies that arranges for hunters to go to Nunavut, in which this appears: "In 1950 the estimated World Population of Polar Bears was 5,000. Since the commercialization of sport hunting and culling of the larger males the population of Polar Bears has quadrupled, it is now estimated at 25,000 animals." That is nonsense, of course; the world population of polar bears in 1950 was probably closer to 20,000. An idea introduced by ecologist Warder Allee in 1931—now known as the "Allee effect"—is the phenomenon where individuals benefit from the presence of conspecifics and suffer from a decrease in some component of fitness at low population sizes or densities. As Courchamp, Clutton-Brock, and Grenfell wrote in 1999, "The Allee effect describes a scenario in which populations at low numbers are affected by a positive relationship between population growth rate and density, which increases their likelihood of extinction."

It is ludicrous to claim that sport hunting *increased* the polar bear population; taking a large number of breeding-age males—the hunters' favorite targets—out of the stock can only *reduce* it. A 2007 study by Molnár, Derocher, Lewis, and Taylor suggests that it is indeed trophy hunting, which almost always targets large males, that could lead to a sudden collapse of the breeding rate. The usual rate of males to receptive females is three to one, because so many females are out of commission during the two years they care for their cubs. If the males are removed by hunting, the ratio could drop to one male for every female; given the hard time males have finding females, their chances of acquiring a mate would be substantially reduced, and the number of cubs produced each year would drop. As Molnár et al. put it, "Prolonged sex-selective harvest has significantly reduced the numbers of adult male bears in all Canadian polar bear populations, leading to balanced or even female-biased operational sex ratios." In other words, more males are needed, not fewer, so removing the males is exactly the opposite of what is needed to sustain a viable polar bear population in Nunavut.

Both Nunavut and the Northwest Territories have extensive exposures to the Beaufort Sea (as does the Yukon Territory, which is between the Northwest Territories and Alaska); when frozen, the Beaufort provides a perfect habitat for the bears. Ian Stirling's thirty-five years of studying *Ursus maritimus* have taken him to the remotest corners of Canada. It doesn't get much more remote than Tuktoyaktuk, an Inuit village on a peninsula in the Beaufort. In December 2007, Edmonton journalist Ed Struzik joined Stirling on a helicopter flight out of Tuktoyaktuk, looking for polar bears. By their very nature, these animals define the term "few and far between." And spotting white bears on a white background is difficult, especially if visibility is reduced by haze or sea fog. When searching for bears, Stirling looks for tracks in the snow, and instructs the pilot to follow them. Sometimes they go to the water's edge: "A lead like this is a magnet for bears," said Stirling, "because this is where you tend to get a lot of seals hauling out. So there's no surprise that our guy has gone for a swim." As they looked for bears or tracks, Stirling explained the plight of the bear to Struzik (2007):

We've documented a 22 percent decline in the western Hudson Bay population between 1987 and 2004 . . . The animals we see now are younger and thinner than the typical bear you'd see 20 or 30 years ago . . . the reason why is pretty simple. Bears pile on the fat they need to make it through the year by catching seals on the ice. With the ice melting two or three weeks sooner in spring, as has been hap-

pening in western and southern Hudson Bay, the animals are spending much more time on land, and getting less opportunity to put on
the reserves they need to successfully reproduce and to make it
through the year . . . Less time feeding means more time using up
stored fat.

Andrew Derocher has been studying the bears of the southern Beaufort Sea around Tuktoyaktuk—"Tuk," to the natives—and believes the
population is in decline. The bears are showing other signs of stress:
weight loss, increased drownings, and cannibalism. Quoted in a 2008
article by Colin Campbell and Kate Lunau, Derocher said, "It's going
far, far faster than I ever imagined. My level of unease with the polar
bear situation is growing every day." But Tuktoyaktuk hunter Chucky
Gruben doesn't think the bears need any protection; he says the numbers are holding up just fine. Gruben says, "If something goes wrong
here, we'll know it. We live it . . . Some biologists have studied the
bears for thirty years, but how long have they spent on the ice? Who
is the government going to believe?" Polar bear hunting is one of the
few sources of income to residents of Nunavut and the NWT; some
200 hunters are taken out on the ice every year to go on what is considered the world's most challenging hunt. So it is very much in
Gruben's interest that the bear hunts continue; his two annual permits are worth $60,000 to him. U.S. trophy hunting of polar bears is a
$2 million-a-year business for the people of Nunavut—especially on
Baffin Island.

The fifth largest in the world, Baffin Island covers some 195,000
square miles, an area approximately the size of Spain. It is separated
from the eastern Canadian mainland by Hudson Strait, and from
Greenland by Davis Strait and Baffin Bay. Both shores of Baffin Bay—
and the ice that forms there—are prime habitat for polar bears, which
are hunted by both the Greenlanders and the Baffin Island Inuit. In
1997, the so-called "Baffin" population of polar bears was estimated at
2,100, but it has now dropped to around 1,500, largely attributable
to overhunting. An annual quota of thirty-eight was set in 2004 by
the Nunavut authorities, and although the Greenland hunters claimed
to have taken no more than twenty, they may have killed ten times
that number (Mittelstaedt 2008). When the Nunavut government
announced that it was raising the number of polar bears that could be

killed from thirty-eight to 105, the Humane Society of the United States and the World Wildlife Fund protested loudly, and the U.S. Fish & Wildlife Service announced that it would review the bear's status with regard to the Endangered Species Act. Nunavut raised the quota to 105 anyway. In 2007, the Nunavut Wildlife Management Board rejected proposals to scale it back, in part because a lower quota was unacceptable to the Inuit hunters. Despite falling population numbers and American objections, more than a hundred polar bears will be killed every year in Nunavut.

Canada's polar bears exemplify the contradictions that exist throughout the polar bear nations. As Campbell and Lunau wrote,

> As much as the polar bear war is about saving a species, it's also about climate change and a cause. The polar bear just happens to be the most convenient—not to mention big and handsome—model around. The perfect tool in the fight against global warming. Although Derocher, the World Conservation Union's polar bear biologist, favors a "threatened" listing, he agrees it will be damaging to Inuit who rely on sport hunting for income. "That's the rub of this—people who had the least impact on global warming are going to be the most affected," he says.

During a helicopter ride over Melville Island in 2003, University of Alberta geologist John England spotted what looked like a brown bear on the ice. The following year, when England continued his research on the island, he found a couple of brown bear hairs stuck to a guy-wire outside his cabin; when he submitted them for DNA testing, they proved to be those of a grizzly, a bear not previously known to venture so far north. In their 2007 discussion of northerly grizzlies, Doupé, England, Furze, and Paetkau wrote that

> during the early 1990s there have been numerous reports of grizzly bears on the sea ice off the mainland coast, extending from Hudson Bay in the east to the Beaufort seas in the west . . . The tracks of a grizzly and the remains of two seal pups in the vicinity [of the Dundas Peninsula, Melville Island] suggested that it had been hunting on the sea ice . . . a grizzly had probably killed a two-year-old polar bear whose partly eaten carcass had been found nearby.

When biologist Charles Francis was flying across Melville Island on a shorebird survey in early 2008, he saw what he thought was a polar bear feeding on a musk ox. If it was a polar bear, he thought, it was a very dirty one. Quoted in Ed Struzik's article in the *Edmonton Journal,* Francis said, "Initially we thought it was a hybrid like the grizzly bear–polar bear that had been shot in the Arctic a couple of years earlier," but a careful look at the photographs showed that it was pure grizzly. Melville Island, part of Nunavut, is about 800 miles north of the grizzly's usual range, and covered with ice for nine months of every year, so it is unclear what a grizzly would be doing there. It might have been feeding on musk oxen, berries, bird's eggs, seal carrion, or even the leftovers from polar bear kills, but even so, sea ice is not their normal habitat, and the big brown bears would be in for a hard time trespassing into polar bear territory. Derocher, who is now studying barren-ground grizzlies in the Arctic, opined that the bears might be following the herds of barren-ground caribou *(Rangifer tarandus groenlandicus)* that range through the Canadian territories of Nunavut and the Northwest Territories, but he also observed that the caribou populations are on the decrease. In Struzik's 2006 *National Wildlife* article ("Grizzly Bears on Ice"), he said that Derocher is concerned that oil and gas pipelines planned for this area could affect both species of Arctic bears, polar and grizzly.

During his visit to Kaktovik in September 2007, *Vanity Fair* reporter Michael Shnayerson witnessed a grizzly feeding on a whale carcass as a group of polar bears looked on. Kaktovik is one of the northernmost settlements on Alaska's North Slope, fronting on the Beaufort Sea, far from the grizzly's normal range. "For a while," wrote Shnayerson, "the grizzly fed alone at the bone pile. Then, slowly, one or two of the larger polar bears edged back towards him. The largest bear growled and clicked his teeth as he advanced. The grizzly gave no ground . . . the grizzly and the polar bear started cuffing each other, not trying to inflict injury—just posturing . . . it was the polar bear that finally withdrew." Grizzlies usually dominate polar bears in confrontations between the two species. There is no arrangement between them to try each other's territory or diet, but it is more than a little strange to find these two great predators, so far from the habitats in which they functioned so efficiently for thousands of years, suddenly appearing in an environment that is all wrong for them. (Just as polar bears developed all the equipment required to feed almost exclusively on seals, grizzlies, the quintessence of omnivory, are out of place where there is almost nothing to eat but meat.) The presence of grizzly bears on the North Slope and the concurrent appearance of polar bears hundreds of miles from their normal sea ice hunting grounds are just two of the behavior modifications connected with the changing climate of the Arctic.

In *The Origin of Species* (1859), Charles Darwin recognized that environmental conditions are among those influences that define individual fitness and population success. Writing of glacial periods that come and go in Europe, he said,

> As the cold came on, and as each more southern zone became fitted for the inhabitants of the north, those would take the places of the former inhabitants of the temperate regions. The latter, at the same time would travel further and further southward, unless they were stopped by barriers, in which case they would perish. The mountains would be covered with snow and ice, and their former alpine inhabitants would descend to the plains. By the time the cold had reached its maximum, we should have Arctic flora and fauna, covering the central parts of Europe, as far south as the Alps and the Pyrenees, and even stretching into Spain.

Although Darwin understood (and explained) the origin of species as no man before him had ever done, neither he nor anyone else could have foreseen the massive anthropogenic climate changes that now threaten all of the earth's biomes. Still, his analysis is a pretty good explanation of polar bears moving south and grizzlies moving north.

In March 2008, Ian Stirling, Evan Richardson, Gregory Thiemann, and Andrew Derocher published "Unusual Predation Attempts of Polar Bears on Ringed Seals in the Southern Beaufort Sea," their three-year study of the anomalous behavior of bears on the offshore ice from Atkinson Point, in the Northwest Territories, west to the Alaska border. The evidence for "unusual predation attempts" included fourteen holes clawed through solid ice, evidently the work of starving bears whose normal hunting techniques—stalking the seals or waiting by their breathing holes—were not working. At one site, where there was no evidence of a seal kill, there was blood on the ice, probably from the wearing down or breakage of the bear's claws. They also found the carcass of an adult female bear that had been killed and mostly eaten, probably by an adult male, "because only an adult male . . . would have been capable of killing an adult female in this way." The researchers also noted that there were increased incidents of cannibalism, and that three polar bears were discovered to have starved to death. "It is unknown," they wrote, "whether seals were less abundant in comparison to other years or less accessible because they maintained breathing holes below rafted ice rather than snowdrifts, or whether some other factor was involved." They concluded, "We suggest that the dramatic retreat of the pack ice minima in September, the increase in the area of open water adjacent to the coast . . . and the later freeze-up, via mechanisms not yet understood, have had a negative effect on the survival and repro-duction of polar bears." In an interview with the Canadian Broadcast-ing Corporation, Stirling said that if the Beaufort Sea ice keeps changing, people should expect more polar bears to wander inland. He said that polar bears will have a hard time surviving far from the sea, and while "some people say that the bears . . . will just adapt and go onto land . . . That's simply not going to happen."

In April 2008, the Canadian press reported that World Wildlife Fund–Canada had called on Prime Minister Stephen Harper to protect that country's threatened polar bears. Peter Ewins, WWF–Canada's head of species conservation, said, "There is rapidly mounting evidence that polar bear populations are in crisis as a result of sea-ice habitat loss, over-hunting, and industrial pressures." He continued, "The habitat of polar bears and [bowhead] whales in the Beaufort Sea is set to be sold off for oil and gas exploration on June 2, without proper resource plan-ning that would protect such sensitive wildlife habitats." As evidence of the pressure on the bear populations, Ewins cited the mother and cubs that had been shot in Déline, NWT, sixty miles south of the Arctic Cir-cle and more than 250 miles from the Beaufort Sea. Responding to the increase in the Baffin Bay aboriginal polar bear hunting quota, Ewins said, "The hunting pressure in Nunavut and especially in Greenland has been shown to have been much too heavy and unsustainable," and he called for a reduction to sixty-four—or even a temporary ban on the hunt.

When the Committee on the Status of Endangered Wildlife in Canada (COSEWIC) proposed on April 25, 2008, that the polar bear should be designated a species of "special concern," the WWF opposed this suggestion because it maintained that the program would take five

© John Alexander

© John Alexander

© John Alexander

© Nancy Harris

© John Alexander

© John Alexander

© John Alexander

© Norbert Rosing

© Norbert Rosing

© John Alexander

© John Alexander

© Fred Bruemmer

© John Alexander

© Richard Ellis

years to implement. "We don't have to wait to prove that the Arctic ice is melting everywhere before we start acting," said Ewins. "We have to take action now, especially in the areas where polar bears are most highly threatened." The Inuit hunters immediately opposed the suggestion. If the great white bears were protected, they claimed, then rich Americans would no longer be able to hunt bears with Inuit guides, depriving them of thousands of dollars in fees. The same result would come from the United States listing the polar bear as an endangered species, as these great white hunters would not be allowed to bring the skins, mounts, skulls, or any other souvenirs into the U.S. Because Canada is home to approximately two-thirds of the world's polar bears, what happens (or doesn't) in that country will have a significant and lasting effect on the total population. In their 2007 report on Canada's polar bears, Page, Gue, and Moola wrote,

> More than half of the world's polar bears are found in Canada. As both a source of national pride and an issue of global responsibility, the fate of the polar bears, to a large extent, rests on what Canadians do to protect them. Five of Canada's 13 polar bear populations are in trouble, however. Though the other eight populations are thought to be currently not at risk, the polar bear's hunting platform—the sea ice—is melting at an unprecedented rate due to global warming. Without this sea ice the future of all polar bears in Canada is uncertain. And while the current and future stats of specific polar bear populations remains unclear, this report finds that Canada's response to the crisis has been inadequate. In short, Canada has no plan.

GREENLAND

With the exception of Australia, Greenland is the largest island in the world. An autonomous part of the Kingdom of Denmark since 1953, it incorporates some 840,000 square miles, most of which is covered by a permanent ice sheet that can be as much as two miles thick. Most of the island lies within the Arctic Circle, and its northernmost point, Cape Morris Jesup, is 500 miles from the North Pole. The island was first colonized in 985–86 by Erik the Red, who gave it its unlikely name in an effort to induce further settlement, but conditions were too harsh, and the first settlers abandoned the island or died there. At the end of the tenth century, Norsemen from Iceland tried again to settle in the southwestern regions of Greenland, and by the thirteenth century the Norse colonization was at its height, with 280 farmsteads and a population of more than 3,000. The region also had a bishop's see with sixteen churches. The progress and prosperity of this region did not last, however, and because of the political conditions in Europe, ties gradually loosened with the colony and communication ceased altogether until the sixteenth century. As the position of the colony weakened, Eskimos moved down from the north and managed to drive out the few remaining Norse settlers.

In the thirteenth-century *Konungs skuggsjá* ("King's Mirror"), written anonymously in Old Norwegian as a dialogue between a ruler and his heir, the son asks about Greenland,

> With your permission, I also wish to ask what the people who inhabit these lands live upon; what the character of the country is, whether it is ice-clad like the ocean or free from ice even though the sea be frozen; and whether corn grows in that country as in other lands.

Because their dense fur does not mat, water rolls off the polar bears.

The father answers,

> As to whether any kind of grain can grow there, my belief is that the
> country draws but little profit from that source . . . You have also
> asked about the size of the land, whether it is mainland or an island,
> but I believe that few know of the size of the land, though all believe
> it is continental and connected with some mainland, inasmuch as it
> evidently contains a number of such animals as live on the mainland
> but rarely on islands . . . In reply to your question whether the land
> thaws out or remains icebound like the sea, I can state definitely that
> only a small part of the land thaws out, while all the rest remains
> under the ice. But nobody knows whether the land is large or small,
> because all the mountain ranges and all the valleys are covered with
> ice, and no opening has been found anywhere.

Greenland remained inhabited only by Eskimos until Hans Egede
established a settlement there. Born in 1686 in Harstad, Norway, Egede
began his missionary work in 1721 and continued for fifteen years. With
the support of the Bergen Company, Egede established the town of
Godthåb on the southwest coast, which is now Nuuk, the capital of
Greenland. As early as 1722, Egede had written a report to the Bergen
Company; it was printed in 1729 as *Det gamle Grønlands nye perlustration*, "Old Greenland's New Perlustration." (To perlustrate is to travel
through and survey thoroughly.) He begins with a brief narrative of the
founding of the Norse colony and its later history, and then describes the
plant and animal life on Greenland, along with accounts of Eskimo culture, commerce, and religion. Of the dangerous wildlife, Egede wrote,

> There are no venomous serpents or insects, no ravenous wild beasts
> to be seen in Greenland, if you except the bear, which some will have
> to be an amphibious animal, as he lives chiefly upon the ice in most
> northern parts, and feeds upon seals and fish. He very seldom appears
> near the colony, in which I had taken up my quarters. He is of a very
> large size, and of a hideous and frightful aspect, with white long
> hairs: he is greedy of human blood . . .
>
> In the 76th degree of latitude the number of bears is so great, that
> they in droves surround the natives habitations, who then, with their
> dogs, fall upon them, and with their spears and lances kill them. In

winter, instead of dens or caves under the earth, as in Norway and other places, here the bears make theirs under the snow; which, according to the information the natives have given me, are made with pillars, like stately buildings.

Egede's *Perlustration,* translated into many European languages, was almost all that was known about Greenland until the intrepid whalers of the nineteenth century navigated Davis Strait in order to hunt whales and barter with the inhabitants there. (William Scoresby's comprehensive *Account of the Arctic Regions,* published in 1820, includes much information on the Greenland ice, but hardly anything about the island itself; like all other whalers, Scoresby spent most of his time at sea.) For two centuries, Scoresby and the armada of Dutch and British whalers plied the waters of East and West Greenland in pursuit of the bowhead whale, which they all but eliminated. The bowhead was the predominant mammal of Greenland waters, but the white bear dominated the land—until people came along. In his 1928 summary of polar bears in Greenland, Ludwig Mecking wrote,

> Along uninhabited stretches of coast the polar bear wanders about, preferring the ice to the land or water. In their legends the Greenlanders recognize him as their master teacher, as to food, wanderings, and methods of hunting. Like the Eskimo, the polar bear finds his chief food in the seal and has berries for his dainties; he travels extensively, climbs ice hummocks as a lookout, and stalks his prey; and in the same way that a she-bear makes a snow-cave for her young, the Eskimo builds his snow-house.

When Danish zoologist Alwin Pedersen stayed in East Greenland during the 1930s, he observed that

> the migrations of polar bears on the drift ice are determined by those of the seals. During winter, when the seals live under the ice along the coast and in the fjords, the bears have almost completely deserted the shore. They then live far out along the edges of the big patches of open water which appear in the ice, and off the offshore islands such as Sabine, Shannon, and Great Koldewey . . . They also spend the winter at the mouth of the vast Scoresby Sound, where there is often

some open water . . . One year between February 23 and 29, twenty-one bears entered the fjord, and the Greenlanders killed twelve of them, of which eleven were old males.

Greenland appears to be the only place where polar bear hunting for skins occurs with any regularity, a practice that is based entirely on economic considerations: many Greenlanders have no other source of income. As Bjørn Rosing reported on polar bear management in Greenland,

> In certain periods of the year the income from skins may insure a family's upkeep for several months . . . In East Greenland, almost all bear skins are put up for sale in the market and bearskin trousers are uncommon, or even rare in this region . . . The elite hunters may have such trousers, but they are usually the only ones who use skins for this purpose . . . For some hunters, a bear shot in the open-water period may represent a full income for one month, or even for the entire summer . . . The Great Greenland Tannery buys all skins for sale in the market, including summer skins of low quality . . . Many seal-skins would have to be sold to equal the value of a bear-skin.

When he was living with the Greenland Eskimos in 1906, Peter Freuchen went hunting at Cape York with an old man named Angutid-luarssuk:

> One day as a number of us were standing about a blowhole in the ice, a bear approached us. Our dogs were tethered far away in order not to disturb the seals, so we all took off after him on foot. Out in front of us shot old Angutidluarssuk. Before the bear could reach open water the old man had it cornered. Instead of killing it, however, he waited until a little boy, who had never got a bear because he had no dogs, caught up with him. Angutidluarssuk let him spear it first. The boy was unable to kill it, but his harpoon was the first in the beast and the prey was technically his. Angutidluarssuk had killed the animal by the time we caught up with him and those among the first to arrive shared in the skin. But the boy, whose pants were scraped almost clean of hair, got a whole new pair, and the rest half a piece each. There is enough hide for three pairs of pants on a bear. The

meat was divided among all the others, and that evening as we
camped on the ice and cooked the meat there were no words fine
enough to praise the young man whose first bear it was.

Fewer than 60,000 people now live in Greenland—called *Kalaallit
Nunaat* in Greenlandic—virtually all of them in settlements on the
coasts. Nuuk is the capital, with a population of about 11,000. The main
industries are sealing, hunting, fishing, and mining. After *Homo sapiens
groenlandicus,* the predominant land predator in Greenland is the polar
bear, threatened not only by hunting but also by environmental pollution and the destruction of its habitat. Persistent organic pollutants
(POPs) have been discovered in very high concentrations in polar bears
from East Greenland and Svalbard, which has led to concern about
their ability to reproduce.

In a Greenland Ministry of Fisheries report, Rosing wrote that

> until recently, there were no restrictions on hunting of polar bears in
> North-West and East Greenland. Anyone seeing a polar bear was
> entitled to kill it. For this reason, there were, and still are various local
> traditions linked to this animal . . . In East Greenland and to some
> extent in South Greenland, the traditional rule that the person who
> first spots the bear is also the one who "catches" it, i.e. the one who
> gets the skin and the meat irrespective of who actually kills the bear,
> is still upheld. It is therefore possible to encounter very old people
> and small children who talk about bears they have recently caught.

This practice confounds hunting statistics because of multiple reporting of kills, where "several hunters who have participated in the same
hunt are proud that a bear was taken, and each reported the kill regardless of whether they shot the bear" (Jessen 2002).

Polar bears, known in Greenland as *Nanoq,* live and breed in the
northern reaches of this great, ice-covered island, drifting southward in
the summer toward the ice fields of the east coast. Because the bears
live so far north, however, it is extremely rare for either local inhabitants
or tourists to see a living example. An area in Melville Bay has been set
aside as a polar bear reserve, and the largest protected area in the world
is the Northeast Greenland National Park, where only hunting by
native people is permitted. Even with this variance, however, the bears

of northeast Greenland are fairly safe from hunting: there are no people there.* Native hunters are also allowed to kill twenty bears per year in the Ammassalilk district. The Greenland bear's skin is made into long-wearing pants (called *kamik*), which also function as a status symbol, as they do for Inuit everywhere. The strength of the bear has made it a popular symbol in the Arctic world, and Greenland's Home Rule uses the polar bear in the official national coat of arms.

Satellite tracking and mark-recapture information led researchers to conclude that Canada and Greenland shared polar bear subpopulations that are exploited at relatively high levels within both jurisdictions. Because Canada and Greenland have different management schemes, a joint study was initiated to establish a comanagement plan for these shared populations (Born 2002). For the other polar bear nations, the government is not the moving force behind polar bear hunting—and, indeed, in Canada, Russia, Alaska, and Norway it is the government that imposes the restrictions. (The Norwegian Polar Institute published a booklet called *Polar Bears in Svalbard,* which contains a section entitled "Hunting, Laws and Regulations"—but a large part of the book is concerned with how to avoid being attacked, and what to do if you are.) In 2002, the Greenland Institute of Natural Resources issued a twenty-six-page booklet called *The Polar Bear Hunt in Greenland,* which author and bear biologist Aqqalu Rosing-Asvid introduces thus:

Polar bears have probably been hunted in Greenland for as long as the Inuit have inhabited the island. Today modern rifles execute the final kill, but the majority of the hunts are still likely to involve dogs and sledges, as in earlier times. There is no limit to the number of bears that can be taken, but vehicles (including snowmobiles) and large boats may not be used in the hunt or as transportation to or from the hunting place. It is not allowed to use poison, any kind of trap, small-caliber rifles, shotguns or semi- and fully-automatic rifles.

---

* Originally created on May 22, 1974, Northeast Greenland National Park, the only national park in Greenland, is the largest in the world, with an area of 375,000 square miles—approximately the size of Egypt. The park encompasses the entire northeastern coastline and interior sections of Greenland. In 1986, the permanent population of the park was forty, most of whom were involved in cleanup and closeout operations at former mining exploration sites and left soon after. In January 1977 the area was designated an International Biosphere Reserve.

For each of Greenland's hunting districts, data were collected by researchers (one of whom is Rosing-Asvid) and codified as to catch history, method of hunting, and any other relevant details. For the period 1980–1989, a total of 150 polar bear kills were reported, although Rosing-Asvid believes that many went unreported. A system called *Piniarneq* was initiated in 1992, requiring that each hunter, in order to renew his hunting license, report his kills once a year, filling out a form in which he lists the number of kills every month. When I asked Rosing-Asvid why the Greenlanders hunted the bears at all, he answered,

> Inuit still live off the wildlife they can catch in some parts of Green-land. Seals are the daily bread here and polar bears have always been hunted for the meat, the hide, and blubber. In some parts of Green-land the hide is used for pants, in other parts the hide is sold. This might sound strange to the rest of the world, but I believe that it is a tradition, which is important if you want to maintain this kind of life. If for instance the hunters only hunted the seals, it would create a miserable situation. Polar bears would break into the meat depots and it would be pretty dangerous to live in these places. When polar bears are hunted around the settlements it creates a surplus in the seal population, which can be harvested. The important thing is that there still are huge areas without any hunt, where people don't inter-fere with the ecosystem.

Bear meat is eaten mainly in East Greenland and in the north, where the majority of polar bears are caught. The meat is cooked for several hours in order to make it tender, and also to remove any trace of roundworms, a muscle parasite that can cause serious illness in humans. In his description of Greenland hunters, Lonnie Dupre wrote, "From every kill, the meat is eaten and the skin used to make the prized nanus (polar bear pants) that the hunters wear. They are durable and extremely warm." The entire skin, often made into a rug with the head attached and the mouth gaping open, is a most desirable trophy. An intact polar bear skull is another much-sought-after sou-venir. The large canine teeth are items of jewelry. The claws were tra-ditionally an important part of amulets, used to symbolize the strength of the bear. Today the shiny black claws are popular as jewelry in the form of earrings or pendants. In other words, nothing is wasted except the bear.

As John Bonner wrote in 2002, "hunting has always been a way of life for the Inuit in one of the world's great wildernesses, but now they have far greater mobility and firepower . . . Companies set up by the Greenland government will buy the carcasses or valuable parts of any animal that strays within shooting distance of the island's 10,000 registered hunters." In *A Farewell to Greenland's Wildlife,* published in 2002, Danish author and environmentalist Kjeld Hansen documented the wanton and irresponsible slaughter of seabirds, marine mammals, fish, and mollusks, sparing only those species—large terrestrial mammals such as caribou and musk ox—which can be easily counted. Even the Greenland harp seal fishery, so much smaller than its Canadian counterpart, dumps 5,700 tons of skinned carcasses into the sea, because no use for the meat has been found. According to Hansen, almost everyone in Greenland is dedicated to eliminating the island's wildlife. In 1998, hunters killed 221,783 Brünnich's guillemots, 72,109 common eiders, 43,713 black-legged kittiwakes, 746 narwhals, 187 minke whales, 198 polar bears, 610 walruses, 82,108 ringed seals, and 82,491 harp seals. These kills (plus others) amount to 17,500 tons of animals and birds killed annually, which works out to 350 kilos (770 pounds) of meat for every one of Greenland's 58,000 people. "Meat wastage from Greenland kills is enormous," wrote Hansen. "Thousands of tons of meat from killed animals and birds are not used at all. At the same time, the quantity of beef and pork imported from Denmark satisfies three quarters of the population's needs."*

* The Greenland government took issue with Hansen's book, and on its official Web site (www.nanoq.gl) it argued that "it is correct that Greenland is facing certain difficulties in terms of overexploitation of specific species. However, the Danish journalist Kjeld Hansen's book *Farewell to Greenland's Wildlife,* published in 2002 and articles published in foreign media, particularly *Newsweek* and *BBC Wildlife Magazine* in relation to this book, may give the impression that we are ruthlessly overexploiting all species that live in Greenland. That is not the case. A status report issued by the Greenland Institute of Natural Resources shows that the following six species have declined because of overexploitation and for other reasons: guillemot, eider, king eider and Arctic tern (all bird species), narwhals and beluga. According to the Institute of Natural Resources the following four species need protection: polar bear, walrus, harbor seal and porpoise. The other 30 of the about 40 species most exploited in Greenland do not give rise to concern."

Of polar bears, Hansen said,

According to the *Piniarneq 2001* official hunting statistics, 121–198
polar bears are killed annually in the whole of Greenland, though
these figures do not adequately reflect the actual numbers killed. The
estimated figure is higher. Polar bear hunters are required to submit
detailed information about every single kill under Greenland Home
Rule regulations for polar bear hunting, but in the majority of cases
this information is never submitted. In actual fact no one knows how
many animals are killed each year.

In response to Hansen's much-publicized exposé, in the summer of
2004 quotas were introduced for narwhal and beluga, and the government agreed to look into the possibility of offering a trophy hunt for
polar bears, "already practiced in Canada, since it will provide the
hunters in the outlying districts with an alternate source of income,
which has already been shown with the trophy hunting of musk oxen
and reindeer." There are four recognized populations of polar bears in
Greenland, and all are hunted by native people. The catch figures for
2005 were Kane Basin, 10; Baffin Bay, 115; Davis Strait, 1; East Greenland, 70, for a total of 196. The local government hopes polar bear hunts
will help bolster the faltering economy in the northwestern part of the
island by creating jobs for hunting guides.

In early 2005, after Greenland announced its plan to permit sport
hunting of polar bears, conservationists rose up in protest. Most visible
was former French film star Brigitte Bardot, who condemned Greenland's plans to organize polar bear hunts for wealthy tourists. Agence
France-Presse quoted the sex-kitten-turned-animal-rights-activist: "I
have been fighting for years to stop the ice shelf being stained with the
blood of thousands of seals shamelessly exterminated in Canada and
Norway," she wrote in an open letter dated January 18, 2005, to Queen
Margrethe II of Denmark (of which Greenland is a dependent territory). "Your country also seems to want to leave its stamp on the ice
shelf by causing the blood of these innocent bears to flow, bears whose
survival is already threatened by global warming." Paul Watson's Sea
Shepherd Society has written to the U.S. Fish & Wildlife Service to
request that the polar bear be listed as endangered and that bear "trophies" be banned from entering the United States. "The killing of polar

bears for sport is sick and perverse," said Captain Watson. "People who need to kill and destroy such magnificent creatures to satisfy their narcissistic depravity have no place in the 21st Century. All polar bear killing must be outlawed if we are to have any hope of saving this species. The world of global warming requires radical changes in human behavior and eliminating recreational slaughter is a good place to begin."

Instead, the Greenland government decided to set a hunting quota. "The quota was set at 150 animals in 2006, and will be reviewed next year," said Ole Heinrich of the fishing and hunting directorate. As of January 1, 2007, only professional hunters with special permits issued by their local authorities will be allowed to kill polar bears, with the total kills set at 150. That is far fewer than the 200 to 250 bears normally hunted down each year, but more than the level recommended by biologists. Hunters will not be allowed to hunt cubs or their mothers. Aircraft, helicopters, motorized vehicles, and boats larger than forty gross registered tons are not allowed for hunting or for transportation of carcasses. Poisons, traps, foot snares, and self-shooting guns are forbidden, as are shotguns and automatic weapons. (Meanwhile, plans to introduce polar bear safaris, in which tourists would accompany an authorized hunter, are in the planning stages.)

In January 1968 the IUCN organized the first official meeting of the Polar Bear Group, under the aegis of the IUCN Survival Science Commission (now the Species Survival Commission). Scientists from the circumpolar nations of Norway, Canada, the Soviet Union, the United States, and Denmark were invited to attend the meeting, which was held at IUCN headquarters in Morges, Switzerland. No proceedings of the meeting were published, but the polar bear nations all agreed that the main order of business was to try to determine how many polar bears there were. Following the 1972 U.S. Marine Mammal Protection Act, the five nations agreed to draft an Agreement on the Conservation of Polar Bears, which was ratified by all in 1977. The agreement stipulated that the taking (which includes hunting, killing, and capturing) of polar bears shall be prohibited, except for scientific purposes or by local people, and polar bear research programs shall be conducted. In 1981, the agreement was extended indefinitely. The "No Taking" rule appeared to be exactly the protection the ice bear needed, for there were no other imminent threats on its horizon.

But even those Greenland bears that are not being hunted are in trouble. In his 2002 report, Erik Born noted that "a circumpolar study of POPs (persistent organic pollutants, e.g., PCB and DDT) in polar bears found high levels of POPs in polar bears from eastern Greenland and Svalbard," which contributed to morphological anomalies. "Thirteen anomalous polar bears were reported," wrote Born.

> The most striking record was from 10 June 1999 when an adult female bear, with clear signs of pseudohermaphroditism was killed at Scoresby Sound. The female had an enlarged clitoris, while the internal sexual organs apparently were normal. The other 12 cases of aberrant bears included: cases of supernumerary nipples or claws, a collapsed lung, abnormal claws after a healed fracture, partial melanism, and a malformed newborn.

All these abnormalities could have been caused by naturally induced trauma, but examination of these "aberrant" bears showed high concentrations of chemical pollutants. In a 2006 WWF report on chemical pollutants in the Arctic ("Killing Them Softly: Health Effects in Arctic Wildlife Linked to Chemical Exposures"), Brettania Walker wrote, "The greatest concern is that contaminant mixtures may interact with other natural stressors in the Arctic (e.g. climate change, habitat loss, reduced food supply) resulting in wildlife having reduced ability to successfully deal with everyday challenges (harsh winters, hibernation, feeding, nesting predation) leading to reduced reproductive capacity, increased likelihood of disease or even death, and population declines." And population declines, of course, lead to further population declines.

The title of a 2006 study by Danish scientists is framed as a question: "Are Organohalogen Contaminants a Cofactor in the Development of Renal Lesions in East Greenland Polar Bears?" The answer? Probably. Christian Sonne, Rune Dietz, Erik Born, and their colleagues suggested that "long term exposure to OCs may be a cofactor in renal lesion occurrence, although other cofactors, such as exposure to heavy metals and concurrent infection from microorganisms cannot be ruled out." Mercury, one of the so-called heavy metals (defined as any metallic chemical element that has a relatively high density and is toxic or poisonous at low concentrations), has now emerged as one of the main contaminants of Arctic animals. Far from the Arctic, it enters the atmosphere from coal-fired utilities and industrial boilers and comes to rest on land, sea, or ice, where it is incorporated into the food chain. Ringed seals eat mercury-tainted fish, and polar bears eat ringed seals. In a 2007 study, the Danish scientists found that the polar bears of East Greenland were among the most mercury-polluted species in the Arctic. Examining the livers and kidneys of fifty-nine adult and subadult bears, they found lesions that indicated that "the signs and nature of chronic inflammation and statistical relationships points toward age and recurrent infections as the main factor ... These are new and important results in the monitoring and assessment of the potential toxic impact from the increasing mercury concentrations in Arctic wildlife and humans relying on polluted marine species."

A report published in 2008 by Danish environmental scientists identified yet another toxic threat to Greenland's polar bears. After testing 128 bears from East Greenland, the researchers found that industrial chemicals known as perfluoroalkyl contaminants (PFCs) have increased by 27 percent since 1984, more than twice the rate of the PFC increase recorded by Canadian scientists for the polar bears of Baffin Island. Concentrations of PFCs in the livers of Greenland bears are greater than the PCBs recorded earlier, and the bears are being hit by a "triple whammy from the combined effects of PCBs, PFCs, and mercury, which is also widespread in the Arctic." Laboratory experiments with rats have shown that PFCs adversely affect the liver, the immune system, and hormone levels; when adult rats were given high doses, all their babies died within a day (Calamai 2008). In their report, Dietz, Bossi, Riget et al. wrote, "Observed developmental effects [in rats, rabbits, and mice] from exposure to PFCs include increased pup mortality, reduction in fetal weight, cleft palate, placental edema, delayed skeletal ossification, and cardiac abnormalities." Perfluoroalkyls are found in all kinds of everyday products, from windshield washer liquids to the greaseproof paper used to wrap fast foods, but it is not immediately obvious how the PFCs are transmitted to bears in the Arctic. It is possible that they are the degraded products of fluorotelemer alcohols (FTOHs), which are released into the atmosphere by factories.

After the Antarctic, the Greenland ice sheet is the second largest ice body in the world, covering roughly 80 percent of the island, or 672,000 square miles. In 2002, NASA Goddard Space Center climatologist Jay Zwally and his colleagues noted that the Jakobshavn Isbrae (Jakobshavn Glacier), known to be one of the world's fastest-moving glaciers, is speeding up. Located in west-central Greenland, the Jakobshavn Glacier has long released the largest icebergs into the North Atlantic and is believed to have been the source of the iceberg that ripped a gash in the ill-fated *Titanic* in April 1912. The outflowing ice in the Jakobshavn is moving twice as fast as it was a decade ago. Its "tongue" has retreated four miles since 2000, and the ice outflow is now moving at a rate of 120 feet each day, plugging the Ilulissat harbor with random-sized chunks of ice. One of the major drainage outlets of Greenland's interior ice sheet is thinning more than four times faster than it did for most of the twentieth century, and a component of this thinning is a substantial increase in ice speed. In 2004, climatologists Jonathan Gregory, Philippe Huybrechts, and Sarah Raper wrote, "The Greenland ice-sheet would melt faster in a warmer climate and is likely to be eliminated—except for residual glaciers in the mountains—if the annual temperature in Greenland increases by more than 3°C." By December 2007, the AP reported that "Greenland's ice sheet melted nearly 19 billion tons more than the previous high mark, and the volume of Arctic sea ice at summer's end was half of what it was four years earlier."

In 2007, 552 billion tons of surface ice was lost over Greenland, 15 percent more than the average summer melt. It is conceivable that global warming may push Greenland's ice sheet over a threshold where it will melt in less than a few hundred years.* It appears that some of Greenland's water is going to the same place as the ice: back into the ocean. In July 2006, scientists documented the sudden, complete draining of a meltwater lake that measured 2.2 square miles in area and was twenty-five feet deep. The lake, just north of the Jakobshavn Glacier, split open the ice sheet from top to bottom, and, like a draining bathtub, the entire lake disappeared in an hour and a half—exceeding the

---

* What lies under Greenland's thick ice sheet is not known. Like Antarctica, the other continent-sized slab of ice, Greenland's ice sheet gets squashed down under its own weight, and the force squeezes ice outward so there's movement at the sides. Scientists using the Global Ice Sheet Mapping Orbiter (GISMO) found topography matching that of Canada and the northern United States, with much of the land scoured by flowing ice and mountains rising from the bottom. How fast the ice moves depends on whether the bottom of the ice, where it meets the ground, is well lubricated by water. Under-ice rivers and steep terrain down which water can slide could also accelerate speed. When the melting ice drains to the bedrock below, the ice sheet slides faster to the sea, a feedback loop that speeds further ice loss.

flow of Niagara Falls. (The event was documented by Das et al. 2008.) If all of Greenland's ice were to melt, most coastal cities in the world would be inundated, and several small island countries, such as Tuvalu and the Maldives, would disappear completely.

The summer of 2003 was the warmest since 1958 in coastal southern Greenland. The summer of 2005 was even warmer, and while 2006 was somewhat less warm, the runoff from the melting ice sheet was on the increase. The record was broken again in 2007, with the most extreme melting in fifty years. In a 2008 study in the *Journal of Climate*, some of the world's leading glaciologists and climatologists from the United Kingdom, Belgium, Denmark, and the U.S. (Hanna, Huybrechts et al.) announced that "[they] attribute significantly increased Greenland summer warmth and Greenland ice sheet melt and runoff since 1990 to global warming." The melting ice sheet and the meltwater runoff from Greenland's glaciers could trigger an irreversible catastrophe as more and more of Greenland's age-old ice returns to its watery state. Edward Hanna of England's University of Sheffield, in remarks published in *ScienceDaily* on January 16, 2008, said, "Our work shows that global warming is beginning to take its toll in the Greenland Ice Sheet which, as a relict feature of the last Ice Age, has already been living on borrowed time and seems now to be in inexorable decline. The question is can we reduce greenhouse-gas emissions in time to make enough of a difference to curb this decay?"

V

The Eskimo and the Polar Bear

I saw a polar bear on an ice-drift.
He seemed harmless as a dog,
who comes running towards you,
wagging his tail.
But so much did he want to get at me
that when I jumped aside
he went spinning on the ice.
We played this game of tag
from morning until dusk.
But then at last, I tired him out,
and ran my spear into his side.

Eskimo poem, collected by Knud Rasmussen

The Bering land bridge, also known as Beringia, stretched for roughly 1,000 miles north to south at its greatest extent, joining western Alaska and eastern Siberia at various times during the Pleistocene. The bridge is believed to have enabled human migration from Asia to the Americas about 15,000 years ago. Seagoing coastal settlers may also have crossed earlier, but opinion remains divided on this point, and the coastal sites that would offer evidence now lie submerged under hundreds of feet of water. Indigenous Asians are thought to have occupied the northern territories for at least 18,000 years, and when some of them crossed into North America, they brought their culture with them. As Ian Stirling (1988) wrote,

> Where these people came from is unclear but the structure of tools found in the middens in Alaska suggests that the Paleoeskimos came from northeastern Siberia. They probably crossed to North America on the frozen ice of the Bering Sea. Possibly they came in boats, although there is no evidence of it. Most dramatic, though, is that radiocarbon dating of artifacts collected all across the Arctic gives a very similar age. This indicates that once the Paleoeskimos figured how to exploit this unoccupied niche as human predators, they spread extremely rapidly from Alaska to Greenland in much the same way as the polar bears must have done some 200,000 years earlier.

Eskimo is a Native American word that is widely believed to mean "eater of raw meat," although this definition is disputed. Many Inuit consider the word *Eskimo* offensive, but it is still generally used to refer to all Eskimo peoples, though it has fallen into disuse throughout Canada, where Canadians use the term Inuit. In Inuktitut, the language of the Inuit, the word *Inuit* means "the people." I am using the words Inuit and Eskimo interchangeably, because there were many people who used *Eskimo* before the more politically correct *Inuit* was selected, and I cannot change a quote or a reference for political reasons. Besides, *Eskimo* refers to the Arctic and sub-Arctic people in Alaska, while *Inuit* is the name of the people of the Canadian Arctic. Regardless of where they live, however, Inuit and Eskimos are the same people, with the same language and much the same culture.

The Inuit were traditionally hunters of whales, walruses, caribou, and seals, although polar bears, musk oxen, birds, and any other edible animal might be taken when available. The Arctic has very little edible vegetation, although Inuit occasionally supplemented their diet with seaweed. Sea animals were hunted from single-passenger, covered seal-skin boats called *qajait* (singular *qajaq*) that were extraordinarily buoyant and could easily be righted by a seated person even if they completely overturned. The Inuit design was copied—along with the Inuit word—by Europeans, who called them *kayaks*. Depending on location, various Arctic peoples concentrated on one or more food items; the Chukchi of Chukotka were divided into two distinct groups, culturally and economically: the maritime sea hunters, and the reindeer herders (Arutiunov 1988). Across the Bering Strait in Alaska, the north coast and Bering Strait groups specialized in hunting whales, walruses, and seals, while the interior people were mostly after caribou. The art and culture of these people emphasized the animals they hunted, but one hardly ever sees an image of a polar bear. Nanook was too scarce and too fierce to build a culture around.*

Franz Boas (1858–1920) was born in Minden, Germany; he earned his baccalaureate from the University of Heidelberg in 1881 and, in the same year, his PhD from the University of Kiel. In 1899 he became a professor at Columbia University. Long regarded as one of the most influential anthropologists, he published *The Central Eskimo* in 1888, in which he discussed in detail the distribution, social and religious life, tales and traditions, arts, clothes, and hunting and fishing practices of the Eskimo. Although he was quite specific about the various tribes, he wrote,

> The mode of life of all Eskimo tribes of Northeastern America is very uniform . . . All depends upon the distribution of food at the different seasons. The migrations or the accessibility of the game compels the natives to move their habitations from time to time, and hence the distribution of the villages depends, to a great extent, upon that of the animals which supply them with their food . . . In Arctic America, the abundance of seals found in all parts of the sea enables them to withstand the inclemency of the climate and the sterility of the soil. The skins of seals furnish the material for summer garments and for the tent; their flesh is almost the only food, and their blubber the indispensable fuel during the long dark winter.

* *Nanook of the North* was a documentary made in 1922 by pioneer filmmaker Robert Flaherty. It was shot in Inukjuak, on the eastern shore of Hudson Bay, almost directly opposite Churchill. The title character is not a bear but a man, who is shown leading his small family through a sequence of typical "Eskimo" activities: kayaking, ice fishing, harpooning a walrus in the surf, trapping a fox, building an igloo, and harpooning a seal through its breathing hole. The only mention of Nanuk (the bear) occurs when the family arrives at a fur-trading post, and we learn that Nanook (the man) has "killed seven great polar bears with nothing more formidable than his harpoon."

Not unlike the polar bear, the Central Eskimo was totally dependent on the seal. Because the bears appeared irregularly—or sometimes not at all—it was only when they saw a bear or its tracks that the Eskimos went after Nanook. "The Eskimo pursue them in light sledges," wrote Boas, "and when they are near the pursued animal the traces of the most reliable dogs in the team are cut, when they dash forward and bring the bear to bay. As the hunter gets sufficiently near the last dogs are let loose and the bear is killed with a spear or with a bow and arrow . . . Its skin and flesh are highly prized by the Eskimo."

In the seventeenth century, Dutch and English whalers who wintered on Arctic islands like Spitsbergen and Jan Mayen tried to eat a local grass to ward off scurvy, but Eskimos, who live almost exclusively on meat and fish, do not get the disease. Fruits, vegetables, and other carbohydrates—the usual sources of vitamin C—account for as little as 2 percent of their total calorie intake. The meat and liver of the ringed seal contains 20 and 180 milligrams of vitamin C per kilogram respectively. The traditional Eskimo diet also includes various plants, seaweeds, and the skin of the beluga and the narwhal (known as *muktuk*), which are all rich in vitamin C. There is also vitamin C in the liver of reindeer and smaller amounts in bear meat.

The Inuit hunt seals by making holes in the ice and waiting for the air-breathing mammals to use them when they need air. According to Inuit tradition, they learned to do this by observing the polar bear, who hunts in this same manner. The Inuit have hunted *nanuq* for millennia. The bears are too scarce and too dangerous to be considered a common prey item, but there is a lot of meat on a thousand-pound bear, and the thick-furred pelts are without equal for clothing and sleeping skins. The Inuit will track the bears for days, analyzing the footprints in the snow to ascertain how big the bear is, how recently it passed, and if it is worth pursuing. The bears often make the same determinations about the Inuit: many a bear hunter has been following a bear, only to glance behind him and see another bear tracking him. In recent years, Inuit hunters, still permitted to take polar bears in most areas, can use rifles, but before Europeans brought firearms to the people of the ice, they had to confront the bear armed only with a spear or harpoon.

While stationed at the Hudson's Bay Company's headquarters near the Churchill River in Manitoba in 1784, David Thompson had the rare opportunity to observe what he referred to as the "Indian superstition of the Polar Bear." (The region around Churchill, far to the south of the usual Eskimos and polar bear territory, was inhabited by the Chipewyan and Cree peoples.) Spotting a polar bear "prowling about in the ebb tide," Thompson reported, "the Indians set off to kill it as the skin could be taken to [York] Factory in the canoe." After the bear was shot, the Indians skinned it and cut off the head, which they dragged away from the incoming tide, "each man having hold of an ear, with the utmost speed in the mud . . . on the first grass they laid down the head, with the nose to the sea, which they made red with ochre; then made a speech to the Manito of the Bears, that he would be kind to them as they performed all his orders."

When Elisha Kane's brig *Advance* was trapped in the ice of Etah Bay in northwestern Greenland in the spring of 1855, and he and his men were starving, they were taken in by "the Esquimaux." During that time, Kane had the opportunity to observe the aboriginal polar bear hunt:

> Let us suppose a bear scented at the base of an iceberg. The Esquimaux examines the track with sagacious care, to determine its age and direction, and the speed with which the animal was moving when he passed along. The dogs are set upon the trail, and the hunter courses over the ice at their side in silence. As he turns the angle of the berg the game is in view before him, stalking probably along with quiet march, sometimes snuffing the air suspiciously, but making nevertheless, for a nest of broken hummocks. The dogs spring forward, opening in a wild wolfish yell, the driver shrieking "Nanook! Nanook!" and all straining every nerve in pursuit.
>
> The bear rises on his haunches, inspects his pursuers, and starts off at full speed. The hunter, as he runs, leaning over the sledge, seizes the traces of a couple of his dogs and liberates them from their burden. It is the work of a minute; for the motion is not checked, and the remaining dogs rush on with apparent ease. Now pressed more severely, the bear makes for an iceberg and stands at bay, while his foremost pursuers halt at a short distance and quietly await the arrival of the hunter. At this moment the whole pack are liberated; the hunter grasps his lance, and, tumbling through the snow and ice prepares for the encounter.

Many wounds are received by the Etah Bay Esquimaux in these encounters: the bear is looked upon as more fierce in that neighborhood, and about Anoatok and Rensselaer Bay, than around the broken ice to the south. He uses his teeth much more generally than is supposed by systematic writers. The hugging, pawing, and boxing, which characterize the black and grisly bears, are resorted to by him only under peculiar circumstances . . . It is only when absolutely beset, or when the female is defending her cub, that the Polar bear shows fight upon his haunches. Among seven hunters who visited the brig last December, no less than five were scarred by direct teeth-wounds of bears. Two of these had been bit in the calves while running; and one, our friend Metek, had received a like dishonorable wound somewhat higher.

Kane's men ate the meat of the bears they killed, but for the Esquimaux, Nanook was more than food; because of its importance in aboriginal culture, the great white bear was assigned a role of supernatural significance. Killing one was a major event, requiring ceremonial propitiation of its spirit. Sometimes it was the bear who killed the person, for the predator-prey relationship went both ways. Norwegian polar bear expert Thor Larsen lists some examples of the superstitions associated with the great bear:

> The polar bear is a dangerous animal, but we need it. We must hunt it and kill it, but we also have to take some precautions so that the bear's soul will not return and harm us.
> The bears hear everything and know everything Man talks about.
> If it is a male bear, one must hang a rope over the bear's nose, and in the rope there must be a harpoon, some blubber and meat and some pieces of leather. Everything is for the bear's soul. The leather is for the repair of the bear's boots, because a bear walks a lot.
> Everything must remain like this for at least five days. Furthermore, all bones from the bear must be collected as its meat is eaten, and the bones must be piled up by the skull, in the window-frame. The skull must face inwards.
> All this is done in order to help the bear find its home. The bear gets human tools and equipment, because bears can often change themselves into humans.

It was sometimes claimed that the bears came to the humans voluntarily because they wanted gifts from the hunters. Some said that after the bear's skull, hide and bones have been in the house for five days—these were the bear's visiting days—and received gifts, the skull should be boiled and thrown into the sea. Only thus treated, could the bear return home.

It was commonly believed that when somebody ate Polar Bear meat and lost the piece of meat on the floor, he could not pick it up right away. He had to pick it up from behind the legs, beneath his crooked knee; if not he would be eaten by a bear.

In Eskimo mythology, Tornarsuk is a god of the underworld and the leader of the Torniat, the protective pantheon. Tornarsuk is as long as a big seal, but much thicker. His head and back paws resemble those of the seal, but his forearms are as long as those of a man, which description brings it rather close to a polar bear. (A skinned-out polar bear, especially on its back, looks surprisingly human.) The spiritual guardian of shamans was Tornarsuk, and it was believed that the spirits of people and bears could be interchanged. When something goes

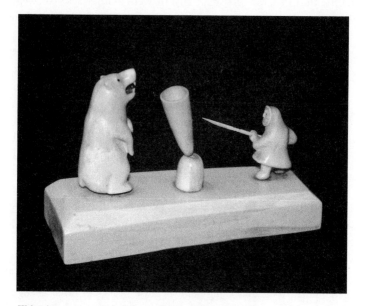

Walrus ivory pen stand, depicting an Eskimo polar bear hunter

wrong or when something interferes with well-made plans, the failure is often attributed to the evil spirit Tornarsuk. During a polar bear hunt with Eskimos in northern Greenland in 1906, Robert Peary was told that a bear that kept on running when the dogs reached him "was almost certain proof that the great devil himself—terrible Tornarsuk— was in that bear." Later in the hunt, Peary (who regarded himself as an excellent shot) fired twice at the bear, "but the bear kept right on up the canyon side. Surely Tornarsuk was in him!"

Polar bears were—and still are—an important part of Eskimo life and culture. For different Eskimo societies living in different regions, other animals have taken precedence: the seal (a generic term for all Arctic pinnipeds, even though there are many different kinds) supplies clothing, food, and even heat and lighting oil. For Eskimos of the tundra—whom Farley Mowat called "people of the deer"—the caribou is the most important wild animal. Where walruses and whales are available, they furnish food, oil, bones, and sinews for sewing. Many of the artifacts of the Eskimo's animal-dependent culture have been replaced: dogsleds by snowmobiles; ivory-tipped spears by rifles; harpoons by shoulder guns; igloos by prefabricated houses; sealskin parkas by nylon and Gore-Tex; and kayaks by aluminum motorboats. But even if there were a McDonald's in the village, many would still follow the old ways of hunting, and no more so than with the polar bear.

VI

Hunting the Hunter

It makes no difference to polar bears if they are shot for food, for sport, or as adjuncts to a walrus hunt. In the case of "sportsmen," the thick white pelt is likely to end up as a rug spread out in front of a fireplace—you don't see ladies (or men) of fashion wearing polar bear coats. In *Why Elephants Have Big Ears*, Chris Lavers wrote, "Curiously, the fur of polar bears has never been popular for clothing, partly because of the hazards of removing it from its rightful owner but mainly because the hairs are rather coarse." The entire bear could be mounted in an upright stance like the one at the head of the stairs in the Explorers Club in New York City—a taxidermied bear that rears up to its full height with forepaws extended and fangs bared. Sometimes, bears were shot opportunistically, simply because they were there, but only if "there" happened to be north of the Arctic Circle. "The whalers, and subsequently the sealers, killed everything that could be sold for a profit; polar bear skins became very popular in Europe during Victorian times as a sign of wealth and thereby increased the demand. Between 1905 and 1909, Dundee whalers alone killed more than 1,000 bears off the ice of eastern Greenland in the Davis Strait and Hudson Bay" (Ward and Kynaston 1999). As Barry Lopez observed in *Arctic Dreams*,

> Thousands of miles from familiar surroundings, genuinely frightened, and perhaps strained by the grim conditions of shipboard life, Europeans took to killing any polar bear they saw. They shot them out of pettiness and a sense of rectitude. In time, killing bears became

the sort of amusement people expected on an arctic journey. Travelers regularly shot them from the ship's deck, for target practice. One idle summer in 1896, a whaling captain with nothing else to do shot thirty-five for sport.

Aboard the British steamwhaler *Diana* out of Hull (Captain John Gravill commanding), Charles Edward Smith, the ship's surgeon, kept a careful record of the daily events of the voyage of 1866–67, most of which was spent trapped in the ice of northern Baffin Bay. The journal was transcribed by his son, C. E. Smith Harris, and published in 1923 as *From the Deep of the Sea: An Epic of the Arctic*. Before he died on December 26, 1866 (of "brain fever, asthma, and bronchitis"), Gravill described many of his experiences with polar bears, including these, where the bears were killed for no other reason than because they were in shooting range:

Old John, one of the men, tells me he remembers a bear attacking a ship's company of forty men sealing on the ice. Two years ago, the *Constantia* fell in with a dead whale covered with bears. The ship's crew shot no fewer than sixty of these bears, out of which number they got forty-five . . .

Well, I went and struck a lance into the bear, but didn't kill it. It dived below a very large and broad piece of ice that happened to be near, and then came up on the other side of the ice. The bear actually kept the boat's crew pulling round that ice for more than an hour. It kept on diving and coming up again on the opposite side before I could get another lance into it, and it was wounded and bleeding and weakening all the time from the first lance . . .

When you are pulling after a bear in the water and are coming up to him fast, in nine cases out of ten he will turn around and face you, though I have seen them dive and come up astern of the boat. They are nasty things, you know, for they will get hold of your oars or anything with their tusks. Old Captain Hawkins, when he had the *William*, was pulled clean over his boat's bow by one of them bears.

Although thirteen of the men aboard the *Diana* had already died of scurvy, starvation, and other causes, they did not intend to eat the meat of the bears they killed, according to an entry in Dr. Smith's diary dated

March 6, 1867, two weeks before they broke out of the pack ice. A bear had been spotted immediately ahead of the ship, and several of the men shot at it. "I am very glad the bear escaped us," wrote Smith.

> Had we shot him and kept his hindquarters for dog's meat, I am perfectly certain that no fear of illness or disease or even death would have deterred some of our crew from eating the flesh. I am assured that bear's meat is extremely unhealthy. When the S.S. *Eider* was wintered in this country, her crew shot some bears also, and it is a remarkable fact that the only men that died were those who had eaten bear's meat. The skin of their arms and hands came off in flakes. Neither the Esquimaux nor their dogs will touch the flesh of a bear.

(It is in fact the consumption of the *liver* of a polar bear that causes the skin to peel off.)

Anything that looks as if it might be edible might be sampled by a hungry bear. A seal, walrus, dog, or human that crosses the path of a bear that hasn't eaten for a while would probably be considered fair game. Hungry bears will try to catch anything that moves, and many things that don't move, such as dead walruses, whale carcasses, sleeping seals, or men in tents or igloos. Although it is of little consolation to a person whose leg is being gnawed on, in defense of the anthropophagous polar bear it must be said that many more people have eaten bear meat than bears have eaten people meat. Over a two-year period beginning in August 1896, for instance, Frederick Jackson and his men killed eighty-three polar bears to feed the members of their expedition to Franz Josef Land.

Born in Pennsylvania in 1856 and educated at Bowdoin College* in Maine, Robert Edward Peary is probably the most controversial figure in the annals of polar exploration. In 1886, he crossed Greenland on foot, becoming the first to demonstrate that it was an island. Fully committed to Arctic exploration, he sailed to Greenland on the research vessel *Roosevelt* in 1905, where he and his party reached 87°6'N on foot,

---

* According to the Bowdoin College Web site, the polar bear was selected as the official mascot in 1913 in recognition of the exploration of the polar regions by Bowdoin alumni Thomas H. Hubbard of the Class of 1857, Robert E. Peary of the Class of 1877, and Donald B. MacMillan of the Class of 1898.

Renowned explorer and polar bear hunter Robert E. Peary

setting the record. In August 1908, the *Roosevelt* headed back to Green-land, with Peary determined to reach the North Pole. He set off from Ellesmere Island on March 1, 1909, with his servant, Matthew Henson, seventeen Eskimos, nineteen sledges, and 133 dogs. When he went back to the *Roosevelt*, on April 27, he claimed to have reached the pole (with Henson and four Eskimos) on April 6. Peary returned in triumph, and was honored as the greatest explorer of all time. However, in a letter to the New York *Herald*, Frederick Cook, a surgeon on Peary's earlier Greenland expedition, asserted that he himself had reached the North Pole almost a year earlier, but had spent the year on Devon Island, not returning until April 15, 1909. Their conflicting claims ignited a battle that still rages, although recent examination of diaries, photographs, meteorological data, and other pertinent material suggests strongly that neither man actually reached the North Pole and that both fabricated their accounts. Because Peary's claim was accepted for so long, nobody else tried to reach the pole on foot until British explorer Wally Herbert did so on April 6, 1969—exactly sixty years after Peary's alleged accomplishment.

Whether or not he ever reached the North Pole, Peary unquestionably spent a lot of time on the Arctic ice, and there recorded several encounters with polar bears, including a hunt during which the Eskimos trapped *Nanook* in a snow canyon and shot it with Peary's rifle. "If there is anything that starts the blood lust in an Eskimo's heart more wildly than the sight of a polar bear, I have yet to discover it," he wrote. "Hardened as I am to arctic hunting, I was thrilled myself." After the 1910 publication of *The North Pole,* the book in which he detailed his triumph, he published *Secrets of Polar Travel,* an instruction book for aspiring explorers, in which he said this about the bear:

> To most travelers and explorers, and to all readers, the polar bear, sometimes called the "Tiger of the North," has loomed largest as the "big game" par excellence of the North. I know of nothing that will excite an Eskimo so much as the sight of one of these huge creatures in the distance; but a contest with even three or four bears and a man armed with a Winchester is always one-sided and tame sport in comparison with a lively walrus hunt.
>
> In 1886, at Ravenscraig Harbor, on the south side of Eglinton Fiord, a fleet of four whalers and the *Eagle* obtained ten bears, two of these being harpooned in the water by the crew of the *Eagle.* So enraged was one of the animals that the crews of three boats were required to keep the bear from climbing into the *Eagle*'s boat to wreak vengeance on the occupants. Just north of Cape Hooper we got three more bears in the ice-pack. It is not always possible to bring a bear down with the first shot when he is traveling over rough ice, but there need be no doubt as to whether a shot has reached its mark or not, for a wounded bear will always make savage snaps at the spot stung by a bullet.

Although his claim to have reached the North Pole before Peary was more than dubious, Frederick Cook had little reason to fabricate his encounters with polar bears, and when he and his team were camped on the ice, they saw a huge bear nosing around their fireplace:

> We had left there a walrus joint, weighing about one hundred pounds, for our next meal. We jumped up, all of us at once, shouting and making a pretended rush. The bear took up the meat in his forepaws and walked off, man-like, on two legs, with a threatening grunt. His movement was slow and cautious, and his grip on the meat was secure. Occasionally he veered about. With a beckoning turn of his head, and a challenging call . . . After moving away about three hundred yards on the sea ice, he calmly sat down and devoured our prospective meal.

Cook's party had almost no ammunition for their rifles, so brandishing bows, arrows, and stones, and yelling at the tops of their lungs, they charged the bears who had found their food cache, and managed to drive them off, but discovered that the animals had already eaten everything—so, "baffled and unable to resent our robbery, starvation again confronted us."

Upon encountering the fresh tracks of a bear, Cook and his companions artfully arranged "pieces of skin to imitate the dark outline of a recumbent seal," and made a snare through which the bear would have to pass his head to get at the bait. Then they waited in a sturdy igloo for the bear to take the seal: "Soon a crackling sound on the snows gave the battle call, and with a little black nose extended from a long neck, a vicious creature emerged . . . Apparently as hungry as we were, he came in straight rushes for the bait . . . Wela and Etuk emerged, one with a lance, the other with a spiked harpoon shaft." But Cook knew that the lance, the looped line, and the bow and arrow would be futile. Luckily, he had hidden his last four cartridges in his parka ("to be used in the last stages of hunger to kill something—or ourselves"), and as the men drew the loop tight around the neck of the bear and Etuk stabbed it with his lance, Cook handed the loaded rifle to Wela, who shot the bear. "When the smoke cleared, the bleeding bear lay on the ground. We skinned the animal, and devoured the warm, steaming flesh. Strength revived. Here were food and fuel in abundance. We were saved!" (I am not sure that this story is any more accurate than the one of his conquest of the North Pole. Cook's is the only account of a polar bear carrying a haunch of meat in its paws while walking upright. In addition to the unlikely sequence of Cook loading his rifle and handing it to another man as the bear was charging, there is the eating of raw polar bear flesh, which Cook, as a doctor, would know was likely to contain Trichinella parasites.)

Because the vast wasteland of the Arctic is the perfect habitat for ringed seals, adventurers like Peary and Cook were more than likely to encounter polar bears during their travels. So too was Naomi Uemura, who made the first solo assault on the North Pole in March 1978. Chronicled in the *National Geographic*, Uemura's story begins with these words: "Shortly before dawn the polar bear attacks." Very dramatic, except that the bear didn't really attack. Uemura was awakened by the barking of his dogs—"In the Arctic, there are few creatures a sled dog instinctively fears: One is man, another is the polar bear"—and hears the ominous shuffling of a bear outside his tent. "It's all over," he thinks. "I'm going to be killed." After ransacking Uemura's food supplies (pemmican, frozen seal meat, a bucket of nourishing whale oil—a perfect menu for a hungry bear), the unseen animal begins ripping the terrified man's nylon tent. "Now it is surely over," thought Uemura. "Live human meat is tastier than pemmican or frozen seal. He's found my scent. I'm finished." Apparently the bear didn't agree about "live human meat"; he took one sniff of Uemura in his sleeping bag, turned, and padded away. When the bear returned the next day, Uemura was ready: "At the first yip from the dogs, now tightly secured, I station myself beside the sled and train my telescopic sight on the bear. He comes toward me, dignified, massive through the eyepiece. At a range of fifty meters I squeeze the trigger; the bear stands upright. Then with a groan he is down, dragging his great body toward the safety of the ice hills. Several more shots for good measure, and it is over."

Uemura generously repaid the bear's sparing his life by shooting it. That the bear didn't even bother him in his sleeping bag didn't change his mind about the ferocity of the polar bear; he knew that bears were man-eaters, and the way to ensure a successful assault on the North Pole was to eliminate anything that might stand in his way. As in so many comparable situations, the curious bear was seen as an aggressive bear, and Uemura didn't want to be the one to satisfy the bear's curiosity about what human meat might taste like.

Spread out as they are across millions of square miles of ice, polar bears were not really threatened by Inuit or Eskimo hunts. But when Europeans, Canadians, and Americans took it into their heads that hunting the largest carnivore in the Arctic would provide the same kind of thrill as shooting a lion or a tiger, the numbers of bears began to fall. In *Wild Life Beyond the North,* Frank Illingworth described the way men thought about bears—in 1952, anyway:

> The polar bear is hunted mercilessly. Henry Rudi, the Norwegian trapper, shot one hundred and twenty-five in one winter in Spitzbergen. The remoteness of the animal's hunting grounds renders it wellnigh impossible to enforce game laws; particularly would it be difficult where the natives hunt the bear for its meat and its flesh . . . In the past, the white hunter did not differentiate between the gnarled old bachelor and the she-bear with cubs. A recognized practice in Greenland was to place poisoned meat on floes frequented by bears, and if the cubs died with their mother then the trapper was that much richer in furs and tender steaks. Today he is more circumspect. Furthermore in some parts of the Arctic the polar bear is protected

Stefansson drags a seal across the ice, Eskimo-style.

during the breeding season, and the sale of cub-sized pelts brings the
law down on the offending trapper—which is indeed fortunate for
the future of an animal with such fascinating characteristics.

After his ship *Karluk* became trapped in the sea ice north of Alaska
in August 1913, Vilhjalmur Stefansson and a small group left the ship to
hunt for food, and never went back to the westward-drifting ship,
which was eventually crushed. Most of the crew survived while Stefansson and his party drifted on ice floes, living among the Inuit and
exploring northern Canada, eventually returning in 1918. He wrote up
his adventures in several books, including *My Life with the Eskimo; The
Stefansson-Anderson Expedition, 1909–1912;* and *Hunters of the Great
North.*

To survive in the Arctic, Stefansson learned to live like an Eskimo.
Although he hated fish, he lived on nothing but fish and meat for a
year, and remained so healthy—and put on weight, just as Nansen had
done eating only bear meat and walrus blubber—that he was able to
live and work in relative comfort.* In *Hunters of the Great North* (1922),
Stefansson wrote chapters called "How I Learned to Hunt Caribou,"
"How I Learned to Hunt Seals," and "How We Hunt Polar Bears." Stefansson and his hosts hunted bears for food: "When I first arrived at
Tuktoyaktok," he wrote, "we had bear fat to eat with our fish. Two or
three bears had been killed in the early fall before I arrived and their
meat had been eaten immediately but some of the fat had been saved
against winter." Eskimo bear hunts are conducted in the traditional
fashion, where the dogs are loosed to harass the bear, enabling the
hunters to get close enough to shoot it. But, says Stefansson, "the more
I see and the more I read, the less inclined I am to favor the method. It
is too dangerous to the dogs and if you are a good bear hunter you can
get the bear well enough without the use of dogs."

---

* Stefansson's experience with the Eskimo "no-carb" diet became a subject of great interest to the medical profession, because the conventional wisdom at the time was that too
much meat was unhealthy and a balanced diet should include fruits, vegetables, and grains.
Stefansson agreed to have his all-meat diet observed under the auspices of the American
Medical Association, and the results, published in the *Journal of the American Medical Association,* showed that he was perfectly healthy after a year on a diet without any vegetables,
grains, salt, or even vitamin supplementation. (See Clarence W. Lieb, "The Effects of an
Exclusive Long-Continued Meat Diet," *JAMA,* July 23, 1926, and "The Effects on Human
Beings of a Twelve Months' Exclusive Meat Diet," *JAMA,* July 6, 1929.)

In *My Life with the Eskimo*, Stefansson tells the story of his first—and almost his last—polar bear hunt. He was out hunting alone, hoping to catch sight of a sleeping seal or a bear. In the distance, he "noticed a spot which seemed more yellow than the ice ought to be," but when it disappeared, he realized it must have been a bear. So he put his binoculars away, and stealthily headed toward the spot where he thought the bear might be. When he arrived, there was no bear to be seen:

> My rifle was buckled in its case slung across my back, and I was slowly and cautiously clambering down the far side of a pressure ridge, when I heard behind me a noise like the spitting of a cat or the hiss of a goose. I looked back and saw, about twenty feet away and almost above me, a polar bear. Had he come the remaining twenty feet as quietly and quickly as a bear can, the literary value of the incident would have been lost forever; for, as the Greek fable points out, a lion does not write a book. From his eye and attitude, as well as the story his trail told afterward there was no doubting his intentions: the hiss was merely his way of saying, "Watch me do it!" Or at least that is how I interpreted it; possibly the motive was chivalry, and the hiss was his way of saying *Garde!* Whichever it was, it was the fatal mistake of a game played well to that point; for no animal on earth can afford to give warning to a man with a rifle.

On another occasion, north of Alaska, Stefansson and his exploring party "were sitting around their campfire enjoying a meal of boiled seal meat, when the dogs all at once commenced a great racket." The smell of burning seal blubber and cooking seal meat had attracted a bear, and the dogs were going crazy. The bear was on the other side of an open lead, which he would have to cross to get at the dogs.

> The white shaggy monster was only twenty-five feet from the dogs . . . He did not appear to be in the least afraid of the dogs, which were rearing, plunging and barking in their eagerness to be at him. But he completely ignored them, and merely stood facing them with his head hanging downward and swinging slowly from side to side. Then he would peer into the water for a moment, as if trying to make up his mind to plunge in and swim across. Just as it appeared that the bear had made up his mind to swim over and kill our dogs,

Storkerson took aim and quickly fired. The bullet, a .30-.30, hit the bear in the right foreleg, and knocked that member out from under him, so that he turned a complete somersault into the water . . .

By this time, Stefansson had unstrapped his rifle: "The bear was wounded, and while it might not menace our dogs again, it would be better to end its misery." Stefansson shot it again in the water, "but the thoroughly frightened King of the Arctic clambered out on the ice and began to limp away. This bullet knocked him over, but he got up again in spite of a second hit from Storkerson's rifle, he disappeared behind a pressure ridge and was lost to view leaving a broad trail of blood." The "hunt" ended with the badly wounded bear being shot three more times before it finally died. Stefansson blamed the bear for getting killed:

> In a sense, this misfortune to the bear was his own fault. The smell of burning seal blubber . . . had attracted him from five miles away, as we later learned by studying his trail. On cutting him up, we saw that he had not been hungry. Had he the sense to study us from a distance of a hundred yards or even twenty five yards, we should not have fired at him. But we had seen him first only a few feet from our dogs and apparently hesitating only a moment before plunging in to swim the narrow water lane that separated them from him. We fired the first shot to protect our dogs, and the others merely to put a wounded animal out of its misery.

Like so many hunters before and after him, Stefansson believed that the polar bear was an extremely dangerous animal. He wrote,

> Among land animals the polar bears are the most powerful of all beasts of prey. When full-grown they may be three times as big as the biggest African lion. Their white color makes them difficult to see against a background of snow or ice, and few animals have more intelligence. It is important therefore that the hunter . . . shall understand their nature and habits thoroughly.

It is possible that Stefansson in fact completely *misunderstood* the nature and habits of the polar bear. Because the smell of cooking seal meat attracted the bear from a great distance, and even though the bear merely peered into the water "as if trying to make up his mind to plunge in and swim across," Stefansson read the bear's mind about what it intended, and shot it. He might have taught himself to think like an Eskimo, but unfortunately, he couldn't teach himself to think like a polar bear.

The first International Scientific Meeting on the Polar Bear, held in Fairbanks, Alaska, in 1965, was attended by delegates from all the polar bear nations. In his summary of the proceedings, Danish-born American biologist Vagn Flyger suggested a way of hunting polar bears that would be more sportsmanlike than shooting them on the ice or in the water. He wrote,

> The most exhilarating way to hunt is with a gun that fires a syringe filled with an immobilizing drug. With this weapon the animal is not killed, but merely drugged into unconsciousness for a short period. In contrast to hunting, where the excitement ends with the squeeze of the trigger, most of the fun here begins after the syringe-gun trigger is pulled . . . Catch-them-alive hunters could bring back photographs as evidence of their prowess, and at the same time, contribute to science by marking the bears with ear-tags before releasing them.

Because they believed that bringing home a trophy was the whole point of hunting, the bear hunters never adopted this method—but scientists did. Immobilizing bears to mark and measure them, and then outfitting them with radio collars, has become the standard operating procedure for scientists who study the lives of polar bears.

In 1966, with Martin Schein, Flyger overflew the pack ice off Point Barrow, Alaska, to put his suggestions into practice. In a small plane they followed bear tracks until the bear was spotted, and then landed well in front of it. From behind a pressure ridge, they shot the bears with a syringe filled with succinylcholine chloride, "which paralyzed the bear within a few minutes . . . The bears were examined, measured, and marked with ear tags and dye so they could be recognized if later seen." Flyger and Schein immobilized five bears, "but of these four died because of a combination of overdoses of the drug and circumstances connected with chasing the bears with aircraft." The following year, another expedition was mounted, this time in Svalbard. Four bears were shot from a seal-hunting boat, so they were not so heavily stressed, and a different drug—M99, a synthetic opiate—was used. All the bears were marked and released alive (Flyger 1967a).

Any confrontation with a wild polar bear has to be (correctly) interpreted as potentially perilous, but hindsight might enable one to put another spin on it. What if the bear was just attracted by cooking smells? What if the bear was just curious? In *New Scientist* for November 17, 2007, Alun Anderson interviewed Dixie Dansercoer, a Belgian explorer who had just completed a 1,200-mile walk from Siberia to Greenland:

Q. What do you fear?

A. A polar bear knocking at the door when you are asleep. We had two very intense confrontations with bears. When you meet these animals in their own habitat they do not hesitate to come very close. We carry Magnum .44 handguns but we have to scare them off without killing them.

Q. How did you deal with them?

A. On the first encounter, we were sitting on the sledge drinking our tea when suddenly a polar bear came running. He approached us from downwind, sniffing us out. He came on until he was 2 metres from us. We had a hard time in scaring him away. You have six bullets in the Magnum, so you know how many you can waste on just making a loud noise. The first one we fired in the air. But bears are used to moving ice and loud cracking sounds. The second one went near his paws to really make him feel the detonation. The third one was closer and had to be the one that scared him off. On the second encounter I awoke during the night; I'd sensed something in my sleep. We pitch the tent with the door facing downwind so it will face an approaching bear. I opened the door and there was a mother bear with two cubs. They walked toward the tent. Again we had to fire three shots before they left.

Obviously, there is no way of knowing what these particular bears had in mind, but there is nothing—no charge, no growl, no aggressive moves—that makes the events appear like anything but curiosity. As Downs Matthews wrote, "Aside from a fondness for sleep and a passion for eating, polar bears share a compelling curiosity about anything that

Curious bears investigating the nuclear submarine USS Honolulu, *which has just appeared in their icy world*

enters their hostile environment. Given the opportunity, a polar bear will find a way into any house, cache, or vehicle and having examined the contents, attempt to eat whatever he can get his teeth around." It is certainly possible that the curiosity that propelled the bear to investigate people in a tent could turn into a "desire to get his teeth around" whatever part of the person is available, thus initiating an "attack." The extent of polar bears' curiosity was demonstrated in October 2003, when the nuclear submarine USS *Honolulu* surfaced some 280 miles from the North Pole. As the sub's conning tower broke through the ice, a lookout spotted three polar bears near the part of the vessel that was visible. Although a house-sized object poking through the ice was something the bears had probably never seen before, they showed no fear, and casually ambled right up to it, seeming only mildly curious about the gigantic black thing that had suddenly appeared in their white world.

Early in 2008, a large polar bear wandered into the northwest Alaskan village of Noorvik, about forty-five miles east of Kotzebue. The bear disturbed the townspeople by noisily rooting around in the trash dump, and after several villagers followed its tracks and located it out of town, they decided to shoot it. The man who actually spotted the bear was a non-native, and could not shoot the bear under federal law, so he called Alaska Fish and Game and asked if his half-native son could kill it. He could, and did (Halpin 2008a). There are many villages and villagers (not to mention garbage dumps) in those parts of Alaska that border on the Chukchi or Beaufort seas, and are therefore well within polar bear territory, but to date, the number of "attacks" on people there is close to zero. Statistics notwithstanding—there can always be a first time—a hungry polar bear entering a village is considered a menace, and the villagers feel justified in killing it.

The myth that polar bears were, as James Clarke wrote, "the only animals in the world that count man as their natural prey" made conquering this man-eater an act of exceptional bravado for a man armed only with a high-powered rifle. Clarke wrote *Man Is the Prey*, in which he discussed assorted man-killing animals, including mosquitoes, spiders, birds, snakes, hyenas, elephants, rhinos, and many more. To justify the hunting of polar bears, he described them thus:

> *Thalarctos maritimus* [the bear's earlier name] is a monstrous animal: the great white bear can weigh more than half-a-ton—sometimes a great deal more—and in exceptional cases can rear up to 10 or 11 feet high, which is as high as an elephant. It can crush a man's skull with a single blow (and has done so on occasion) and each of its fur-soled forefeet weigh fifty pounds. Its claws are its main weapons for they are heavy and sharp but its teeth can inflict awful damage.

Peter Hathaway Capstick, who gave up a successful career as a Wall Street stockbroker to move to Africa and become a professional "white hunter" (his term), wrote a book called *Maneaters* in which he "explored the wide world of maneaters—creatures who regard *homo sapien* [sic] as just another meal ticket." No insects or birds for Capstick; he is only interested in those big, toothsome creatures that want to eat people. That includes sharks, lions, crocodiles, leopards, bears, wolves, hyenas, tigers, and, as a bit of an afterthought, cannibals. As he says, the polar bear "is the supreme predator of his world of the Arctic, matched with his physical characteristics as well as the very low population density of people in his range tally up to a most uninhibited general predator. By 'general' I mean that man is fair game." After dismissing shooting bears from the rail of a ship or the cabin of an airplane as "unsporting," Capstick tells us that

> the Barents Expedition in the late 16th Century recorded many attacks by polar bears and at least one witnessed case of a member of the company being eaten . . . Surely, polar bears in the wild run across precious few humans and fewer live to pass the information along. Plain curiosity may be the reason for such persistent digging-up of Eskimo graves, the bodies exhumed, not eaten. So, precisely why the white bear is a confirmed maneater may not be so important as just knowing that he is.

Wherever there are large, potentially dangerous mammals, there will be hunters ready to hunt them down and kill them.

Alaska Hunting Safaris is based in Wasilla, Alaska, but because it is the agent for two native village hunting corporations, it is able to offer polar bear hunting in Canada's Northwest Territories. The native villages are Tuktoyaktuk, in the Mackenzie River delta, and Sachs Harbour, the only settlement on Banks Island, a large, treeless, mostly snow-covered island in the Canadian archipelago. Alaska Hunting Safaris' Web site (www.polarbearhunting.net) informs you that

> this is, by far, the toughest hunt on earth and not for the weak at heart! Hunting the arctic pack ice by dog team and sled you can experience temperatures to minus 40°F with nothing between you and the elements but a canvas tent and the clothes on your back. But if you are a dedicated hunter, willing to endure the physical and mental challenges required, the reward can be the most prestigious of all trophies.

Prospective hunters are taken to Tuktoyaktuk, and then taken to the hunting site by snowmobile, but the actual hunting "must be done in the traditional manner with an Inuvialuit native guide and dog team." The Web site continues: "Polar Bear hunting is very rigorous. Only dedicated hunters in excellent physical condition should undertake this hunt. Hunters and guides camp on the ice pack and cover miles every day via dog sled. Hunters will ride, glass, and spend up to 12 hours a day searching for bears. Weather conditions are unpredictable and often severe." Sometimes a polar bear hunt turns up surprises.

On a fourteen-day safari on Banks Island in April 2006 that cost him close to $50,000,* Jim Martell of Salmon Springs, Idaho, shot the only grizzly–polar bear hybrid ever found in the wild. Martell's "polar grizz," now mounted and occupying a place of honor in his trophy room, was a dirty white color, with dark rings around its eyes, a slight hump on its shoulders, long brown claws, and a slightly indented profile. The DNA of the bear showed that it was indeed a hybrid and not a light-colored grizzly. Quoted by Alicia Wittmeyer in the *Santa Fe New Mexican* on January 21, 2007, Ian Stirling said, "It was not a case of—to use a very crude term—a one-night stand. They've had to interact socially and very intensely for a very extended period of time. That's what makes this so surprising. Grizzlies and polar bears obviously look different, you'd think they would recognize that they were dealing with a different kind of animal." The DNA analysis showed that the bear's mother was a polar bear and the father a grizzly. Polar and grizzly bears have been bred together in zoos, but in the wild they rarely cross paths. Canadian wildlife officials are now thinking up a name for the creature. Some of the suggestions they have come up with so far are "pizzly," "grolar bear," or "*nanulak*," after the Inuit names for polar bear *(nanuq)* and grizzly bear *(aklak)*.

Have you ever thought about hunting a polar bear with a bow and arrow? Pat Lefemine's Web site "Everything You Need to Know About Polar Bear Bow Hunting" will answer any questions you might have:

Q. Where can I go to bow hunt a polar bear?
A. Unlike Russia, Greenland, US (Alaska) and Norway, sport hunting for Polar Bear is only allowed in the farthest reaches of the Canadian Arctic—in what is now called Nunavut (formerly part of the Northwest Territories) and the Northwest Territories.
Q. How does one go about bow hunting a polar bear?
A. You and your guides will hit the ice every day in search of polar bears. You look for fresh tracks and begin to follow them. A lot of polar bear hunting is done by glassing long distances over the ice.

* Martell's invoice probably included a lot of extras. He did not go with Alaska Hunting Safaris, but assuming their prices are competitive, the fee for a fourteen-day hunt is $30,000, but to that one must add airfares, hotels, excess baggage, shipping of trophies, licenses and import fees, and the cost of whatever celebrations one chooses to add to the total for a successful hunt. (The full fee is charged whether a bear is killed or not; Alaska Hunting Safaris claims that in 2006 it took six bears for seven clients.)

Very often, a bear will simply wander into camp. Once a bear has been spotted, you will move in for a closer look. If it appears to be a large male, and you wish to take it, the dog team is cut loose and the team will hopefully bay the Polar Bear. You and your guide move in for a clean shot. The hunt is not without its risks. Many times the polar bear will be bayed, but as the hunter moves in the dogs may abandon the bear leaving you and your guide alone with the irritated boar. Also, a bear can seriously injure the dogs, or run right through them to get to the bowhunter. In all cases the Inuit guides are backing you up with a rifle.

Q. How much does it cost?

A. Actual hunt: $30,000; Airfare to Yellowknife: $800; Airfare to northern community: $1500; Northern Outfitter clothing: $2000; Tags, tips, hotel fees: $2000; USFWS importation fee: $1000; taxidermy fee (optional): $4000. Total: $41,300.

No matter how one shoots a polar bear, there are certain regulations that apply to the import of the trophy into the United States, since the bear is protected under the Marine Mammal Protection Act (MMPA) and the Convention on International Trade in Endangered Species of Wild Fauna and Flora (CITES). The International Agreement on the Conservation of Polar Bears allows sport hunting only in Canada, and then only in Nunavut and the Northwest Territories. The U.S. Fish & Wildlife Service defines a trophy as "parts that are traditionally considered to comprise a trophy, including the hide, skull, teeth, claws, baculum, other bones, rugs, and full mounts." (Articles such as clothing, curios, or jewelry cannot be imported or created from imported parts. Polar bear hides purchased in Canada or received as gifts cannot be imported.) Before the trophy can be imported, the hunter must obtain a CITES* export permit from the Canadian Management Authority

---

* CITES is an international agreement between governments, drafted as a result of a resolution adopted at a meeting of members of the World Conservation Union in 1963. Its aim is to ensure that international trade in specimens of wild animals and plants does not threaten their survival, and it accords varying degrees of protection to more than 33,000 species of animals and plants. Appendix II of the agreement lists some 32,500 species that are not necessarily threatened with extinction but may become so unless trade is subject to strict regulation. In practice, many hundreds of thousands of Appendix II animals are traded on an annual basis. No import permit is necessary for these species under CITES, but individual governments may impose import restrictions.

and a MMPA import permit from the U.S. Fish & Wildlife Service. Only native Greenlanders are allowed to hunt polar bears on their island; if a tourist buys a souvenir rug or skull in Greenland, a CITES certificate is required to take the products to any other CITES signatory country.

What happens to sport-hunted polar bears? A successful hunter with a big enough house (or trophy room) may have the bear mounted and stood in the corner, but most people don't have room for a ten-foot-tall bear in their house, so they might have a rug made out of the skin, or donate it to a local museum. There probably isn't a large natural history museum in the world that doesn't have a polar bear on the premises, often part of a diorama of the "Frozen North." In some circles, sport hunting is a competition, with hunters vying for the record antlers of a mule deer or moose, or the biggest mountain lion or grizzly bear. Under the direction of William T. Hornaday, the National Collection of Heads and Horns opened at the Bronx Zoo in 1922; the collection now belongs to the Boone and Crockett Club and is on display at

Diorama of a polar bear (with a ribbon seal) at the American Museum of Natural History in New York: the background has since been repainted.

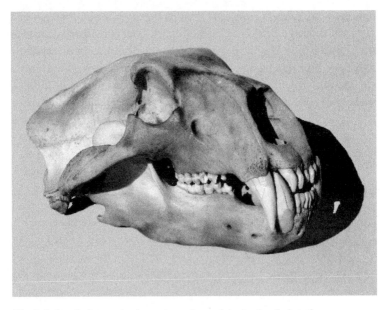

The skull of a polar bear: notice the massive canines and the shearing cheek-teeth

the Buffalo Bill Historical Center in Cody, Wyoming. Most of the collection consists of horned animals from North America—whitetails, mule deer, bighorn sheep, moose, elk, and caribou—but also houses the skull of a jaguar, a walrus, and a polar bear, shot by Shelby Longoria in Kotzebue, Alaska, in 1963. Bears don't have horns or antlers, of course, so the length of the skull determines the record, and the record polar bear measured eighteen and a half inches without the lower jaw. (The world's record grizzly skull was 17.8 inches.)

Sport hunting for polar bears is not permitted in U.S. territory. Because of a worldwide decline in their populations, as of January 1, 2008, the United States was preparing to list the polar bear as an endangered species. If this would curtail hunting, why do Canadians think the listing would be a very bad idea? In a December 29 article in the *Toronto Globe & Mail*, Brodie Fenlon wrote, "The most vociferous objections, apart from the burgeoning oil and gas industry, came from Canadians, including the government of Nunavut, the Inuvialuit Game Council, the president of an Ontario based travel company, and several other aboriginal agencies." If the polar bear is added to the Endangered

Species Act, American tourists, who pay up to $40,000 for a guided hunt in Nunavut, would not be allowed to import their trophies into the United States. Unless they were willing to display a photograph of a dead bear over the mantelpiece, the incentive for hunting the animals would vanish. (And the Inuit who guide the hunters would be denied a substantial part of their annual income—perhaps all of it.) With about 15,000 of the world's estimated total of 22,000 polar bears, Canada exemplifies our contradictory attitudes toward the white bear: do we love it enough to kill it, or do we love it enough to save it?

VII

In the Zoo and at the Circus

And now, for the first time in three decades, RINGLING BROS.
AND BARNUM AND BAILEY CIRCUS is featuring a "Comic Section" in its presentation of caged wild animal acts. Fancy-
footed, solemn-faced, funny white bears. They are nature's own
comedians. Her favorite jesters. Polar bears as big and white as
the biggest snowman you ever saw. These white monsters from
the Arctic have been reduced from a state of ferocity to intellec-
tual perfection by superb training.

Circus program, 1977

Because not everybody can get to see the bears of Churchill, let
alone Spitsbergen, Wrangel Island, or Nunavut, innumerable
movies and television programs have been made to show polar bears in
action. Still, the most impressive thing about polar bears, young or old,
is their powerful presence, and nothing can communicate this as well as
a real live bear. This is the entry for "The Polar Bear" in the 1907 *Popular Official Guide* to the New York Zoological Park (Bronx Zoo), written by William T. Hornaday, director and general curator:

In nearly every collection of living bears the individuals of this
species are the most showy and attractive. Their white coats quickly
catch the eye of the visitor, and whether young or old, they are gener-

The cover of the Ringling Brothers' circus program for 1977, dominated by polar bears

ally the most active and playful of all captive bears. In cold weather, when other bears lie in the sun, or, if permitted, curl up in the straw of their sleeping dens, the Polar Bear will disport himself in the freezing cold water of his swimming pool, and joyously play with a cake of ice until the sight of it makes one shiver.

The world's supply of captive Polar Bears comes almost wholly from whalers and sealers, who improve every opportunity to capture cubs. A great number thus find their way into the hands of Mr. Carl Hagenbeck, of Hamburg, who supplied the large specimen now exhibited. The grizzly bear of the United States will soon cease to exist, but not so with the Polar Bear. Thanks to the "Frost King," he needs no protection against man's propensity to exterminate all wild creatures. There will be hundreds of bears around the northern end of Franz Josef Land as long as the seals and walrus remain for them to feed upon.

Carl Hagenbeck, the father of the modern zoo

In the diary he kept from March 22 to December 26, 1866, Captain Gravill of the Hull whaler *Diana,* operating in the Davis Strait and Baffin Bay, reminisced about how they collected polar bear cubs:

Bears is very affectionate animals. I remember in 1860, when I had this ship, wee saw a she-bear and her cub on a piece of ice. I sent Clarke and Byers away after them, with orders to shoot the old bear and bring the young one aboard alive. Byers shot the old bear dead. The young one laid itself down on the body of the mother, and never took the least notice of the men. Well, they made the old bear fast to a rope and rowed away, towing the body. The young bear came to the edge of the ice, and when it saw its mother swimming away, it jumped in the water and followed close astern of her. When the boat was well clear of the ice, the man lay to and "snickled" the cub with a rope at the end of a boat-hook easy enough. They towed the dead bear alongside the ship, with the young one swimming after her without requiring to be dragged along by the rope . . . We took that young bear home and sold him for £12. I've known good ones to fetch £20. I suppose they are bought for the Zoological Gardens.

Carl Hagenbeck (1844–1913) was a German animal collector, dealer, and exhibitor who is considered the father of the modern zoo. His father, Gottfried, a Hamburg fishmonger, occasionally brought home exotic animals from the docks, and young Carl, reluctant to take over his father's business, chose to become an animal collector instead. He traveled the world with hunters to add to his menagerie, sometimes "collecting" people as well. In Hagenbeck's *Volkershauen* ("people shows") Zulus, Samoans, Nubians, Laplanders, and Eskimos performed their customary activities as part of the show, wearing their traditional dress (or lack thereof). However bizarre it seems today, exhibitions of these exotic "savages" were extremely popular in those pre-photography days.*

When his show arrived in America on April 16, 1883, the *New York Times* described "Mr. Carl Hagenbeck's Pursuit of Rare Beasts from All over the World":

Mr. Hagenbeck intends to stop in this country only a fortnight. He will visit Philadelphia, Washington, Chicago, St. Louis, Cincinnati, Buffalo, and Niagara Falls, see the various shows on exhibit along the route, sell them what they want, and buy from them what they do not need. Hagenbeck said to the reporter: "You think I am rather young to have so extensive a business? I am 38 years old and began when I was 15. My father was a large fish-dealer. The fishermen began to

---

* In 1904, Samuel Phillips Verner bought nine pygmies from a Congolese slave trader and took them to America to be exhibited in the "Anthropology Exhibit" at the St. Louis World's Fair. In 1906, Hermon Bumpus, director of the American Museum of Natural History in New York, took one of them, Ota Benga, gave him a place to sleep, and allowed him to roam the halls of the museum. Then socialite and amateur anthropologist Madison Grant, head of the New York Zoological Society, put the pygmy on display in the Monkey House at the Bronx Zoo. At the behest of Grant, an avowed racist, zoo director William Hornaday placed Ota Benga (who stood four foot eleven, and whose teeth had been filed to points) in a cage with an orangutan and labeled him "The Missing Link," illustrating that Africans were closer to apes than to Europeans. The *New York Times* (September 9, 1906) called it "the most interesting exhibit in Bronx Park," but there were so many protests that Ota Benga was released from the cage and allowed to roam the grounds of the zoo, as a sort of interactive exhibit. After he was removed from exhibition and put to work in a factory, he committed suicide, with a stolen pistol, in 1916.

catch seals alive and bring them to my father. Once someone sold him a polar bear, which he exhibited. That is how he came to look into the business."

When the show returned to New York in September 1894, the *Times* was again effusive in its praise:

Never since the time when Noah battened down his hatches, drew in his gangplank, and let the ark go adrift has there been seen such a well-behaved, quiet, willing, and obedient lot of animals from the jungles under one roof as are at present at Madison Square Garden . . . Their performances are most wonderful. Immense Siberian [polar] bears jump hurdles, pose on pedestals, and march and perform in other ways at the word of command . . . The lioness Helena is a famous equestrian, and by the manner in which she rides the horse Columbus, she shows that she is a great judge of pace.

Historically, Hagenbeck is regarded as a lover and savior of wildlife, but his "collectors" killed many more animals than they brought back alive. In *Savages and Beasts,* Nigel Rothfels's 2002 history of the Hagenbecks, we read that

Carl Hagenbeck did not become the leading animal dealer in the world simply because he loved animals. He became so because of his extraordinary business sense, the accelerating growth of a market for the animals, his location at one of the hubs of international exchange, his carefully nurtured contacts in the zoological and circus world, his desire to bypass the traditional lines of bringing animals to Europe by sending his own catchers into the field, and his plain hard work.

A zoo usually isn't mobile, but a circus is supposed to travel. With his younger brother Wilhelm, Hagenbeck combined the two concepts, and traveled his zoological collection around the world as if it were a circus. The Hagenbeck collection was a popular attraction in various European capitals, and returned to New York City in 1902. On October 5, the *Times* welcomed the collection with an article subtitled "Chorus Girls Stop Rehearsing and Get Information About Fierce Beasts and Polar Bears":

Two polar bears side by side, began to rock to and fro in unison, as polar bears do.

"Oh wouldn't he make a lovely set of furs—and a rug besides," a pretty girl cried, pointing to the biggest.

Two days later (October 7, 1902), the *Times* reported that

Carl Hagenbeck's assortment of trained animals performed last night before a large crowd of spectators at the New York Theatre . . . A novelty was an act introduced by Herman Boger. He brought in the iron-barred cage on the stage several varieties of wild beasts, all considered as natural enemies of each other, and before he ended grouped them together and laid on them while the two monster lions, mounted on either side, looked out at the audience through the gratings. The applause was vociferous, and the animals seemed to enjoy it, for they bowed to the audience and gave a roar of apparent delight.

Boger's group comprised the giant hybrid, half lion and half tiger; one Somali lion, one African lion, two Royal Bengal tigers, one Congo panther, one Indian leopard, two South American pumas, two polar bears, and four German boar hounds. Some sea lions he has taught to play ping-pong.

An eye of one of the polar bears was closed last night after fifteen minutes of constant chastisement in order to get him in a docile mood.

Wilhelm (aka Willy or William) was in charge of the Hagenbeck Circus, which also traveled throughout Europe. Hornaday wrote that

the most astounding animal group ever turned out of the Hagenbeck establishment . . . consisted of *75 full-grown polar bears!* Now, polar bears either for the cage or the stage, are bad citizens. Instinctively I always suspect their mental reservations and for twenty-one years have carefully kept our keepers out of their reach. But Mr. William Hagenbeck, brother of the great Carl, actually trained and performed with a huge *herd* of dangerous polar bears . . . they were taught to form pyramids, shoot the chutes, ride in pony carriages, draw and ride in sleds, drink from bottles, and ride a see-saw . . . The star per-

A 1922 poster for Ringling Brothers' Circus

former was Monk, the wrestling bear, who went with his trainer through a fearsome wrestling performance.

In *Beasts and Men,* Carl Hagenbeck described his brother as "one of the early pioneers of modern methods and by his long experience become a past-master in the art of training wild beasts. Nearly all the troupes which he now exhibits have been collected and broken in by himself, though of late years he has received some assistance from his son." Wilhelm was the first to introduce troupes of polar bears into the circus. Before his time it was held that the bears were untrainable; and to him belongs the credit of showing the error of this view. According to Hornaday, William Hagenbeck "found the polar bear a most awkward beast to train. In the first place its character is difficult to understand. He is by nature very suspicious, and without the least warning is apt to turn on his trainer. Among the seventy bears that have been taught to do tricks, *only two* of them are really fond of their work." When the explorer Roald Amundsen saw the polar bear act, he was so impressed that he asked Hagenbeck if he could train the bears to pull a large sled. Of course, said Hagenbeck, and in nine weeks, twenty-one

A polar bear towers over the diminutive Ursula Böttcher

bears were trained and ready to work in the north as a team. But when neither Hagenbeck nor the bears' keeper, Reuben Castang, was willing to go on polar expeditions, the idea was abandoned.

The sled-pulling bears were eventually sold to Ursula Böttcher, an animal trainer whose polar bear act was featured in several circuses in Europe and Ringling Brothers in the United States. Only five feet tall, Ursula ("bear" in German) would work in a cage in the center ring as ten adult polar bears performed their tricks with a ponderous, teddy-bear charm. Ursula Bottcher—whose name lost the umlaut when she made her American debut at Ringling Bros. and Barnum & Bailey Circus in 1977—was described in the program for that year as the

winner of a Circus Oscar in 1973 . . . began as an usher in a German circus, and worked her way into animal training . . . She progressed from lions and tigers to polar bears, usually considered as the most dangerous of all beasts because of their strength, speed, size, and expressionless faces that give no indication of an impending attack . . .

The "Northern Panorama" at Hagenbeck's Hamburg Tierpark: the reindeer are on the plateau to the left and the bears on the "ice"-bedecked rocks to the right of center. The seals are out of sight in a foreground moat.

She has no delusions about their relationship. "If I gave them the chance, they would eat me." (Fox 1977)

Ursula was attacked only once during her act, when a female bear named Nixe knocked her down and began biting her on the neck and shoulders. Bottcher pushed the bear off, and continued the act. "I had to do the trick again," she said. "I had to dance with her right away. If I didn't then she would have known she was stronger than I" (Davids 1982). By and large, polar bears were rarely used in "animal-trainer" acts because they neither roar nor look particularly threatening; it is possible for the audience to see them as oversize plush toys rather than dangerous man-eaters.

Although there was already a zoo in Hamburg, Hagenbeck constructed a new facility outside the city, which he called Tierpark Hagenbeck. Of his concept for the zoo at Stellingen, he wrote,

> I desired above all things, to give the animals the maximum of liberty. I wished to exhibit them not as captives, confined within narrow

spaces, and looked at between bars, but as free to wander from place to place within as large limits as possible, and with no bars to obstruct the view and serve as a reminder of captivity. I wished also to show what could be accomplished in the way of acclimatization. I desired to refute the prevailing notion that luxurious and expensive houses with complicated heating apparatus were necessary for keeping wild animals alive and healthy. I hoped to show that far better results could be obtained when they were kept in the fresh air and allowed to grow accustomed to the climate.

True to his principles, Hagenbeck invented the "panorama" exhibit, the first attempt to exhibit zoo animals in an approximation of their natural surroundings. In the foreground of the "Northern Panorama," for instance, there was a pool for seals and walruses, and behind that, a moat hidden from sight. Beyond the moat were the reindeer, and beyond a second hidden moat were the polar bears. Successive enclosures were higher than those in front of them, so by hiding the moats, the animals appeared to be together in a single landscape.* Hagenbeck's designs were employed at the St. Louis World's Fair in 1904, "where the exhibits are said to have featured a polar bear, a walrus, and an Eskimo" (Coe 1986), and at the Rome Zoo in 1911. "The ideas of Carl Hagenbeck," said European zoo historian Harro Strehlow, "had started to change the design and animal maintenance systems of the zoo world."

It took some time for those ideas to cross the Atlantic. "American zoo directors remained cautious about constructing moated displays in their own zoos," wrote Elizabeth Hanson in *Animal Attractions* (2002). "William Hornaday was dead set against them. In his opinion, the educational value of the zoo decreased in direct proportion to the increase in distance between animal and viewer. Hagenbeck tried to persuade Hornaday to build a moated bear display, but Hornaday found that it

* In *Animal Gardens,* her 1967 book about zoos, Emily Hahn described her impressions of the polar exhibit: "Polar bears walked around a rocky hillside, and just as we got there, one dived into the water beneath. It all looked craggy and very cold. To the left, in what I would have sworn was the same water, seals were diving after fish a keeper threw for them. And at this point, in spite of my resolution earlier in the day, I blotted my copy book and was caught. Earnestly I said, 'But you can't keep those animals all together in one place, Mr. Hagenbeck! [Carl-Heinrich, the original Hagenbeck's grandson]. Don't the bears eat the seals?' He smiled triumphantly. 'Of course they would if they could get across, but they can't. Clever isn't it?' "

Polar bear in the Alaska Zoo (Anchorage)

would push the animals so far away from the visitors that fully one half of their potential educational value would be lost. In the 1920s he tried to persuade other zoo directors to protest the 'Hagenbeckization' of American zoos." (In later years, of course, the Bronx Zoo would become renowned for its "moated" or panoramic exhibits, beginning with the 1941 "African Plains," where antelope and zebras graze unconcernedly, separated from the lions by an invisible moat.)

In his time, Hornaday was regarded as America's foremost authority on zoos and zookeeping. He was named director of the New York Zoological Society in 1896, and as founder and president of the American Bison Society from 1907 to 1910 was instrumental in saving the "buffalo," which by the turn of the century had been slaughtered into near nonexistence. Hornaday's reputation was somewhat tarnished by his participation in the unfortunate Ota Benga affair, but he is now regarded as one of the few professionals in America who cared as much as Carl Hagenbeck about the well-being of the animals in his charge. Here is the epigraph for his 1923 book, *The Minds and Manners of Wild Animals:*

If every man devoted to his affairs, and to the affairs of his city and state, the same measure of intelligence and honest industry that every warm-blooded wild animal devoted to its affairs, the people of this world would abound in good health, prosperity, peace and happiness.

To assume that every wild beast and bird is a sacred creature, peacefully dwelling in an earthly paradise, is a mistake. They have their wisdom and their folly, their joys and their sorrows, their trials and tribulations.

As the alleged lord of creation, it is man's duty to know the wild animals truly as they are in order to enjoy them to the utmost, to utilize them sensibly and fairly, and to give them a square deal.

In 1907, the "lords of creation" at the Bronx Zoo gave their polar bears a literally square deal: they kept them in cages. Two male bears had been purchased from Carl Hagenbeck some seven years earlier, and when one of them died, Hornaday bought a female, and introduced her into the cage of the large male. Immediately the big male attacked the little female. Hornaday reported later that he and the keepers "beat him over the head; we drove big steel spikes into him, we rammed him with planks, not caring how many bones we might break. But each time that we beat him off, and the poor harried female rose to her feet, he flung himself on her anew, crushed her down against the snow, and fought to reach her throat!" The he-bear dragged the female away from the bars where the men were beating him, took the female into the center of the cage, and killed her. Hornaday, who had earlier written that "polar bears in captivity are courageous, treacherous, and dangerous," now wrote, "It is my belief that at first the male did not intend to murder the female. I think his first impulse was to play with her, as he had always done with the male comrade of his own size. But the *joy of combat* seized him, and after that his only purpose was to kill. My verdict was, not premeditated murder, but murder in the second degree."

The word *menagerie* (from the French *ménage,* a domestic establishment or a sexual relationship) is popularly used to refer to a collection of wild animals, usually maintained for the pleasure of the owner. After the Middle Ages, menageries were maintained by popes, bishops, sovereigns, and wealthy patricians, some of whom collected and traded animals like postage stamps. The more exotic the animal, the more desirable it was for a private menagerie. Some of the more exotic animals, like elephants, rhinos, and giraffes, were traveled around Europe in an oxymoronic one-animal menagerie. An Indian rhinoceros nicknamed "Clara" toured Europe from 1741 to 1758, visiting Paris, Berlin, Rome, Naples, Venice (where her famous portrait was painted by Pietro Longhi), and London. Until Clara's Grand Tour, the only rhinoceros most people knew was Dürer's 1515 engraving, and he had never seen a rhino—he worked from secondhand descriptions.

Successor to Hagenbeck's traveling zoo-cum-circus was the circus that traveled with a menagerie, which consisted of a collection of exotic animals, permanently incarcerated in cages, and usually positioned close to the freak show. In this zoo on wheels, one might find baboons, giraffes, rhinos, hippos, zebras, and other animals that were not expected to perform—they just had to look exotic or dangerous. The most famous of these nonperformers was Gargantua, a gorilla that had been captured in Africa and first exhibited by Ringling Brothers and Barnum & Bailey in 1938. His face was twisted into what was perceived as a horrid snarl, but was actually the result of acid that had been thrown in his face by a crewman aboard the ship that brought him to America. Ringling Brothers billed him as "The Most Terrifying Creature in the World," and when he appeared on circus posters, he was usually shown with a scantily clad woman in his hand—à la *King Kong*. As we've seen, polar bears sometimes attack people, but they are not particularly scary (unless you're a seal). Until fairly recently, polar bears were regarded as curiosities—white where most bears are dark, envoys from an unknown world of ice. No zoo was considered complete unless it exhibited a polar bear.

There are five boroughs that comprise New York City, and each one has its own zoo: the Staten Island Zoo; the Prospect Park Zoo, in Brooklyn; the Central Park Zoo, in Manhattan; the Queens Zoo; and the Bronx Zoo. Three of these (Queens, Prospect Park, and the Bronx) are operated under the aegis of the Wildlife Conservation Society, as is the New York Aquarium at Coney Island. The Bronx and Central Park zoos exhibit polar bears. A census assembled by the conservation group Polar Bears International (www.polarbearsinternational.org) lists 245 in zoos around the world, from Singapore to San Diego, Denmark to Denver. The number is probably much higher—the PBI figure comes from zoos that responded to their inquiries. Conditions differ widely from zoo to zoo; some, like SeaWorld in Florida, have created a facsimile of the Arctic environment, while others put the bears in nasty barred cages with concrete floors. The Novosibirskii Zoopark in Siberia does not have much of a problem approximating the polar bear's natural environment, but the hot, tropical climate of Singapore has caused algae to grow in the hollow hairs of its two bears, turning them green. If polar bears in captivity do not get the high fat content of the seals they normally eat in the wild, they may become fat, lose muscle tone, and even experience hair loss, which, because the bear's skin is black under its white coat, gives the bear an unattractive, blotchy appearance. The Philadelphia Zoo feeds its bears (Klondike and Coldilox) fish, apples, raisins, peanut butter, honey, and dehydrated fruit, and they are also given beef bones to gnaw on.

Mazuri, a subsidiary of Purina Mills, manufactures special diets for zoo animals, such as Elephant Supplement, Llama Crumbles, Marmoset Jelly, Ferret Diet, Kangaroo/Wallaby Diet, and so on. It also makes Polar Bear Diet, "formulated to feed as [the] sole source of the diet for polar bears . . . animals can be fed approximately 2 pounds of Mazuri Polar Bear Diet per 100 pounds of body weight." It contains:

ground corn, fish meal, porcine meat meal, porcine animal fat preserved with BHA, dehulled soybean meal, corn gluten meal, dried beet pulp, ground soybean hulls, salt, taurine, soybean oil, pyridoxine hydrochloride, choline chloride, chole-calciferol (vitamin D3), menadione dimethylpyrimidinol bisulfite (vitamin K), dl-alpha tocopheryl acetate (vitamin E), vitamin A acetate, calcium pantothenate, biotin, zinc oxide, ethoxyquin (a preservative), nicotinic acid, thiamin mononitrate, riboflavin, folic acid, cyanocobalamin (vitamin B2), manganous oxide, ferrous carbonate, copper sulfate, zinc sulfate, calcium iodate, calcium carbonate, cobalt carbonate, and sodium selenite.

At a 2004 conference on polar bear husbandry, Else Poulsen, head zookeeper of the "Arctic Ring of Life" exhibit at the Detroit Zoo, gave a presentation entitled, "Captive Polar Bear Diets: What Are We Doing?" She said, "Currently zoos in the captive community do not agree on what to feed polar bears. What we do seem to agree on is a lack of confidence in our diet plans." Like many captive polar bears, those at the Detroit Zoo gain a lot of weight in the summer, "followed by an extensive appetite loss and weight free-fall for 6–8 months throughout the fall and winter." The summer weight gain renders the bears listless, and during the summer months, when zoo attendance is highest, they spend most of their time lying motionless or lolling in warm, stagnant pools. Wild polar bears usually experience weight loss in the summer, and during this period, some even become vegetarian (Derocher et al. 1993). During the fall, when they hunt seals on the ice, they put the weight back on; they also improve their muscle tone by their constant movement and hunting, not to mention the complete change in diet to seal fat and meat. Paulsen concluded,

> Polar bears are highly specialized feeders. Adults feed largely on seal blubber and skin, and subadults and females with young feed on the muscle meats left behind on a seal carcass. In the zoo community, we have capitalized on the fact that superficially polar bears appear to be adaptable omnivores . . . yet we house polar bears without considering feeding them legal sources of seal meat, blubber and skin . . . Behavior-based husbandry dictates that we at least consider the option of obtaining legal sources of seal product and offering it to our bears.

The only way for a bear in a zoo to express its dissatisfaction with its diet is to refuse to eat what it's offered, and such behavior will obviously result in even more health problems. Regardless of their diet, polar bears in zoos can live more than forty years, far longer than a wild bear. But increased longevity notwithstanding, there are times when keeping polar bears in zoos just doesn't seem like a very good idea.

William Hornaday truly believed that he had a special insight into the behavior of animals, and in his book he had a go at psychoanalyzing a polar bear named Silver King. "At this moment," he wrote,

> we have a huge polar bear who refuses to forget that he was captured in the water, at Kane Basin, and who now avoids the water in his swimming pool almost as much as any burned child dreads fire. Through-out the hottest months of midsummer old Silver King lies on the rock floor of his huge and handsome den, grouching and grumbling, not more than once a week enjoying a swim in his spacious pool . . . Evidently the chase of Silver King through green arc-

tic water and over ice floes, mile after mile, his final lassoing, and the drag behind a motor boat to the ship were, to old Silver King, a terrible tragedy. Now he regards all deep water as a trap to catch bears, but strange to relate, the winter's snow and ice seem to renew his interest in the swimming pool.

The tragedy, dear Hornaday, is not in our bears, but in ourselves. Poor old Silver King, traumatized by his chase and capture, not to mention his transportation from Arctic Canada to the Bronx in a boxcar, obviously preferred a cool rock floor in the midsummer heat to a dip in a tepid (and probably filthy) pool. Wrenched from his environment and placed in alien and discomforting circumstances, the real surprise was that he didn't decide to attack William Hornaday, the man who was responsible for putting him there in the first place.

As Carl Hagenbeck realized a century ago, exhibiting large animals in small cages is bad for the animals and worse for communicating to the public their true nature. There are some species that are wide-ranging by nature and necessity, so keeping them penned up in cages or enclosures will be detrimental to their health and well-being. In a study published in *Nature* in 2003, Oxford University scientists Ros Clubb and Georgia Mason wrote, "Some species—ring-tailed lemurs and snow leopards, for example—apparently thrive in captivity, while others, such as elephants and polar bears, are prone to problems that include poor health, repetitive stereotypical behavior and breeding difficulties." Gus, the polar bear who lives in the Central Park Zoo, spent most of his time swimming in circles in the pool in his enclosure, which was redesigned in 1998 to include a gravel pit for digging and a snowbank. His actions were described by John Kifner (*New York Times* 1994) as "swimming in a tight little figure 8, gracefully pushing off his artificial rock pile with a huge hind paw, languorously backstroking, then turning a neat diving flip by the underwater window. Over and over and over." Of all captive large carnivores, polar bears are most likely to adopt repetitive behaviors when they are in small enclosures. Clubb and Mason pointed out that brown bears, with a typical home range far smaller than that of a polar bear, do not pace nearly as much as polar bears. They wrote, "a polar bear's typical enclosure size is about one-millionth of its minimum home range size," so any artificial enclosure will automatically be too small. Animals that need a lot of land (or ice,

In his swimming pool, Gus demonstrates that polar bears are pigeon-toed swimmers as well as pigeon-toed walkers.

in the case of polar bears) are often the hardest to conserve in the wild, and may be the most vulnerable in captivity. One solution, say Clubb and Mason, is to "stop housing large carnivores and concentrate instead on species that respond better to being kept in captivity." Unfortunately, all zoos want to feature bears, lions, and tigers; they aren't going to be willing to just include small mammals and colorful birds, no matter how interesting. So they have to find ways to improve the way the large carnivores are exhibited.

New York seems an odd place for polar bear attacks, but the city has had its share—all in zoos, of course. In 1922, at the old Central Park Zoo, a thirteen-year-old boy was trying to feed a peanut to a polar bear by poking it through the wire screen around the cage, when the bear chewed off half of his finger. Sixty years later, in September 1982, at the same zoo, a homeless Cuban immigrant identified as Conrado Mones was killed by a bear named Scandy after the man scaled three fences to get into the bear's pen. It was reported that Mones had been escorted from the zoo several times earlier because he kept trying to climb into the enclosures of other animals. There were no witnesses to the attack, so we will never know what actually happened, but zoo officials said that the cage was designed to keep people out and bears in—so the man couldn't have gotten out, however he managed to get in. The body was discovered lying in a pool of water at seven a.m. when guards made their morning rounds; Scandy was standing by quietly (Shipp 1982).

Five years later, at Brooklyn's Prospect Park Zoo, three boys climbed a fence outside the zoo and climbed into the polar bear enclosure. It was May 21, 1987, warm enough for them to think that a dip in the bear's two-foot-deep moat would be a cool idea. Eleven-year-old Juan Perez removed his pants and shoes, threw them over the spiked fence, and then waded into the moat. Two bears, named Teddy and Lucy, evidently disturbed by the commotion, came out of their den and clambered down to the moat. While one of them grabbed Perez, the other tried to pull the body away. Perez was dead by the time the guards arrived and shot both bears with a twelve-gauge shotgun and a .38 caliber pistol (Rangel 1987).*

Why captive bears attack people is not known. That the bear's "territory" was invaded seems to be the most popular explanation, but polar bears are not particularly territorial animals. Bears in zoos rarely go hungry (even if they have to eat fish and carrots instead of seal meat), so they probably don't intend to eat their victims. It might be that bears in cages or enclosures, having already been deprived of their customary surroundings, develop aberrant behavior patterns, including pacing, swimming in circles—and attacking.† In the wild and in captivity, man-

---

* There are polar bears in many American zoos, and there are probably stories from every one. At the Alaska Zoo at Anchorage, an adult male named Binky became famous for biting zoo visitors. In 1994, an Australian tourist named Kathryn Warburton climbed over the safety rails to get a close-up photograph and was bitten on the leg. Binky kept her shoe for three days before it could be retrieved by zoo officials. Six weeks later, a local teenager who apparently hoped to swim in Binky's pool was mauled when he got too close to the bear's cage. After these attacks, Binky became an Anchorage celebrity. Merchandise was sold, including T-shirts, mugs, and bumper stickers, often adorned with the iconic shoe photo or with the slogan "Send another tourist, this one got away."

† Probably the most celebrated case of a "tamed" animal attacking its handler occurred in Las Vegas on October 5, 2003. Onstage at the Mirage hotel, Roy Horn (the "Roy" of Siegfried and Roy) was attempting to pull one of their white tigers, Montecore, forward with a leash; when Montecore wouldn't come, Roy whacked him on the head with his microphone. The 600-pound cat then grabbed Roy's arm; when the tiger wouldn't release him, Roy hit him on the head again. This evidently angered the tiger to the point where it grabbed Roy by the neck and nearly killed him, picking him up and dragging him off, just as it would do with a prey animal. Three weeks later, Roy was taken off the critical list in a Las Vegas hospital, the tiger was in isolation, and Siegfried and Roy's show was canceled indefinitely.

killing polar bears are in the vast minority, and indeed, there are many bears in zoos that have developed a bond with their keepers, allowing the men (or women) into their cages and enclosures to play with them, the very opposite of attacking. There have even been some polar bears that—with the help of the media—were beloved by everyone who came into contact with them and just about everybody who saw them.

While a zoo may not be the best place for a polar bear, it is better than the Suarez Brothers Circus. Based in Guadalajara, Mexico, this poor excuse for a circus traveled throughout Central America, Mexico, and the southern United States. Included in its menagerie were seven polar bears, whose origins were cloudy at best. One was said to have come from the Atlanta Zoo, but administrators there said that its bear had died in Germany in 1994. Three others were from Churchill, but officials in Manitoba said they didn't know how some of their bears ended up in a Mexican circus. In June 2001, the U.S. Department of Agriculture cited Suarez "for failure to provide minimum space or access to a pool of water, failure to maintain suitable temperatures, and failure to provide veterinary care for sick bears." (In 1998, a Suarez bear named Yiopa died in Mexico of untreated dirofilariasis, a heartworm infection.) A videotape taken by PETA in Puerto Rico in July 2001 showed that the bears were repeatedly hit in the face with a stick or whip to make them perform. In Puerto Rico on August 16, when rangers found bears living in cages with excessive accumulation of feces, without access to water or shade in 113-degree heat for twenty-four hours, Suarez was charged with two counts of cruelty to animals. According to an animal control officer, "All were with their tongues hanging out, breathing really hard."

On August 30, 2001, Canadian singer Sarah McLachlan urged the USDA to seize the Suarez bears, and wrote, "It is heartbreaking to see these beautiful bears, regarded in Canada as a natural treasure, belittled and mistreated by the owners of a traveling show, who only seek to profit from their misery." Pedro Nunez, a Puerto Rican veterinarian, observed "bears caged individually in spaces too small for their size . . . They didn't have access to a pool and you could see that some bottles of water were dirty with tomato, lettuce and carrot. A large quantity of bloody diarrhea, with lots of mucus, was draining from one of the cages, accumulating on the floor" (Roberts 2004a). The U.S. Marine Mammal Commission attempted to intervene, but the Fish &

Wildlife Service allowed Suarez to keep the bears in transit facilities without access to water or cool air. After discovering that Suarez had filed false documents for a bear named Alaska, Fish & Wildlife confiscated the bear and shipped her off to the Baltimore Zoo (providing much-needed company for its formerly solitary male, Magnet). Citing violations of the Marine Mammal Protection Act, the other six bears—known as the "Suarez Six"—were confiscated shortly thereafter.

On March 12, 2002, Congressman Earl Blumenauer of Oregon and thirty-eight of his colleagues in the House of Representatives introduced the Polar Bear Protection Act of 2002, "to make sure that the other six [Suarez] bears are not forgotten and that polar bears will not suffer like this in the future." The legislation prohibits anyone from knowingly making "available any polar bear for use in a traveling show or circus." Blumenauer said, "The bottom line is that the circus is just not an appropriate place for a polar bear. We have the power to stop this outrage, end the cruelty and prohibit future mistreatment of these amazing animals." Homes were found for all of the Suarez bears, but Royale, who was already debilitated, died on the FedEx flight from Puerto Rico to Memphis. (FedEx transported the bears at no cost to the recipient zoos.) Wilhelm and Masha went to the North Carolina Zoological Park; Kenneth and Boris to the Port Defiance Zoo in Tacoma, Washington; and Barle to the Detroit Zoo. In Detroit, after mating with a male named Triton, Barle gave birth in 2005 to a healthy cub, Talani. Masha was euthanized in June 2007, after exploratory surgery revealed gastric ulcers, bladder and kidney infections, pneumonia, and other physical problems.*

Until the Suarez Brothers, polar bear acts in circuses had been largely discontinued. The white bears were usually part of the menagerie—if the concept of a menagerie hadn't also been discontinued—and relegated to curio status: a (usually dirty) big white bear that sat quietly in a cage or, if there was enough room, paced incessantly. Here, Paul Rodgers describes his 2006 visit to the Edinburgh Zoo:

---

* This account is drawn from several Web sites, including those put up by PETA (People for the Ethical Treatment of Animals), HSUS (the Humane Society of the United States), and AWI (the Animal Welfare Institute), in addition to many contemporaneous newspaper articles. I have woven together details from these accounts to make a coherent story, but there is no way of confirming every date, fact, or quote.

Mercedes, the only captive polar bear in Britain, is lying on her back, playing with a broken elderberry branch in her enclosure next to the pygmy hippos. The yellowing fur on her belly is thinner than on her back, so this posture is cooler in the 22°C sunshine [71.5°F] at Edinburgh Zoo. It's still too hot for her usual, abnormal behaviour—walking in a tight circle next to three heavy logs in her pen. Perhaps later she'll practice her other unnatural activity, repetitively swimming laps in the shallow, stagnant, algae-clogged moat.

Nowadays there has been a dramatic change in the way zoos are designed and built; it is no longer considered satisfactory to stick the animal in a cage and let people gawk at it. In many cases, the iron-barred cages have been replaced by open areas landscaped to resemble the animal's natural habitat, presumably with something, such as a moat or a fence, that will keep the animals in and the public out. Almost by definition, the zoo has become an educational and conservation institution, emphasizing the life and status of the animal in the wild. In a 1993 *National Geographic* article by Cliff Tarpy on the zoo's role in today's world, a zoo director was quoted as saying, "Twenty-five years ago, a zoo was rated on how many species it had in its collection. The thought that species were going to become extinct had not penetrated. The idea of conservation is, by and large, new stuff."

George Schaller, a renowned field biologist affiliated with the Wildlife Conservation Society, is quoted in Tarpy's article: "Zoos have no validity nowadays, no purpose, except to help protect and raise endangered animals and to raise public consciousness about the plight of wildlife. Zoos need to get outside their own walls more often and put more effort into saving the animals in the wild." But William Conway, in 1993 the director of the WCS and overseer of the five New York City zoos, argued passionately for the validity of the concept: "At a zoo or conservation park, you do not confront a photograph or a video. You confront the living, breathing animal. There is an immediacy of enormous value and importance. It's something that cannot be Xeroxed. The power of that confrontation—as concerns our feeling about wildlife and our struggle to preserve it—cannot be gainsaid, ever." (Just as there can be no self-respecting zoo without polar bears, there can be no self-respecting article about zoos without polar bears. In Tarpy's article, there is a full-page photograph of three polar bears in the Central Park Zoo—with the Manhattan skyline in the background—with the caption: "Snowflakes and polar bears paint an arctic tableau at the renovated Central Park Zoo.")

Some years ago, the Bronx Zoo (officially the New York Zoological Park) tried to change its name to the Wildlife Conservation Center, but because everybody continued to call it the "Bronx Zoo" anyway, the name-change idea was dropped. By this time, concern for the zoo animals' welfare has taken precedence over the idea that they were put here to amuse us. Some animals adjust to limited space, but others require open areas in which to walk, climb, run, fly, swim, or breed. In their 2003 study, Clubb and Mason specifically identified polar bears and elephants as animals prone to substantial problems in captivity. It is obviously impossible to replicate even a small portion of the polar bear's natural habitat; nature has spent millions of years combining ice, snow, rock, land, and water to create the perfect environment for the bear. You cannot build a polar bear enclosure that incorporates thousands of square miles of open ice fields, so if people are going to see live polar bears (anywhere but Churchill), they might have to go to the zoo.

The Milwaukee Zoo was the first to raise to maturity polar bear cubs

Gus and Ida at the Central Park Zoo, New York City

Brumas, the first polar bear cub to captivate a nation

born in captivity. In 1912, four young bears captured by a fishing vessel off Greenland were brought to an animal dealer in New York and purchased by the Washington Park Zoological Society in Milwaukee. Two of these, Sultana and Silver King, mated and produced eleven cubs, among them three sets of twins. Sultana II, born on December 10, 1931, followed in her mother's footsteps and produced three healthy cubs from 1944 to 1948, when George Speidel, the zoo's director, published "Milwaukee's Polar Bears" in the journal *Parks & Recreation:* "Even though Sultana II herself was born in captivity," he wrote, "her cubs are taught to swim, dive for fish, and attain other proficiencies that she feels are necessary to promote interesting living. This, of course, includes begging for peanuts and other tid-bits. She is fortunately endowed with exceptional maternal qualifications in rearing her cubs to great physical development."

At the London Zoo in November 1949, a cub was born to a female named Ivy and a male named Mischa. The newborn cub was named Brumas after her keepers Bruce Smith and Sam Giddins. (Why didn't they just name her Brusam?) The first polar bear to be successfully reared in Britain, Brumas was an immediate sensation with the public, and in those pre-television days, people flocked to the zoo to get a glimpse of the baby bear. In 1950 the zoo's attendance rose to three million, roughly a million more than had been recorded for any previous year. The bear's popularity was explained in a souvenir booklet published by the *Daily Graphic:* "Brumas is an ideal and an affection, like Father Christmas. She stands for kindness to animals; she stands for the love of pets . . . Brumas is the spirit of gentleness and fondness." Brumas lived for nine years at the zoo, and generated an avalanche of newsreels, books, postcards, and toys, demonstrating the enormous drawing power of the polar bear—even after it has outgrown the "cute" phase.

On November 6, 1994, two polar bear cubs—subsequently named Klondike and Snow—were born to a female named Ulu at the Denver Zoo. When the cubs were abandoned by their mother, zookeepers found the two tiny babies nearly frozen on the floor of the cage.* Given only a fifty-fifty chance of survival, the cubs were fed with eyedroppers and swaddled in warm towels. At first Klondike's belly swelled up like a balloon because he was unable to digest the man-made formula; then Snow developed rickets, dragging one leg behind her. The drama of the two baby bears was played out on Denver television, then fed to TV stations nationwide, resulting in the video *Saving Klondike and Snow,* which sold 90,000 copies in three months. Attendance at the Denver Zoo doubled during the period that the little bears were on exhibit, and the zoo made more than $320,000 in royalties from the sale of plush replicas, oven mitts, baby bibs, napkins, bicycle bottles, and coloring books (Brooke 1995). When they were a year old, the bears had grown to weigh about 300 pounds each, and when Denver Zoo officials conceded that their "Northern Shores" exhibit wasn't large enough for two adolescent polar bears, they were transferred to SeaWorld of Orlando's "Base Station Wild Arctic" attraction. More than a mere zoo exhibit,

---

* We have no way of knowing how many cubs are abandoned by their mothers in the wild, but it happens often in zoos. Polar bear mothers are the very essence of protective motherhood, so abandoning a cub might be another unfortunate function of captivity, like pacing or swimming in circles. An abandoned baby—especially one as adorable as a polar bear cub—tugs at the heartstrings and goes a long way to accounting for the remarkable popularity of the little white bears in captivity.

Souvenir book about the Denver Zoo's hand-reared polar bear cubs

"Wild Arctic" is an adventure ride where visitors take a simulated heli-copter ride through a snowstorm, and then get to see Arctic wildlife, including walruses, harbor seals, beluga whales—and now, Klondike and Snow.

Klondike and Snow never made the cover of *Vanity Fair*—but Knut did. Born in December 2006 to an ex–circus bear named Tosca (part of Ursula Böttcher's troupe), who had been impregnated at the Berlin Zoo by a male named Lars, Knut and his twin sister, who later died, were abandoned on a rock in the polar bear enclosure. Keeper Thomas Dörflein bottle-fed little Knut around the clock for the first four months, and on March 23, 2006, the bear made his first public appearance. Some 400 journalists showed up on "Knut Day." As the cub began appearing in public, Knutmania escalated throughout Germany and subsequently spread across Europe. Naturally, the adorable little bear spawned an industry of gift items, from toys to DVDs, and Steiff, the

German company that made the first teddy bears, turned out several plush versions of Knut, one of which was sold exclusively at the Berlin Zoo. Knut is estimated to be the biggest cash-grossing animal of all time. The German *Vanity Fair* had Knut on the cover in March 2007, and two months later, Leonardo DiCaprio was pictured with Knut for the American edition.*

An animal rights activist named Frank Albrecht was quoted in the German magazine *Bild* as saying that Knut should have been killed rather than suffer the humiliation of being raised as a domestic pet. The Albrecht controversy only served to fuel the already roaring blaze of Knut's publicity and, if possible, enhanced even more the public's perception of the little white bear as a cuddly and defenseless creature. Even when he was a year old, and had ceased to be quite so adorable, Knut was still the main attraction at the Berlin Zoo. His first birthday party, held on December 5, 2007, was an event of national significance. The federal mint produced 25,000 commemorative silver Knut coins. In an article headlined "Germans Go Nuts Over Knut as Zoo Marks Bear's Birthday," the *Guardian*'s Kate Connolly reported,

> The first birthday of a polar bear who captured the hearts of millions around the world . . . is being commemorated in Berlin today with the pomp and gusto generally reserved for a royal wedding or World Cup win . . . Children's street parties, live TV specials and a gourmet cake for the celebrity himself. A trustee of the zoo allowed as how the not-so-little bear still has the ability to "draw attention to the environment in a nice way, not a threatening, scolding way."

German Environment Minister Sigmar Gabriel, who adopted Knut at birth, paid for his upkeep in return for using his logo in the German campaign against global warming, and also as the official symbol of the endangered species conference held in Bonn in 2008.

---

* *Vanity Fair*'s celebrity photographer, Annie Liebovitz, photographed Knut in the Berlin Zoo and DiCaprio on an ice floe in Iceland. The two stars were Photoshopped together, so it appears that DiCaprio, who is properly outfitted for ice climbing, is standing on a hunk of floating ice looking down at the polar bear cub. To their credit, the editors of *Vanity Fair* did not attempt to pass off the cover photograph as genuine, but admitted up front that it was doctored.

For this cover, Leonardo DiCaprio was photographed in Iceland, Knut at the Berlin Zoo, and the two images were combined.

"Move over Brad Pitt and Tom Cruise," said headlines in German newspapers at the end of 2007; "Polar Bear Knut to Become Hollywood Star." He will be featured in a film financed by American producer Ash R. Shah, who underwrote the 2007 animated film *Garfield Gets Real*, about the comic-strip cat. (The first Garfield feature, *Garfield the Movie*, was released in 2004.) A rumor began circulating that Suri Cruise, the eighteenth-month-old daughter of Tom Cruise and Katie Holmes, would do the voice of Knut, but this story turned out to be a ploy to raise money for the film. Because the producers cannot pay the bear, they offered to guarantee the Berlin Zoo $5 million for the rights to tell Knut's story (*Der Spiegel*, December 21, 2007). Pictures of Knut posted in conjunction with this story show that at the age of one, Knut has become a big boy, and has lost virtually all of the cuteness that made him so endearing to the world. If the film actually comes to pass, it will

But when it came to the German Vanity Fair, Knut alone was the cover boy.

be interesting to see how it portrays the bear. Will they use old images of cute little Knut, or will they make him an animated figure like Garfield?

Knut's marketability is fading fast. He is no longer a little fluffball, but a 300-pound dirty-white bear strong enough to knock over a pony—and he is still growing. His snout is longer, and his eyes now seem smaller and less appealing. And worse yet, Frank Albrecht, the man who advocated killing Knut when he was a cub, has now announced that the year-old bear has become "a problem bear who has become addicted to human beings, will never mate, and faces a lonely future." According to Markus Roebke, one of Knut's original handlers, Knut is "a publicity-addicted psycho," who whimpers and cries when there is nobody outside his compound (Kucharz 2008). Knut killed the carp that had been put in the moat surrounding his enclosure by scooping them out of the water and leaving them to die. The yearling now lives in an enclosure behind a thick plate-glass window that protects him from the public (and the public from him), and is said to lunge at children with his formidable fangs bared. Of course, Knut lovers have refused to believe anything negative about their favorite animal, and their loyalty to white bear cubs has been rewarded with the appearance of another tiny star in the *Eisbär* pantheon.

Shortly after the press release about the possible Knut movie, officials at the Nuremberg Zoo announced that three cubs just born to two female polar bears would not be hand-reared like Knut; if their mothers continued to ignore them, they would be allowed to starve to death. In an interview on January 6, 2008, deputy zoo director Helmut Mägdefrau said, "We expect to be branded as cruel to animals. The fact is, in nature if something goes wrong, it goes wrong. If you don't let the mothers practice, they'll never learn how to bring up cubs . . . Berlin Zoo did a terrific job in hand-rearing Knut from day one. But we want to avoid Knutmania at all costs. If people spend hours queuing up to see a polar bear cub, there's something wrong. We've got a baby giraffe, too, that's just as cute." But a newborn giraffe, all legs and neck, can be six feet tall, and it would be really uncomfortable to try and cuddle one in your arms. Baby polar bears, however, define the terms *furry* and *cute,* and as was demonstrated with Brumas, Klondike, Snow, and Knut, they can generate unprecedented publicity for the zoo that capitalizes on the cuteness factor. The title of the *Observer* article by Allan Hall that contained Mägdefrau's comments was "Zoo Leaves Polar Bear Cubs to Starve," clearly exemplifying our overemotional and overprotective attitude toward the poor little orphans. A zoo that lets its baby polar bears starve to death will not only be vilified, it will lose a lot of money.

A couple of days after Mägdefrau's announcement, Vera, the mother of one of the Nuremberg cubs, brought her tiny baby out of the cave in which it had been born; carrying the tiny creature by the scruff of the neck, as a cat will carry its kitten, she dropped it on the stone surface. (The other mother, named Vilma, was still in the cave, and was believed to have eaten her cubs.) Once Vera's cub, identified as a female, was brought out of the cave, she was seen to be much too small to feed herself, and if the mother was going to reject her, an intervention would be necessary. The cub certainly could not be left to die in full view of the public. At this point, Mägdefrau reversed himself, and announced that zoo personnel would bottle-feed the cub (Chivers 2008), and the Nuremberg version of Knutmania was about to begin. Newspapers around the world covered the story of the abandoned and then not-abandoned bear cub with a tone usually reserved for stories of major international significance. As soon as the decision to save the cub was announced, the *Guardian* published "Our Soft Spot for the Serial Killer of the Arctic," which author Laura Barton opened with:

> The news that Vilma, a polar bear at Nuremberg Zoo, appears to have eaten her newborn cubs will no doubt confuse our relationship with our new favorite animal. For some time now, the world has been in the throes of an enormous polar bear crush—they've been there in adverts and in films, in coffee-table books and children's stories, and most of all, in the cautionary tales of global warming, clinging to a block of melting ice, looking sweet sad and lovable.

Before the little bear was rescued, she was quite dirty, because she had been in a den with a matted-straw floor, but as soon as they could, keepers cleaned her up, and before long, there were photographs of a snow-white, helpless little creature, her eyes still closed, being fed from a baby bottle. On January 12, the Associated Press reported that the Nuremberg Zoo had opened a Web site for the little bear (www.eis baer.nuernberg.de), and that suggestions for naming the four-week-old baby were pouring in at the rate of fifteen per minute. Keepers started calling the cub "Flocke," which is German for "flake"—as in snowflake—and after some 30,000 e-mail suggestions were considered, that became the little bear's official name. Flocke (pronounced "*flock-eh*") made her public debut in April 2008.

In a discussion of Snowflake in the European edition of *Business-Week*, Frank Thadeusz wrote, "In terms of zoology, the year 2007 was deceptive. Berlin Zoo's baby polar bear Knut became the darling of Germany and the world—and gave the general public the impression that one of the most dangerous and powerful predators on earth is in fact a cuddly creature with a cute little button nose and soft, fluffy ears." Dangerous predator or cuddly creature, the polar bear has indeed become our new favorite animal. The rivalry between the German zoos is symptomatic of our strange love affair with the polar bear. On April 8, 2008, when Flocke was introduced to the public, 350 press photographers showed up to document the event, and Nuremberg Zoo workers plastered their city with posters that pictured adorable Flocke and said, "Knut was yesterday." Nuremberg city fathers "insisted that the baby bear was excellent publicity for a city hitherto famous for Nazi party rallies and the post–Second World War trial of Nazi war criminals" (Paterson 2008). In May 2008, the Nuremberg Zoo named UN Environment Program chief Achim Steiner Flocke's official patron. As with Knut, when German Environment Minister Sigmar Gabriel used the (then) cute little bear to symbolize global warming, five-month-old Flocke's celebrity was being parlayed into an environmental message.

In time, of course, Flocke will also become "yesterday," and, like Knut, will outgrow the "cute" phase and become just another big white

Wilbaer and his mother, Corinna

March 3, 2008: at the Tiergarten Schönbrunn (Vienna), the polar bear mother appears out of her den with her two cubs for the first time.

bear in a zoo. Another cub was born in Stuttgart's Wilhelma Zoo in December 2007, and was brought out of the den in February 2008 by his mother, Corinna. She showed no signs of abandoning her male cub, which was named Wilbaer—"Wil" for the Wilhelma Zoo, and "baer," German for "bear." In April 2008, at the age of four months, Wilbaer (or Wilbar, as he is sometimes known) made his first public appearance at the Stuttgart Zoo. As his mother watched, more than 10,000 polar bear fanatics gathered around, trying to get a glimpse of the cub. Also in April 2008, officials at St. Petersburg's Leningrad Zoo announced the debut of two four-month-old cubs named Krasin and Peter, born in December of the previous year. Like their American and German counterparts, the Russian cubs will make appearances in magazines, television advertising, and newspaper stories.

As bear cubs grow, they lose their appeal, so every zoo wants to capitalize on its baby polar bears. This fad will probably continue as long as captive bears give birth in artificial dens. But as they mature, they will acquire a different role altogether.

Adult polar bears—in captivity or in the wild—now stand (or swim) for global warming, considered the major threat to the planet today. Combining the cute and cuddly image of the babies with that of an endangered carnivore, the white bear represents our ambiguous attitude toward wild animals. At the same time that we fall in love with the cubs, we fear the adults—and we may well fear *for* them. Keeping polar bears in zoos is probably not good for the bears, but we can't just let newborn cubs starve, can we? Besides, a baby polar bear does wonders for the zoo that exhibits it and, in protecting them from harm (or extinction) in the wild, might even provide a justification for keeping animals in captivity in the first place. "Sportsmen" still shoot defenseless polar bears on the ice, but we worry that the shrinking Arctic ice cap will endanger the bears' way of life. Will drilling for oil in the bears' Chukchi Sea habitat be necessary to supply more oil and gas that we need to continue our industrialized way of life? Never mind that more oil and gas consumption means more greenhouse gases, and more greenhouse gases means more global warming. Even if it is somnolent or overweight, the polar bear still serves as a reminder of our precarious relationship with nature; in its whiteness, it might be the beacon that can light the way to a better understanding of our place—and our responsibilities—in the world.

VIII

On the Whiteness of the Bear

The polar bear is a totemic, iconic creature. We have witnessed how in living human memory, the image of the polar bear has been expropriated and put to the most varied and unlikely purposes—selling dreams, sweets, lifestyles, travel. In all cases except for seemingly the most contemporary and chilling— its role as iconic representative of the demise of its own environment—its appeal is dependant upon an almost inescapable anthropomorphism. The bear stands on two legs. It plays and wrestles, it sits, it rests, all in ways that are suggestively "human."

Nanoq: Flat out and Bluesome,
Snæbjörnsdóttir and Wilson

I n *Moby-Dick,* Herman Melville wrote,

This elusive quality it is, which causes the thought of whiteness, when divorced from more kindly associations, and coupled with any object terrible in itself, to heighten that terror to the furthest bounds. Witness the white bear of the poles, and the white shark of the tropics; what but their smooth, flaky whiteness makes them the transcendent horrors that they are? That ghastly whiteness it is which imparts an abhorrent mildness, even more loathsome than terrific, to the dumb-gloating of their aspect. So that not the fierce-fanged tiger in his heraldic coat can so stagger courage as the white-shrouded bear or shark.

To the chapter called "The Whiteness of the Whale," Melville then added this footnote:

> With reference to the Polar bear, it may possibly be urged by him who would fain go still deeper into this matter, that it is not the whiteness, separately regarded, which heightens the intolerable hideousness of that brute; for, analysed, that heightened hideousness, it might be said, only arises from the circumstance, that the irresponsible ferociousness of the creature stands invested in the fleece of celestial innocence and love; and hence, by bringing together two such opposite emotions in our minds, the Polar bear frightens us with so unnatural a contrast. But even assuming all this to be true; yet were it not for the whiteness, you would not have that intensified terror.

Melville follows the footnote with a disquisition on why the "white gliding repose" of the white shark "strangely tallies with the same quality in the Polar quadruped." Herman Melville probably never saw a polar bear, and certainly never saw a white shark, which despite its inclusion in the chapter on fearful white animals is not white, but dark gray above with white underparts. (It is highly unlikely that he ever saw a white sperm whale either. The malevolent creature in *Moby-Dick* is based on whalers' tales that Melville had heard about a whale named "Mocha Dick" that was attacking ships off the coast of Chile in the 1830s, and was described by Jeremiah Reynolds in 1839 as "white as wool.")

Like the bears themselves, the first men to see polar bears were probably swaddled in heavy fur coats. The earliest human inhabitants of the Arctic regarded *Nanuk* first as a dangerous predator, then as a rival hunter, and lastly as an animal to be hunted for its red meat and white coat. Somewhere along the line, the proto-Inuit assigned to the ghostly white bear supernatural qualities—it was surely the ruler of the Arctic, as mere humans could never be, comfortable in a perpetually frozen world of ice and snow. The Inuit—then as now—feared and worshipped the great bear. They occasionally killed and ate them, but only after the bear spirits had been appropriately propitiated. The first Europeans to visit the desolate homeland of *Ursus maritimus* shot them whenever an opportunity presented itself. Sometimes bears were captured and brought back to European menageries or zoos, where they were exhibited to visitors who looked upon the great white bears as emissaries from a world where the sun shines dimly for half the year and the land is made of ice.

In his biography of Henry Hudson, the British historian Llewelyn Powys romantically sums up how people thought about the great ice bear around 1927:

> In all stories of polar expeditions these bears play an important part. With their long necks and small heads, with hair growing at the bottom of their feet to prevent them from slipping on the ice, with a coat white as milk except in the case of very old animals, when it takes on a yellow hue, these formidable creatures manage to sustain life in the peculiar territory they inhabit, whose only escarpments are icebergs, and whose only earth is snow. In those seas porpoises often carry upon their backs their claw-marks; sometimes, however, these bears kill a walrus, sometimes a seal, sometimes a white fox; in an hour of extremity they will even eat lichen and seaweed, and then get them away to some sheltered crevice, to sleep the profound sleep of an animal who fears no enemy. Little do they wot of forests with sheltering tree trunks and delicate articulate leaves. A long crepuscular winter, amid the blanched shadows of moonlit ice, to be replaced by the glittering light of the summer sun that never sinks, such is the cosmos they know.

"Teddy bears" are said to have begun with American president Theodore "Teddy" Roosevelt, who was hunting in Mississippi in 1902 when he found a black bear cub that had lost his mother. His kindness to the cub was noticed by the *Washington Star* newspaper cartoonist Clifford Berryman, whose cartoon inspired a Brooklyn toy store owner to make two stuffed bears. The owner asked Roosevelt if he would mind if they were called "Teddy's bears," and a worldwide phenomenon was launched. More or less simultaneously, Margaret Steiff, a disabled German seamstress with a soft-toy factory in Giengen, had added a soft plush bear to the Steiff catalog. Between 1903 and the First World War,

Steiff sold literally millions of bears, with their trademark button in the left ear, in the United States, Germany, and Britain, as the teddy bear became the toy craze of the early 1900s. It required no stretch of the creative imagination to transform the cuddly brown teddy bears into cuddly white bears. You might even say that the white version was cuter.

New York Times science writer Natalie Angier wrote "The Cute Factor," an article in which she identified some of the qualities that make something look cute: "bright, forward-facing eyes set low on a big round face, a pair of big round ears, floppy limbs, and a side-to-side, teeter-totter gait." The paradigm, of course, is the human toddler, but also fulfilling these criteria are puppies of many dog breeds, koalas, young lions, tigers, and leopards, and bear cubs of all species, including pandas. A polar bear cub is arguably the cutest animal of all. The cub's eyes are big, black, and round, giving them the appearance of toys, while the eyes of adults are more almond shaped and proportionally smaller. Cubs have a short little snout that lengthens into the Roman nose of the adult—many have described the long neck and small head of an adult polar bear as "serpentine." Steven Kazlowski, who has studied and photographed Alaskan polar bears for almost a decade, points out that "the head of a female polar bear, larger in circumference than her neck, is one characteristic that distinguishes females from males."

Female polar bears have also assumed iconic status, but in a way that is not usually acknowledged. The next time you see one of those familiar photographs of a mother bear and her two adorable cubs, tear your eyes from the cubs and look at the mother. From the moment she leads her cubs from their birth den, she is the personification of protective motherhood. She looks on benignly as her babies clamber all over her, she provides them with food, she drives off much larger males that might do her children harm, she curls up around them in bad weather, she calls them back if they wander off. Many mammals nurse their young from a standing or lying position, but a mother polar bear sits upright as her cubs nurse. Those given to anthropomorphizing the behavior of wild animals could be excused for identifying her attitude as unconditional love. Few mothers—of any species—are so unabashedly devoted to their offspring, and few offspring are as endearing as polar bears.

It is highly unlikely that the word *cute* was popular with Arctic explorers or whalers, but once the public was able to see a baby polar bear, everything changed. Introducing the polar bear in *Wild Life Beyond the North,* Frank Illingworth wrote, "Here among the contorted polar ice, are to be seen the roly-poly bear cubs, no larger than a rabbit when born, in October, and weighing 400 pounds by the following September, tripping along between mother's feet or clinging to her absurd little tail when tired of swimming." Of course, there are those who refuse to be seduced by the polar bear's warm, fuzzy image, and who think the use of the bear is a cheap attempt to garner support for what they regard as the completely bogus issue of global warming. In a Web posting for December 29, 2002, Miceal [sic] O'Ronian published an elaborate attack on the science and the motives of those who would alert us to the dangers of the melting Arctic ice cap (www.johndaly .com/p-bears/index.htm):

> In an apparently successful effort to convince the people of Canada that, unless they ratified the Kyoto Protocol,* they face an Arctic meltdown of apocalyptic proportions, the greenhouse industry launched a media blitz which was large, even by their standards. The stars of the campaign were the polar bears of Canada, with particular attention to the population about Churchill. There is nothing cute or lovable about one of the most formidable predators on the planet; all of the stories about polar bears included the obligatory photographs of polar bear cubs, which are adorable by any criteria. Given the propensity of the greenhouse industry to craft subsets of data which support their positions, while carefully ignoring contradictory data, the question which begs to be asked is: How real is anthropogenic global warming in the area about Hudson Bay?

O'Ronian's objections notwithstanding, the image of the polar bear—adult and roly-poly cub—has become the very symbol of the Arctic. It appears in the coat of arms of Greenland and on the license

---

* On December 17, 2002, Canada ratified the Kyoto Protocol, which addresses climate change and, more specifically, the speed at which the earth is warming up. For the record, when the Kyoto Protocol went into effect on February 16, 2005, 141 countries had ratified it, including every major industrialized country—except the United States. After being sworn in as Australia's new prime minister in November 2007, Kevin Rudd of the Labour Party immediately signed documents to ratify the Kyoto Protocol on climate change, reversing a decade of Australian environmental policy and leaving the United States standing alone among industrialized nations in its refusal to ratify the treaty.

For Coca-Cola, polar bears come in all shapes and sizes.

plates of Nunavut, and constitutes a large proportion of the items sold in the gift shops and airports of Churchill, Anchorage, Nome, Sitka, Juneau, and smaller settlements in between. (Many of the little ivory souvenir bears are carved from walrus ivory, which American Eskimos and Canadian Inuit can harvest legally.) Polar bears appear on caps, sweatshirts, T-shirts, place mats, jigsaw puzzles, mouse pads, charms, jewelry, night-lights, figurines, pillows, blankets, calendars, Christmas tree ornaments, Christmas cards, and any other knickknack you could possibly think of. The most popular items are little stuffed bears.

Early in the 1990s, the Coca-Cola company began using the polar bear in its advertising, and produced several television commercials that showed the bears drinking Coke ("Always Cool, Always Coke"). The campaign was so successful that Coke went on to fashion a whole line of gift items that had polar bears on them, including drinking cups (naturally), storage tins, statuettes, collector spoons, stationery, stickers, lunch boxes, and legions of little stuffed bears wearing the Coca-Cola logo. According to Linda Lee Harry and Jean Gibbs-Simpson, whose book *Coca-Cola Collectible Polar Bears* celebrates the successful union between the bears and the soft-drink company, "The Coca-Cola Company has found the perfect four-legged promoter in the polar bear. His Arctic homeland reminds us that Coke is best served 'Ice Cold' while his play-ful antics symbolize fun and good times spent with family and friends." On the heels of the phenomenal success of the documentary *March of the Penguins* and the animated film *Happy Feet* (which featured tap-dancing penguins), some of Coke's polar bear television spots showed Coke-swilling bears cavorting with penguins. In advertising, "cute" trumps zoogeographical accuracy, so despite their polar separation, pen-guins and polar bears continue to laugh it up together for Coke.* "The only downside for the polar bears," wrote Simon Garfield in the British newspaper the *Observer*, "is that they didn't own their image rights."

These commercials contributed substantially to the recent transfor-mation of the polar bear from killer of seals and attacker of men to cute, furry, beloved icon. Rather than Melville's "transcendent horror," whiteness today is commonly used to symbolize purity and cleanliness. Think of "pure as the driven snow" or the white garments of hospital workers. In early Hollywood Westerns, the bad guys always wore black hats, the good guys, white. White is the color of wedding dresses and angel's wings; a white flag is an international symbol of either surrender or truce, a sign of peaceful intent. Moby-Dick† was unquestionably malevolent, but he was fictional, and in various cultures, real (and rare)

---

* *The Golden Compass*, a Hollywood fantasy film based on a novel by Philip Pullman, uses a great many computer-generated animals, among them giant polar bears in armor. In her *New York Times* review (December 7, 2007), Manohla Dargis wrote, "Among other things, I would have liked to spend some quality time with Lyra's friend and protector the warrior bear Iorek Byrnison, a gorgeous creature whose ferocity is, alas, tempered by his resem-blance to some familiar cuddly polar bears. It is, I discovered, hard to keep your mind off the concession stand when you are waiting for Iorek to offer Lyra a Coke."

† As I've noted earlier, "Moby-Dick" wasn't actually white. (The title of the novel is "Moby-Dick, or the Whale," not "Moby-Dick, or the White Whale.") Melville describes him as having "a peculiar snow-white wrinkled forehead, and a high pyramidal white hump. . . . The rest of his body was so streaked and spotted, and marbled with the same shrouded hue, that, in the end he gained the distinctive appellation of the White Whale; a name, indeed, literally justified by his vivid aspect, when seen gliding at high noon through a dark blue sea, leaving a milky-way wake of creamy foam, all spangled with golden gleamings."

white elephants, white buffalos, and white tigers are heralded as omens of good luck. The humble brown weasel becomes the white ermine in winter, providing its soft, white fur for the cloaks of royalty. (The snow-shoe hare also turns white in the winter, but its fur is not so highly esteemed.) Dall sheep and mountain goats are white, and so are some Arctic wolves; and of course, in the winter, the little Arctic fox is as white as the snow it cavorts in. Many Arctic birds are white: the ivory gull, the snowy owl, the gyrfalcon. In Arctic waters, there can be found the little white whale, also known as the beluga. Reaching a maximum length of twenty feet, *Delphinapterus leucas* (*leucas* means "white" in Greek) frequents the polar waters of the Northern Hemisphere, and like most other Arctic mammals, it is hunted by the Eskimo. The beluga—from the Russian *byelo*, which also means "white"—is born gray, but as it matures it turns creamy white. (*Belorus* is White Russia.)

The Arctic animals—the fox, the hare, the ermine, and especially the polar bear—are white because they have to be, not because somebody thought they ought to be. In a world made of glaring ice and snow, white is the best color to be. The ice bear is an integral part of its environment, as white as the snow and ice it lives in. The bear draws its

It is not only the bear that is out of place, it is the place *that is out of place.*

power from its whiteness; it is an all-conquering, heavy snowstorm of a creature, fearing nothing. Is it an accident that this powerful, beautiful—and now endangered—white beast has become the poster child for global warming?

Most bears are dark-colored creatures of temperate or tropical forests, although there are some that live in the mountains of South and North America. Foremost among the reasons for the elevation of the polar bear to its current prominence is its glaring incongruity. It is not only the bear that is out of place—it is the *place* that is out of place. Whitened out, horizon-less landscapes are not the world we know. The great white bear is an alien being in a setting that might be on a frozen planet somewhere in space. Through art, photographs, and moving images, we have become familiar with the polar bear, but its lifestyle is radically different from that of any other species of bear—or any other animal, for that matter. The polar bear is a grand, handsome beast, the epitome of strength, power, and dominance—but, at least in what we call "popular culture," the adults have been supplanted by the adorable little cubs.

The 1958 Disney film *White Wilderness* shows what "nine daring photographers" got after three years in the Arctic filming walruses, polar bears, and lemmings, as well as wolves, wolverines, and other "vicious predators." As soon as it was released, the film was criticized for its depiction of the lemmings' "mass suicide," which 1) was staged by herding captive lemmings off a cliff and into the ocean, and 2) doesn't actually happen anyway. Polar bears, described in the film as "the largest, most powerful and most ferocious of all Arctic animals," are sometimes shown as menacing adults, but much more frequently as little cubs that love to frolic in the snow. For Disney's "True-Life Adventures" (which included *Nature's Half Acre, Beaver Valley,* and *The Living Desert*), the filmmakers often resorted to staged events when the wild animals didn't behave the way they wanted them to. In *White Wilderness,* for example, whenever we see walruses or polar bears in the water, it is obvious that they have been driven there by cameramen harassing them from helicopters. From the human bootprints in the snow around the gaping den in which a mother bear is "hibernating," we can see that the den was dug open by men and the cubs released. (The immobile, unblinking female looks very much as if she has been tranquilized or shot; with cubs old enough to venture out of the den, she would certainly have been wide awake.) Another sequence, designed to demonstrate how playful polar bear cubs are, includes one rolling a big snowball over a cliff to land on its sibling, but doesn't bother to explain where the "snowball" came from. A young bear, tumbling down a steep, snowy hillside and crashing heavily into a rock pile is an unlikely conclusion to a playful tumble unless the bear was pushed. This "True-Life Adventure" serves up its natural history in clichés, and incorrect ones at that. As the film ends, the polar bear is seen "patrolling his beat as usual, unmindful of the cold. Winter and summer he remains what nature intended him to be: lord and sovereign of this frosty domain."

By the time National Geographic released *Polar Bear Alert* in 1982, the great white bears were considered very dangerous—especially in Churchill, where the film was shot. As we see the bears wandering ominously through the streets of the "polar bear capital of the world," the narrator (Jason Robards) tells us that "each fall the largest, most deadly carnivore in the Arctic migrates through this isolated Canadian village on an annual northward trek. For scientists, the migration presents a unique chance to observe the bears. For residents, it is a season of apprehension." After poking its nose into a closed door, a bear is wounded by a hysterical home owner, and then finished off by a bear-patrol officer. (As with Stefansson, we hear that "we can't have a wounded polar bear wandering around," especially if we are the ones who wounded it in the first place.) The bloody carcass is thrown into the back of a truck. Later, Ian Stirling and Dennis Andriashek tag polar bears from helicopters, the beginning of a study that began in the 1970s. As if to demonstrate how truly dangerous the bears are, two of the film-makers (one at a time) enter a tiny cage and wait for the bears to get at them. You see the bears mouthing the heavy mesh of the cage, poking a paw into it, and trying to tip it over.* (I've heard that the bars of the cage were smeared with sardine oil.) "Really scary," says Jim Lipscomb, the movie cameraman and director of the film. The film ends with Robards intoning, "In the next score of years, few of the world's great

---

* The use of the cage was the inspiration for *The Cage,* a 1994 novel by Audrey Schulman, in which a young woman nature photographer joins an expedition to Churchill, where she will, because of her small stature, sit in a cage and film the bears. In the novel, the Churchill bears are especially vicious, stalking and attacking anybody outside a house or a cage. In an unfortunate misreading of the seasons, the photographers encounter the dangerous bears of Churchill in the dead of winter, by which time they would have been long gone.

beasts, including the polar bear, will not survive without the active collaboration of man. Once shielded by the inaccessible reaches of the Arctic, the polar bear is one of the last to come under pressure."

A really good portrayal of polar bears in action takes place in the 2007 National Geographic film *Arctic Tale*. Advertised as a story of Nanu the baby polar bear and Seela the baby walrus, it is actually a patchwork of many unrelated sequences of different polar bears and walruses (as well as Arctic foxes, belugas, narwhals, and bowhead whales), stitched together to create a narrative that purports to follow a bear and a walrus as they grow up, brave the dangers of a hostile world, then find mates and have their own babies. Anyone paying even a modicum of attention will see that the bears and the walruses change from sequence to sequence: they are smaller as they get older in some instances; the tusks of the walruses become both longer and shorter and occasionally disappear altogether; and the background changes completely in what is supposed to be a single sequence of a young bear—Nanu's twin brother—dying from malnutrition. The little bear collapses in the middle of a blowing snowstorm, then we see a close-up of him lying in a calm snowfield full of dwarf willow brush (in Churchill?), and finally it's back to the storm for the death scene. After Nanu grows up, she is represented by probably ten to fifteen different bears—some larger, some smaller; some clean white, some (in the same sequence) brownish around the head and paws; some with an all-black muzzle, some with just a black nose. The sensational sequence of a mother walrus hugging baby Seela soon after she's born is repeated frame for frame at the end, when *Seela* is supposed to be the one having a baby.

Despite these inconsistencies and the silly narration, this is the best filming of wild polar bears and walruses ever accomplished. Of course there are the obligatory images of the impossibly cute babies emerging from the den, followed by their mother (who looks a little surprised to see a cameraman in front of her). Nanu's mother pounding the ice with her forepaws as a young ringed seal cowers below it is a classic of wildlife filming—or, rather, film editing, as the bear and the seal never appear in the same shot. Cameraman Adam Ravetch managed to get incredible shots of polar bears and walruses underwater, not to mention the images of a bear swimming into a walrus colony, climbing up the rocks where the giant pinnipeds are resting, and, as they panic and lumber past him into the water, seizing an adult female walrus and killing her. (So much for those who maintained that a bear would never attack a full-grown walrus.) When yearling Nanu is starving, she approaches a huge male who is feeding on a carcass, and at first he drives her off—making more noise than polar bears are supposed to make—but finally relents and lets her eat. In this film, you don't know where you are. The narrator (Queen Latifah) tells you only that this is "Rock Island" or "Snow Mountain," so the opportunity to understand that the events have occurred in a real place is lost. If you can get past the anthropomorphic narrative and see that this should never have been marketed as a story for kids, you will witness a sensationally shot film that brings the plight of the bears and the walruses into sharp—sometimes even painful—focus.*

Another way to see a polar bear is to visit a natural history museum. In many of the large museums of Europe and America, the bears are usually posed in a diorama with a painted background and a bloody seal carcass on the fake ice. In the earliest museum displays, the polar bear skins were stuffed with straw or some other material, giving them a lumpy, unrealistic appearance. For example, Ole Worm, a Danish doctor who lived from 1588 to 1654, built one of the most well-known *Wunderkammern*—"wonder cabinets"—in Europe. The objects on display were marvels of nature, antiquities, and ethnographic items, ranging from minerals, fossils, and preserved plants to bones, tusks, tortoise shells, taxidermied animals, and runic texts. The frontispiece from his 1655 *Museum Wormianum,* a posthumously published catalog of the collection in his Copenhagen home, is one of the iconic images of the seventeenth-century wonder cabinet. The collection includes a narwhal

---

* A "bonus feature" on the *Arctic Tale* DVD is a twenty-nine-minute piece called "How *Arctic Tale* Was Made." It might even be better than the film, not only because of the hardships the crew suffered during the *fifteen years* required to make the movie, but because their interactions with the animals, underwater or on the ice, are far more revealing of the animals' nature than any invented story. Sometimes the crew got in two days of filming weather in a month, sometimes none; sometimes they waited for days in a sleetstorm and nothing happened that they could shoot. You wouldn't know that the shots of the bear attacking the walrus herd were made after a month of waiting in a tower in a freezing storm on a tiny island in Foxe Basin, north of Hudson Bay. During the bonus, you hear that "nobody knew where the walruses were," and "for the first three years, we never saw a bear," and only then do you learn about the people of the village of Igloolik, who were immeasurably helpful to the filmmakers, getting them out on the ice, bringing the boat, and, most important, telling them where to look for the animals.

Ole Worm's 1655 Museum Wormianum in Copenhagen. Exhibiting the fascination with all things Arctic, there is a walrus skull just inside the near left window, a narwhal skull (complete with horn) to the right of the next window, and a little stuffed polar bear hanging from the ceiling.

skull (Worm was the first to identify the narwhal as the source of the legendary unicorn's horn) and a small polar bear suspended from the ceiling. More recently, photographer Rosamond Purcell reconstructed Worm's *Wunderkammern* using ethnographic objects and natural history specimens borrowed from collections around the country, including a narwhal skull, a swordfish sword, ostrich eggs, and a hanging polar bear. The Purcell reconstruction has been shown at the Santa Monica Museum of Art and the Harvard Science Center in Cambridge, Massachusetts.

When British artists Bryndís Snæbjörnsdóttir ("Snow-Bear's Daughter" in Icelandic) and Mark Wilson found a polar bear behind the bar in a pub in Wensleydale, they set out to catalog every taxidermied polar bear they could find in the UK. In three years, they found a total of thirty-four, photographed every one, and incorporated the pictures into a book that they called *Nanoq: Flat Out and Bluesome: A Cultural Life of Polar Bears.* Ten of the bears were exhibited for six weeks (February 17 to March 31) in 2004, at Spike Island, a large exhibit space in Bristol.

An exhibit of photographs of the bears as Snæbjörnsdóttir and Wil-

Exhibit of ten polar bear mounts, found by Bryndís Snæbjörnsdóttir and Mark Wilson in various museums, private houses, and pubs in England

son had found them was presented at the University Museum of Natural History in Oxford in 2004, and in 2006, the photographs were exhibited at London's Horniman Museum, which once housed a magnificent taxidermied polar bear that seems to have gone missing.* The archive of photographic images of the mounted polar bears in situ has been exhibited at the Fram Polar Expedition Museum in Oslo, the Tromsø (Norway) Polar Museum, the University of Iceland, Nordic House in the Faeroes, and the Scott Polar Institute in Cambridge.

In the 1920s, Carl Akeley, a preparator and taxidermist at the American Museum of Natural History in New York, developed a method of sculpting an animal's body in wax and plaster over the skeleton, retaining the shape of every muscle, and then stretching the skin over the plaster manikin, giving the animal a "lifelike" appearance. (Akeley also

---

* Before the exhibit opened at the Horniman Museum in London, the museum's Web site sounded this plaintive note: "The museum is hunting for one of its favourite attractions—a polar bear. The taxidermied grizzly [sic] has been missing from the museum since it was taken off display in the 1940s. The bear had been amazing audiences since the Horniman opened in 1901, and its disappearance has been baffling staff since it went awol nearly 60 years ago." Janet Vitmayer, director of the Horniman Museum, said, "The fate of the Horniman's Polar Bear has long been of interest to us—it was, after all, one of the largest animals on display and very popular with visitors."

One of the photographs of a "stuffed" polar bear from Snæbjörnsdóttir and Wilson's project. This is Nina, who lived at the Bristol Zoo for twenty-nine years. She stands on a model iceberg mounted on wheels.

designed the cameras used by Robert Flaherty to shoot *Nanook of the North.*) Of course, nothing is *less* lifelike—more dead, if you will—than a stuffed animal. Of the taxidermied bears in *Nanoq: Flat Out and Bluesome,* Michelle Henning, lecturer in cultural studies at the University of the West of England (Bristol), wrote,

> The tragedy of the polar bear is not just its hunting down, but also its sad resurrection as these taxidermy artifacts, and the indifference and forgetfulness associated with the places in which the artists find them. The photographic part of the project documents the fate of these taxidermied bears; the terrible incongruity of their surroundings compared to the icy place where they originate, and where their white fur would camouflage them. One bear keeps company with a grandfather clock, a mounted pheasant in a glass case, china polar bears, and a bust on a pedestal.

Diorama at the Denver Museum of Nature and Science, showing a polar bear family: mom, pop, and the kids, with a ribbon seal

When the taxidermied bears are exhibited, as at Spike Island, there are no labels or other identifying text; only an upside-down map of the British Isles with the thirty-four places of origin marked with a star. In the book, however, each of the color photographs is accompanied by a detailed caption, in which Snæbjörnsdóttir and Wilson explain not only how they got the photograph and where, but also where the bear originally came from and how it happened to be in that particular museum or house. At Somerleyton Hall, in East Anglia, for example, the current Lord Somerleyton showed the bears to Snæbjörnsdóttir and Wilson and told them that these two bears were shot by his grandfather during an 1897 expedition to Spitsbergen in which a total of fifty-five polar bears were killed.

Bears of all species can—and often do—walk upright on their hind legs. In the circus, we have seen everything from elephants and horses to dogs, cats, tigers, and lions trained to rear up and walk on two legs, but the only mammals that regularly exhibit bipedal locomotion are the primates (including us), and the bears.* The bears' upright stance is strongly reminiscent of human standing or walking positions, and this

---

* Kangaroos cannot actually "walk," but move by placing their forefeet on the ground and then swinging their powerful haunches forward together. At speed, of course, the kangaroo "hops" bipedally. Birds all walk on two legs because they only *have* two legs.

resemblance has often led to a mythical or even practical congruence between bears and people. There are many cultures where bears—or their spirits—are worshipped, and some where the line between bears and people is so faintly drawn as to be indistinguishable. For centuries, the Eskimos and Inuit thought of the polar bear as the reigning demon of their world—an animal that might be killed occasionally, but whose spirit had to be propitiated. In his 2007 book, *Bears*, Bernd Brunner wrote,

> The idea that people were descended from bears played an important role not only in North America but in Europe and Asia as well . . . For the southwestern Yavapi, in what is now Arizona, the only difference between men and bears was that humans could make fire. For this reason they did not hunt bears, and the animals could supposedly be found living in the immediate vicinity of the tribe's settlements as a result. The situation was similar among the Pueblo: their rule against eating one's own kind also made bear meat taboo . . . Many tribes believed that bears could transform into humans, other animals, or even objects.

Bears will rear up on their hind legs to get a better view of their surroundings, but they will also rise to their full height—which in big brown bears and polar bears can be more than ten feet—to intimidate rivals or perceived threats. The play-fighting of polar bears is usually conducted on hind legs, and more than one observer has likened this activity to humans wrestling. Brunner tells us that Ludwig Heck, director of the Berlin Zoo, believed that the bear "serves as a caricature of mankind, as our own distorted reflection." Such moments of recognition occur, Heck claimed, "when he stands on his hind legs and toddles around like a portly old man in his underwear, when he sits on his backside, and 'lays his hands in his lap,' or when he, with astounding dexterity, gestures with his front paws, which resemble human hands in thick gloves and which are capable of the same rotational movement that makes our own hands the ready tools of our minds." In Philip Pullman's "His Dark Materials" trilogy, giant polar bears form one of the warring groups, and although they spend a lot of time on all fours, they can, if the occasion demands, handle delicate objects with their paws, make their own armor, fight with swords, and even talk. Indeed, the polar bear king Iorek Byrnison is one of the many "heroes" of these books. The popularity of *The Golden Compass, The Subtle Knife,* and *The Amber Spyglass* (so far, only *The Golden Compass* has been made into a movie) suggests that even fake animals (think *Jaws*) can be worked into our contemporary mythology.

In India, Asian black bears are captured as cubs and trained to perform as "dancing bears" while their owners collect a few rupees. In American and European circuses, bears (dancing, black, polar, and other) have long been featured performers. Ursula Böttcher was probably the most famous of all polar bear trainers, but Brunner reminds us of Cate Pallenberg, a German circus performer of the 1920s whose bears "roller-skated, drove a car, walked on stilts, played the drums and even rowed a boat." A tape of the Ringling Brothers circus of 1980 includes a performance by Ursula and her ten polar bears. Motivated mostly by voice commands, the bears leap ponderously from pedestal to pedestal and allow Ursula to ride on one while another jumps over her through a flaming hoop. She waltzes with one bear while the others drink "milk" from bottles. The bears climb aboard a sort of polar bear carousel, which consists of a ring of five connected platforms pushed around in a circle by another bear. In the finale of the act, all the bears climb up a ladder to a slide, and come down backward or forward. Throughout the act, as the bears walk on their hind legs or career down the slide, it is obvious that they are real, but they look uncannily like men in polar bear suits. It might very well be their sometime resemblance to humans that, at least in part, is the reason we feel as we do about polar bears. It is true that a long-nosed white bear with big teeth and claws and fur on the soles of its feet doesn't much resemble a human, but except for the anthropoid apes, few animals do. The bear doesn't actually look like a person—it looks like an ursine version of a person. As Paul Ward and Suzanne Kynaston wrote, "The most convincing factor of the kinship between bears and Man was probably the resemblance that the skinned corpse of a bear has to a human body; the Inuit tell stories of polar bears that become human when they 'take their coats off' as they enter a house, becoming bears again when they put them back on to go outside." This preternatural similarity—not evident in any other mammals except apes—may be one of the reasons that we think of bears so differently from other animals.

The menagerie at the Jardin des Plantes in Paris was founded in 1793

The great American wildlife painter Carl Rungius (1869–1959) paints the polar bear.

to display exotic animals to a public eager for novelty. Artists like Antoine-Louis Barye and Eugène Delacroix were among the first to take advantage of the animals on display. François Pompon (1855–1933) conceived his polar bear after seeing the bears brought back from the north by Philippe, Duke of Orléans. One of the few polar bear sculptures regarded as "art" is Pompon's marble *ours blanc,* now in Paris's Musée d'Orsay. Previously Pompon hewed marble for such artists as Auguste Rodin and Camille Claudel, but around 1905 he began sculpting animals that he saw in the Jardin des Plantes. He was fascinated by the polar bears, but abandoned any realistic rendering, focussing instead on the essence of the animal. "I first do the animal with almost all its trappings," he said, "then I gradually eliminate them."

In late 2007, the American Museum of Natural History opened an exhibit entitled "Water: H_2O = Life." With its living animals (mostly fish), videos, interactive exhibits, dramatic graphics and models, this was a most comprehensive show, incorporating everything about our "Water Planet": lakes, rivers, oceans, icebergs, ice caps, and glaciers; circulation and conservation; ordinary ocean waves and tsunamis; irrigation and drought; and many other relevant subjects. The only animal (except for us) that was featured was the polar bear. Dominating the section on climate change, this piece explained how the loss of the Arctic ice will affect polar bears—and everything else on the planet. A video of bears hunting dominated this part of the exhibit, and again, *Ursus maritimus* was selected as the poster child for global warming. In fact, the bear was the symbol of the entire show: the shop that visitors passed through at the exit sold every kind of polar bear item, including T-shirts and plush replicas the size of a Labrador retriever. Symbolically, the price tag on every item in the shop had a polar bear on it.

"Not so long ago," wrote Simon Garfield,

> polar bears were a symbol of cold, but these days they are a symbol of warmth. In the past few weeks it has become difficult to open a newspaper or web page without seeing photographs of the beautiful yellow-white animals leaping, or lying on sea ice in the Arctic, the newly helpless emblem of climate change. The traditional threats to

Reflections in a frozen sea

the polar bear—hunting, toxic waste, offshore drilling—have been overshadowed by a new one: the ice around them is melting, and we are to blame.

So we need polar bears, because they are more than big white animals that live in an alien world, or little fuzzballs that are shamelessly used to sell Coke. They are the envoys from the real world, sent to remind us of our obligations as stewards of this planet and its fragile ecosystems. They stand for the elemental beauty of nature, for wildness, for the preservation of the earth's endangered habitats—for everything that human beings need to protect in order to survive. As Thoreau said, "In wildness is the preservation of the world."

Global Warming and the Bear

Average global surface temperatures are to increase further from 1.1 to 6.4 degrees Celsius (around 2 to 11.5 degrees Fahrenheit) by the year 2010. The magnitude and the rate of this increase, unprecedented for the last 10,000 years, will threaten the survival of many species, especially those unable to migrate to new ranges or otherwise adapt. Global climate change, by itself or acting synergistically with other environmental changes secondary to human activity, could well become the factor most responsible for species extinctions within the next 100 years.

Chivian and Bernstein, 2008

Secretary of Defense Donald Rumsfeld was responsible for the phrase "fighting a war with the army we have," and was referring to the Iraq War. But on today's environmental battlefields, "the army we have"—mammalogists, conservation biologists, climatologists, atmospheric scientists, and reporters—may not be up to the task of saving the polar bear. The bears' habitat is disappearing, and human beings are responsible. We have filled the skies with poisonous fumes and chemical aerosols that effectively trap heat in the atmosphere and warm the surface of the planet. The principal greenhouse gases that enter the atmosphere because of human activities are carbon dioxide (CO_2), methane (CH_4), nitrous oxide (N_2O), and the synthetic hydrofluorocarbons, perfluorocarbons, and sulfur hexafluoride. These gases are typically emitted in smaller quantities, but because they are potent greenhouse gases, they are sometimes referred to as High Global Warming Potential gases ("High GWP gases"). Some greenhouse gases, such as carbon dioxide, occur naturally and are emitted to the atmosphere through natural processes and human activities, but others, such as fluorinated gases, are created and emitted solely through human activities.

The industrial revolution is usually cited as the beginning of major human insults to the land and the atmosphere, as the burning of fossil fuels for factories, trains, and automobiles spewed pollutants into the air, and their creation and maintenance altered the landscape. Prior to that—say, up to the eighteenth century—the conventional wisdom is that people lived in harmony with their surroundings, rather like a colony of gorillas, who modify their environs only to build sleeping nests. There are those, however, who identify the beginning of human effects on the landscape and the atmosphere at much further back in time, perhaps when man turned from hunting to planting. Our influence on the planet has been dated at 8,000 to 5,000 years ago, when land exploitation for agriculture and animal husbandry led to increased emissions of carbon dioxide, methane, and nitrous oxide—the beginning of the greenhouse gas modifications of the atmosphere. Changes that will be visible to future historians include greenhouse gas emissions, the paving over of much of the earth, the diversion of rivers, the death of coral reefs, the rise (and fall) of cities, deep mining, and anthropogenic extinctions. In *GSA Today*, the popular journal of the Geological Society of America, a consortium of twenty-one British geologists wrote that because humans have had such a visible effect on the planet in recent years, the current epoch, now considered part of the Holocene, ought to be named the "Anthropocene." They concluded, "Sufficient evidence has emerged of stratigraphically significant change (both elapsed and imminent) for recognition of the Anthropocene—currently a vivid yet informal metaphor for global environmental change—as the new geological epoch to be considered for formalization by international discussion." The lead author of the *GSA Today* paper, Leicester University's Jan Zalasiewicz, said, "It's extraordinary how a single species could have such an effect on the whole planet."

"Let us hope," wrote Paul Crutzen and Will Steffen (2003),

that the fourth phase of the "Anthropocene," which should be developed during this century, will not be further characterized by continued human plundering of Earth's resources and dumping of excessive amounts of anthropogenic waste products in the environment, but more by vastly improved technology and environmental management, wise use of Earth's remaining resources, control of human and domestic animal population, and overall careful treatment and restoration of the environment—in short, responsible stewardship of the Earth System.

At first, it doesn't seem that a rise in temperature of a few degrees— or even a few fractions of degrees—would be particularly harmful. But climate change is usually held to be one of the major factors in the extinction of the so-called charismatic megafauna of North America during the Pleistocene, 20,000 to 10,000 years ago. The mammoths, mastodons, saber-toothed tigers, cave bears, woolly rhinos, and numerous other species disappeared during that era, eliminated, some say, by their inability to adapt to changes in their environment. Others hold that the arrival of Man the Hunter across the Bering land bridge from Asia was the actual cause of the eradication of the mammals of Pleistocene North America. Whatever caused their downfall, all these great creatures are gone, and only their fossils remain to remind us of their existence.

"Global warming" is currently a catchall term that refers to the rising temperature of the earth over the past 100 years or so, for a variety of reasons. Observations collected over the period suggest that the average land surface temperature has climbed 0.8–1.0°F (0.45–0.6°C) in the century. The surface of the ocean has also been warming at a similar rate. Studies that combine land and sea measurements have generally estimated that global temperatures have warmed 0.5–1.0°F (0.3–0.6°C). About two-thirds of this warming took place between 1900 and 1940. Global temperatures declined slightly from the 1940s through the 1970s, but have been getting higher more rapidly during the last twenty-five years than in the time before 1940. Surface temperatures are not rising uniformly. Nighttime low temperatures are increasing on average about twice as rapidly as daytime highs. The winters in areas between 50° and 70° north latitude (the latitude of Canada and Alaska) are warming relatively fast, while summer temperatures show little upward trend. Urban areas are warming somewhat more rapidly than rural areas, because of the changes in land cover and the consumption of energy that take place in densely developed areas (a feature known as the "urban heat island" effect). Frequent and severe heat waves lead to increases in heat-related illness and death, especially in urban areas and among the elderly, the young, the ill, and the poor.

It is possible—even likely—that warming in the future will melt the polar ice packs and the world's glaciers, raising the worldwide sea level enough to drown many coastal areas and cities. As Ward and Brownlee (2000) put it,

> At the start of the twenty-first century, there is a planetary consensus emerging that rapid global warming of the planet, caused by human air pollution, is a significant global threat. A warming world will bring about rising sea levels, changing plant communities, and the migration of tropical diseases into temperate regions. There may be an increase in the violence of storms, more droughts and floods, and disruption of agriculture. As Earth heats up, wars over food, water, and habitable land may increase.

Warmer temperatures allow mosquitoes that transmit diseases such as malaria and dengue fever to extend their ranges and increase both their biting rate and their ability to infect humans.

Warmer temperatures increase melting of mountain glaciers, increase ocean heat content, and cause ocean water to expand. Largely as a result of these effects, global sea level has risen four to ten inches over the past 100 years. With additional warming, sea level is projected to climb from half a foot to three feet more during the next 100 years. On average, fifty to 100 feet of beach are lost for every foot of sea level rise. Local land subsidence (sinking) and/or uplift due to geologic forces and coastal development will also affect the rate of coastal land loss. Measurements suggest that sea level has risen worldwide approximately six to eight inches in the last century. Part of that rise has been attributed to the historic warming of the atmosphere and the oceans. Approximately one to two inches resulted from the melting of mountain glaciers. Another one to two inches came from the expansion of ocean water that resulted from warmer ocean temperatures. A number of factors unrelated to greenhouse gases may be responsible for part of the historic rise in sea level, including the pumping of groundwater, and melting of the polar ice sheets in response to the global warming that has taken place since the last ice age. Nevertheless, scientists are currently unable to account for all of the measured sea level increase of the last century.

By its very definition, global warming affects every place on earth, from the tallest mountains to the deepest ocean trenches and everywhere in between. Our weather will change, agriculture and fishing will have to be modified, and the way of life of all creatures on earth will be affected. Already in the offing, a warming ocean will have the most profound—and predictable—effect on ice that comes into contact with it. Antarctica is twice as large as Australia and contains 70 percent of the earth's freshwater resources. The ice, which covers about 98 percent of the continent, and averages about 6,500 feet thick (well over a mile), constitutes most of the entire Antarctic landmass. Floating ice shelves make up about 11 percent of the continent. In March 2006, University of Colorado (Boulder) researchers used data from a pair of NASA satellites orbiting earth to determine that the Antarctic ice sheet, which harbors 90 percent of our planet's ice, has lost significant mass in recent years. The team used measurements taken with the Gravity Recovery and Climate Experiment (GRACE) to conclude that the Antarctic ice sheet is losing up to thirty-six cubic miles of ice, or 152 cubic kilometers, annually. By comparison, the city of Los Angeles uses about one cubic mile of freshwater annually. At the measured rate of melting it would take about six years for the oceans to rise an inch, or seventy-two years to rise a foot. Launched in 2002 by NASA and Germany, the two GRACE satellites whip around earth sixteen times a day at an altitude of 310 miles, sensing subtle variations in the planet's mass and gravitational pull. Separated by 137 miles at all times, the satellites measure changes in earth's gravity field caused by regional changes in the planet's mass, including such things as ice sheets, oceans, and water stored in the soil and in underground aquifers.

The Arctic Ocean is the smallest of the world's oceans, only one-sixth the volume of the next smallest, the Indian Ocean. Its area is 5,440,000 square miles, and its depth averages 3,240 feet. (The deepest point, on the Pole Abyssal Plain, is 14,800 feet below sea level.) The total includes the marginal Chukchi, East Siberian, Laptev, Kara, Barents, White, Greenland, and Beaufort seas. The Arctic Ocean is almost completely surrounded by the landmasses of North America, Eurasia, and Greenland. While there are small gaps in this encirclement—the Bering Strait, for example—the major part of the water inflow and outflow takes place in the Greenland Sea, roughly 80 percent leaving and entering the Arctic passes through the narrow channel between Greenland and Spitsbergen. Within 80° north latitude, there are several landmasses (the northernmost part of Greenland is Cape Morris Jesup, at 83°40'N), including islands in the Canadian archipelago, Severnaya Zemlya, Franz Josef Land, and northern Spitsbergen, but the North Pole is in the middle of the Arctic Ocean.

Between 60° north and 75° north the occurrence of sea ice is seasonal (it appears in the fall, and remains through the winter and early spring), but most of the region above 75° north is (or used to be) permanently ice covered. The ice of the northern Arctic Ocean is not solid like that of the Antarctic or even the Greenland ice cap; it floats in the ocean, put in motion by the prevailing currents and winds. (Sea ice is frozen salt water; it is different from icebergs, which are freshwater, and have broken off from glaciers.) Because of the ice (and the enduring winter night) the Arctic Ocean is poorly explored. (Those who sought the North Pole did very little exploration.) The exception is Nansen, whose *Fram* expedition in 1893–96 was the first scientific study of the contours and conditions of the Arctic Ocean. In 1928, Sir Hubert Wilkins made the first airplane flight across the Arctic Ocean; in 1937, the Soviet Union set up the first floating scientific station; and now airplane and satellite observations have provided accurate images of this previously uncharted region.

One important factor in the global warming scenario is the reduction of the earth's albedo (Latin for "white"), the overall average reflection coefficient, which affects the planet's equilibrium temperature. The greenhouse effect, by trapping infrared radiation, can lower the earth's albedo, and therefore raise temperatures. Because the Arctic sea ice cover acts as a giant mirror, reflecting the sun's rays back into space, its disappearance can only serve to accelerate the earth's warming trend. In *Science* (December 5, 2003), climatologists Thomas Karl and Kevin Treberth wrote,

Ice-albedo feedback occurs as increased warming diminishes snow and ice cover, making the planet darker and more receptive to absorbing solar radiation, causing warming, which further melts snow and ice. This effect is greatest at high latitudes. Decreased snow cover extent has significantly contributed to the earlier onset of spring in the past few decades over northern-hemisphere high latitudes. The feedback is affected by changes in clouds, thus complicating the net feedback effect.

In the last two decades, temperatures have been rising in the Arctic at a rate twenty times faster than the warming that occurred over the previous century, and the thickness of the ice sheet has decreased by about half (down from fifteen feet in the 1980s to eight feet in 2003). Spring comes earlier and fall is arriving later, which, combined with higher summer temperatures year after year, contributes to the gradual shrinking of the permanent ice sheet. Surface temperatures are increasing at a rate of two degrees per decade over the region, and the result is pooling of liquid water on the surface of the ice sheets. Because water absorbs heat (rather than reflecting most of the radiation, as ice does), this results in accelerated ice melt, and also causes deep fractures to develop in ice shelves and glaciers, leading to such events as the splitting of the Ward Hunt Ice Shelf (in the Antarctic) into huge state-sized chunks, and eventually to iceberg calving events, as the ice sheet splits along these fissures. Arctic sea ice set a new record for minimum size in 2002. All over the world, warming temperatures are causing a reduction in ice. Because ice reflects back into space almost all the energy it receives, while water absorbs energy and thus warms, as the ice decreases, the surface area of water increases, and the amount of warming rises in direct proportion to this increased absorption. As the ice sheet continues to retreat, the rate of warming can be expected to increase, and we will see an ever more rapid retreat of the ice cap.

If all the ice in Greenland and Antarctica melted, it would cause a rise in sea level of around 230 feet (seventy meters.) Such a nightmare is extremely unlikely under any circumstances, but even the melting of a small proportion of these ice caps could have devastating effects, flooding low-lying coastal regions and reducing the safety margin of coastal defenses. New calculations by Philippe Huybrechts of Vrije Universiteit, Brussels, and Jan de Wolde of the University of Utrecht, the

Netherlands (a country with a vested interest in sea level), put limits on how much sea level could rise due to melting ice over the next millennium. Huybrechts and de Wolde wrote,

New calculations were performed to investigate the combined response of the Greenland and Antarctic ice sheets to a range of climatic warming scenarios over the next millennium . . . The experiments were initialized with simulations over the last two glacial cycles to estimate the present evolution and were subsequently forced with temperature scenarios resulting from greenhouse emission scenarios which assume equivalent CO_2 increases of two, four, and eight times the present (1990 A.D.) value by the year 2130 A.D. and a stabilization after that. The calculations brought to light that during the next century (short-term effect), the background evolution trend would dominate the response of the Antarctic ice sheet but would be negligible for the Greenland ice sheet. On that timescale, the Greenland and Antarctic ice sheets would roughly balance one another for the middle scenario (similar to the IPCC96 IS92a scenario), with respective contributions to the worldwide sea level stand on the order of about ±10 cm. On the longer term, however, both ice sheets would contribute positively to the worldwide sea level stand and the most important effect would come from melting on the Greenland ice sheet.

In *Nature* (March 11, 2004), Quirin Schiermeier wrote "A Rising Tide," a discussion of the melting of the Greenland ice cap. "It has become clear in recent years," he wrote, "that climate warming is beginning to trigger rapid and substantial changes in the polar ice caps. In Greenland, these changes may be irreversible." Floating sea ice has been on the decline in recent years, which means less ice to reflect sunlight, and therefore the oceans absorb more solar energy, leading to further warming. The Greenland ice sheet has been in balance for the past 20,000 years, but there is growing evidence that it is losing its equilibrium. Huybrechts's "worst-case scenario" has Greenland's mean annual temperature rising by 8°C by 2100, which would mean that by the end of the millennium, "the ice sheet would shrink to a small glaciated area, and the sea level would rise by six meters."

"A Worrying Trend of Less Ice, Higher Seas" is the title of Richard Kerr's article in *Science*, dated March 26, 2006. He wrote,

> The summertime Arctic Ocean could be ice-free by century's end, 11,000-year-old shelves around Antarctica are breaking up over the course of weeks, and glaciers there and in Greenland have been galloping into the sea . . . And the speeding glaciers, at least, are surely driving up sea level and pushing shorelines inland . . . Some of the glaciers draining the great ice sheets of the Antarctic and Greenland have speeded up dramatically, driving up sea level and catching scientists unawares. They don't fully understand what is happening. And if they don't understand what a little warming is doing to the ice sheets today, they reason, what can they say about the ice's fate and rising seas in the greenhouse world of the next century or two?

In January 2003, Terry Root and several colleagues published a study they called *Fingerprints of Global Warming on Wild Animals and Plants*. These "fingerprints" consist of temperature-related factors identifiable in species ranging from mollusks to mammals, from grasses to trees. They found that in over 80 percent of the animal and plant species studied, "a significant impact of global warming is already discernible," and concluded, "The synergism of rapid temperature rise and other stresses, in particular habitat destruction, could easily disrupt the connectedness among species and lead to a reformulation of species communities, reflecting differential changes in species, and to numerous extirpations and possibly extinctions."

In May 2004, Sir David King, chief scientific adviser to the British government's Office of Science and Technology, gave an interview to the *Guardian*, in which he asserted, "Antarctica is likely to be the world's only habitable continent by the end of this century if global warming remains unchecked." He said the earth was entering the "first hot period" since sixty million years ago, when there was no ice on the planet and "the rest of the globe could not sustain human life." Furthermore, Sir David said that levels of carbon dioxide in the atmosphere—the main greenhouse gas causing climate change—were already 50 percent higher than at any time in the past 420,000 years. The last time they were at this level—379 parts per million—was indeed sixty million years ago, during a rapid period of global warming. Levels soared to 1,000 parts per million, causing a massive reduction of life. As Sir David said, "No ice was left on Earth. Antarctica was the best place for mammals to live." King warned that if the world did not curb its burning of fossil fuels "we will reach that level by 2100."

In Vagn Flyger's 1967 essay on the status of the polar bear, we encounter this statement:

> The reason for the decline in numbers of polar bears over the past 100 years is not entirely clear. It is true that the polar ice cap has receded and that the consequent disappearance of pack ice has caused bears to become a rare sight in areas such as southeast Greenland and Iceland. Pack ice is the habitat of the polar bear and the seals which are his food. So naturally, as the ice goes, so go the bears. But this cannot be the whole explanation for the general decrease; on some arctic islands, excessive hunting has definitely eliminated the animal or has sharply reduced his numbers. However, the overall picture is not clear, and the polar bear, perhaps the world's largest carnivore, may go the way of the world's largest mammal, the blue whale.

In 1967, it was generally believed that the blue whale was headed for extinction—commercial hunting for this species had been halted by the International Whaling Commission only a year earlier—and while its diet of living crustaceans (krill) would technically classify *Balaenoptera musculus* as a carnivore, the title of largest carnivore that has ever lived is usually awarded to the sixty-ton sperm whale. The polar bear, then, is only the world's largest *terrestrial* carnivore, but Flyger's comments on the receding ice pack as a factor in the decrease in polar bear numbers were unusually prescient. Flyger was renowned for his work on squirrels, but it is obvious that he also cared deeply about *Ursus maritimus*, for he wrote, "Although it is the nations bordering the polar seas that demonstrate greatest interest in the polar bear, he actually belongs to everyone. Surely the peoples of the world would want to assure this great animal a place on the globe, not because he is something for hunters to shoot, but because he is the symbol of the Arctic and a worthy companion of mankind." Even more than the bear, however, the ice itself is the symbol of the Arctic, and the ice is in serious trouble. In her 2008 article "Losing Greenland," a summary of the science of measuring ice loss, Alexandra Witze wrote, "Climate change elsewhere in the Arctic has been swifter than anticipated. The remarkable shrinkage of the ice is the largest change in Earth's surface that humans have probably ever observed."

In 1988, when he was a senior editor at *Discover* magazine, Andrew Revkin wrote what was probably the first major article warning of the imminent dangers of global warming. In "Endless Summer—Living with the Greenhouse Effect," Revkin quoted NASA's James Hansen, speaking before a U.S. Senate committee on June 23, 1988: "Global warming has reached a level such that we can ascribe with a high degree of confidence a cause and effect relationship between the greenhouse effect and observed warming. It is already happening now."* Inspired by Hansen's testimony, Revkin explained in *Discover,* "Comparable climate shifts have happened before, but over tens of centuries, not tens of years. The unprecedented rapid climate change could accelerate the already high rate of species extinction as plants and animals fail to adapt quickly enough. For the first time in history humans are affecting the ecological balance of not just a region but the entire world, all at once." He quoted University of California oceanographer/climatologist Roger Revelle (who would figure significantly in Al Gore's 2006 *Inconvenient Truth*): "Average climate would certainly get warmer, but what's more serious is how many more hurricanes we'll have, how many more droughts we'll have, how many days above 100 degrees." We have had more hurricanes, more cyclones, more droughts, more floods, more storms, and more overheated days, but nobody expected the Arctic ice cap to melt.

James Hansen did not discover global warming, nor was he the first to warn of its dangers. That discovery, recounted in Spencer Weart's 2003 book *The Discovery of Global Warming,* was a complex process, involving scientists from many diverse disciplines, over a significant period of time. More than a century ago, the Swedish scientist Svante

---

* Hansen had actually begun warning of the dangers of anthropogenic climate change in 1981. As the senior author of a paper in *Science,* he wrote, "It is shown that the anthropogenic carbon dioxide warming should emerge from the noise level of natural climate variability by the end of the century and there is a high probability of global warming in the 1980s. Potential effects on climate in the 21st century include the creation of drought-prone regions in North America and Central Asia as part of shifting climatic zones, erosion of the West Antarctic ice sheet with a consequent rise in sea level, and opening of the fabled Northwest Passage."

Arrhenius (1859–1927) coined the term "greenhouse effect" as he pointed out that the combustion of fossil fuels might increase the level of CO_2 in the atmosphere, and thereby warm the earth several degrees. No one knows who coined the term "global warming," but Roger Revelle's discovery that the oceans did not absorb much of the excess carbon dioxide produced by people was one of the early wake-up calls. In 1957, with Hans Seuss, Revelle published "Carbon Dioxide Exchange Between Atmosphere and Ocean and the Question of Atmospheric CO_2 During the Past Decades," in which they wrote, "Human beings are now carrying out a large-scale geophysical experiment." Then Charles David Keeling published a report sponsored by the Conservation Foundation, in which he (and several other scientists) suggested that "the doubling of CO_2 projected for the next century could raise the world's temperature by 4°C (more than 6°F). They warned that this could be harmful; for example, it could cause glaciers to melt and raise the sea level so that coastlines would get flooded" (Weart 2003). Awareness of a phenomenon (or a problem) within the narrow confines of the scientific community is admirable—and vital—but without public and/or governmental acknowledgment, it cannot produce the changes required to fix the problem.

Revkin's *Discover* article appeared at about the same time that Bill McKibben was preparing *The End of Nature* (1989), considered the first book about global warming for a general audience. McKibben wrote,

Perhaps the most famous of the computer programs is in the hands of James Hansen and his colleagues at NASA's Goddard Institute for Space Studies, in, of all places, Manhattan. NASA used an early version of the model around 1970 to study the accuracy of predictions from satellite weather observations; when the Goddard weather group moved to Washington, Hansen, who was staying on in New York, decided he'd try the model on longer-term problems—on climate as opposed to weather. Over the years, he and his colleagues have fine-tuned the program, and even though it remains a rough simulation of the mightily complex real world, they have improved it to the point where they are willing to forecast not just the effects of a doubling of carbon dioxide but the incremental effects along the way—that is, the forecast not just for 2050 but for 2000.

Then, in their 1990 assessment of the relative roles of sun and dust versus greenhouse gases in global climate change, Hansen and Lacis observed that "steadily increasing concentrations, principally man-made, of greenhouse gases, have led to the expectation of global warming during coming decades. Computer simulations, supported by paleoclimate studies, suggest that the potential greenhouse climate change could rival the difference between today's climate and the last great ice age of 20,000 years ago." Hansen and Lacis concluded that solar variability will not counteract greenhouse warming, and that tro-pospheric aerosols—greenhouse gases—would have to be substan-tially reduced in order to avoid the incipient dangers of global warming. "It seems imperative that governments give much higher priority to research and development on energy sources that produce little or no greenhouse gases," wrote the authors. "Otherwise we risk the danger of soon finding ourselves, in the mid-American vernacular, up the prover-bial creek without a paddle." They wrote this scenario eighteen years before Hansen would testify again before a congressional subcommit-tee, pointing out that the problem had only gotten worse.

Virtually all of Hansen's studies had been published in scientific journals, but in 2004 he wrote "Can We Defuse the Global Warming Time Bomb?" for the popular magazine *Scientific American*. (The edi-tors of the magazine identified Hansen as "best-known for his testi-mony on climate change to congressional committees in the 1980s that helped raise broad awareness of the global warming issue.") He wrote, "The dominant issue in global warming, in my opinion, is sea level change and the question of how fast ice sheets can disintegrate. A large proportion of the world's people live within a few meters of sea level, with trillions of dollars of infrastructure. The need to preserve global coast lines, I suggest, sets a low ceiling on the level of global warming that would constitute dangerous anthropogenic interference." He believed that reduced CO_2 emissions "might be accomplished via improved energy efficiency and increased use of renewable energies, but a long-term decline of emissions will require development of energy technologies that produce little or no CO_2 or that capture and sequester CO_2." In other words, to defuse the global warming time bomb, Amer-ica had to reduce its emissions of CO_2 by curtailing the burning of coal, oil, and other fossil fuels, and resorting to other sources of energy:

"Realistic moderate global energy growth rates," wrote Hansen, "coupled with near-term emphasis on renewable energies could keep global CO_2 emissions flat in the near term and allow the possibility of long-term reductions, as may be required to avoid dangerous anthropogenic interference with climate."

More than twenty-five billion tons of CO_2 are released into the atmosphere every year: four tons for every man, woman, and child on the planet. America's cars, trucks, and coal-burning factories produce far more than the global average, and there is one source that has escaped front-page attention: underground coal fires. Underground coal fires in China alone produce as much carbon dioxide annually as all the cars and light trucks in the United States. Fires in other countries, including the United States, are smaller but still add significantly to the total burden. Since Hansen began beating the global warming drum, the U.S. government has done nothing to curtail CO_2 emissions (and, as noted in a previous chapter, remains one of two major countries that have not signed the Kyoto Protocol). It has, however, gone to great lengths to curtail James Hansen. In a speech at the American Geophysical Union in San Francisco in 2006, Hansen suggested that motor vehicles should be modified to reduce emissions. (He also said that 2005 was the warmest year in the past century.) The Bush administration tried to muzzle him by arranging for NASA officials to review his future lectures, papers, and postings on the Goddard Web site. According to a *New York Times* article by Andrew Revkin, Hansen said he would ignore the restrictions.

They couldn't muzzle Hansen, so they tried to rewrite what he said. On March 20, 2007, the House Committee on Oversight and Government Reform displayed documents that "appear to portray a systematic White House effort to minimize the significance of climate change." Philip Cooney, chief of staff at the White House's Council on Environmental Quality (CEQ) from 2001 to 2005, said this editing was part of the normal review process between agencies. (Before he joined the White House, Cooney was a lobbyist for the American Petroleum Institute, and he now works for ExxonMobil.) In a ten-year policy plan, Cooney and Brian Hannegan (also at CEQ) made at least 181 edits to emphasize scientific uncertainty regarding the effects of climate change and 113 changes to minimize the importance of human contributions to global warming, according to the committee's memo. For example,

Cooney replaced "will" with "may" in the sentence "Warming temperatures will also affect Arctic land areas," and he deleted this sentence:
"Climate change has global consequences for human health and the
environment." In his written testimony, Hansen said, "In my more than
three decades in government, I have never seen anything approaching
the degree to which information flow from scientists to the public has
been screened and controlled as it has now."

Undeterred by attempts at government censorship and sentence
modification, Hansen et al. published "Climate Change and Trace
Gases" in 2007. They wrote,

> Paleoclimate data show that the Earth's climate is remarkably sensi-
> tive to global forcings. Positive feedbacks predominate. This allows
> the entire planet to be whipsawed between climate states . . . Inertia
> of ice sheet and ocean provides only moderate delay to ice sheet dis-
> integration and a burst of added global warming. Recent greenhouse
> gas emissions place the Earth perilously close to dramatic climate
> change that could run out of control, with great dangers for humans
> and other creatures.

They included a section entitled "Dangerous Climate Change": "Emergence of human-caused global warming raises the question: what level
of further warming will be 'dangerous' for humanity? . . . There is little
doubt that the projected warnings under BAU [business-as-usual]
would initiate albedo-flip changes as great as those that occurred at earlier times in the Earth's history." They concluded, "The imminent peril
is initiation of dynamical and thermodynamical processes of the West
Antarctic and Greenland ice sheets that produce a situation out of
humanity's control, such that devastating sea-level rise will inevitably
occur."

On the twentieth anniversary of his June 23, 1988, testimony before
Congress, Hansen was invited by Democratic Representative Edward
Markey to address the House Select Subcommittee on Energy Inde-
pendence and Global Warming. In the unrestrained language for which
he has become notorious, Hansen said (among other things),

> Special interests have blocked transition to our renewable energy
> future. Instead of moving heavily into renewable energies, fossil com-

panies choose to spread doubt about global warming, as tobacco companies discredited the smoking-cancer link. Methods are sophisticated, including funding to help shape school textbook discussions of global warming.

CEOs of fossil energy companies know what they are doing and are aware of long-term consequences of continued business as usual. In my opinion, these CEOs should be tried for high crimes against humanity and nature.

Conviction of ExxonMobil and Peabody Coal CEOs will be no consolation, if we pass on a runaway climate to our children. Humanity would be impoverished by ravages of continually shifting shorelines and intensification of regional climate extremes. Loss of countless species would leave a more desolate planet.

There are those who do not share Hansen's view that ecological Armageddon is imminent, and some who do not even believe that global warming is a legitimate threat. According to AP reporter Seth Borenstein, "Longtime global warming skeptic Sen. James Imhofe, R.-Okla, citing a recent poll, said in a statement, 'Hansen, Gore and the media have been trumpeting man-made climate doom since the 1980s. But Americans are not buying it.' " Canadian essayist Rex Murphy wrote that Hansen called for a tribunal,

or as I prefer to call it, an Inquisition, to put on trial for crimes against nature and humanity, the CEOs of the big oil companies, who, according to Dr. Hansen's frantic view of things, feed the public "misinformation" about the climate crisis . . . Science has no need of tribunals or trials, no need of Nuremberg justices, or analogies with the Holocaust. James Hansen's words this week were an offense, an offense against inquiry, against science, against moral seriousness. They were a plea or insolence against the idea of debate itself.

The critics and deniers notwithstanding, the unnatural forcing of the climate is a result of man-made emissions of carbon dioxide and other greenhouse gases, and threatens to generate a "flip" in the climate that could spark a cataclysm in the ice sheets of Antarctica and Greenland. Hansen et al., 2007:

Earth's climate is remarkably sensitive to forcings, i.e. imposed changes of the planet's energy balance. Both fast and slow feedbacks turn out to be predominately positive. As a result, our climate has the potential for large rapid fluctuations. Indeed, the Earth, and the creatures struggling to exist on the planet, have been repeatedly whipsawed between climate states. No doubt this rough ride has driven progression of life via changing stresses, extinctions and species evolution. But civilization developed, and constructed extensive infrastructure, during a period of unusual climate stability, the Holocene, now almost 12000 years in duration. That period is about to end.

Seventeen years after his groundbreaking *Discover* article, Revkin, now a science reporter for the *New York Times,* began reporting on the subject of retreating polar ice. In 2005, he wrote an article entitled "In Melting Trend, Less Ice to Go Around," and since then he has written regularly about the problem with a growing sense of crisis, as seen in this succession of headlines, a drumroll of impending doom:

MARCH 3, 2006:
"Loss of Antarctic Ice Increases"

MARCH 15, 2006:
"Ice Retreats in Arctic for 2nd Year;
Some Fear Most of It Will Vanish"

JUNE 13, 2006:
"Biologists Note Polar Bear Cannibalism"

AUGUST 11, 2006:
"Greenland: Ice Cap Melting Faster"

SEPTEMBER 14, 2006:
"NASA Scientists See New Signs of Global Warming"

DECEMBER 12, 2006:
"By 2040, Greenhouse Gases Could Lead
to an Open Arctic Sea in Summers"

DECEMBER 26, 2006 (WITH BARRINGER):
"Agency Proposes to List Polar Bear as Threatened"

FEBRUARY 3, 2007 (WITH ROSENTHAL):
"Science Panel Calls Global Warming 'Unequivocal' "

AUGUST 10, 2007:
"Analysts See 'Simply Incredible' Shrinking
of Floating Ice in the Arctic"

SEPTEMBER 8, 2007 (WITH BRODER):
"Warming Is Seen as Wiping Out Most Polar Bears"

SEPTEMBER 21, 2007:
"Scientists Report Severe Retreat of Arctic Ice"

OCTOBER 2, 2007:
"Grim Outlook for Bears"

OCTOBER 2, 2007:
"Arctic Melt Unnerves Experts"

In 2006, Revkin wrote a book called *The North Pole Was Here,* the story of his visit (by plane) in the spring of 2003 to a landing sixty miles from the pole. In the book he wrote,

> To celebrate getting here, one scientist who arrived a couple of days before us, Jim Johnson, erected a red-and-white-striped barber pole and a sign that said NORTH POLE IS HERE. But after a day or so, Johnson changed the wording, so that the sign now reads NORTH POLE *WAS* HERE. The past tense is meant as a joke. The drift of the ice guarantees that anyone who is at the North Pole at one moment is not there a few minutes later. But the sign also reflects the broader and much more profound idea that confronts everyone up here: that the unreachable, unchanging North Pole of our imagination, history, maps and lore, no longer exists.

In his *Scientific American* article in 2004, James Hansen warned that "global warming is real, and the consequences are potentially disastrous." He continued, "Human-made forces, especially greenhouse gases, soot and other small particles, now exceed natural forces, and the world has begun to warm at a rate predicted by climate models . . . Halting global warming requires urgent, unprecedented international cooperation, but the needed actions are feasible and have additional benefits for human health, agriculture and the environment." After a detailed discussion of global warming, Hansen asked, "Will we act soon enough?" Al Gore answered: "Not under the present administration." In a paid ad in the *New York Times* on February 20, 2004, the advocacy group MoveOn quoted a speech that Gore gave in New York City on January 15, in which he said,

Although the Earth is vast, its most vulnerable point is the atmosphere, which is surprisingly thin. As the late Carl Sagan used to say, it's like a coat of varnish on a globe. Today, there is no longer any credible basis for doubting that our atmosphere is heating up because of global warming caused by human activities: The earth's environment is sustaining severe and potentially irreparable damage from an unprecedented accumulation of pollution in the atmosphere. The evidence is overwhelming and undeniable. Glaciers are melting almost everywhere in the world. Within 15 years there will be no more snows of Kilimanjaro. In our own Glacier National Park, most of the glaciers have already melted. Soon it will be "the park formerly known as Glacier." The Arctic ice pack has thinned by 40 percent in the last half century, and is still receding. Scientists project that within another 50 years, we may well see the complete disappearance in summertime of the Arctic ice cap. At present, this massive ice cap works like a giant mirror, reflecting 95 percent of the sun's energy. But without it, 90 percent of that energy will be absorbed. Since temperature variations between the equator and the poles help shape ocean currents and jet streams, pole-melting threatens massive disruption of our entire global weather pattern.

"No Escape: Thaw Gains Momentum" was the title of a 2005 *New York Times* article by Andrew Revkin. "Many scientists," he wrote,

say it has taken a long time for them to accept that global warming, partly the result of carbon dioxide and other heat-trapping gases in the atmosphere, could shrink the Arctic's summer cloak of ice. But many of those same scientists have concluded that the momentum behind human-caused warming, combined by the region's tendency to amplify change, has put the familiar Arctic past the point of no return . . . Even with just modest growth in emissions of the greenhouse gases, almost all of the summer sea ice is likely to disappear by late in the century.

At meetings sponsored by the National Science Foundation, Arctic scientists from all involved disciplines convened to discuss the scenario of a retreating ice sheet. In *Eos,* a publication of the American Geophysical Union, twenty-one scientists collaborated on a report they called "Arctic System on Trajectory to New, Seasonally Ice-Free State." Their statement:

> The Arctic system is moving toward a new state that falls outside the envelope of glacial-interglacial fluctuations that prevailed during recent Earth history. This future Arctic is likely to have dramatically less permanent ice than exists at present. At the present rate of change, a summer ice-free Arctic Ocean within a century is a real possibility, a state not witnessed for at least a million years. The change appears to be driven largely by feedback-enhanced global climate warming, and there seem to be few, if any, processes or feedbacks within the Arctic system that are capable of altering the trajectory toward this "super interglacial" state.

As Hansen predicted in 1981, global warming has seen to it that the heretofore impassable Northwest Passage may soon be open to ships for its entire length, perhaps even rendering the Panama Canal obsolete for Atlantic/Pacific traffic. (It was the Panama Canal, opened in 1914, that enabled ships to sail from one ocean to the other without passing through the treacherous waters and winds of Cape Horn.) The Northwest Passage—a direct shipping route from Europe to Asia across the Arctic Ocean—is ice free in summer for the first time since satellite records began in 1979. Climate models had projected that the passage would eventually open as warming temperatures melted the Arctic sea ice, but no one had predicted it would happen this soon.

In the *New York Review of Books* (July 13, 2006), Hansen reviewed three books on global warming (Tim Flannery's *The Weather Makers,* Elizabeth Kolbert's *Field Notes from a Catastrophe,* and Al Gore's *An Inconvenient Truth*) and said,

> The species most at risk are those in polar climates and biologically diverse slopes of alpine regions. Polar animals, in effect, will be pushed off the planet. Alpine species will be pushed to higher altitudes, and toward smaller, rockier areas with thinner air; thus, in effect, they will be also pushed off the planet. A few such species, such as polar bears, will no doubt be "rescued" by human beings, but survival in zoos or managed animal reserves will be small consolation to bears or nature lovers.

Hansen then took to the soapbox to defend his stance on—and the science of—global warming, and to show that those who profess to believe that the planet is not in crisis are playing politics to the detriment of the world and everything that lives on it. He asked, "Why are the same scientists and political forces that succeeded in controlling the threat to the ozone layer now failing miserably to deal with the global warming crisis?" His answer:

> Scientists present the facts about climate change critically, failing to stress that business-as-usual will transform the planet. The press and television, despite an overwhelming consensus concerning global warming, give equal time to fringe "contrarians" supported by the fossil fuel industry. Special interest groups mount effective disinformation campaigns to sow doubt about the reality of global warming. The government appears to be strongly influenced by special interests, or otherwise confused and distracted, and has failed to provide leadership. The public is understandably confused or disinterested.

In the review, Hansen took the opportunity to present Gore, his film and his book, as correct in all particulars. The book and the movie, he said, "are filled with pictures—stunning illustrations, maps, graphs, brief explanations, and stories about people who have important parts in the global warming story or in Al Gore's life. The movie seems to

me powerful and the book complements it, adding useful explanations . . . the story is scientifically accurate and yet should be under-
standable to the public, a public that is less and less drawn to science."

An Inconvenient Truth is an Academy Award–winning documentary
about climate change, specifically global warming, presented by former
Vice President Al Gore and directed by Davis Guggenheim. It takes
the form of an illustrated lecture—or an elaborate PowerPoint presentation—with Gore shown speaking to a live audience. The film earned
$49 million worldwide in theaters, and was released on DVD by Para-
mount Home Entertainment on November 21, 2006; it has been well
received by film critics, scientists, and politicians, and is now being used
in school science curricula around the world. A companion book with
the same title has been on the *New York Times* paperback nonfiction
best-seller list since June 11, 2006, and reached number one within two
weeks. The book is essentially a printed version of the film, incorporating the graphs, charts, photographs, and narration. Of polar bears,
Gore says,

> The melting of the ice represents bad news for creatures like polar
> bears. A new scientific study shows that, for the first time, polar bears
> have been drowning in significant numbers. Such deaths have been
> rare in the past. But now, these bears find they have to swim much
> longer distances from floe to floe. In some places the edge of the ice
> is 30 to 40 miles from shore.*

In October 2007, Gore added another accolade to the Oscar he and
his producers received. Together with the Intergovernmental Panel on
Climate Change (IPCC), Gore was awarded the Nobel Peace Prize for
2007. The IPCC is a United Nations body of about 2,500 atmospheric
scientists, oceanographers, ice specialists, economists, and other experts,
considered the world's top scientific authority on global warming and
its impact. Established in 1988, following a demand by the Group of

---

* In the book, this quote appears opposite a full-page photo of two bears on an ice floe. In
the film, however, Gore's reading of the same lines is voiced-over an animated sequence of
a forlorn bear looking for ice, failing to find any, and swimming off into the distance. That
this sequence had to be animated has given Gore's critics ammunition to criticize him and
the film. No one has ever managed to film a bear in the act of drowning, but carcasses floating or washed ashore with no visible injuries suggested that they might have drowned.

This bear is swimming from one ice floe to another, but there have been cases in which bears swam in search of ice floes and, not finding any, died from exhaustion.

Seven (the seven richest countries in the world: the United States, Japan, Germany, France, Great Britain, Canada, Italy), under the auspices of the World Meteorological Society and the United Nations Environment Program, the IPCC assesses "the scientific, technical and socio-economic information that relates to human induced climate change."

After losing the contest for the White House in 2000, Gore reinvented himself, with *An Inconvenient Truth,* as a passionate student of climate change. Then he collected the International Emmy Founders Award, presented by the International Academy of Television Arts & Sciences, an organization of broadcasters from seventy countries, for launching Current TV, a cable/satellite channel, and for calling attention to global warming. The IPCC does no research or experiments; instead, its people gather, sift, and summarize the best information available and then issue "comprehensive, objective, open, and transparent" assessments of the state of scientific knowledge on climate change. The 2007 *Synthesis Report of the IPCC Fourth Assessment* included these statements about world climate change:

Warming of the climate system is unequivocal, as is now evident from observations of increases in global average air and ocean temperatures, widespread melting of snow and ice, and rising global average sea level.

Observational evidence from all continents and most oceans shows that many systems are being affected by regional climate changes, particularly temperature increases.

Global atmospheric concentrations of CO_2, methane (CH_4) and nitrous oxide (N_2O) have increased markedly as a result of human activities since 1750 and now far exceed pre-industrial values determined from ice cores spanning many thousands of years.

For the polar regions, the IPCC concluded:

The main projected biophysical effects is reductions in thickness and extent of glaciers and ice sheets and sea ice, and changes in natural ecosystems with detrimental effects on many organisms, including migratory birds, mammals and higher predators.

In both polar regions, specific ecosystems and habitats are projected to be vulnerable, as climatic barriers to species invasions are lowered.

Following the IPCC Fourth Assessment Report (and its Nobel Prize), a multidisciplinary group of researchers (Rosenzweig et al. 2008) analyzed data from published papers on 829 physical systems and 28,000 plant and animal systems going back to 1970, and wrote that "there has been significant anthropogenic warming over the past 50 years averaged over each continent except Antarctica, and [they concluded] that anthropogenic climate change is having a significant impact on physical and biological systems globally and in some continents." Ninety-five percent of the "anthropogenic climate change," wrote the authors, is "in the direction expected with warming temperatures"—that is, global warming. As lead author Cynthia Rosenzweig put it, "Humans are influencing climate through increasing greenhouse gas emissions, and the warming world is causing impacts on physical and biological systems attributable at the global scale." The changes include wastage of glaciers, melting permafrost, earlier spring runoff, increases in coastal erosion, warming of water bodies (and the concurrent shifting of marine life from cold-adapted to warmer-adapted communities), changes in species interactions, and the massive reduction of the Arctic ice cap, probably the most egregious anthropogenic climate change in the history of the earth.

In the early years of this century, there has been a rapid decrease in the amount of sea ice in place during the summer, and within the last two years more than 600 square miles of water has been opened up. Here's what climatologists Mark Serreze, Marika Holland, and Julienne Stroeve wrote in March 2007:

> Linear trends in arctic sea-ice extent over the period 1979 to 2006 are negative in every month. This ice loss is best viewed as a combination of strong natural variability in the coupled ice-ocean-atmosphere system and a growing radiative forcing associated with rising concentrations of atmospheric greenhouse gases, the latter supported by evidence of qualitative consistency between observed trends and those simulated by climate models over the same period.

As of November 2007, researchers studying the fate of the Arctic sea ice drastically revised their predictions. Early studies indicated that the summer ice would disappear by the end of the twenty-first century; shortly thereafter, the collapse was predicted for mid-century. The Arctic Ocean ice cover for 2005 had been the lowest on record, but the summer of 2007 was far worse: the ice had receded 43 percent from the 1979 level—a loss "equivalent to two Alaskas," wrote Richard Kerr in *Science*. Kerr also explained the "feedback loops" that might account for this calamitous acceleration of ice loss:

> In one [feedback loop] thinner ice one year made ice melt more easily the next year. In another, when white, highly reflective ice melted, the darker, more absorptive open water that replaced it absorbed more solar energy. The added heat could help melt more ice and keep new ice thinner that year—and even the next if the heat lingered through the winter.

Kerr's article is entitled "Is Battered Arctic Sea Ice Down for the Count?" Even the most optimistic researchers did not expect that the ice might go quickly into an abrupt and possibly irreversible decline.

Recent articles and studies about the decline of the Arctic ice are concerned with a global phenomenon; the subject is much too large to
address individual animals, but surely the diminution of the ice perforce
raises the question, "What about the polar bears?"

When Ian Stirling published *Polar Bears* in 1988, global warming had
not surfaced as a threat to the Arctic ice cap or its inhabitants. He concluded the book with an essay on "Conservation and Environmental
Concerns," in which he identified hunting, offshore drilling, oil spills,
and toxic chemicals as potentially harmful to polar bears—but he naturally assumed that the ice wasn't going anywhere. Five years later, with
polar bear specialist Andrew Derocher, Stirling speculated about the
possible impacts of climatic warming on polar bears: "In recent years,"
they wrote, "there has been a growing scientific consensus that increasing concentrations of greenhouse gases in the atmosphere are causing
the climate of the earth to warm. Of particular importance to the Arctic Ocean is how climatic warming may affect ice cover. One dramatic
consequence, speculated to be in as little as 100 years, is that the arctic
ice cap might disappear completely." They predicted the effect of such
an event on polar bears:

> The presence of sea ice is critical to polar bears because it provides
> the platform from which they hunt the seals they feed on. Similarly,
> the seals, especially the ringed seal that are the main food of polar
> bears, depend on the sea ice to provide a platform on which they can
> give birth and nurse their pups . . . Should the Arctic Ocean become
> seasonally ice free for a long enough period, it is likely that polar
> bears would become extirpated from at least the southern part of
> their range. If climatic warming occurs, the polar bear is the ideal
> species through which to monitor the cumulative effects in arctic
> marine ecosystems because of its position at the top of the arctic
> marine food chain.

In 2004, joined by Nicholas Lunn of the Canadian Wildlife Service,
Derocher and Stirling wrote another article about polar bears in a
warming climate, in which they gloomily concluded that, "given the
rapid pace of ecological change in the Arctic, the long generation time,
and the highly specialized nature of polar bears, it is unlikely that polar
bears will survive as a species if the sea ice disappears completely as has

been predicted by some." The Arctic ice sheet always diminishes in summer and increases in winter. The average minimum area of sea ice from 1979, when satellite mapping began, was 2.69 million square miles, roughly the size of the contiguous United States. Cooler winter temperatures allow the sea ice to "rebound" after summer melting, but with the exception of May 2005, every month since December 2004 has set a new record low ice extent for that month. Research from the National Snow and Ice Data Center (NSIDC) revealed that as of September 2005, the ice cover dropped to 2.05 million square miles, 20 percent below the average. As we have seen above, the ice reflects sunlight and open water absorbs it, so the smaller the ice cover, the greater the area of water that is warmed. More warm water melts more ice. More melting ice means fewer places for seals to dig lairs. Fewer seal lairs means fewer seals born. And fewer seals born is very bad for hungry polar bears.

"Polar bears depend on sea ice for survival," wrote Stirling and Claire Parkinson in 2006. "Climate warming in the Arctic has caused significant declines in total cover and thickness of sea ice in the polar basin and progressively earlier breakup in some areas. Inuit hunters in the areas of four polar bear populations in the eastern Canadian Arctic (including Western Hudson Bay) have reported seeing more bears near settlements during the open-water period in recent years." More bears seen near settlements leads to the incorrect assumption that there are more bears everywhere, but in fact the earlier breakup of the ice shortens the spring hunting season for females, so they eat less, and thinner bears are more likely to push into human settlements in search of food. Stirling, interviewed for a 2006 NASA news feature ("Warming Climate May Put Chill on Arctic Polar Bear Population"), said, "If the climate continues to warm as projected by the Intergovernmental Panel on Climate Change (IPCC), and the ice continues to break up progressively earlier, it is likely that in 20–30 years polar bear reproduction in Western Hudson Bay will be significantly limited." As the population declines, interactions between bears and humans will likely increase. Stirling and Parkinson concluded that their data suggest "that a precautionary approach be taken to the harvesting of polar bears and that the potential effects of climate warming be incorporated into planning for the management and conservation of this species throughout the Arctic."

With the melting of the Arctic ice cap, a red flag has been raised: the polar bear is in trouble. As of May 2006 the polar bear was listed in the IUCN Red List of Threatened Species for the first time. It has been assigned the category of "Vulnerable," which is one of three categories for being threatened: Critically Endangered, Endangered, and Vulnerable. The polar bear has also been listed as "Vulnerable" on several national Red Lists and as "Threatened" on the Russian national Red List.

At the UN climate talks in 1998, Greenpeace warned that the impacts of global warming were already appearing and endangering species living in the Arctic, especially polar bears. In a CNN news story dated November 4, 1998, we read that

> the melting and retreat of Arctic sea ice has already had an effect on polar bear habitat and may ultimately contribute to extinction of the species . . . Scientists studying Arctic sea ice have recently documented significant changes there and say the Arctic is warming at least twice as fast as the rest of the globe . . . the Nansen Environmental Remote Sensing Center in Norway found a 4.6 percent decline in ice extent and a 5.8 percent decline in actual ice area between 1978 and 1994 . . . Polar bears feed almost exclusively on ringed seals, which they hunt from the ice edge to the pack ice itself.

The article quotes Charles Jonkel, an experienced bear researcher, and founder of the Great Bear Foundation: "If they lose their ice platform, we lose their habitat, and we're not going to have any polar bears."

Unfortunately, unqualified statements like that fueled a firestorm of almost hysterical sympathy for the bears; people began to believe that they were all in immediate danger of extinction and drowning because of global warming. Al Gore's repeated use of the image of a polar bear swimming to nowhere contributed to the all-too-common fatalistic interpretation of the plight of the bears. "The Incredible Shrinking Polar Bears" appeared in *National Wildlife* in March 2004, and stated: "In Canada's Hudson Bay, a long-term study confirms that [polar bears] are losing weight and bearing fewer cubs, as global warming melts away their icy habitat. Is this a preview of what other populations of polar bears will soon be facing?" A *Time* magazine cover for April 3, 2006, showed a lone polar bear staring down at a piece of floating ice, with the headline "Be Worried. Be Very Worried," with the word

Time *cover, April 3, 2006*

"Very" in red. A typical example of emotional, tear-inducing prose appeared in the German magazine *Der Spiegel* on December 23, 2005, where Annika Thomé wrote,

> Global warming is causing famine-like conditions for polar bears in the Canadian province of Manitoba. The feeding season is shorter and the ice is thinner—bears are slowly starving, weak bears are drowning and they are leaving behind orphans. Scientists are trying to save the species by finding foster families for orphaned cubs.

While it is true that the shrinking ice cap is a result of global warming, and the loss of the ice is a real threat to the bears, there are still a lot of polar bears left, and not all of them are swimming into oblivion. There have always been orphaned bear cubs, and there's not much even the most dedicated scientists can do about them, except maybe transport a couple of them to a zoo. Still, the warming climate of the Arctic is indeed having a noticeable effect on polar bears, particularly those of Alaska and Nunavut.

After three decades of studying the wildlife of Cooper Island, a barrier island north of Barrow, Alaska, George Divoky has noticed a remarkable change. From 1975 to 2002, he saw a total of three polar bears, but in 2005, he saw twenty in three days. "Now the polar bears are annual and regular," he said in a 2008 interview with Sebastian Lander of the *Sun*. Unable to hunt for seals on the ice—because there is no ice—the bears are coming ashore to forage. "Having a polar bear show up in your front yard is one of the more compelling pieces of evidence that climate change is real," Divoky said.

Lander's article was entitled "Boffins Fear Arctic Ice Melting Could See the Rise of a Polar Bear and Grizzly Hybrid—Dubbed the 'Grolar Bear.' " ("Boffin" is British slang for an expert, and all that time with the wildlife of Cooper Island certainly qualifies Divoky.) With regard to the "grolar bear," the grizzly–polar bear hybrid shot in northern Canada in 2006, Divoky said, "One of the real things that is happening is that grizzlies are moving north at the same time that polar bears are forced to be on the beach and we have found a number of grizzly-bear polar-bear hybrids." The hybrid bear is probably the accidental outcome of a male grizzly that just happened upon a female polar bear, but there is no question that climate change is responsible for both species changing their habits—and their habitats.

Morphologically an odd candidate for the title of "canary in a coal mine," the polar bear has begun to serve that function in the High Arctic, heralding the possible destruction of an entire ecosystem. As Revkin wrote in the *New York Times* on October 2, 2007, "The Arctic ice cap shrank so much this past summer that waves briefly lapped along two long-imagined shipping routes, the Northwest Passage over Canada and the Northern Sea Route over Russia. Over all, the floating ice dwindled to an extent unparalleled in a century or more, by several estimates." In another article in the *Times* on the same date, he said,

Two-thirds of the world's polar bears will disappear by 2050, even under moderate projections for shrinking summer sea ice caused by greenhouse gases in the atmosphere . . . Scientists concluded that, while the bears are not likely to be driven to extinction, they would be

largely relegated to the Arctic archipelago of Canada and spots off
the northern Greenland coast, where summer sea ice tends to persist
even in warm summers like this one, a shrinking that could be
enough to reduce the bear population by two-thirds.

He quoted polar bear expert Steven Amstrup of the U.S. Geological
Survey: "It appears that they've reached a point where the earlier departure of the sea ice and their earlier appearance onshore is starting to
affect their survival . . . an abrupt collapse could occur as well."

In a November 2007 interview in *Smithsonian,* Amstrup answered
Laura Helmuth's question about the continued shrinking of the polar
bear population by saying, "We looked only at the end of this century.
And based on the best estimates of future sea ice, we forecast that there
would still be polar bears remaining in the Canadian Arctic islands.
Humans caused the problem and humans can fix the problem. We predict that there will be polar bears around to repopulate their territory if
the sea ice comes back. It's an expression of hope."

The year 2007 was a unequivocal disaster for the Arctic ice. In "Portrait of a Meltdown," *Science News* writer Sid Perkins summed it up this
way: "A variety of climatological factors converged this year in a perfect
storm that dramatically melted the Arctic Ocean's ice cover to a record
low. The abrupt downturn could be a harbinger of ice-poor summers
for decades to come." Perkins quoted Donald Perovich, a geophysicist
at the U.S. Army Cold Regions Research and Engineering Laboratory
in Hanover, New Hampshire: " 'In some parts of the Beaufort Sea,
north of Alaska and western Canada, ice that started the summer
3.3. m [10 feet] thick ended up measuring just 50 centimeters [19.5
inches] . . . About 70 cm of that shrinkage resulted from the melting of
the ice's upper surface—a typical amount for the summer, but a whop-
ping 2 m or so of that erosion, about five times the normal summer loss,
occurred from below.' The Arctic meltdown may be self-perpetuating;
in some areas the average date for winter freeze-ups is now 2 months
later than usual. Has the meltdown reached a point of no return? Perovich believes it has: 'Years from now, we'll look back at 2007 and be
amazed,' he says."

For climatologists, a "tipping point" is defined as the point at which
a small increase in temperature or other change could trigger a dispro-
portionately larger change in the future. Lenton et al. (2008) intro-

duced the concept of a "tipping element," which they described as "those components of the Earth System that are at least sub-continental in scale and can be switched—under particular condi-tions—into a qualitatively different state by small perturbations." They identified nine tipping elements that could be triggered by global warming: the Arctic sea ice, the Greenland ice sheet, the West Antarc-tic ice sheet, Atlantic thermohaline circulation, El Niño Southern Oscillation, the Sahara/Sahel and the West African monsoon, the Amazon rain forest, and the boreal forest. In the study, published in the *Proceedings of the National Academy of Sciences,* Lenton and his col-leagues concluded that "a critical threshold for summer Arctic sea ice may exist, whereas a further threshold for year-round ice-loss is more uncertain and less accessible this century. Given that the IPCC models significantly underestimate the observed rate of Arctic sea ice decline, a summer ice-loss threshold may be very close and a transition could occur well within this century." In other words, we are getting danger-ously close to tipping the polar bears into the Arctic Ocean, where they will swim toward extinction.

The cracking of the vast ice shelves was thought to be strictly an Antarctic phenomenon until 2007, when David Shukman of the BBC reported that Canadian scientists had found that the Ayles Ice Island, an iceberg the size of Manhattan that had calved off the Ayles Ice Shelf in 2005, had split in two and was wedged into the Sverdrup Channel, an inlet between two of the Queen Elizabeth Islands in the High Cana-dian Arctic. The following year, the Canadian military found a network of ten-mile-long cracks on the Ward Hunt Ice Shelf (WHIS), one of the largest ice shelves in Canada. A front-page story in the *Toronto Globe & Mail* by Jessica Leeder on July 29, 2008, was headlined "Huge Chunk Snaps Off Storied Ice Shelf." The WHIS—the largest remain-ing such structure in the Arctic—is now breaking up. Once joined to Ellesmere Island, which is part of the Queen Elizabeth Islands (along with Melville, Devon, Bathurst, and Cornwallis islands), WHIS is north of Disraeli Fjord, which is warming, and attached—but not for long—to the northernmost point of land in Canada before the Arctic Ocean. (Cape Aldrich on Ellesmere is Canada's most northerly point, only thirty miles farther south than Cape Morris Jesup in Greenland, the most northerly point of land in the Northern Hemisphere.)

Formed by accumulating snow and freezing meltwater, ice shelves are large platforms of thick, ancient sea ice that float on the ocean's surface. At 275 square miles in size, the WHIS is larger than the Wilkins shelf that collapsed in the Antarctic in March 2008, and seven times the size of the Ayles Ice Shelf chunk that broke off in 2005 from Ellesmere's western coast. The first major crack in the WHIS was discovered in 2002, and another huge crack appeared in 2005. The newest cracks, more than ten miles long and 100 feet wide, indicate that a breakup is coming, bringing the Arctic ice closer to the tipping point, from which regeneration is impossible. In July 2008, an eight-square-mile platform broke off the WHIS, and is destined to melt. Derek Mueller, Canada's foremost authority on ice shelves, said,

> It may weaken over time; it may melt away slowly, then all of a sudden you pass this threshold . . . The take-home message for me is that these ice shelves are not regenerating. If we're looking at an indication of whether climate is to blame, it really is the lack of regeneration that convinces me. They're breaking away so rapidly that there's no hope of regeneration; that is pretty strong evidence that suggests this is related to global warming. (Leeder 2008)

Introducing their 2008 discussion of "Conservation of Arctic Marine Mammals Faced with Climate Change," Ragen, Huntington, and Hovelsrud wrote,

> On a daily basis, societies are making decisions that will influence the effects of climate change for decades or even centuries to come. To promote informed management of the associated risks, we review available conservation measures for Arctic marine mammals, a group that includes some of the most charismatic species on earth. The majority of available conservation measures (e.g., restrictions on hunting, protection of essential habitat areas from development, reduction of incidental take) are intended to address the effects of increasing human activity in the Arctic that are likely to follow decreasing sea ice and rising temperatures. As important as those measures will be in the effort to conserve Arctic marine mammals and ecosystems, they will not address the primary physical manifestations of climate change, such as loss of sea ice. Short of actions to prevent climate change, there are no known conservation measures

that can be used to ensure the long-term persistence of these species
and ecosystems as we know them today.

Mark Serreze of the National Snow and Ice Data Center in Colorado believes that the Arctic ice cap will disappear entirely from the
North Pole by 2009. According to Serreze (quoted in an article by
Steve Connor in the British newspaper the *Independent*), during the
winter of 2007, the pole was covered by thin, first-year ice, which will
melt by the summer of 2008, and the area of open water will increase to
an unprecedented extent. Serreze said, "The issue is that, for the first
time that I am aware of, the North Pole is covered with extensive first
year ice—ice that formed last autumn and winter. I'd say it's even odds
whether the North Pole melts out."* In another article about Serreze's
startling prediction ("North Pole, No Ice"), Randy Boswell of the Canwest News Service wrote that "three young Scandinavian royals—
Prince Haakon of Norway, Princess Victoria of Sweden, and Prince
Frederick of Denmark—set off on June 22 from Norway's Svalbard
Islands aboard a pole-bound icebreaker, their joint mission to make
first hand observations of the melting polar ice cap."

In 2008, two stories appeared that will, in time, have an impact on
polar bear populations, but in both cases, the situations are unresolved.
First came an announcement that the Arctic ice cap was melting much
faster than had been estimated, and that "the North Pole could be free
of ice in five years' time instead of 60." In the *Observer* for August 10,
2008, Robin McKie wrote, "Scientists say that the disappearance of sea
ice at the North Pole could exceed last year's record loss . . . 'It is a
neck-and-neck race between 2007 and this year over the issue of ice
loss,' said Mark Serreze . . . The Beaufort Sea storms triggered steep
ice losses and it now looks as if it will be a very close call indeed whether
2007 or 2008 is the worst year on record for ice cover over the Arctic."
Serreze: "We always knew it would be the first region on earth to feel

* How does Mark Serreze's prognostication jibe with the experience of McCarthy and
McKenna, who reported open water at the North Pole in August 2000? I asked Serreze if
his report was in conflict with what had been reported in 2000, and he answered, "No real
conflict here—I remember well the story of 2000 and indeed was contacted by media about
it . . . Yes, there was a lot of open water at or near the North Pole that year, but most likely
dynamically-produced patterns of winds and ocean currents made those leads or polynyas.
This year we are talking about an open North Pole due to melting of the ice cover such that
you could get to the pole in a sailing ship—a different thing."

the impact of climate change, but not at anything like this speed." Then it was announced that the Bush administration was planning to bypass the scientific review process critical to the Endangered Species Act, and allow federal agencies to approve their own projects (Cappiello 2008). The logic behind this attempt to render the ESA useless goes like this, according to the *Seattle Post-Intelligencer:* "Say the Department of Transportation wants to fund a highway. That agency would decide— without the help of scientists—that the project meets ESA standards. It's a smooth review, a done deal, so the highway would be built right away . . . In other words, we didn't like the polar bear listing and want to make certain that it doesn't happen again." In time, these questions and editorials will be answered one way or another, but whatever the outcome, none of this bodes well for the beleaguered polar bears.

In August 2008, there was a report that ten polar bears were spotted swimming in the open Chukchi Sea on a single day, from fifteen to sixty-five miles offshore. An Associated Press article in the *New York Times* for August 28 was headlined "As Arctic Sea Ice Melts, Experts Expect New Low" and illustrated by a photograph of one of the bears swimming uncomfortably in a helicopter's backwash. In the article, Mark Serreze said, "We could very well be in that quick slide downward in terms of passing a tipping point . . . It's tipping now. We're seeing it happen now." Serreze observed that we are witnessing another effect, known as "Arctic amplification," where the warming up north is increased in a feedback mechanism and the effects spill southward starting in autumn. Over the last few years, the bigger melt has meant more warm water, which releases more heat into the air during fall cooling, which makes the atmosphere warmer than normal. The *Times* article concluded with a discussion of another potential threat: "On top of that, researchers are investigating 'alarming' reports in the last few days of the release of methane from long-frozen Arctic waters, possibly from the warming of the sea . . . Giant burps of methane, which is a potent greenhouse gas, is a long-feared effect of warming in the Arctic that would accelerate warming even more, according to scientists."

Do we really need a *reason* to preserve polar bears? In their 2008 chapter on "Threatened Groups of Organisms Valuable to Medicine," Eric Chivian and Aaron Bernstein (both MDs) looked at seven groups of organisms—amphibians, nonhuman primates, gymnosperms (a group of plants that includes the conifers, cycads, and the ginkgo tree), cone snails, sharks, horseshoe crabs—and bears. Ursodeoxycholic acid (UDCA) is present in the gallbladders of many species of bears, including polar bears, and this substance is currently being used to treat several human diseases, including the prevention of complications from the thickening of bile that can occur in pregnancy. It can also help dissolve certain kinds of gallstones. "Its most important use," Chivian and Bernstein wrote, "is in patients with primary biliary cirrhosis, a disease that can lead to destruction of the liver from inflammation of its internal bile ducts." The authors correctly point out that the bears most threatened by the harvesting of bile are the Asiatic black bears *(Ursus thibetanus),* which are kept in squeeze cages on bear farms in China. Steel catheters are inserted into their gallbladders, and the bile is siphoned off for medical applications. (See Ellis, *Tiger Bone & Rhino Horn: The Destruction of Wildlife for Traditional Chinese Medicine.*) UDCA was discovered in 1901 by Olaf Hammarsten, a Swedish chemist who was examining the composition of polar bear bile, but polar bears' unique ability to process waste products internally makes them prime subjects for medical research—and qualifies them for inclusion in Chivian and Bernstein's short list of organisms valuable to medicine. They wrote,

> The remarkable physiological processes that allow polar bears to survive the extreme privations of "denning" are not found in any other animal. Understanding these processes, which involve the recycling of essentially all their body wastes, and identifying the substances that mediate them may lead to new insights for treating a number of human diseases . . . The loss of polar bears, as well as other denning bears, not only deprives us of these magnificent creatures, but also results in the potential loss of potential medicines and prime biomedical research models for understanding and treating several human diseases that have caused much human suffering and large numbers of deaths worldwide, such as osteoporosis, kidney failure, and diabetes types 1 and 2.

Unfortunately, however, its value in medical research will probably not save the polar bear.

The other great land predators, including lions, tigers, and brown bears, are endangered because they are perceived as a threat to human survival. Wild tigers, unquestionably a menace to humans, have added a weird twist to this equation: they are being hunted out of existence in India because their bones are believed to enhance male sexual prowess. We are eliminating the tigers in order to enable humans to procreate more expeditiously. But polar bears do not represent that much of a threat to humans; it is our planet-endangering activities that will be responsible for their demise. If polar bears were not so highly specialized, living an isolated, wandering life and feeding almost exclusively on one (also threatened) prey item, they could probably adapt more easily to changing conditions around them. As it is, modifying their environment, even by just raising the temperature a couple of degrees, will spell doom for the great white bear.

The polar bear is the world's largest living land predator, and this alone would seem to qualify it for eradication at the hand of man. In *Monster of God*, David Quammen wrote,

The near presence of big predators—dangerous, flesh-eating beasts— has been a fearful reality throughout human history . . . We could be

Farewell, Nanook

killed and consumed by this or that ferocious creature—a lion, a tiger, a leopard, a crocodile, a shark, a giant lizard (on the island of Komodo), or a bear . . . Around the planet today, big predators are in most places either gone or endangered. Under current trends, they can't last much longer.

Probably because they inhabit regions where there are relatively few people for them to eat, polar bears are not included in Quammen's extensive discussion of man-eating predators, but they have been traditionally regarded as dangerous—think of the bears in Iceland and Iqaluit that were shot simply because they had the temerity to appear where people could see them—and so they were killed whenever possible. Brave "big-game hunters" pit themselves against the "dangerous" polar bear, often shooting them from a distance so great that the bear never knew it was being hunted. Although people have been killing bears for centuries, often under the rubric of "self-defense," the bears are now threatened by anthropogenic climate change, a far more insidious and wide-ranging effect, initiated by humans.

Is the Polar Bear Doomed?

Why not just transfer the poor bears to the Antarctic?

In 2007, in the journal *Conservation Biology*, McLachlan, Hellmann, and Schwartz wrote "A Framework for Debate of Assisted Migration in an Era of Climate Change." Their discussion of the efficacy of moving animals or plants susceptible to anthropogenic climate change was discussed by Carl Zimmer, who wrote, "In 2004, an international team of scientists estimated that 15 percent to 37 percent of species would become extinct by 2050 because of global warming." Assisted migration—more correctly called "assisted colonization," according to Malcolm Hunter (2007)—is something that conservation biologists are beginning to identify as a possible stopgap to species depletion and even extinction. So far, the experiment has not been tried, but some biologists see it as a way to rescue some animals and plants whose home climate is threatened. As per "global warming," rising temperatures might be detrimental to some species, and a cooler location might be sought. Certainly, however, no one entertains the idea of moving threatened species from pole to pole, and besides, as Zimmer points out, "Some species threatened by climate change, including polar bears and other animals adapted to very cold climates, may have nowhere to go."

There are plenty of seals in the Antarctic, of course: Weddells, Rosses, leopards, and one species, the crabeater, said to be the most numerous large mammal in the world. (Crabeaters do not eat crabs; they eat krill, the food of the great whales; like the whales, they feed exclusively at sea.) Why couldn't the polar bears hunt them? They probably could, if we could transport the bears, but transportation to another hemisphere would present more problems than just wear and tear on the bears. Antarctic seals are very different from their northern counterparts. They forage at sea, which means that they spend a considerable amount of time away from the ice floes where they might be hunted. While the Arctic ringed and bearded seals are loners, crabeaters congregate in groups, so the appearance of a bear would drive them all into the water, where the bear would be unable to catch them. Along with the killer whale, the leopard seal is the major predator of seals and penguins in the Antarctic, and, given its aggressive nature and large size—leopard seals can weigh up to a thousand pounds—a polar bear trying to attack an adult would be in for a rude surprise. While the trackless wastes of the Arctic are—or were—frozen ocean, the corresponding area in the Antarctic is the ice cover of a continent, a sheet of solid ice, most of it far from the water and the seals. It seems unlikely that polar bears would modify their hunting behavior to catch different seals—but if we've learned anything about polar bears, it is that they are adaptable, at least up to a point.

Could they eat penguins? Penguins would be much easier prey for polar bears, because they can't fly and have no land predators, so the bears could just walk up and grab them. However, with the exception of kings and emperors, most penguins would make only a snack for a polar bear, and it is likely that once they learned that they had a predator that could catch them on land, they would quickly take to the water when a bear appeared. (Penguins could easily outswim a polar bear.) Their nesting grounds would be a different problem altogether, for it is possible that the bears could learn to eat penguin eggs, which are abundant and would be completely unprotected in a rookery.

Polar bears are solitary animals; males have to search long and hard for a receptive female in the Arctic's trackless wastes. As we saw in an earlier chapter, after mating, the impregnated female has only a few short months in which to acquire the fat deposits she will need to live on and support the cubs during the fall and winter. After delivering nearly naked cubs that weigh no more than a pound and a half, she nurses them until about April, when she breaks out of the den, ready to lead her cubs onto the ice. Notice the regular sequence of events in the lives of polar bears: mate in April, eat all summer, den up in the fall, emerge with cubs in April. What would happen if the seasons were suddenly reversed?

Millennia of evolution have honed the bears' systems to coincide with the seasons and sunlight of the North, and relocating polar bears to the Antarctic would engender a permanent case of jet lag. Every hormonal and behavioral stimulus keyed to the seasons would be reversed. Even if the bears could be successfully transported, they would be in a state of confusion, as the times of daylight and darkness appeared at exactly the wrong times of the year. Also, the mating and breeding behavior of the polar bears is closely affiliated with that of the ringed seals. The seals of the South could not be counted on to behave like their northern counterparts to accommodate the eating habits of the bears, and it is unlikely in any case that they could provide an adequate substitute for the bears' traditional diet.

Of all nonmigratory animals, bears are probably the most dependent upon the clock of the seasons. The concept of hibernation is almost synonymous with the behavior of bears, even though not all species hibernate. The bears of the tropics, such as spectacled bears, sloth bears, sun bears, and Asiatic black bears, are active all year round, but American black bears and all species of brown (grizzly) bears den up for some or all of the winter. American black bears sleep for months without eating, drinking, urinating, or defecating. The bears' body heat is lost very slowly, enabling them to cut their metabolic rate in half and still make it through winter, maintaining temperatures above 88°—within twelve degrees of their normal summer temperature. New knowledge of the hibernation process has led biologists to redefine mammalian hibernation as simply a specialized, seasonal reduction of metabolism concurrent with the environmental pressures of food unavailability and low environmental temperatures. Hibernation for the black bear, as for other mammals, is primarily a mechanism to conserve energy through seasons when there is no food or water. Hibernation in the true sense of the word does not apply to polar bears. True hibernators, such as raccoons, skunks, woodchucks, and chipmunks, experience a marked drop in heart rate and a body temperature that plunges to nearly 0°C (32°F). It may take some time to wake them up. The ice bears do not enter a state of deep hibernation because they need a higher body temperature in order to meet the demands of pregnancy, birth, and the nursing of their young.

Those who aren't really paying attention believe that the poles incorporate similar habitats of ice and snow, and therefore what could live at the North Pole could (or did) live at the South Pole. This misunderstanding is not helped by the fact that some species, particularly birds like skuas and gulls, do occur in both the southern and northern polar regions, while others, like the Arctic and Antarctic terns, look so much alike that to the untrained eye, they might as well live in both places. Some shearwaters, to confuse matters even more, migrate from one polar region to the other and back again. The Arctic tern is the world's champion long-distance migrator, seeing two summers each year as it migrates from its northern Arctic breeding grounds to the oceans around Antarctica and back, a round trip of some 24,000 miles. Although most albatross species are seen soaring over Southern Hemisphere waters, there are some North Pacific species, and there is one record of a black-browed albatross, known almost exclusively from southern climes, showing up in a gannet colony on the Scottish Shetland Islands, where it was nicknamed "Albert Ross." Some whales, such as blues, fins, humpbacks, and minkes, are found in both southern and northern polar waters (and many areas in between), while killer whales, the most cosmopolitan of all cetacean species, live in almost every ocean. There are northern elephant seals and southern elephant seals, and many smaller pinnipeds can be found at the extremes of both hemispheres. The eared seals (otariids) of the north include fur seals and sea lions, with corresponding (but different) species in the south. Ditto for the earless seals (phocids). Walruses are only found in the Northern Hemisphere. Penguins, which live only in the Southern Hemisphere (except for Galápagos penguins, which live almost on the Equator), have become the darlings of popular commercials and movies.

Predators that historically have wreaked havoc in new environments are cats, rats, dogs, and goats, which were, sometimes accidentally, introduced to new surroundings, and then quickly changed those surroundings to suit themselves, preying on or displacing the local species. The cane toad *(Bufo marinus)* was introduced into Australia to eat the cane beetles that were ravaging sugar crops, but the toad quickly became more of a problem than the beetles. One hundred and one toads arrived at Edmonton in North Queensland in June 1935, and within six months over 60,000 young toads had been released. The toad has become one of Australia's worst environmental disasters, spreading across Queensland and throughout the Northern Territory. The giant toads, which can be a foot long and weigh more than five pounds, are omnivorous, and will eat anything they can get hold of—amphibians, reptiles, birds, and even small mammals. Unlike most other frogs and toads, cane toads eat things which do not move, and will climb into a bowl of dog food left outside and eat it. They do not only eat the food normally available to Australian frogs, they eat the frogs as well. The giant toad is poisonous to any animal unfortunate enough to try to eat one. Fish that eat the "toadpoles" die, and other animals that eat adult toads die too. When the toad is threatened, it secretes a highly toxic milky substance from large glands in the back of its head, which will burn the eyes, inflame the skin, and kill cats and dogs if they ingest it.

Consider, too, the case of the Burmese python, now an established resident of Florida. One of the world's largest snakes, this python can reach a length of twenty feet and weigh more than a grown man. They are often bought as pets by people who think it is cool to own a giant snake, but when the snake gets too big and too hard to handle, the owner surreptitiously releases it into the nearest swamp. The pythons feed on small mammals, such as mice, rats, rabbits, squirrels, possums, raccoons, and even bobcats. Florida game wardens are trying to trap the pythons, but finding snakes in a swamp is considerably more difficult than finding needles in haystacks, and it now appears that they are establishing a firm foothold in the Everglades; clutches of fertile eggs have been found and destroyed, but there are undoubtedly more where they came from. According to an article by Andrew Revkin, "Some rough estimates put the state's pet python population above 5,000. More than 350 have been found in the park [the Everglades] since 2002, with others showing up in mangroves along Florida's west coast." Skip Snow, a federal biologist, told Revkin that there are perhaps ten more for every one that is seen.

The record of introduced species—sometimes known as bio-invaders—is almost endless, and virtually every instance ends badly. Mongooses that were introduced into the Hawaiian Islands to eat the rats ate the birds instead. In Florida, in addition to the pythons, pet owners have released such exotic animals as African monitor lizards, Caribbean cane toads (the same species that has wreaked such havoc in

Australia), and carnivorous fish such as the evil-looking snakehead, which can move from pond to pond by slithering overland. Even though we have messed things up, sometimes irrevocably, relocating an animal that we have endangered smacks of arrogant anthropocentrism—as if we could put Humpty Dumpty together again, just because we were the ones that tossed him off the wall. Remember the old TV margarine ad, "It's not nice to fool Mother Nature"? Whenever we've tried, the results have been calamitous. Maybe we should learn to control ourselves before we try to control the bears.

Much has been made of the story that polar bears, unable to find ice on which to hunt seals, take to the water in search of food, but because the ice has melted there is no ice, and therefore no seals, so the bears swim until they drown. Al Gore presented the story particularly dramatically in *An Inconvenient Truth,* and while it may be true, its importance has been greatly exaggerated and it is far from the primary threat to polar bears. The real threat is the loss of habitat as a function of global warming. Greenhouse gases in the atmosphere cause rising temperatures in the Arctic, which means that the Arctic's ice cover is shrinking. The loss of sea ice may indeed cause individual bears to swim in search of a floe, and there already is some documentation of this happening. Two biologists from Alaska, Charles Monnett and Jeffrey Gleason, published the results of aerial surveys conducted in September 2004, where they had spotted fifty-five bears, ten of them in open water. "In addition," they wrote, "four polar bear carcasses were seen floating in open water and had, presumably drowned." We can't tell for sure that these bears drowned, but Monnett and Gleason speculate that "mortalities due to offshore swimming during late-ice (or mild ice) years may be an important and unaccounted source of natural mortality given energetic demands placed on individual bears engaged in long-distance swimming."

Because pregnant females dig dens in the snow, warming weather can cause these little caves to collapse, trapping the mother and cubs inside. In June 1989, Doug Irish saw the head of a dead polar bear sticking out of the snow along the Yukon Territory coastline of the Beaufort Sea. After excavating the den, two three-to-four-week-old cubs were found, also dead. Peter Clarkson and Irish (1990) wrote up the discovery in the journal *Arctic,* and suggested that the den must have collapsed in January, when a warm spell weakened its walls, and a heavy snowstorm followed, adding weight to the fragile structure. Another result of Arctic warming is a predictable increase in forest fire activity (though obviously not in the environs of the Beaufort Sea, East Greenland, or other polar bear habitats where no trees or plants grow). In western Hudson Bay, from 2001 to 2003, Evan Richardson, Ian Stirling, and Bob Kochtubajda examined 149 maternity denning sites, forty-eight of which had been burned. They found that "fire significantly altered vegetation composition and increased the depth of the active layer, resulting in a decrease in the stability of the den sites, the collapse of dens, and a degradation of the surrounding habitat." They found no bears trapped in burned dens, but because bears avoid burned areas for denning, the fires effectively limit the possible denning sites.

A completely unexpected response to the bears' loss of habitat and the corresponding shortage of food has been the turn to cannibalism—bears eating bears. Taylor, Larsen, and Schweinsburg commented on this phenomenon in 1985, and, from mostly anecdotal evidence, concluded that males sometimes killed cubs or attacked incapacitated individuals. But in a 2006 study, Steven Amstrup and his colleagues "confirmed three instances of intraspecific predation and cannibalism in the Beaufort Sea," which had nothing to do with cubs or injured bears. Searching for maternity dens on January 24, 2004, researchers found one where a recently killed female had been dragged out over the snow and partially eaten. Multiple bite wounds on the carcass and the tracks and blood in the snow left no doubt that the killer was a large male polar bear. Spotting from a helicopter two months later, they found another dead female on the sea ice, killed by a much larger bear. Three days later, they saw an adult male feeding on a dead yearling bear, and their analysis of the footprints indicated the animal had been lying in a snow pit on a pressure ridge and that a predatory bear had stalked it in its bed and overwhelmed it there. In the past, polar bears had been seen feeding on carcasses of dead bears, but these were the first known instances of bears killing other bears for food in the Beaufort Sea area. (The only previously reported cannibalism occurred in Svalbard.) "In the cases we observed," wrote Amstrup et al., "the motivation for the attacks appears to be nutritional . . . Because adult male polar bears feed little during the spring when they focus on breeding, they enter the summer in poor condition. Therefore, adult males may be the first population segment to show adverse effects of the large ice retreats of recent years and the potentially reduced foraging opportunities it presents."

Even more than the drowning of the bears, however, a reduction in the ice cap will deprive most of the bears of their traditional habitat and drive those that remain to areas where ice persists, such as the Arctic archipelago of Canada and the northern coast of Greenland. In a September 2007 *New York Times* article, John Broder and Andrew Revkin quoted biologist Steven Amstrup: "As the ice goes, so goes the polar bear." Broder and Revkin wrote, "Two thirds of the world's polar bears will disappear by 2050, even under moderate projections for shrinking summer sea ice caused by greenhouse gases in the atmosphere." As sea ice becomes more unstable, the bears have to expend more energy to maintain contact with their preferred habitats. Eventually, reproductive rates will begin to fall, because the females will not be able to store enough fat to fast through the winter when the cubs are born and nursed. So far, the only visible sign of a drop in polar bear populations is the occasional drowning of swimming bears and the signs of intraspecies cannibalism. Habitat modification has always been considered a major element in endangering species—think of burning the Amazon rain forests or building hotels on turtle-nesting beaches—but the shrinking Arctic ice is not just modifying the bears' habitat, it is destroying it completely. The polar bear could become the first mammal to lose its habitat to global warming. Because every living thing in the Arctic ecosystem is (or will be soon) affected by the reduction of the ice cap, the bears, the seals, the walruses, the whales, and even the birds are threatened.

Throughout the world's history, many—make that *most*—species have gone extinct. And because the vast majority of those extinctions occurred long before Mr. *Homo sapiens* arrived to wreak his special kind of havoc, we cannot take the blame for them. We had nothing whatever to do with the extinction of the trilobites, the pterodactyls, T. rex, Archaeopteryx, or the host of other creatures that were gone millions of years before our ancestors climbed down from the trees. But there are no more dodos, passenger pigeons, Tasmanian tigers, Carolina parakeets, Eskimo curlews, Steller's sea cows, or Chinese tigers because human beings killed them all. The power to eliminate a species from the face of the earth is not a license to do so. Sometimes when we have realized that certain animals were on the brink of extinction—the California condor and the whooping crane, for example—people have gone to extraordinary lengths to see that the last of their kind did not die off, and through protection and breeding programs small but viable populations have been restored.

When biologist David Ehrenfeld wrote *Biological Conservation* in 1970, he meant it to be a text for college students as an introduction to conservation biology, now considered one of the most important of all biology subsets. Ehrenfeld, a founding editor of the journal *Conservation Biology*, believed the outlook was glum for animal conservation because there were going to be too many people, making too many changes to the environment, and leaving room only for small, herbivorous, widely distributed, and highly fecund species, such as sparrows, squirrels, and rats. For those large species that had a restricted distribution, a low reproductive rate, and identifiable hunting pressure, it was just about hopeless. To illustrate his hypothesis, he concocted a "most endangered animal" composite, identifying the unfortunate creature that had all the components required for imminent extinction in the modern world:

> It turns out to be a large predator with a narrow habitat tolerance, long gestation period, and few young per litter. It is hunted for a natural product and/or for sport but is not subject to efficient game management. It has a restricted distribution, but travels across international boundaries. It is intolerant of man, reproduces in aggregates, and has nonadaptive behavioral idiosyncrasies. Although there is probably no such animal, this model, with one or two exceptions, comes very close to being a description of a polar bear.

Life on earth depends on energy from the sun. About 30 percent of the sunlight that beams toward our planet is deflected by the outer atmosphere and scattered back into space. The rest reaches the planet's surface and is reflected upward again as a type of slow-moving energy called infrared radiation. As infrared radiation is carried aloft by air currents, it is absorbed by greenhouse gases such as water vapor, carbon dioxide, ozone, and methane, which slows its escape from the atmosphere. Although greenhouse gases make up only about 1 percent of the earth's atmosphere, they regulate our climate by trapping heat and holding it in a kind of warm-air blanket that surrounds the planet. This phenomenon is what scientists call the "greenhouse effect." Without it, scientists estimate that the average temperature on earth would be colder by approximately 30 degrees Celsius (54 degrees Fahrenheit), far too cold to sustain our current ecosystem. While the greenhouse effect is an essential environmental prerequisite for life on earth, there can be too much of a good thing. The problems begin when human activities distort and accelerate the natural process by creating *more* greenhouse gases in the atmosphere than are necessary to warm the planet to an ideal temperature.

Nowadays, greenhouse gases in the atmosphere are raising the temperature of the entire planet, and as the oceans warm, the ice melts. And as the ice melts, the habitat of the polar bear is eroding away. The 1997 Kyoto Protocol was designed to achieve "stabilization of greenhouse gas concentrations in the atmosphere at a level that would prevent dangerous anthropogenic interference with the climate system." The ratifying countries are allowed to use emissions trading to meet their obligations if they maintain or increase their greenhouse gas emissions. Emissions trading allows nations that can easily meet their targets to sell credits to those that cannot. The goal of the Kyoto Protocol is to reduce worldwide greenhouse gas emissions to 5.2 percent below 1990 levels between 2008 and 2012. Compared to the emissions levels that would occur by 2010 without the Kyoto Protocol, however, this target actually represents a 29 percent cut.

"U.N. Report Describes Risks of Inaction on Climate Change" was the lead story on the front page of the *New York Times* for November 17, 2007. Elisabeth Rosenthal wrote,

Valencia, Spain, Nov. 16—In its final and most powerful report, a United Nations panel of scientists meeting here describes the mounting risks of climate change in language that is both more specific and forceful than its previous assessments, according to scientists here.

Synthesizing reams of data from its three previous reports, the United Nations Intergovernmental Panel on Climate Change for the first time specifically points out important risks if governments fail to respond: melting ice sheets that could lead to a rapid rise in sea levels and the extinction of large numbers of species brought about by even moderate amounts of warming, on the order of 1 to 3 degrees.

One such area is the future melting of ice sheets in Greenland and western Antarctica. In earlier reports, the panel's scientists acknowledged that their computer models were poor at such predictions, and did not reflect the rapid melting that scientists have recently observed. If these areas melt entirely, seas would rise 40 feet, scientists said. While scientists are certain that the sheets will melt over millennia, producing sea-level rises, there is now evidence to suggest that it could happen much faster than this, perhaps over centuries.

Chantal Kreviazuk, a popular Canadian singer-songwriter, visited Churchill in the fall of 2007, and in a December 29 article in the Toronto *Globe & Mail* she wrote, "I dread the fact that one day I may have to tell my grandchildren how great white creatures once roamed Canada's north and then disappeared. But unless we do something, the polar bear will go the way of the dinosaur." On her tundra-buggy rides ("imagine a subway-car on tractor wheels," she wrote) Kreviazuk was accompanied by Robert Buchanan of Polar Bears International, an organization that supports research projects that benefit the world's polar bears, and whose overhead is covered by gift shop sales and administrative grants; and biologist Steven Amstrup of the U.S. Geological Survey, who has studied polar bears for twenty-seven years. Of the bears they could see from the vehicle, they told her

that their summer fast has grown longer and longer because climate change has caused a remarkable delay in the formation of the sea ice they need to reach the seals and walruses they prey upon . . . The late freeze is even more significant because the ice is breaking up earlier. It now melts about three weeks sooner than it did just three decades ago, meaning the bears have less time to put on fat to sustain them in the summer . . . the average adult female now comes ashore 60 kilograms [130 pounds] lighter than she used to, and . . . most litters are now limited to one cub, and triplets, once fairly common, are no longer seen.

In November 2007, the journal *Science* published a Richard Kerr article with the title "How Urgent Is Climate Change?" running below a photograph of a polar bear on the ice. The article began:

The latest reports from the Nobel Prize–winning Intergovernmental Panel on Climate Change (IPCC) were informative enough. Humans are messing with climate and will, sooner or later, get burned if they keep it up. But just how urgent is this global warming business?

IPCC wasn't at all clear on that, at least not in its summary reports. In the absence of forthright guidance from the scientific community, news about melting ice and starving polar bears has stoked the public climate frenzy of the past couple of years. Climate researchers, on the other hand, prefer science to headlines when considering just how imminent the coming climate crunch might be. With a chance to digest the detailed IPCC products that are now available, many scientists are more convinced than ever that immediate action is required. The time to start "is right now," says climate modeler Gerald Meehl of the National Center for Atmospheric Research in Boulder, Colorado. "We can't wait any longer."

In December 2006, Secretary of the Interior Dirk Kempthorne announced that the U.S. Fish & Wildlife Service was proposing to list the polar bear as a "threatened" species under the Endangered Species Act, and initiated a scientific review to determine the status of the species. One way to provide some level of security for a species considered to be in trouble, at least in the United States, is to change the rules on hunting or disturbing the animals—in other words, to put them on the Endangered Species List. In 1972, President Nixon called on Congress to pass comprehensive endangered species legislation. Congress responded by creating the Endangered Species Act (ESA), which was signed into law on December 28, 1973. That same year also saw the establishment of the Convention on International Trade in Endangered Species of Wild Fauna and Flora (CITES), an international agreement restricting commerce in plant and animal species believed to be actually or potentially harmed by trade. The U.S. CITES list includes all species protected by the ESA as well as species which are vulnerable but not yet threatened or endangered. The stated purpose of the Endangered Species Act is to safeguard species and also "the ecosystems upon which they depend." Listing the polar bear, with its diminishing population and its disappearing habitat, would seem to be a no-brainer. There are some people in Alaska and elsewhere who disagree.

If the polar bear is listed as endangered, subsistence hunting and oil prospecting (not to mention oil drilling), considered to have an adverse effect on the bears, would be prohibited under the MMPA. "The state of Alaska," wrote Tom Kizzia in the *Anchorage Daily News* (September 8, 2007), "fearing consequences for subsistence hunting and oil production, has strenuously opposed a federal threatened-species listing, arguing, among other things, that bear populations have been stable and that too much uncertainty surrounds global warming trends." But there is no uncertainty in the 2006 report by Hansen et al. in which they wrote that in the past thirty years, average world surface temperatures have increased by 0.2°C per decade but parts of the Arctic have experienced tenfold the average warming. The U.S. Geological Survey Reports that Secretary Kempthorne requested have now been issued (see Durner et al. 2007 and Hunter et al. 2007), and the overall conclusion reads as follows:

> Projected changes in sea ice conditions, if realized, will result in loss of approximately ⅔ of the world's polar bear population by the mid-21st century. Because the observed trajectory of Arctic sea ice decline appears to be underestimated by current available models, this assessment of future polar bear status may be conservative.

It's much worse than we thought. "Ultimately," the report concludes, "we projected a 42% loss of optimal bear habitat during summer in the polar basin by mid century." And no, the bears will not fare well converting to land-based hunting; they are poorly equipped for chasing reindeer or musk oxen, and in any case those herbivores do not provide the high-fat, high-calorie nutrition that the bears need. Listing the polar bear as endangered will not cool the Arctic and stop the ice from melting—but encouraging sport hunting and oil drilling in the bears' Alaska habitat will speed them along the slippery slope toward extinction.

"This is a complex issue," said Chris Tollefson of the U.S. Fish & Wildlife Service, "because we have most polar bear populations not showing significant declines at the moment, but we have a lot of climate models and data showing great losses in the foreseeable future." (One population that has shown a decline is the highly visible one west of Hudson Bay, where the shortage of denning areas has resulted in a 22

percent decline in the number of bears.) Sarah Palin, Republican governor of Alaska and former vice presidential candidate, is opposed to the
endangered species listing, because she believes that it will cause economic hardship to the oil industry—Alaska's biggest and most important—if the bears are protected in areas where the industry wants to
prospect or drill. At the moment, the world's polar bears are not endangered, but if the climate modeling is accurate—and most scientists
believe it is—the bears will be in big trouble in the very near future.
Andrew Derocher believes the science is solid, and that governments
have to act before it is too late. "For some people, the proof of this won't
be reliable until the last polar bear drowns," he said (Azios 2008).

On January 2, 2008, the *New York Times* ran an editorial they entitled
"Of Two Minds on Polar Bears."

> Listing the polar bear would trigger a series of protections, including,
> in time, identifying habitat critical to the bears' survival. It would also
> impose obligations on all federal agencies to avoid actions that could
> hurt the bears' prospects. But the minerals service, where the wishes
> of the oil and gas industry carry great weight, has a history of doing
> as it pleases. Environmental groups and members of the House and
> Senate are thus asking Dirk Kempthorne, the interior secretary, to
> declare a timeout, postponing Chukchi Sea lease sales for three years
> pending further scientific study . . .
>
> The urgent and immediate question, though, is the future of the
> polar bear, which is bleak enough without further stresses. Everyone
> agrees that the overwhelming threat is the loss of sea ice, where the
> bears hunt for food and nurture their young. Yet there is also wide
> recognition among federal scientists, even in the minerals service,
> that the many activities associated with oil drilling—the seismic
> tests, the vast increase in ship traffic, the noise, the potential spills—
> can only weaken the bear's resilience.

The U.S. government was not likely to heed such editorials, and two
days after its publication, the Minerals Management Service announced
that it would be seeking bids for petroleum licenses in the Chukchi
Sea on February 6. Under consideration is a 46,000-square-mile area
located between Alaska and the coast of the Russian Far East that is

said to hold fifteen billion gallons of recoverable oil and a huge volume of natural gas. It is also the home of one of the main populations of polar bears in U.S. and Russian territory, as well as large walrus herds. In response to the announcement, WWF's Margaret Williams said, "The chances for survival of this icon of the Arctic will be greatly diminished if its last remaining critical habitat is turned into a vast oil and gas field" (Usborne 2008). Brendan Cummings of the Center for Biological Diversity in San Francisco responded to the announcement even more dramatically, saying, "The polar bear is in need of intensive care, but with this lease sale the Bush administration is threatening to burn down the hospital."

Governor Palin responded by submitting an op-ed piece to the *New York Times* (January 5, 2008), in which she argued against listing the polar bear, saying that "polar bears are more numerous than they were 40 years ago" and don't need government protection. She suggested that "climate change" is the only threat to the bears, not mentioning the real reason that environmental groups are in favor of the listing: because oil and gas drilling will wreak havoc with the bear's Alaskan habitat. Writing in the *San Francisco Chronicle*, Jane Kay said,

> Environmental groups fear that political meddling and a rush to sell oil leases in Arctic waters are behind the Bush administration's announcement that it will miss a legal deadline to determine whether to list the polar bear under the Endangered Species Act . . . Major environmental groups, including the Sierra Club, National Resources Defense Council, and Greenpeace, as well as some congressional leaders . . . fear that the polar bear decision has been purposefully delayed to allow a first-time oil lease sale to go forward Feb. 6 in Alaska's pristine Chukchi Sea, which provides one-tenth of the habitat for the world's polar bears.

The oil and gas industry has contributed millions of dollars to Alaskans; the polar bear hasn't contributed much except a few pretty pictures and an uncomfortable controversy about endangered species. One of the Alaskans who has benefited from the pipeline and its ancillary benefits has been Alaska's Ted Stevens, the longest-serving senator in the history of the Republican Party. In the *Fairbanks Daily News-*

Miner (January 10, 2008), Stevens said that listing the polar bear under the Endangered Species Act would impact oil and gas leasing on Alaska's North Slope and possibly offshore, and could even block the development of a natural gas pipeline. "If the polar bear is listed," he said, "its habitat will be subject to new criteria as far as any development, and the major development being considered today in the polar bear habitat is the natural gas pipeline." The listing is unnecessary, he continued, "and backed largely by environmentalists bent on blocking development projects" (Milkowski 2008). Those darned environmentalists! Worried about a few bears when there are millions to be made from another pipeline!*

It's not difficult to understand why Alaskans would want another pipeline. After oil was discovered in 1968 by the Atlantic-Richfield Company at Prudhoe Bay on the Arctic coast of Alaska, a Trans-Alaska Pipeline was proposed to carry the oil south from Prudhoe Bay to the port of Valdez. The land across which the pipeline was to be built would cross property involved in a Native Rights dispute, and the pipeline could not be constructed until the claims had been settled. In 1971 the Alaska Native Claims Settlement Act was signed into law by President Nixon, under which the Natives relinquished aboriginal claims to their lands in return for access to forty-four million acres of land and $963 million, to be divided among regional, urban, and village corporations. The land claimed by the government is now the National Petroleum Reserve–Alaska, a twenty-three-million-acre area (about the size of Indiana) that comprises the entire North Slope of Alaska and includes the villages of Point Hope, Wainwright, Barrow, Prudhoe Bay, and Kaktovik. This area has been managed by the Bureau of Land Management since 1976.

Most Alaskans—and all Alaskan politicians—are in favor of the oil leases, and opposed to the listing of the polar bear. If the Chukchi Sea wells come in, it would likely mean another pipeline and another bonanza for Alaskans. Don Young, the sole congressman from Alaska in the U.S. House of Representatives since 1973, said in an Associated

---

* Senator Stevens was convicted in October 2008 of seven counts of lying on Senate disclosure forms by failing to report more than $250,000 in home improvements and other gifts from an oil executive. The eighty-four-year-old senator, confident of reelection in November 2008, refused to relinquish his Senate seat, but was defeated by Anchorage mayor Mark Begich.

Press interview, "This is yet another example of how a law with the best of intentions has been subverted by the lawyers for the extreme environmental organizations and the liberal Democratic leadership." (Young, a Republican, is under federal investigation for possibly taking bribes, illegal gratuities, or unreported gifts.) The same politicians are ardently supporting the opening of oil drilling in the Arctic National Wildlife Refuge, despite opposition from environmentalists and politicians in the Lower 48.

Canadian Inuit leaders criticized environmentalists for pushing Washington to declare the polar bear a threatened species, saying the move was unnecessary and would hurt the local economy by deterring American hunters who spend millions of dollars a year for the right to shoot the animals in northern Canada. Mary Simon, president of the Inuit Council (Tapiriit) of Canada, said, "The polar bear is a very important subsistence, economic, cultural, conservation, management, and rights concern for Inuit in Canada. It's a complex and multilevel concern. But it seems the media, environmental groups, and the public are looking at this in overly simplistic black-and-white terms as the demise of the polar bear from climate change and sports hunting."

January 15, 2008: In another *New York Times* editorial ("Regulatory Games and the Polar Bear") we read,

> Although Congress and the courts have largely frustrated the Bush administration's efforts to open up Alaska to oil and gas drilling, Vice President Dick Cheney and his industry friends remain determined to lock up as many oil and gas leases as they can before the door hits them on the way out. They are certainly not going to let the struggling polar bear stand in their way.
>
> The Interior Department's Minerals Management Service has announced that early next month it will sell oil and gas leases on nearly 30 million acres of prime polar bear habitat in the Chukchi Sea. Meanwhile, the department's Fish and Wildlife Service has postponed a long-awaited decision on whether to place this iconic and troubled animal on the list of threatened species . . .
>
> That would give scientists more time to assess the threats to the bear and other fragile wildlife. The department could also use the time to figure out how and where drilling may safely proceed, if at all. There is no urgency to lease Alaskan waters. President Bush's sugges-

tion that new oil production will bring short-term relief at the pump
is nonsense, since oil fields take years to develop. It is urgent to help
the bears.

Two weeks later, as if in response to this impassioned editorial, the
Wall Street Journal chimed in with an editorial of its own, called "The
Polar Bear Express," in which they took exactly the opposite position
from everyone who believed that the bears were threatened: "The problem is that polar bear populations have been rising over the past four
decades and may be at an historic high." But polar bear populations
throughout the Arctic have fallen precipitously over the past four
decades, and some are at 60 percent of what they were in 1960. The edi-
torialists at the *Journal* were prepared to argue that global warming isn't
really a problem at all, writing, "These projections are speculative, however, and tend to underestimate the dynamism of the environment.
Animals adapt to changing conditions, which might mean a shift in
population patterns to areas where pack ice is more robust year round."
But every climatologist knows that there has been a drastic loss of the
Arctic sea ice, and that this loss will only increase. To suggest that it is
up to the bears to "adapt to changing conditions" flies smack in the face
of evolutionary history: failure to adapt to changing conditions is one of
the primary causes of extinction. Said the *Journal*, "The logical—and
dangerous—leap here is that the greens are attempting to re-write the
Endangered Species Act without actual legislation. If the 'iconic' polar
bear is classified as threatened, and the harm is formally attributed to
warming caused by humans, then their gambit would lead to all sorts of
regulatory mischief." But as written, and without any modification, the
Endangered Species Act protects the habitat of a species classified as
threatened (not to mention endangered), and the very act of drilling in
the Chukchi Sea is hazardous to the bears—think of oil spills, which
are part of the process—and nobody, except perhaps the editorial writers at the *Journal*, denies that global warming is caused by humans.
What the *Journal* calls "a modest sale of oil and gas leases" is actually an
auction of leases in nearly 46,000 square miles—an area the size of
Pennsylvania—of prime polar bear habitat in the Chukchi Sea.

The world's largest oil companies, ExxonMobil, Royal Dutch Shell,
BP, ConocoPhillips, and ChevronTexaco, prepared bids on these
potentially lucrative oil fields. The *Journal* wrote that "the acreage is

WAR OF THE DRONES   QUINDLEN ON GAY MARRIAGE

Newsweek

THE POLITICS OF
**ENDANGERED
SPECIES**
WHAT MAKES THE LIST—
AND WHAT DOESN'T

Newsweek, *June 6, 2008*

estimated to contain 15 billion barrels of oil and 76 trillion feet of natural gas. In 2005, Exxon became the first U.S. company ever to ring up quarterly sales of $40 billion. The company's third quarter revenue was greater than the annual gross domestic product of some of the largest oil-producing nations, including the United Arab Emirates and Kuwait."

In opposition to the listing of the bear as an endangered species, people like Governor Palin have pointed out that polar bear populations have risen in the last several decades. In many cases they have, but that may have to do with the reduction in sport hunting, and in any case, an increase in the populations is not a justification for leaving them unprotected. The threat to the bears lies in the realization that the disappearing ice cap will endanger their habitat and their lives, and an increased population only means that more bears will have less food.

After weeks of anxious waiting, and the hope that somebody would care more about endangered species than oil-company profits, the decision was made on February 6, 2008, to allow the Department of the Interior to move ahead with the auction of oil leases in the Chukchi Sea. Immediately, Royal Dutch Shell bid $105 million for a single exploration block, and $2.1 billion for 275 tracts. The last lease sale in the Chukchi, held in 1991, brought in a total of only $7.4 million. About twenty-five years ago, Shell had explored some of the same regions it leased in 2008, but relinquished the leases as uneconomic. In 2008 high oil prices transformed previously undesirable high-cost regions into exploration possibilities for oil companies, and extinction possibilities for polar bears.

On March 11, 2008, a coalition of environmental groups sued the Bush administration for delaying a decision to protect polar bears threatened with extinction because of the Arctic ice melt. The Center for Biological Diversity, Greenpeace, and the Natural Resources Defense Council filed the suit for missing the legal deadline for issuing a final decision on whether to list the polar bear under the Endangered Species Act. Had the Fish & Wildlife Service listed polar bears as threatened on January 9, the Chukchi Sea lease sale could not have gone ahead without critical studies to assess the potential impacts on polar bears. Should the polar bears be listed as threatened in the near future, the U.S. government would have an obligation to protect their habitat, which might mean having to buy back the Chukchi leases from the energy companies—and at a premium price (Leahy 2008).

On April 17, having missed its deadline by more than three months, the Interior Department announced that it needed another ten weeks because of "the complexity of the legal and scientific issues." Kassie Siegel, an attorney and spokesperson for the Center for Biological Diversity, said, "These are not questions for attorneys, they're questions for scientists." She also said that "the request for more time is likely a tactic by political appointees to delay a decision until the Minerals Management Service can finish issuing offshore petroleum leases in the Chukchi Sea . . . to further protect the leases from legal challenges" (Joling 2008). On April 29, 2008, U.S. District Court Judge Claudia Wilkin ruled that the Bush administration had two weeks to decide whether polar bears deserve protection under the Endangered Species Act because of impacts from the warming climate. "Today's decision is a huge victory for the polar bear; by May 15th the polar bear should receive the protection it deserves," said Siegel. The court rejected a request by the Interior Department for more time, saying, "Defendants offer no specific facts that would justify the existing delay, much less further delay. To allow defendants more time would violate the mandated listing deadlines under the ESA and congressional intent that time is of the essence in listing threatened species." The Bush administration argued in various courts, including the Supreme Court, that such efforts will fail because, among other things, the "remedy" for limiting global warming must be applied globally, not just in the United States (Revkin 2008).

One day before the Interior Department was to appear in court to respond to the environmentalists' lawsuit, Dirk Kempthorne declared the polar bear "threatened" under the Endangered Species Act. Even though it took pressure from environmental groups to force the release of the report, Interior had known for a long time that the bears were in trouble. At 368 pages, "Determination of Threatened Status for the Polar Bear Throughout Its Range" is longer than this book, and, like this book, could not have been assembled overnight. It incorporates a complete natural history of the polar bear; a detailed discussion of the condition of polar bear populations around the world; a comprehensive analysis of the decline of the Arctic sea ice; inclusion of the relevant statutes and acts; and specific recommendations under the law. (The primary authors are Scott Schliebe of the Marine Mammals Management Office and Kurt Johnson of the Branch of Listing, Endangered Species Program.) The ruling reads as follows:

> We, the U.S. Fish and Wildlife Service (Service), determine threatened status for the polar bear *(Ursus maritimus)* under the Endangered Species Act of 1973, as amended (Act) (16 U.S.C. 1531 et seq.). Polar bears evolved to utilize the Arctic sea ice niche and are distributed throughout most ice-covered seas of the Northern Hemisphere. We find, based upon the best available scientific and commercial information, that polar bear habitat—principally sea ice—is declining throughout the species' range, that this decline is expected to continue for the foreseeable future, and that this loss threatens the species throughout all of its range. Therefore, we find that the polar bear is likely to become an endangered species within the foreseeable future throughout all of its range. This final rule activates the consultation provisions of section 7 of the Act for the polar bear. The special

rule for the polar bear, also published in today's edition of the Federal Register, sets out the prohibitions and exceptions that apply to this threatened species.

At the May 14 press conference at which he announced the decision, Kempthorne said,

> Today I am listing the polar bear as a threatened species under the Endangered Species Act. I believe this decision is most consistent with the record and legal standards of the Endangered Species Act— perhaps the least flexible law Congress has ever enacted. I am also announcing that this listing decision will be accompanied by administrative guidance and a rule that defines the scope of impact that my decision will have, in order to protect the polar bear while preventing unintended harm to the society and economy of the United States . . . This has been a difficult decision. But in the light of the scientific record and the restraints of the inflexible law that guides me, I believe it was the only decision I could make.

On its face, this seemed like a victory for the environmentalists and the bears—indeed, in the *Wall Street Journal,* Ian Talley wrote, "The Bush Administration handed environmentalists a major victory"—but it was in fact a ruling that provided almost no protection for the bears, and nothing that would stand in the way of oil prospecting in their habitat. Listing the polar bear as "threatened" under the ESA meant that bears shot in Canada could not be brought into the United States (whole or in parts), so in that reading, a few bears were protected, but otherwise, those bears at risk because the sea ice was melting were no better off than they were before Kempthorne's announcement. Acknowledging that global warming has caused the retreat of Arctic ice, and that human activities had "some impact" on climate change, he said that no link could be made between any individual power plant or effort to drill for gas or oil, and the fate of the bear. "The loss of sea ice, and not oil and gas exploration or subsistence activity, is the primary threat to the bear," he said (Brown 2008). Via Kempthorne, the administration is invoking a loophole called the 4(d) rule that limits protection for the ice bears and their shrinking sea ice habitat in areas where oil and gas development is planned or proceeding. Essentially the administration has signaled that it will extend the bears no greater protection from oil and gas development than they previously had under the Marine Mammal Protection Act.

Denying the obvious connections between greenhouse gases, global warming, and the loss of the bears' hunting grounds, Kempthorne said that his ruling "should not open the door to use the ESA to regulate greenhouse gases from automobiles, power plants and other sources. That would be a wholly inappropriate use of the Endangered Species Act. ESA is not the right tool to regulate global climate change." Kempthorne was parroting the words of George W. Bush, who announced in April 2008 that "the Clean Air Act, the Endangered Species Act, and the National Environmental Policy Act were never meant to regulate global climate change."

Kassie Siegel of the Center for Biological Diversity, one of the litigants in the lawsuit against the Department of Interior, said, "It's not too late to save the polar bear, and we'll keep fighting to ensure that the polar bear gets all the help it needs through the full protections of the Endangered Species Act." In a statement to CNN, Representative Edward Markey, who chaired the earlier hearings on polar bears and oil drilling, said,

> After years of delay, the Bush administration was forced to face the reality that global warming has endangered the polar bear and that the polar bear needs to be placed on the Endangered Species list. But the administration has also simultaneously announced a rule aimed at allowing oil and gas drilling in the Arctic to continue unchecked even in the face of the polar bear's threatened extinction. Essentially, the administration is giving a gift to Big Oil, and short shrift to the polar bear.

Those who opposed the listing of the polar bear did so because they felt it would be bad for business. According to Felicity Barringer's May 15, 2008, article in the *New York Times*, "Some officials in the Interior Department speculated that the office of Vice President Dick Cheney had tried to block the listing of the bear." Canadian Inuit saw the disappearance of the large fees they had been getting from American sportsmen, because the Endangered Species Act prohibits the import of polar bear trophies into the U.S. The oil companies expected to go to court to ensure that the listing would in no way interfere with the newly acquired leases, and Alaska's legislators—Governor Palin, Representative Don Young, and the two Republican senators, Lisa Murkowski and Ted Stevens—came out as strongly anti-bear and pro–oil drilling. In a prepared statement issued a day after the ESA listing, Stevens said, "I am disappointed and disturbed by the ... decision to weaken the Endangered Species Act by listing the polar bear as a threatened species despite the steady increase in the species' population ... Alaskans must stand together and fight attempts to exploit the public's fear of climate change as a means to impose unreasonable burdens on our state." A week after the Interior Department's announcement, Governor Palin announced that the State of Alaska would sue the U.S. government to stop the listing, arguing that the listing will slow the state's economic development—for which one can read: more oil prospecting (Rosen 2008).

On May 18, 2008, the *New York Times* devoted another editorial to the plight of the polar bear. In "Not Much Help for the Polar Bear," they wrote,

> Boxed into a corner by the courts and its own scientists, the Bush administration agreed last week to place the polar bear under the protection of the Endangered Species Act. The decision was the clearest official acknowledgment that the bear, its hunting grounds diminished by shrinking summer ice, is seriously at risk ... The act—designed to protect specific animals from chain saws, bulldozers and, yes, oil rigs—probably should not have to carry the burden of solving global warming. But President Bush has denied the problem for so long, refusing to offer serious remedies, it is little wonder that people are tempted to grab at any lever ... This leaves the polar bear much as before: living precariously in a changing world, and facing the added stresses of exploratory drilling with no real protection.

Kempthorne has reassured the oil industry that the listing will not prevent drilling in prime polar bear habitat and that the administration will continue to develop these resources in "an environmentally sound way"—a world-class oxymoron. There is no environmentally sound way to drill for oil in the polar seas. Pipelines, boat traffic, drilling platforms, and ice-breaking vessels are just a few of the risks that come with oil development. Drilling also brings seismic blasting—a process one scientist referred to as "the most severe acoustic insult to the marine environment, short of naval warfare." And then there is the threat of oil spills. The oil industry's record with spills is not good, and even the Interior Department admits there could be more than a fifty-fifty chance of a major spill in the area. If a spill did occur, it would be disastrous. There is no proven method for cleaning up oil in the Arctic's broken sea ice, and once a bear makes contact with even a small amount of oil, it loses its ability to insulate and can die of hypothermia and ingestion.

Only a month after the polar bear was declared an endangered species, the Fish & Wildlife Service gave permission to the oil companies to annoy and harm the bears of the Chukchi Sea if the bears interfered with oil exploration. According to Associated Press writer Dina Cappiello (June 14, 2008), "exploring in the Chukchi Sea's 29.7 million acres will require five drill ships, one or two icebreakers, a barge, a tug, daily helicopter flights . . . and the creation of hundreds of miles of ice trails and roads along the coastline." This cannot help but disturb the bears. (On the same date, a headline on the blog *Raw Story* read, "Bush Gives OK for Oil Companies to Harm Polar Bears.") The materiel and activity will incite the natural curiosity of the bears, and there is no question that bears that come too close to oil workers or road builders will be seen as threats. As the men will surely be armed to protect themselves from marauding bears, any bear the comes within rifle range will be shot. It is hard to imagine any more flagrant disregard of the Endangered Species Act than shooting the species that has just been declared endangered—and then holding the shooters harmless.*

In 2008, Shell Oil spent more than $2 billion for exploration rights in the Chukchi Sea, over and above the $44 million they had already spent

---

* To ensure that its members would not be deprived of the opportunity to shoot a polar bear in Canada and bring home the trophy head or hide, Safari Club International (SCI), a Dallas-based organization dedicated to "protecting the freedom to hunt and protecting hunting heritage," sued the U.S. government too, requesting that the polar bear be removed from the Endangered Species List. The Humane Society of the U.S., the International Fund for Animal Welfare, and Defenders of Wildlife filed a motion to intervene in the SCI lawsuit; as Michael Makarian of HSUS said, "Safari Club International has made a game of encouraging its members to shoot rare animals around the world, the rarer the better. But there is no reason why the federal government should condone this perverse practice" (HSUS, June 16, 2008).

since their purchase of leases from the Minerals Management Service in 2005. In November 2008, the U.S. Court of Appeals for the Ninth Circuit (Alaska, Arizona, California, Hawaii, Idaho, Montana, Nevada, Oregon, Washington) ruled that the MMS had failed to review environmental impacts when it authorized Shell's plan to explore drilling sites in the Beaufort Sea. In March 2009, when the court ruled that MMS must review the Shell plan all over again, Shell canceled its drilling program, hoping for a more favorable ruling in the future (Rosen, 2009).

If polar bears evolved from brown bears that moved north in response to their changing surroundings and learned to hunt seals on the ice, wouldn't it be possible for the white bears to respond to the loss of ice by modifying their eating habits again and go back to hunting on land? In other words, could they de-evolve from polar bears? For the most part, evolution takes its subjects in one direction—not necessarily forward, but rarely backward. An adaptation, once lost, is usually not reacquired. There is even a "law" in evolutionary theory that says that an organism is unable to return, even partially, to a previous stage already realized in the ranks of its ancestors. "Dollo's Law," formulated by Belgian evolutionist Louis Dollo (1857–1931), is also known as the Law of Irreversible Evolution. It basically states that organisms cannot re-evolve along lost pathways, but must (because the same fortuitous train of mutational events, being totally random, will never repeat) find alternate routes. Perhaps the seals that also depend on the ice could change concurrently to breed on land, which might be regarded as a beneficial modification, or at least one that would keep them from going extinct when the ice totally disappears. (Ringed, bearded, harp, ribbon, and hooded seals pup on the ice.)

There is no question that killing off most of the individuals in a given species will result in dangerously low population levels—we killed all the passenger pigeons and almost succeeded in killing off the American bison—but removing the food source by habitat modification can produce the same result. In recent times, many vertebrate species became such specialized feeders that reducing their food source by altering their habitat becomes an imminent threat to the survival of the species—think of how the loss of bamboo forests in China has led to the giant panda's downfall in the wild. Brown bears are regarded as generalists, or omnivores, able to eat almost anything, from roots and leaves to berries and nuts, from mammals of every size to carrion. Polar bears too can vary their diet, sometimes eating walruses, caribou, birds, eggs, or whale carrion, but they rely heavily on seals for the high fat content that supplies their thick layers of insulating body fat, enabling them to function in their inhospitable habitat. Species can continue to exist as long as they are not killed off in too-large numbers, and as long as their habitat and food source remains available. If the habitat is modified and the food source threatened, the very existence of the specialized feeders is at risk. And although the polar bear may have been perceived as an evolutionary success story, it now may be the exact opposite: a too-highly specialized animal doomed to extinction because its habitat and food source are disappearing. As Ian Stirling put it in Shnayerson's *Vanity Fair* article, "Polar bears are too big, thanks to their diet of seal and salmon. They could never adjust back to a brown bear's partial diet of roots and berries. Either the polar bear with all its amazing adaptations survives as it is—or it doesn't."

Afterword

In the past, if someone asked me, "Why polar bears?" about the best I could come up with was "I like polar bears." I like other animals too; for a long time I drew and painted nothing but horses, and more recently, I have been painting whales, sharks, and dolphins. Except for a couple of rubber whales that somebody once gave me, there is no physical evidence of my love affair with whales, sharks, or dolphins. (I suppose you could count the big blue whale model that I designed for the

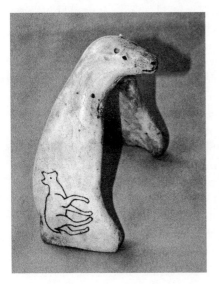

Walrus jawbone carved with the face of a polar bear

Hall of Ocean Life at the American Museum of Natural History, or the murals I painted for the New Bedford Whaling Museum—but those were commissioned.) But I have been collecting polar bears for years. I have little bears made of ivory, glass, wood, stone, porcelain, and bone. I have an oosik carved with a polar bear head on one end and a walrus (the original owner) on the other. I designed a series of crystal animals for the Franklin Mint, one of which was a polar bear. I once bought a two-foot-high porcelain bear from a store that sold garden furniture because I thought it would be a nice thing to have, but in its thirty-five years in my possession, I have never found a good place to put it. I once painted a polar bear picture for a marine-mammal veterinarian who paid for it with a polar bear skull. I own a tie with polar bears on it, bought in the general store at Churchill.

I like the way polar bears look, but there's more to it than that. There is something very special about the white bear. It's big and strong—but so are elephants and rhinoceroses. The bear is white, of course, and this somehow contributes to its fascination. I began this project believing that Nanook was the maximum predator of the Arctic ice; that polar bears wantonly killed seals and walruses; that they would chase down travelers in sledges, swat their dogs away, and attack the people; that they prowled the streets of Churchill looking for luckless tourists and townspeople to eat, because it was too early for the bears to go out on the ice; and that en route to the North Pole in 1994, it would have been suicidal to leave our Russian icebreaker without a soldier armed with a rifle accompanying us. But the more I looked into the life history of the polar bear—particularly its interactions with humans—the more I realized that it has a far more complex personality than most people realize. Nanook has been vilified more because of what people thought he could do than for what he actually did. While certainly capable of all those horrific historical acts, the polar bear probably committed very few of them—and none out of bloodlust or malice. I wrote this book in the same spirit that I wrote *Great White Shark* and *The Search for the Giant Squid:* I wanted to pay homage to a wild spirit, and I wanted to correct the misconceptions that surrounded it.

As I became steeped in polar bear lore, history, and psychology, I realized that the great white bear had already become a conflicted and contradictory symbol: at the same time that it could be used to demonstrate our veneration of wildlife, it also represented our disrespect for nature, crystallized as global warming. Somehow the corporeal reality of *Ursus maritimus* trumped our petty (and often incorrect) interpretations of its behavior; its lonely, ice-bound existence transcended our attempts to imprison or understand it. The great bear, dominant over its environment as no other wild creature ever was before or since, now finds itself threatened by the careless and uncaring predator that has—usually at the expense of the natural world—become the only creature in history that can drive other species to extinction and modify the earth to suit his needs. Although he was speaking of all animals, Henry Beston could have been referring to the polar bear nation when he wrote,

> We need another and a wiser and perhaps a more mystical concept of animals. Remote from universal nature, and living by complicated artifice, man in civilization surveys the creature through the glass of his knowledge, and sees thereby a feather magnified and the whole image in distortion. We patronize them for their incompleteness, for their tragic fate of having taken form so far below ourselves. And therein we err, we greatly err. For the animal shall not be measured by man. In a world older and more complete than ours they move finished and complete, gifted with extensions of senses we have lost or never attained, living by forces we shall never hear. They are not brethren, not underlings; they are other nations, caught with ourselves in the net of life and time, fellow prisoners of the splendor and travail of the earth.

I wrote this book because I had to.

Why another polar bear book? There already are any number of them, every one illustrated with better photographs than I ever took. (In fact, some of those books are almost all photographs.) In 2008, Steven Kazlowski published *The Last Polar Bear*, which, along with his spectacular photographs, includes essays by several writers and conservationists, all deeply concerned about the fate of the great white bear. With this exception, most of those other books were published before the threat of global warming got everybody believing that the Arctic ice cap was going to melt before the end of the decade, leaving the poor polar bears searching for ice that was no longer there, and swimming until they drowned. That was hyperbole, of course; while the melting of the Arctic ice is a fact, and there have been some bears swimming off into eternity, all the world's 22,000 polar bears are threatened by the irreversible loss of sea ice. As opposing camps debate the necessity of protecting the polar bear and its habitat, the bear has assumed an unexpected political significance, comparable to that of various cetaceans during the "whale wars" of the 1980s.

When I was writing *The Book of Whales*, which was published in 1980, I was serving on the American delegation to the International Whaling Commission, and news about whales and whaling was being made right before my eyes in a hall in Brighton, England. From the meeting I would call in what I considered essential updates on the quotas for minke whales, the position of the Japanese on scientific-research whaling, or what the Peruvians wanted. (The recipient of those calls was my editor, Ash Green, who also happens to be the editor of this book.) After many phone calls, during which I told him that we had to change what was on page 82 or 191 or 247 (the book was in galleys by that time), he finally said, "We're running a publishing house here, not a newspaper; you can't keep telling us to stop the presses." At that point I had to let the book go, regardless of what happened at the IWC. Although I didn't believe it at the time, the book was all right even without the latest updates.

More or less the same thing happened a decade later, as I was finishing up *Men and Whales* (same editor, same publisher). This time, I was trying to complete a manuscript that covered the entire history of whaling, and in an afterword not unlike this one, I wrote,

> Future IWC meetings will demonstrate if the anti-whaling coalition is strong enough to withstand the pressure, or if the whaling nations can overthrow world opinion on the agonizingly interminable argument about humankind's "right" to slaughter whales. Rather than writing about the end of whaling, I may have produced only a long interim report. I seriously hope not.

The book was published in 1991, and that wasn't the end of whaling by a long shot. The Japanese would continue "research whaling" well into the first decade of the new century; Alaskan Eskimos were still killing bowheads; and the Norwegians, who took an exception to the 1983 moratorium, were not affected by the worldwide ban on commercial whaling and have continued killing whales to this day. But when the Japanese announced that they were going to kill humpbacks and minkes in Australian sanctuary waters, the Australian government said they most assuredly were not, and the Japanese backed down. They still plan to kill whales in the Antarctic, over the dramatic protests of Paul Watson and the Sea Shepherd Society, who continue to try to stop the Japanese whaleships any way they can—including by ramming them, if necessary. As the controversy about Japanese whaling continued well into 2008, it appears that I did produce a "long, interim report."

By the time you read this, the Japanese will have killed however many whales they decided they needed for "research," and as always, the meat of those whales will end up for sale in Japanese meat markets. That the Australian government found the Japanese in contravention of Australian laws by hunting in a whale sanctuary may or may not keep the whalers from killing whales, since it is not clear how the Australians can actually stop the whalers. Paul Watson may or may not have rammed Japanese whaleships, and these and other stories will be extensively covered in newspapers and other media. I can't do much about *Men and Whales*, but I am trying to keep this book as up to date as possible. The world's polar bears are threatened by the continued melting of the Arctic ice cover, which changes their behavior and habits in ways that may be detrimental to their health and perhaps even to their continued existence. Reports and news articles appear daily, predicting the end of the ice and therefore the end of the polar bears, or the possibility of drilling for oil in the Chukchi Sea. There are therefore an inordinate number of media references in this book and its bibliography; many of them contain predictions or possibilities that appeared imminent to the writers but, in fact, may not actually come to pass. The Arctic ice cap may disappear. The polar bear may be listed as an endangered species. Knut might or might not star in a movie.

In trying to keep up with developments in the ever-changing news of polar bears, I subscribed to "Google Alerts," a service that brings to my computer a daily collection of polar bear news stories from around the world. (Some of them are about "polar bear swimmers"—people who enjoy swimming in ice-cold water—but I haven't figured out how to refine the search to eliminate those.) Craig Van Note's Monitor Consortium supplies a daily compendium of news articles about all subjects environmental, and in recent times many of these have been about global warming, polar bears, or a newsworthy combination of the two. The bear's iconic and political significance has meant that the more traditional news sources—television, magazines, newspapers—run stories on the plight of the polar bear as they develop. At one point, the *New York Times* was publishing impassioned editorials about the situation with the bears, the oil leases, and the Interior Department. To date, there have been dozens of news stories about the listing of the polar bear as an endangered species, as proponents of the sale of oil and gas leases in the Chukchi Sea argue that oil company profits are more important than polar bears. I'm willing to bet that by the time this book is published, the oil companies will have begun exploratory drilling and the polar bear will be more endangered than ever. By the time you read this, the German bear cubs, whose show-business careers have been chronicled in such detail, will have long outgrown the "cute" phase of their lives, and there will probably be other fluffy white cubs that will capture the public's attention. In late March 2008, polar bears began appearing in Newfoundland, where they hadn't been seen for many years. Their appearance may signal a general southward migration because of changes in the ice cap far to the north, but five sightings in two weeks may not yet constitute a trend.

During the time I was working on this book, the Republican administration in Washington was as blatantly anti-environment as any administration in American history. Wildlife, forests, waterways—even the *atmosphere,* for God's sake—were unprotected, ignored, or destroyed in the interests of big business. I fervently hope that the election of Barack Obama will turn this disastrous policy around and restore our faith in government to protect our natural heritage.

Up to the moment I have to sign off on this manuscript, I have tried to keep track of current events and current opinions. I hope to be able to bring the material up to date, but like that of the whales, the bears' situation is in flux, and will, I'm afraid, continue to deteriorate. I write these books to make people aware of what's happening to their wildlife birthright; no one should be able to deny us or our grandchildren the right to coexist with sharks, whales, dolphins, tuna, or polar bears.

In my first book, *The Book of Sharks,* published in 1975, I included an "afterword," which was supposed to be sort of an explanation—or even an apology—for what I had presented in the preceding pages. I wrote about how much I had learned about sharks, and how much there was still to learn. I spoke about the process of conducting research, and how writing or painting couldn't really capture the essence of the shark: "Only when it is in the ocean," I said, "swimming silently with measured strokes of its tail, and looking out through sleepless eyes, is it real." Then I said, "In a way it has been like climbing a great mountain. There is a certain measure of personal gratification, but the mountain is unchanged by man's puny attempts to 'conquer' it. Like Everest, the shark will remain indomitable." I had written about "shark tournaments," where the fins of the captured sharks were lopped off by Asian restaurateurs to be made into shark-fin soup—but at the time only a couple of hundred sharks were killed per tournament, so it wasn't a problem for shark populations in general. Thirty years after I wrote that book, shark-finners throughout the world's oceans are slaughtering sharks by the hundreds of thousands for soup. Many shark species became endangered during that period, and the oceanic whitetip, which I had called "probably the most numerous large animal in the world," is rare over most of its previous range and extinct in the Gulf of Mexico. Not only were the sharks not indomitable, they were, like so many of Beston's "other nations," catastrophically susceptible to the predations of *Homo sapiens*.

Anything that is covered herein, no matter how ancient or recent, has undergone the meticulous scrutiny of Ash Green, my longtime editor and even longer-time friend. He will have retired by the time you read this, and I want to thank him for his dedication and loyalty—not to mention his superb editing skills—on this and eight of my other books. You might think that an association that began in 1980 with Knopf's publication of my *Book of Whales* and, two years later, with *Dolphins and Porpoises*, would have no need of an agent for future books, but as with the tuna book that immediately preceded this one, Steve Wasserman brought me and the books back to Knopf—whence I had strayed, I am embarrassed to admit. I am not embarrassed, however, to admit my gratitude to Stephanie Guest, whose support has always been unwavering even as I tried to corral the peripatetic white bears into a coherent book.

Andrew Derocher read an early version of the manuscript and made many helpful comments. Because he has been studying polar bears for many years, he knows a lot more about the animals than I do, and I made many of the changes he suggested—even when they sounded wrong to me. If someone reads your manuscript and makes corrections or suggestions, it is customary just to thank them for reading it, but some of Andy's observations were so prescient that I just had to include them. Contrary to the rules of acknowledgments, I have incorporated some of his remarks into the text, with only an "Andrew Derocher said" as an attribution. But despite expert advice from Derocher and others, I alone am responsible for mistakes or misinterpretations.

At a chance meeting with my friend John Alexander, he allowed as how he had a number of photographs of the polar bears of Churchill, so I asked if I could see them. I expected maybe twenty slides, but when the package arrived, I found that he had sent me three hundred, each one better than the next. I had already positioned many of the photos in the text (the body of the book, as you can see, uses black-and-white

Felix Leo Ellis Adams, age three, wearing a shirt with one of the few representations of a polar bear that shows an adult bear rather than a cute little cub

images), but because the editors had granted my request for a color insert, I decided to use John's spectacular color photographs there. I wish I could have used more, but in many cases there are other images that I was obliged to use because I had already bought and paid for them. There's simply not enough space to do justice to John's magnificent portfolio, but even their limited number greatly enhances this book.

Thanks also to George Amato, Jack Brink, Fred Bruemmer, Amanda Byrd, Klaus Gille, Nancy Harris, Jürgen Holfort, Chuck Jonkel, Jim McCarthy, Lawrence Millman, Martin Mittelstaedt, Paul Nicklen, Nikita Ovsyanikov, Andy Revkin, Norbert Rosing, Aqqalu Rosing-Asvid, Rick Sammon, Mark Serreze, Ian Stirling, Ed Struzik, Shelley Wanger, Priscilla Watson, George Wenzel, Ian Whitaker, Margaret Williams, Simon Winchester, Bryndís Snæbjörnsdóttir and Mark Wilson, and Bruce Foster and Celia Ackerman of the Central Park Zoo. Andy Williams of the photo agency CritterZone not only provided some spectacular photographs, he also helped with a particularly tricky download. Dugald Wells invited me to join the Cruise North expedition in July 2008, where we were surprised to see the juvenile polar bear on the road in Churchill.

I hope that wild polar bears will be around long enough so that my grandchildren, Lochlan, Stella, Felix, and Michael, will be able to see them, but at least they can read this book, which, I now realize, was written for them.

Updates to the Text

The news for polar bears has not been good. Since the original publication of this book (November 2009), events affecting the bears—almost all of them negatively—have transpired. Ranging in scale from the shooting of an individual bear to the removal of protection for the entire species, these events sadly support my original contention that the future for polar bears is bleak—and getting more so.

Page 125. Isle of Mull, Scotland. April 1, 2010: A conservation officer on the Isle of Mull in Scotland came across an exhausted polar bear lying on the beach. He snapped a couple of pictures and went off to get help, but when he came back, the bear was gone. Mull is about six hundred miles south of Iceland.

Page 220. Ulukhaktok, Northwest Territories, Canada. May 2, 2010: Inuit hunter David Kuptana was hunting on Victoria Island in April, when he shot what appeared to be an ordinary polar bear. Upon closer examination, the bear had the large head and ears of a brown bear, brown rings around its eyes, and no hair on the soles of its feet. DNA tests showed that it was a second-generation hybrid, suggesting that "pizzly" or "grolar" bears are becoming more common.

Page 328. Doha, Qatar. March 18, 2010: At the Convention on International Trade in Endangered Species (CITES), a U.S. proposal to restrict trade in polar bear parts and products was overwhelmingly defeated, largely through the efforts of Canada and Greenland, where polar bear hunting contributes to the subsistence economy of native peoples.

Page 342. Washington, D.C. March 30, 2010: The Obama administration proposed to open vast expanses of water to offshore oil and gas drilling along the Atlantic coast, the Gulf of Mexico, and the northern coast of Alaska. The administration has been forced to reconsider these reckless proposals, however, in the light of the catastrophic accident on April 20, 2010, when the Deepwater Horizon offshore rig blew up, killing eleven men and spewing oil into the Gulf of Mexico at the rate of at least 210,000 gallons a day, putting it in the running for largest oil spill in history. (The largest spill began on January 23, 1991, when Saddam Hussein's Iraqi forces opened the valves at the Sea Island oil terminal and dumped some 11,000,000 barrels of oil into the Persian Gulf.) There are no polar bears in or near the Gulf of Mexico, but on May 15, 2010, we learned that Shell Oil was planning to drill at five sites in the Chukchi and Bering Seas, both prime polar bear habitats. Shell paid $2.1 billion for its oil and gas leases off Alaska's coast in 2007, in a region estimated to hold nearly as much oil as Alaska's North Slope oil fields. In the past couple of years, Shell's efforts to drill in those areas have been rife with setbacks due to opposition from many North Slope community leaders and environmentalists who doubt the company's ability to clean up oil spills in Arctic waters and worry about increased industrial activity hurting marine mammals. On May 27, almost six weeks after the busted wellhead began spewing oil into the Gulf of Mexico, President Obama announced a moratorium on deepwater offshore drilling in the Chukchi Sea among other Arctic areas. Subsequently, the moratorium was struck down by a federal judge, and offshore drilling rights in the Arctic are still unresolved.

Bibliography

Aars, J., M. Andersen, and K. M. Kovacs. 2005. *Polar Bears in Svalbard*. Norwegian Polar Institute.

Agusti, J., and M. Anton. 2002. *Mammoths, Sabertooths, and Hominids: 65 Million Years of Mammalian Evolution in Europe*. Columbia University Press.

Allee, W. 1931. *Animal Aggregations: A Study in Sociology*. University of Chicago Press.

Amstrup, S. C. 1993. Human disturbances of denning polar bears in Alaska. *Arctic* 46(3): 246–50.

Amstrup, S. C., and G. M. Durner. 1998. Polar bear research in the Beaufort Sea. Pp. 131–39 in *Proceedings of the Twelfth Working Meeting of the IUCN/SSC Polar Bear Specialist Group, February 3–7, 1977, Oslo, Norway*. IUCN.

Amstrup, S. C., I. Stirling, and J. W. Lentfer. 1986. Past and present status of polar bears in Alaska. *Wildlife Society Bulletin* 14:241–54.

Amstrup, S. C., G. M. Durner, I. Stirling, N. J. Lunn, and F. Messier. 2000. Movements and distribution of polar bears in the Beaufort Sea. *Canadian Journal of Zoology* 78(6): 948–66.

Amstrup, S. C., I. Stirling, T. S. Smith, C. Perham, and G. W. Theimann. 2006. Recent observation of intraspecific predation and cannibalism among polar bears in the southern Beaufort Sea. *Polar Biology* 29(11): 997–1002.

Andersen, M., E. Lie, A. E. Derocher, S. E. Belikov, A. Bernhoft, A. N. Boltunov, G. W. Garner, J. U. Skaare, and Ø. Wiig. 2000. Geographic variation of PCB congeners in polar bears *(Ursus maritimus)* from Svalbard east to the Chukchi Sea. *Polar Biology* 24(4): 231–38.

Anderson, A. 2007. 100 days on thin ice. *New Scientist* 96(2630): 54–55.

Anderson, C. J. R., J. D. Roth, and J. M. Waterman. 2007. Can whisker patterns be used to identify individual polar bears? *Journal of Zoology* 273:333–39.

Angier, N. 2004. Built for the Arctic: A species' special adaptations. *New York Times*, Jan. 27.

———. 2006. The cute factor. *New York Times*, Jan. 3.

Anon. 1883. A trader in wild animals: Mr. Carl Hagenbeck's pursuit of rare beasts all over the world. *New York Times,* Apr. 16.

———. 1894. Hagenbeck's performing animals: Wonderful and thrilling exhibitions at the Madison Square Garden. *New York Times,* Sept. 4.

———. 1906. Hope for Ota Benga: If little, he's no fool. *New York Times,* Sept. 30.

———. 1922. Polar bear in Central Park bites boy's finger nearly off. *New York Times,* Nov. 26.

———. 1975. Splashing debut for first polar bear born in the Bronx. *New York Times,* Apr. 18.

———. 1986. Memo to the hunter, editorial. *New York Times,* Aug. 8.

———. 2003. Woman helps bears claw their way to freedom. *National Enquirer,* Sept. 20.

———. 2006a. Censoring truth, editorial. *New York Times,* Feb. 9.

———. 2006b. Plight of polar bears might force US action on climate. *Nature* 439:775.

———. 2007a. Stuffed and mounted: Are polar bears finished in the Arctic? *New Scientist* 196(2591): 48.

———. 2007b. Fair play for polar bears. *New Scientist* 196(2627): 4.

———. 2008. Of two minds on polar bears, editorial. *New York Times,* Jan. 2.

Appenzeller, T. 1991. Fire and ice under the deep sea floor. *Science* 252:1790–92.

———. 2007. The big thaw. *National Geographic* 211(6): 56–71.

Arlov, T. 1989. *A Short History of Svalbard.* Norsk Polarinstitutt.

Arutiunov, S. A. 1988. Chukchi: Warriors and traders of Chukotka. Pp. 39–42 in W. W. Fitzhugh and A. Crowell, eds., *Crossroads of Continents: Cultures of Siberia and Alaska.* Smithsonian Institution.

Associated Press. 1982. Man polar bear killed identified as Cuban. *New York Times,* Sept. 28.

———. 2007. Ominous Arctic melt worries experts. *New York Times,* Dec. 12.

———. 2008a. Alaskan sea drilling plans criticized. *New York Times,* Jan. 3.

———. 2008b. As Arctic sea ice melts, experts expect new low. *New York Times,* Aug. 28.

———. 2008c. 19-square-mile ice sheet breaks loose in Canada. *New York Times,* Sept. 4.

Atkinson, S. N., M. R. L. Cattet, S. C. Polischuk, and M. A. Ramsay. 1996. A case of offspring adoption in free-ranging polar bears *(Ursus maritimus). Arctic* 49(1): 94–96.

Austen, I. 2007. Canada announces plans for 2 new bases in its far north. *New York Times,* Aug. 11.

Azios, T. 2008. Do polar bears need U.S. protection? *Christian Science Monitor,* Jan. 2.

Balikci, A. 1970. *The Netsilik Eskimo.* Natural History Press.

Barringer, F. 2008. Polar bear is made a protected species. *New York Times,* May 15.

Barringer, F., and A. C. Revkin. 2006. Agency proposes to list polar bear as threatened. *New York Times,* Dec. 26.

Barron, J. 1987. Polar bears kill a child at Prospect Park Zoo. *New York Times,* May 20.

Barton, L. 2008. Our soft spot for the serial killer of the Arctic. *The Guardian*, Jan. 10.

Belikov, S. E., and A. N. Boltunov. 1998. Research and management of polar bear populations in the Russian Arctic 1993–1995. Pp. 113–14 in *Proceedings of the Twelfth Working Meeting of the IUCN/SSC Polar Bear Specialist Group, February 3–7, 1977, Oslo, Norway.* IUCN.

Bergreen, L. 2007. *Marco Polo: From Venice to Xanadu.* Knopf.

Bernhoft, A., Ø. Wiig, and J. U. Skaare. 1997. Organochlorines in polar bears (*Ursus maritimus*) at Svalbard. *Environmental Pollution* 95(2): 159–75.

Berta, A., and J. L. Sumich. 1999. *Marine Mammals: Evolutionary Biology.* Academic Press.

Best, R. C. 1982. Thermoregulation in resting and active polar bears. *Journal of Comparative Physiology* 146:63–73.

———. 1984. Digestibility of ringed seals by the polar bear. *Canadian Journal of Zoology* 63:1033–36.

Beston, H. 1928. *The Outermost House.* Holt, Rinehart and Winston.

Biggar, H. P. 1903. *The Voyages of the Cabots and the CorteReals to North America and Greenland 1497–1503.* Tome X. Paris. Revue Hispanique.

Blankesteijn, H., and L. Hacquebord. 1993. God and the Arctic survivors: Without modern medicines, windcheaters or ski boots, explorers still managed to survive the Arctic winters of 400 years ago. Who was their unseen ally? *New Scientist* 1867:38–45.

Blix, A. S., and J. W. Lentfer. Modes of thermal protection in polar bears: At birth and on emergence from the den. *Ecological Applications* 6:311–17.

Boas, F. 1888. *The Central Eskimo.* Smithsonian Institution. Elibron Classics reprint, 2005.

Bockstoce, J. R. 1977. *Steam Whaling in the Western Arctic.* New Bedford Whaling Museum.

———. 1986. *Whales, Ice, and Men: The History of Whaling in the Western Arctic.* New Bedford Whaling Museum.

Bodfish, H. H. 1936. *Chasing the Bowhead.* Harvard University Press.

Borenstein, S. 2008. NASA warming scientist: "This is the last chance." *Associated Press*, June 23.

Born, E. W. 2002. Research on polar bears in Greenland 1997–2001. Pp. 67–74 in *Proceedings of the Thirteenth Working Meeting of the IUCN/SSC Polar Bear Specialist Group, June 23–28, 2001, Nuuk, Greenland.* IUCN.

Born, E. W., A. Renzoni, and R. Dietz. 1991. Total mercury in hair of polar bears (*Ursus maritimus*) from Greenland and Svalbard. *Polar Research* 9(2): 113–20.

Boswell, R. 2008. North Pole, no ice. *Canwest News Service*, June 23.

Bowen, M. 2005. *Thin Ice.* Henry Holt.

Brach, B. 2008. Save polar bears now, urges group. *Canada.com*, Apr. 26.

Broder, J. M., and A. C. Revkin. 2007. Warming is seen as wiping out most polar bears. *New York Times*, Sept. 8.

Brook, R. K., and E. S. Richardson. 2002. Observations of polar bear predatory behaviour toward caribou. *Arctic* 56(2): 193–96.

Brooke, J. 1995. A Rocky Mountain high: Twin polar bears. *New York Times*, Dec. 26.

Brown, K. 2004. *The North Pole*. Crown Point Press.

Brown, S. 2007a. Polar bears dying in years of early ice melt. *NatureNews*, May 13.

———. 2007b. Trophy hunting may push polar bears to "tipping point." *National Geographic News*, Nov. 21.

———. 2008. Polar bears listed as threatened. *NatureNews*, May 14.

Bruemmer, F. 1972. *Encounters with Arctic Animals*. American Heritage.

———. 1981. Two weeks in a polar bear prison. *Audubon* 83(6): 28–37.

———. 1984. How polar bears break the ice. *Natural History* 12/84: 38–47.

———. 1986. *Arctic Animals*. NorthWord.

———. 1989. *World of the Polar Bear*. Key Porter.

Bruemmer, F., and T. Mangelsen. 1997. *Polar Dance: Born of the North Wind*. Images of Nature.

Brunner, B. 2007. *Bears*. Yale University Press.

Buell, J. W. 1887. *Sea and Land: An Illustrated History of the Wonderful and Curious Things of Nature Existing Before and Since the Deluge. A Natural History of the Sea, Land Creatures, the Cannibals, and Wild Races of the World*. Historical Publishing Co.

Burek, K. A., F. M. D. Gulland, and T. M. O'Hara. 2008. Effects of climate change on Arctic marine mammal health. *Ecological Applications* 18(2): Suppl. S126–34.

Burland, C. 1973. *Eskimo Art*. Hamlyn.

Burn-Murdoch, W. G. 1917. *Modern Whaling & Bear-Hunting*. Seeley, Service & Co. Ltd.

Calahane, V. H. 1947. *Mammals of North America*. Macmillan.

Calamai, P. 2008. Bears face new toxic threat. *The Star* (Canada), Mar. 24.

Calvert, W., and I. Stirling. 1990. Interactions between polar bears and overwintering walruses in the central Canadian high Arctic. *International Conference on Bear Research and Management* 8:351–56.

Calvert, W., M. Taylor, I. Stirling, S. Atkinson, M. A. Ramsay, N. J. Lunn, M. Obbard, C. Elliott, G. Lamontagne, and J. Schaefer. 1998. Research on polar bears in Canada 1993–1996. Pp. 69–92 in *Proceedings of the Twelfth Working Meeting of the IUCN/SSC Polar Bear Specialist Group, February 3–7, 1977, Oslo, Norway*. IUCN.

Campbell, C., and K. Lunau. 2008. The war over the polar bear. *Maclean's* 121(4–5): 46–52.

Canadian Broadcasting Corporation (CBC). 2008a. "Frank, it's a polar bear!" Mar. 31.

———. 2008b. N. L. woman in staring match with polar bear. Apr. 14.

———. 2008c. Children run for cover before polar bear shot near Iqaluit. June 25.

Cappiello, D. 2008a. Companies get OK to annoy polar bears. *Associated Press*, June 14.

———. 2008b. Bush to relax protected species rules. *Associated Press*, Aug. 11.

Capstick, P. H. 1981. *Maneaters*. Safari Press.

Chamberlain, G. 2007. Iceland fears bears that go with the floe. *Telegraph* (UK), Apr. 2.

Charles, D. 2008. Polar bear listing opens doors to new lawsuits. *Science* 320:1000–01.

Chivers, T. 2008. Polar bear mother a danger to her cub. *Telegraph* (UK), Jan. 8.

Chivian, E., and A. Bernstein. 2008a. How is biodiversity threatened by human activity? Pp. 28–75 in E. Chivian and A. Bernstein, eds., *Sustaining Life: How Human Health Depends on Biodiversity.* Oxford University Press.

———. 2008b. Threatened groups of organisms valuable to medicine. Pp. 202–85 in E. Chivian and A. Bernstein, eds., *Sustaining Life: How Human Health Depends on Biodiversity.* Oxford University Press.

Clark, D. 2003. Polar bear–human interactions in Canadian national parks, 1986–2000. *Ursus* 14(1): 65–71.

Clark, D., and I. Stirling. 1998. Habitat preferences of polar bears in the Hudson Bay lowlands during late summer and fall. *Ursus* 10:243–50.

Clarke, J. 1969. *Man Is the Prey.* Andre Deutsch.

Clarke, J. S., and J. McArthur. 1809. *The Life of Admiral Lord Nelson.* Cadell and Davies.

Clarkson, P. L., and D. Irish. 1991. Den collapse kills female polar bear and two newborn cubs. *Arctic* 44(1): 83–84.

Clarkson, P. L., and I. Stirling. 1994. Polar bears: Damage prevention and control methods. Pp. C25–C34 in S. E. Hyngstrom, R. M. Timm, and G. E. Larson, eds., *Prevention and Control of Wildlife Damage.* University of Nebraska, U.S. Department of Agriculture, and Great Plains Agricultural Committee.

Clarkson, T. W. 1998. Human toxicology of mercury. *Journal of Trace Elements in Experimental Medicine* 11(2–3): 303–17.

———. 2002. The three modern faces of mercury. *Environmental Health Perspectives* 110(Suppl. 1): 11–23.

Clubb, R., and G. Mason. 2003. Captivity effects on wide-ranging carnivores. *Nature* 425:473–74.

Coe, J. C. 1986. Towards a co-evolution of zoos, aquariums, and natural history museums. Pp. 366–76 in *AAZPA 1986 Conference Proceedings, American Association of Zoological Parks and Aquariums, Wheeling, WV.*

Cone, M. 2005a. Dozens of words for snow, none for pollution. *Mother Jones* 30(1): 60–67.

———. 2005b. *Silent Snow: The Slow Poisoning of the Arctic.* Grove Press.

Connolly, K. Germans go nuts over Knut as zoo marks bear's birthday. *The Guardian,* Dec. 6.

Connor, S. 2008a. The Earth today stands in imminent peril. *The Independent,* June 19.

———. 2008b. No ice at the North Pole. *The Independent,* June 27.

Conway, M. 1906. *No Man's Land: A History of Spitsbergen from Its Discovery in 1596 to the Beginning of the Scientific Exploration of the Country.* Cambridge University Press.

Cook, F. A. 1951. *Return from the North Pole.* Pellegrini & Cudahy.

Corwin, J. A. 2007. Russia: Hunting polar bears to save them. *Radio Free Europe/Radio Liberty,* Jan. 18.

Cosimo, J. C. 2002. A rapidly declining perennial sea ice cover in the Arctic. *Geophysical Research Letters* 29(20): 1956.

Courchamp, F., T. Clutton-Brock, and B. Grenfell. 1999. Inverse density dependence and the Allee effect. *Trends in Ecology and Evolution* 14:405–10.

Courtland, R. 2008. Polar bear numbers set to fall. *Nature* 453:432–33.

Cowan, E. 1970. Curbs on hunting polar bear eased. *New York Times,* Mar. 22.

Crutzen, P. J. and W. Steffen. 2003. How long have we been in the anthropocene era? *Climate Change* 61: 251–57.

Crystall, B. 2008. Go with the floe. *New Scientist* 198(2659): 42–45.

Dargis, M. 2007. Bless the beasts and children, movie review. *New York Times,* Dec. 7.

Das, S. B., I. Joughin, M. D. Behn, I. M. Howat, M. A. King, D. Lizarralde, and M. P. Bhatia. 2008. Fracture propagation to the base of the Greenland Ice Sheet during supraglacial lake drainage. *SciencExpress,* Oct. 20.

Davids, R. C., and D. Guravich. 1982. *Lords of the Arctic.* Macmillan.

Davies, L. E. 1962. Alaskan safaris: Organized big-game hunting grows in state—polar bears among prey. *New York Times,* July 15.

———. 1964. Polar bear prey of Alaska hunts. *New York Times,* Aug. 25.

———. 1966. Alaska curbs hunting licenses to save polar bear population. *New York Times,* July 9.

Degerbøl, M., and P. Freuchen. 1935. *Mammals: Report of the Fifth Thule Expedition 1921–24.* Gyldendalske Boghandel, Nordisk Forlag.

DeMaster, D. P., and I. Stirling. 1981. Ursus maritimus [Polar Bear]. *Mammalian Species* 145:1–7. American Society of Mammalogists.

Derocher, A. E. 1990. Supernumerary mammae and nipples in the polar bear *(Ursus maritimus). Journal of Mammalogy* 71(2): 236–37.

———. 1999. Latitudinal variation in litter size of polar bears: Ecology or methodology? *Polar Biology* 22:350–56.

———. 2005. Polar bear. Pp. 1656–58 in M. Nuttall, ed., *Encyclopedia of the Arctic.* Routledge.

Derocher, A. E., and I. Stirling. 1990. Distribution of polar bears *(Ursus maritimus)* during the ice-free period in Hudson Bay. *Canadian Journal of Zoology* 68(7): 1395–1403.

———. 1994. Age-specific reproductive performance of female polar bears *(Ursus maritimus). Journal of Zoology* 234(4): 527–36.

———. 1995. Estimation of polar bear population size and survival in western Hudson Bay. *Journal of Wildlife Management* 59(2): 215–21.

———. 1996. Aspects of survival in juvenile polar bears. *Canadian Journal of Zoology* 74(7): 1246–52.

———. 1998. Maternal investment and factors affecting offspring size in polar bears *(Ursus maritimus). Journal of Zoology* 245:253–60.

Derocher, A. E., and Ø. Wiig. 1999a. Infanticide and cannibalism of juvenile polar bears *(Ursus maritimus)* in Svalbard. *Arctic* 52(3): 307–10.

———. 1999b. Observation of adoption in polar bears *(Ursus maritimus). Arctic* 52(4): 413–15.

Derocher, A. E., M. Andersen, and Ø. Wiig. 2005. Sexual dimorphism of polar bears. *Journal of Mammalogy* 86(5): 895–901.

Derocher, A. E., D. Andriashek, and I. Stirling. 1993. Terrestrial foraging by polar bears during the ice-free period in Hudson Bay. *Arctic* 46(3): 251–54.

Derocher, A. E., N. J. Lunn, and I. Stirling. 2004. Polar bears in a warming climate. *Integrative and Comparative Biology* 44(2): 163–76.

Derocher, A. E., Ø. Wiig, and M. Andersen. 2002. Diet composition of polar bears in Svalbard and the western Barents Sea. *Polar Biology* 25(6): 448–52.

Derocher, A. E., Ø. Wiig, and G. Bangjord. 2000. Predation of Svalbard reindeer by polar bears. *Polar Biology* 23(3): 675–78.

Derocher, A. E., R. A. Nelson, I. Stirling, and M. A. Ramsay. 1990. Effects of fasting and feeding on serum urea and serum creatinine levels in polar bears. *Marine Mammal Science* 6(3): 196–203.

Derocher, A. E., Ø. Wiig, I. Gjertz, K. Bøkseth, and J. O. Scheie. 1998. Status of polar bears in Norway 1993–1996. Pp. 101–11 in *Proceedings of the Twelfth Working Meeting of the IUCN/SSC Polar Bear Specialist Group, February 3–7, 1977, Oslo, Norway.* IUCN.

Derocher, A. E., H. Wolkers, T. Colborn, M. Schlabach, T. S. Larsen, and Ø. Wiig. 2003. Contaminants in Svalbard polar bear samples archived since 1967 and possible population level effects. *Science of the Total Environment* 301(1–3): 163–74.

Derr, M. 2003. Big beasts, tight space and a call for change. *New York Times,* Oct. 2.

De Veer, G. 1598. *A true Description of three Voyages by the North-East towards Cathay and China, undertaken by the Dutch in the Years 1594, 1595, and 1596 by Gerrit de Veer. Published at Amsterdam in the Year 1598, and in 1609 translated into English by William Phillip.* Hakluyt Society reprint, 1853.

Dieck, H. 1885. *The Marvelous Wonders of the Polar World. Being a Complete and Authentic History of Voyages and Discoveries in the Polar Regions . . . etc.* National Publishing Company.

Dietz, R., R. Bossi, E. F. Riget, S. Sonne, and E. W. Born. 2008. Increasing perfluoroalkyl contaminants in East Greenland polar bears *(Ursus maritimus):* A new toxic threat to the Arctic bears. *Environmental Science and Technology* 42(7): 2701–07.

Dijksman, R. 1986. Death on Jan Mayen: A whaling tragedy of 1634. *Polar Record* 23(143): 196–201.

Di Menna, J., and S. Flick. 2004. Arctic meltdown. *Canadian Geographic* 124(5): 44–45.

Dodge, E. S. 1961. *Northwest by Sea.* Oxford University Press.

Doupé, J. P., J. H. England, M. Furze, and D. Paetkau. 2007. Most northerly observation of a grizzly bear *(Ursus arctos)* in Canada: Photographic and DNA evidence from Melville Island, Northwest Territories. *Arctic* 60(3): 271–76.

Doutt, J. K. 1940. Polar bears in the Gulf of St. Lawrence. *Journal of Mammalogy* 21:90–92.

———. 1967. Polar bear dens on the Twin Islands, James Bay, Canada. *Journal of Mammalogy* 48(3): 468–71.

Doyle, A. C. 1897. Life on a Greenland whaler. *Strand Magazine* 13:16–25.

Doyle, L. 2008. US enacts law to protect polar bears, but only from hunting. *The Independent* (UK), May 15.

Drew, L. 1997. Tales of the great white bear. *National Wildlife* 35(1): 14–20.

Dufresne, F. 1946. *Alaska's Animals & Fishes.* A. S. Barnes and Company.

Dupre, L. 2000. *Greenland Expedition.* NorthWord.

Durner, G. M., and S. C. Amstrup. 1995. Movements of a polar bear from northern Alaska to northern Greenland. *Arctic* 48(4): 338–41.

Durner, G. M., S. C. Amstrup, and J. Ambrosius. 2001. Remote identification of polar bear den habitat in northern Alaska. *Arctic* 54:115–21.

Durner, G. M., S. C. Amstrup, and A. S. Fishbach. 2003. Habitat characteristics of polar bear terrestrial den sites in northern Alaska. *Arctic* 56(1): 55–62.

Durner, G. M., D. C. Douglas, R. M. Nielson, S. C. Amstrup, and T. L. McDonald. 2007. Predicting the future distribution of polar bear habitat in the polar basin from resource selection functions applied to 21st century general circulation model projections of sea ice. *U.S. Geological Survey Administrative Report.*

Dyck, M. G. 2006. Characteristics of polar bears killed in defense of life and property in Nunavut, Canada, 1970–2000. *Ursus* 17(1): 52–62.

Dyck, M. G., and R. K. Baydack. 2004. Vigilance behaviour of polar bears *(Ursus maritimus)* in the context of wildlife-viewing activities at Churchill, Manitoba, Canada. *Biological Conservation* 116:343–50.

Dyck, M. G., and K. J. Daley. 2002. Cannibalism of a yearling polar bear *(Ursus maritimus)* at Churchill, Canada. *Arctic* 56(2): 190–92.

Dyck, M. G., and S. Romberg. 2007. Observations of a wild polar bear *(Ursus maritimus)* successfully fishing Arctic charr *(Salvelinus alpinus)* and fourhorn sculpin *(Myoxocephalus quadricornus). Polar Biology* 30(12): 1625–28.

Dyck, M. G., W. Soon, R. K. Baydack, D. R. Legates, S. Baliunas, and L. O. Hancock. 2007. Polar bears of western Hudson Bay and climate change: Are warming spring air temperatures the "ultimate" survival control factor? *Ecological Complexity* 4(3): 73–84.

Eaton, R. D. P., and J. P. Farant. 1982. The polar bear as a biological indicator of the environmental mercury burden. *Arctic* 35(3): 422–25.

Eber, D. H. 2002. Recording the spirit world. *Natural History* 111(7): 54–62.

Egede, H. 1729. *Det gamle Grønlands nye perlustration.* Copenhagen. English edition, T. and J. Allman, London, 1818.

Ehrenfeld, D. W. 1970. *Biological Conservation.* Holt, Rinehart and Winston.

Ehrlich, G. 2006. Last days of the ice hunters? *National Geographic* 209(1): 78–101.

Eilperin, J. 2007. Interior reviewed studies weighing risks to polar bear. *Washington Post,* Apr. 15.

Eliasson, K. 2006. *Polar Bears of Churchill.* Munck's Cafe.

———. 2008. Polar Bear Alley Web site, www. polarbearalley.com

Eliot, J. L. 1998. Polar bears: Stalkers of the High Arctic. *National Geographic* 193(1): 52–71.

————. 2004. White on white: Polar bears. *National Geographic* 205(2): 30–47.

————. 2005. Refuge in white: Winter in a Canadian National Park. *National Geographic* 208(6): 46–57.

Ellis, R. 1975. *The Book of Sharks*. Grosset & Dunlap.

————. 1991. *Men and Whales*. Knopf.

————. 2005. *Tiger Bone & Rhino Horn: The Destruction of Wildlife for Traditional Chinese Medicine*. Island Press.

Evans, T. J., A. Fischbach, S. Schliebe, B. Manly, S. Kalxdorff, and G. York. 2003. Polar bear aerial survey in the eastern Chukchi Sea: A pilot study. *Arctic* 56(4): 359–66.

Farnsworth, C. H. 1992. Social season for bears: Not in the kitchen, please. *New York Times*, Nov. 23.

Fay, F. H. 1960. Carnivorous walrus and some Arctic zoonoses. *Arctic* 13(2): 111–22.

————. 1982. Ecology and biology of the Pacific walrus, *Odobenus rosmarus divergens* Illiger. *U.S. Fish and Wildlife Service North American Fauna* 74:1–279.

————. 1985. Odobenus rosmarus [Walrus]. *Mammalian Species* 238:1–7. American Society of Mammalogists.

Feazel, C. T. 1990. *White Bear*. Henry Holt.

Federal Register. 2007. *Endangered and Threatened Wildlife and Plants; 12-Month Petition Finding and Proposed Rule to List the Polar Bear (Ursus maritimus) as Threatened Throughout Its Range*. 50 CFR, part 17. Department of the Interior, Fish and Wildlife Service.

Fenlon, B. 2007. Terror of the north on the brink. *Toronto Globe & Mail*, Dec. 29.

Ferguson, S. H., M. K. Taylor, and F. Messier. 2000. Influence of sea ice dynamics on habitat selection by polar bears. *Ecology* 81(4): 761–72.

Ferguson, S. H., M. K. Taylor, A. Rosing-Asvid, E. W. Born, and F. Messier. 2000. Relationships between denning of polar bears and conditions of sea ice. *Journal of Mammalogy* 81(4): 1118–27.

Fertl, D., M. Reddy, and E. D. Stoops. 2000. *Bears*. Sterling.

Fischer, J. 1903. *The Discoveries of the Norsemen in America with Special Relation to their Early Cartographical Representation*. Translated from the German by Basil H. Soulsby. Henry Stevens, Son & Stiles.

Fishbach, A. S., S. C. Amstrup, and D. C. Douglas. 2007. Landward and eastward shift of Alaskan polar bear denning associated with recent sea ice changes. *Polar Biology* 30(11): 1395–1405.

Fisher, J., N. Simon, and J. Vincent. 1969. *Wildlife in Danger*. Viking.

Flyger, V. 1967a. Polar bear studies during 1966. *Arctic* 20(1): 53.

————. 1967b. The polar bear: A matter for international concern. *Arctic* 20(3): 147–53.

Fox, C. P. 1977. Awesome Arctic ice bears. Pp. 5–11 in *106th Edition Souvenir Program and Magazine*. Ringling Bros. and Barnum and Bailey Circus.

Freeman, M. R. 1973. Polar bear predation on beluga in the Canadian Arctic. *Arctic* 26(2): 163–64.

Freeman, M. R., and G. W. Wenzel. 2006. The nature and significance of polar bear conservation hunting in the Canadian Arctic. *Arctic* 59(1): 21–30.

Freuchen, P. 1935. *Arctic Adventure*. Farrar & Rinehart.

Frey, D. 2002. George Divorky's planet. *New York Times,* Jan. 6.

Friedlander, A. S., D. W. Johnston, S. L. Fink, and D. M. Lavigne. 2007. Variation in ice cover on the east coast of Canada, February–March, 1969–2006: Implications for harp and hooded seals. *IFAW Technical Report* 2007-1:1–8.

Garfield, S. 2007. Living on thin ice. *Observer Magazine,* Mar. 4.

Gillies Ross, W. 1985. *Arctic Whalers, Icy Seas.* Irwin.

Gingrich, N., and T. L. Maple. 2007. *A Contract with the Earth.* Johns Hopkins University Press.

Gjertz, I., and C. Lydersen. 1986. Polar bear predation on ringed seals in the fast-ice of Hornsund, Svalbard. *Polar Research* 4:65–68.

Gjertz, I., and E. Persen. 1987. Confrontations between humans and polar bears in Svalbard. *Polar Research* 5:253–56.

Gjertz, I., S. Aarvik, and R. Hindrum. 1993. Polar bears killed in Svalbard 1987–1992. *Polar Research* 12(2): 107–09.

Gore, A. 2006. *An Inconvenient Truth.* Rodale.

Gosnell, M. 2005. *Ice.* Knopf.

Gough, W. A., and E. Wolfe. 2001. Climate change scenarios for Hudson Bay, Canada, from general circulation models. *Arctic* 54(3): 142–48.

Graff, J. 2007. Fight for the top of the world. *Time* 170(14): 28–33.

Grambo, R. L., and D. J. Cox. 2000. *Bear: A Celebration of Power and Beauty.* Sierra Club.

Graverson, R. G., T. Mauritsen, M. Tjernström, E. Källén, and G. Svensson. 2008. Vertical structure of recent Arctic warming. *Nature* 541:53–56.

Gregory, J. M., P. Huybrechts, and S. B. Raper. 2004. Threatened loss of the Greenland ice sheet. *Nature* 428:616.

Grüner, T. 2005. Hunters win hike in polar bear quota. *NatureNews,* Apr. 4.

Gurvich, I. S. 1988. Ethnic connections across Bering Strait. Pp. 17–21, 39–42 in W. W. Fitzhugh and A. Crowell, eds., *Crossroads of Continents: Cultures of Siberia and Alaska.* Smithsonian Institution.

Haave, M., E. Ropstad, A. E. Derocher. E. Lie, E. Dahl, Ø. Wiig, J. U. Skaare, and B. M. Jenssen. 2003. Polychlorinated biphenyls and reproductive hormones in female polar bears at Svalbard. *Environmental Health Perspectives* 111(4): 431–36.

Hacquebord, L. 1991. Five early European winterings in the Atlantic Arctic (1596–1635): A comparison. *Arctic* 44(2): 146–55.

———. 1995. In search of *Het Behouden Huys:* A survey of the remains of the house of Willem Barentsz on Novaya Zemlya. *Arctic* 48(3): 248–56.

———. 2005. Whaling, historical. Pp. 2174–79 in M. Nuttall, ed., *Encyclopedia of the Arctic.* Routledge.

Hagenbeck, C. 1910. *Beasts and Men.* Longmans & Co.

Hahn, D. 2004. *The Tower Menagerie.* Tarcher/Penguin.

Hahn, E. 1967. *Animal Gardens.* Doubleday.

Hall, A. 2008. Zoo leaves polar bears to starve. *The Observer,* Jan. 6.

Hall, E. R., and K. R. Kelson. 1959. *The Mammals of North America.* Ronald Press.

Halpin, J. 2008a. Polar bear's village visit ends in its death. *Anchorage Daily News-Miner,* Jan. 5.

———. 2008b. Details emerge on Kenai Peninsula grizzly mauling. *Anchorage Daily News-Miner,* Apr. 24.

Hand, E. 2008. Antarctic ice loss speeding up. *NatureNews,* Jan. 13.

Hanna, E., P. Huybrechts, K. Steffen, J. Cappellen, R. Huff, S. Shuman, T. Irvine-Fynn, S. Wise, and M. Griffiths. 2008. Increased runoff from melt from the Greenland Ice Sheet: A response to global warming. *Journal of Climate* 21(2): 331–40.

Hanna, G. D. 1920. Mammals of the St. Matthew Islands, Bering Sea. *Journal of Mammalogy* 1:18–22.

Hansen, J. 2004. Can we defuse the global warming time bomb? *Scientific American* 290(3): 68–77.

———. 2006. The threat to the planet. *New York Review of Books* 53(12): 14–21.

Hansen, J., and A. A. Lacis. 1990. Sun and dust versus greenhouse gases: An assessment of their relative roles in global climate change. *Nature* 346:713–19.

Hansen, J., M. Sato, R. Reudy, A. Lacis, and V. Oinas. 2000. Global warming in the twenty-first century: An alternative scenario. *Proceedings of the National Academy of Sciences* 97(18): 9875–80.

Hansen, J., M. Sato, P. Kharecha, G. Russell, D. W. Lea, and M. Siddall. 2007. Climate change and trace gases. *Philosophical Transactions of the Royal Society A* 365:1925–54.

Hansen, J., M. Sato, R. Ruedy, K. Lo, D. W. Lea, and M. Medina-Elizade. 2006. Global temperature change. *Proceedings of the National Academy of Sciences* 103:14,288–293.

Hansen, J., D. Johnson, A. Lacis, S. Lebedeff, P. Lee, D. Rind, and G. Russell. 1981. Climate impact of increasing atmospheric carbon dioxide. *Science* 213:957–66.

Hansen, K. 2002. *Farewell to Greenland's Wildlife.* Gads Forlag.

Hanson, E. 2002. *Animal Attractions: Nature on Display in American Zoos.* Princeton University Press.

Harington, C. R. 1968. Denning habits of the polar bear (*Ursus maritimus* Phipps). *Canadian Wildlife Service Report Series* 5:1–32.

———. 2008. The evolution of Arctic marine mammals. *Ecological Applications* 18(2): Suppl. S23–40.

Harrison, G. L. 1939. Polar bear in Quebec. *Journal of Mammalogy* 20(4): 503.

Harrison, R. J., and J. E. King. 1968. *Marine Mammals.* Hutchinson University Library.

Harry, L. L., and J. Gibbs-Simpson. 2000. *Coca-Cola Collectible Polar Bears.* Beckett.

Hatkoff, J., I. Hatkoff, and C. Hatkoff. 2007. *Knut: How One Little Polar Bear Captivated the World.* Scholastic Press.

Hearne, S. 1795. *A Journey from Prince of Wales's Fort in Hudson's Bay to the Northern Ocean in the Years 1769, 1770, 1771, and 1772.* Champlain Society ed., 1911.

Hediger, H. 1950. *Wild Animals in Captivity: An Outline of the Biology of Zoological Gardens.* Butterworths Scientific. Dover reprint, 1964.

Helmuth, L. 2007. Interview with Steven Amstrup. *Smithsonian* 38(8): 28.

Hemingway, E. 1995. "The Snows of Kilimanjaro." In *The Snows of Kilimanjaro and Other Stories.* Scribner's.

Herbert, B. 1994. Bears who swim too much. *New York Times,* July 3.

Hisdal, V. 1985. *Geography of Svalbard.* Norsk Polarinstitutt.

Hobson, K. A., and I. Stirling. 1997. Low variation in blood δ^{13} among Hudson Bay polar bears: Implications for metabolism and tracing terrestrial foraging. *Marine Mammal Science* 13(3): 359–67.

Holmes, B. 2007. Special deliverance. *New Scientist* 196(2624): 46–49.

Holobitsky, J. 2007. Overhunting of male polar bears could put species at risk—study. *Edmonton Journal,* Nov. 22.

Hopkin, M. 2006. Polar bears sink deeper into danger. *NatureNews,* May 1.

Hornaday, W. T. 1907. *Popular Official Guide to the New York Zoological Park.* New York Zoological Society.

———. 1922. *The Minds and Manners of Wild Animals.* Scribner's.

Hotton, N. 1968. *The Evidence of Evolution.* American Heritage.

Howat, I. M., I. Joughin, and T. A. Scambos. 2007. Rapid changes in ice discharge from Greenland outlet glaciers. *Science* 315:1559–61.

Hunter, C. M., H. Caswell, M. C. Runge, E. V. Regehr, S. C. Amstrup, and I. Stirling. 2007. Polar bears in the southern Beaufort Sea II: Demography and population growth in relation to sea ice conditions. *U.S. Geological Survey Administrative Report.*

Hunter, M. L. 2007. Climate change and moving species: Furthering the debate on assisted colonization. *Conservation Biology* 21(5): 1356–58.

Huybrechts, P., and J. de Wolde. 1999. The dynamic response of the Greenland and Antarctic ice sheets to multiple-century climatic warming. *Journal of Climate* 12(8): 2169–88.

Illingworth, F. 1952. *Wild Life Beyond the North.* Scribner's.

IPCC. 2007. *Summary for Policymakers of the Synthesis Report of the IPCC Fourth Assessment Report.* Intergovernmental Panel on Climate Change.

Izvestia. 2006. Hungry polar bear sieges Russians for 2 days. Dec. 15.

Jackson, F. G. 1899. *A Thousand Days in the Arctic.* Harper & Brothers.

Jackson, H. T. T. 1939. Polar bear in Lake St. John District, Quebec. *Journal of Mammalogy* 20(3): 253.

Jakobsson, T. E. 2003. Curse of the drift ice. *Iceland Geographic* 1(1): 70–81.

Janes, P. 2006. On thin ice. *Science World* 63(7): 12–14.

Jenness, R., A. W. Erickson, and J. J. Craighead. 1972. Some comparative aspects of milk of four species of bears. *Journal of Mammalogy* 53(1): 34–57.

Jessen, A. 2002. A note on the management of polar bears in Greenland. P. 64 in *Proceedings of the Thirteenth Working Meeting of the IUCN/SSC Polar Bear Specialist Group, June 23–28, 2001, Nuuk, Greenland.* IUCN.

Johnson, C. 2002. Polar bear co-management in Alaska: Co-operative management between the US Fish and Wildlife Service and the native hunters of Alaska for the conservation of polar bears. Pp. 139–41 in *Proceedings of the Thirteenth Working Meeting of the IUCN/SSC Polar Bear Specialist Group, June 23–28, 2001, Nuuk, Greenland.* IUCN.

Joling, D. 2008a. Turf war pits polar bear against pipeline. *Miami Herald,* Feb. 23.

———. 2008b. Alaska officials condemn polar bear listing. *Seattle Post-Intelligencer,* May 14.

———. 2008c. State of Alaska sues over polar bear listing. *Seattle Post-Intelligencer,* Aug. 4.

———. 2009. Court vacates Alaska drilling decision. *Anchorage Daily News,* Mar. 8.

Jonkel, C. 1970. The behavior of captured North American bears (with comments on bear management). *BioScience* 20(21): 1145–47.

Joughin, I., S. B. Das, M. A. King, B. E. Smith, I. M. Howat, and T. Moore. 2008. Seasonal speedup along the western flank of the Greenland Ice Sheet. *Scienc-Express,* Apr. 16.

Kaiser, J. 2002. Breaking up is far too easy. *Science* 297:1494–96.

Kane, E. K. 1856. *Arctic Explorations: The Second Grinnell Expedition in Search of Sir John Franklin, in the Years 1853, '54, '55.* Harper and Brothers.

Karl, T. R., and K. E. Treberth. 1999. The human impact on climate. *Scientific American* 281(6): 100–05.

———. 2003. Modern global climate change. *Science* 302:1719–23.

Kaufman, M. 2008. Escalating ice loss found in Antarctica. *Washington Post,* Jan. 14.

Kay, J. 2008. Groups cite oil leases in U.S. delay on rating polar bear's status. *San Francisco Chronicle,* Jan. 8.

Kazlowski, S. 2008. *The Last Polar Bear.* Braided River.

Keeling, C. H. 2001. Zoological gardens of Great Britain. Pp. 49–74 in V. N. Kisling, ed., *Zoo and Aquarium History: Ancient Animal Collections to Zoological Gardens.* CRC Press.

Keller, M. 2006. The scandal at the zoo. *New York Times,* Aug. 15.

Kellert, S. R. 1999. *American Perceptions of Marine Mammals and Their Management.* Yale University School of Forestry and Environmental Studies.

Kennedy, M., D. Mrfoka, and C. von der Borch. 2008. Snowball Earth termination by stabilization of equatorial permafrost in methane chathrate. *Nature* 453:642–45.

Kenny, D. K., and C. Bickel. 2005. Growth and development of polar bear *(Ursus maritimus)* cubs at Denver Zoological Gardens. *International Zoo Yearbook* 39:205–14.

Kenny, D. K., M. Kenny, C. Bickel, and D. R. Rolling. 2005. *Klondike & Snow.* Roberts Rinehart.

Kerr, R. A. 1989. Hansen vs. the world on the greenhouse threat. *Science* 244:1041–43.

———. 2002a. A warmer Arctic means change for all. *Science* 297:1490–93.

———. 2002b. Whither Arctic ice? Less of it, for sure. *Science* 297:1491.

———. 2006. A worrying trend of less ice, higher seas. *Science* 311:1698–1701.

———. 2007a. Is battered Arctic ice down for the count? *Science* 318:33–34.

———. 2007b. How urgent is climate change? *Science* 318:1230–31.

———. 2008. Greenland ice slipping away but not all that quickly. *Science* 320:301.

Kifner, J. 1994. Stay-at-home SWB, 8, into fitness, seeks thrills. *New York Times,* July 2.

Kiliaan, H. P. L., and I. Stirling. 1978. Observations on overwintering walruses in the eastern Canadian High Arctic. *Journal of Mammalogy* 59:197–200.

Kinne, O. 2003. Climate research: An article unleashed worldwide storms. *Climate Research* 24:197–98.

Kisling, V. N. 2001. *Zoo and Aquarium History: Ancient Animal Collections to Zoological Gardens.* CRC Press.

Kizzia, T. 2007. Alaska polar bears called doomed. *Anchorage Daily News,* Sept. 8.

———. 2008. Polar ice pack loss may break 2007 record. *Anchorage Daily News,* Feb. 8.

Kjelgaard, J. 1949. *Kalak of the Ice.* Holiday House.

Knight, R. J. B. 2006. *The Pursuit of Victory.* Basic Books.

Koon, D. W. 1998. Is polar bear hair fiber optic? *Applied Optics* 37(15): 3198–3200.

Krauss, C. 2006. Bear hunting caught in global warming debate. *New York Times,* May 27.

Kreviazuk, C. 2007. Why 2008 will be the year of the polar bear. *Toronto Globe & Mail,* Dec. 29.

Kristof, N. D. 2007. The big melt. *New York Times,* Aug. 16.

Kucharz, C. 2008. Keeper calls Knut the bear a "psycho." *ABC News.com,* Mar. 26.

Kurtén, B. 1964. The evolution of the polar bear, *Ursus maritimus. Acta Zoologica Fennica* 108:1–26.

Kurtén, B., and E. Anderson. 1980. *Pleistocene Mammals of North America.* Columbia University Press.

Laidre, K. L., and M. P. Heide-Jorgensen. 2005. Arctic sea ice trends and narwhal vulnerability. *Biological Conservation* 121:509–17.

Laidre, K. L., I. Stirling, L. F. Lowry, Ø. Wiig, M. P. Heide-Jorgensen, and S. H. Ferguson. 2008. Quantifying the sensitivity of Arctic marine mammals to climate-induced habitat change. *Ecological Applications* 18(2): Suppl. S97–125.

Lander, S. 2008. Boffins fear Arctic ice melting could see the rise of a polar bear and grizzly hybrid—dubbed the "grolar bear." *The Sun,* May 7.

Larocco, P. 2008. Bear attack sudden, inexplicable. *Press Enterprise,* Apr. 23.

Larsen, T. 1971a. The polar bear: Lonely nomad of the north. *National Geographic* 139(4): 574–90.

———. 1971b. Sexual dimorphism in the molar rows of the polar bear. *Journal of Wildlife Management* 35(2): 374–78.

———. 1978. *The World of the Polar Bear.* Hamlyn.

———. 1984. We've saved the ice bear. *International Wildlife* 14(4): 4–11.

Larson, L. M., trans. 1917. *The King's Mirror (Speculum Regale—Konungs Skuggsjá).* American Scandinavian Foundation, Oxford University Press.

Lavers, C. 2000. *Why Elephants Have Big Ears.* St. Martin's.

Lavigne, D. M., and K. M. Kovacs. 1988. *Harps and Hoods: Ice-Breeding Seals of the Northwest Atlantic.* University of Waterloo Press.

Leahy, S. 2008. Polar bears in limbo as drilling leases go forward. *Inter Press Service News Agency,* Apr. 10.

Leeder, J. 2008. Huge chunk snaps off storied ice shelf. *Toronto Globe & Mail,* July 29.

Lehane, B. 1981. *The Northwest Passage.* Time-Life Books.

Lennox, A. R., and A. E. Goodship. 2007. Polar bears *(Ursus maritimus),* the most evolutionarily advanced hibernators, avoid significant bone loss during hibernation. *Comparative Biochemistry and Physiology* 149(2): 203–08.

Lentfer, J. W. 1975. Polar bear denning on drifting sea ice. *Journal of Mammalogy* 59(3): 716–18.

———. 1978. Polar bear. Pp. 218–25 in D. Haley, ed., *Marine Mammals of Eastern North Pacific and Arctic Waters.* Pacific Search Press.

———. 1979. Solitary sea bear. *Oceans* 12(5): 49–54.

———. 1983. Alaskan polar bear movements from mark and recovery. *Arctic* 36(3): 282–88.

Lentfer, J. W., and W. A. Galster. 1987. Mercury in polar bears from Alaska. *Journal of Wildlife Diseases* 23(2): 338–41.

Lenton, T. M., H. Held., E. Kriegler, J. W. Hall, W. Lucht, S. Rahmstorf, and H. J. Schnellnhuber. 2008. Tipping elements in the Earth's climate system. *Proceedings of the National Academy of Sciences* 105:1786–93.

Lewis, H. F., and J. K. Doutt. 1942. Records of the Atlantic walrus and the polar bear in or near the Northern part of the Gulf of St. Lawrence. *Journal of Mammalogy* 23(4): 365–74.

Lewis-Jones, H. W. G. 2005. Nelson and the bear: The making of an arctic myth. *Polar Record* 219:335–53.

Lipton, B. 1977. *Survival: Life and Art of the Alaskan Eskimo.* Newark Museum/ American Federation of the Arts.

Lønø, O. 1970. The polar bear (*Ursus maritimus* Phipps) in the Svalbard area. *Skrifter 149.* Norsk Polarinstitutt.

Lopez, B. H. 1986. *Arctic Dreams.* Scribner's.

Lunn, N. J., and I. Stirling. 1985. The significance of supplemental food to polar bears during the ice-free period of Hudson Bay. *Canadian Journal of Zoology* 63(10): 2291–97.

Lunn, N. J., I. Stirling, D. Andriashek, and G. B. Kolenosky. 1997. Re-estimating the size of the polar bear population in western Hudson Bay. *Arctic* 50: 234–40.

Lunn, N. J., S. Atkinson, M. Branigan, W. Calvert, D. Clark, B. Doige, C. Elliott, J. Nagy, M. Obbard, R. Otto, I. Stirling, M. Taylor, D. Vandal, and M. Wheatley. 2002. Polar bear management in Canada 1997–2000. Pp. 41–52 in *Proceedings of the Thirteenth Working Meeting of the IUCN/SSC Polar Bear Specialist Group, June 23–28, 2001, Nuuk, Greenland.* IUCN.

Lydersen, K. 2008. Oil group joins Alaska in suing to overturn polar bear protection. *Washington Post,* Aug. 31.

Lyons, R. C. 1992. Weather to make a polar bear glad to be alive. *New York Times,* Feb. 9.

Macdonald, D. 1992. *The Velvet Claw: A Natural History of the Carnivores.* BBC Books.

———, ed. 2001. *The Encyclopedia of Mammals.* Andromeda.

Macleod, I., ed. 1979. *To the Greenland Whaling: Alexander Trotter's Journal of the Voyage of the "Enterprise" in 1856 from Fraserburgh & Lerwick.* Thule Press.

Magnus, O. 1555. *Historia de gentribus septentrionalibus.* Antwerp.

Manning, D. P. 1985. Studies on the footpads of the polar bear *(Ursus maritimus)* and their possible relevance to accident prevention. *Journal of Hand Surgery* 10(3): 303–07.

Manning, T. H. 1961. Comments on "Carnivorous walrus and some Arctic zoonoses." *Arctic* 14(1): 76–77.

Markham, C. R. 1889. *The Life of John Davis, The Navigator, 1550–1605, Discoverer of the Davis Strait.* George Philip.

Martens, F. 1694. *Voyage into Spitzbergen.* In A. White, ed., *A Collection of Documents on Spitzbergen & Greenland.* Hakluyt Society reprint, 1855.

Matthews, D., and D. Guravich. 1993. *Polar Bear.* Chronicle.

Mauritzen, M., A. E. Derocher, and Ø. Wiig. 2001. Space-use strategies of female polar bears in a dynamic sea-ice habitat. *Canadian Journal of Zoology* 77(11): 1704–13.

Mauritzen, M., A. E. Derocher, O. Pavlova, and Ø. Wiig. 2003. Female polar bears *(Ursus maritimus)* in the Barents Sea drift ice: Walking the treadmill. *Animal Behavior* 66(1): 107–13.

Maxwell, G. 1967. *Seals of the World.* Houghton Mifflin.

Mayhew, P. J., G. B. Jenkins, and T. G. Benton. 2007. A long-term association between global temperature and biodiversity, origination and extinction in the fossil record. *Proceedings of the Royal Society B,* Oct. 23, 2007.

McCarthy, J. J., and M. C. McKenna. 2000. How the Earth's ice is changing. *Environment* 42(10): 8–18.

McClintock, F. L. 1875. *The Voyage of the Fox in the Arctic Seas in Search of Franklin and his Companions.* John Murray.

McClintock, J., H. Ducklow, and W. Fraser. 2008. Ecological responses to climate change on the Antarctic Peninsula. *American Scientist* 96(4): 302–10.

McGrath, C. 2006. Commander of sea, myth, and tea towel. *New York Times,* Jan. 2.

McKibben, B. 1989. *The End of Nature.* Anchor Doubleday.

McKie, R. 2008. Meltdown in the Arctic is speeding up. *London Observer,* Aug. 10.

McLachlan, J. S., J. J. Hellmann, and M. W. Schwartz. 2007. A framework for debate of assisted migration in an era of climate change. *Conservation Biology* 21(2): 297–302.

McLaughlin, J. F., J. J. Hellmann, C. L. Boggs, and P. R. Ehrlich. 2002. Climate change hastens population extinctions. *Proceedings of the National Academy of Sciences* 99(9): 6070–74.

McLemore, A. 2008. Bush gives OK for oil companies to harm polar bears. *Raw Story,* June 14.

Mecking, L. 1928. The polar regions: A regional geography. Pp. 93–359 in O. Nordenskjöld and L. Mecking, *The Geography of the Polar Regions.* American Geographical Society.

Mehlum, F. 1990. *Birds and Mammals of Svalbard.* Norsk Polarinstitutt.

Meier, M. F., M. B. Dyurgerov, U. K. Rick, S. O'Neel, W. T. Pfeffer, R. S. Anderson, S. P. Anderson, and A. F. Glazovsky. 2007. Glaciers dominate eustatic sea-level rise in the 21st century. *Science* 317:1064–67.

Meretsky, V. 2008. Do polar bears belong on the endangered species list? *McClatchy-Tribune News Service,* Feb. 17.

Milkowski, S. 2008. Stevens: Polar bear listing could threaten pipeline development. *Fairbanks Daily News-Miner,* Jan. 10.

Mills, W. 1984. White lords of the Arctic. *SeaFrontiers* 30(6): 348–58.

Melville, H. 1851. *Moby-Dick.* 1967 Norton Critical Edition, edited by H. Hayford and H. Parker. W.W. Norton.

Meyers, S. L., A. C. Revkin, S. Romero, and C. Krauss. 2005. Old ways of life are fading as the Arctic thaws. *New York Times,* Oct. 20.

Milius, S. 2003. Carnivores in captivity: Size of range in wild may predict risk in zoo. *Science News* 164(14): 211.

———. 2007a. Den mothers. *Science News* 172(3): 37.

———. 2007b. Hey, what about us? *Science News* 172(22): 346–48.

Mirsky, J. 1970. *To the Arctic! The Story of Northern Exploration from Earliest Times to the Present.* Allan Wingate.

Mittelstaedt, M. 2008a. U.S. to protect polar bears. *Toronto Globe & Mail,* May 15.

———. 2008b. Nunavut rejects call to curb polar bear hunt. *Toronto Globe & Mail,* Nov. 6.

Molnár, P., A. E. Derocher, M. A. Lewis, and M. K. Taylor. 2007. Modeling the mating system of polar bears: A mechanistic approach to the Allee effect. *Proceedings of the Royal Society B,* 275:217–26.

Molnia, B. 2003. Journey to Planet Earth, www. pbs.org/journeytoplanetearth

Monnett, C., and J. S. Gleason. 2006. Observations of mortality associated with extended open-water swimming by polar bears in the Alaskan Beaufort Sea. *Polar Biology* 29(8): 681–87.

Moore, S. E., and H. P. Huntington. 2008. Arctic marine mammals and climate change: Impacts and resilience. *Ecological Applications* 18(2): Suppl. S157–65.

Morrison, J. 2004. The incredible shrinking polar bears. *National Wildlife* 42(2): 18–23.

Mountfield, D. 1974. *A History of Polar Exploration.* Hamlyn.

Mowat, F. 1984. *Sea of Slaughter.* Atlantic Monthly Press.

Mowry, T. 2008. Why did the polar bear cross the Brooks Range? Biologists are baffled. *Fairbanks Daily News-Miner,* Mar. 28.

Muir, J. 1918. *The Cruise of the Corwin: Journal of the Arctic Expedition of 1881 in Search of De Long and the Jeannette.* Houghton Mifflin. Sierra Club edition, 1993.

Murphy, R. 2008. Science by intimidation. *Toronto Globe & Mail,* June 28.

Myers, S. L. 2007. Russia tries to save polar bears with legal hunt. *New York Times,* Apr. 16.

Nansen, F. 1897. *Farthest North.* Archibald Constable.

———. 1925. *Hunting and Adventure in the Arctic.* Duffield.

Nelson, E. W. 1900. *The Eskimo about Bering Strait.* Smithsonian.

———. 1916. The larger North American mammals. *National Geographic* 30(5): 384–472.

Nelson, R. A., G. E. Folk, E. W. Pfeiffer, J. J. Craighead, C. J. Jonkel, and D. L.

Steiger. 1983. Behavior, biochemistry and hibernation in black, grizzly, and polar bears. *Bears: Their Biology and Management,* vol. 5: *A Selection of papers from the Fifth International Conference on Bear Research and Management, Madison, Wisconsin, February 1980,* pp. 284–90.

Nelson, R. K. 1969. *Hunters of the Northern Ice.* University of Chicago Press.

Nicklen, P. 2007. Life at the edge. *National Geographic* 211(6): 32–55.

Norris, S., L. Rosenstrater, and P. M. Eid. 2002. *Polar Bears at Risk.* WWF-World Wide Fund for Nature.

Oleson, T. J. 1950. Polar bears in the middle ages. *Canadian Historical Review* 31(1): 47–55.

O'Neill, K. 2008. U.S. hunters targeting polar bears while they can. *Toronto Globe & Mail,* Apr. 26.

Øritsland, N. A. 1969. Deep body temperatures of swimming and walking polar bear cubs. *Journal of Mammalogy* 50(2): 380–82.

Øritsland, N. A., J. W. Lentfer, and K. Ronald. 1974. Radiative surface temperatures of the polar bear. *Journal of Mammalogy* 55(2): 459–61.

Ormond, R. 1981. *Sir Edward Landseer.* Philadelphia Museum of Art/Tate Gallery.

Overpeck, J. T., M. Sturm, J. A. Francis, D. K. Petrovich, M. C. Serreze, R. Benner, E. C. Carmack, F. S. Chapin III, S. C. Gerlach, L. C. Hamilton, L. D. Hinzman, M. Holland, H. P. Huntington, J. R. Key, A. H. Lloyd, C. M. MacDonald, J. McFadden, D. Noone, T. D. Prowse, P. Schlosser, and C. Vörösmarty. 2005. Arctic system on trajectory to new, seasonally ice-free state. *Eos* 86(34): 309–16.

Ovsyanikov, N. 1996. *Polar Bears: Living with the White Bear.* Voyageur.

———. 1998. *Polar Bears.* World Life Library.

Paetkau, D., S. C. Amstrup, E. W. Born, W. Calvert, A. E. Derocher, G. W. Garner, F. Messier, I. Stirling, M. K. Taylor, Ø. Wiig, and C. Strobeck. 1999. Genetic structure of the world's polar bear populations. *Molecular Ecology* 8:1571–84.

Page, D., L. Gue, and F. Moola. 2007. *Canada's Polar Bear: Falling Through the Cracks.* David Suzuki Foundation.

Palin, S. 2008. Bearing up. *New York Times,* Jan. 5.

Parkinson, C. L., D. J. Cavalieri, P. Gloersen, H. J. Zwally, and J. C. Comiso. 1999. Arctic sea ice extents, areas, and trends, 1978–1996. *Journal of Geophysical Research (Oceans)* 104(C9): 20,837–40,856.

Parks, E. K., A. E. Derocher, and N. J. Lunn. 2006. Seasonal and annual movement patterns of polar bears on the sea ice of Hudson Bay. *Canadian Journal of Zoology* 84(9): 1281–94.

Patent, D. H. 2000. *Polar Bears.* Carolrhoda Books.

———. 2001. *A Polar Bear Biologist at Work.* Wildlife Conservation Society.

Paterson, T. 2008. Polar position? Flocke, Nuremberg Zoo. *The Independent,* Apr. 8.

Payton, B. 2006. *Shadow of the Bear.* Penguin Canada.

Pearce, F. 2003. Doomsday scenario. *New Scientist* 180(2422): 40–43.

———. 2004. Greenland ice cap "doomed to failure." *New Scientist* 184(2742): 28.

Peary, R. E. 1910. *The North Pole: Its Discovery in 1909 Under the Auspices of the Peary Arctic Club.* Frederick A. Stokes Company.

———. 1917. *Secrets of Polar Travel.* Century.

Pedersen, A. 1962. *Polar Animals.* Harrap.

Pelham, E. 1631. *Gods Power and Providence; Shewed, In the Miraculous Preservation and Deliverance of eight Englishmen, left by mischance in Green-land, Anno 1630, nine months and twelve days.* In A. White, ed., *A Collection of Documents on Spitzbergen & Greenland.* Hakluyt Society reprint, 1855.

Perkins, S. 2007. Portrait of a meltdown. *Science News* 172:287.

Perry, R. 1966. *The World of the Polar Bear.* University of Washington Press.

Phipps, C. 1774. *A Voyage Toward the North Pole.* J. Nourse, London.

Pitkin, H. A. 1950. *Brumas Annual Zoo Book.* Daily Graphic.

Polischuk, S. C., R. J. Norstrom, and M. A. Ramsay. 2002. Body burdens and tissue concentrations of organochlorines in polar bears *(Ursus maritimus)* vary during seasonal fasts. *Environmental Pollution* 118:29–39.

Poulsen, E. M. B. 2004. Captive polar bear diets: What are we doing? *International Polar Bear Husbandry Conference Proceedings, Polar Bears International, February 4–7, 2004, San Diego, California.*

Powell, A. 2001. Some don't like it hot: James McCarthy knows what's around the corner. *Harvard Gazette,* Mar. 2001.

Powys, L. 1927. *Henry Hudson.* John Lane, Bodley Head.

Purchas, S. 1610. *Hakluytvs Posthumus, or, Purchas his Pilgrimes. Contayning a history of the world, in sea voyages, & lande-travells, by Englishmen and others . . . Some left written by Mr. Hakluyt at his death, more since added, his also perused, & perfected. All examined, abbreviated, illustrated with notes, enlarged with discourses, adorned with pictures, and expressed in mapps. In four parts, each containing five bookes. Compiled by Samuel Purchas.* H. Fetherston, 1625. Hakluyt Society reprint, 1906.

Quammen, D. 2003. *Monster of God.* Norton.

Quinn, S. 2008. Oil companies expect battles over polar bear listing. *Seattle Post-Intelligencer,* May 14.

Ragen, T. J., H. P. Huntington, and G. K. Hovelsrud. 2008. Conservation of Arctic marine mammals faced with climate change. *Ecological Applications* 18(2): Suppl. S166–74.

Ramsay, M. A., and I. Stirling. 1984. Interactions of wolves and polar bears in Northern Manitoba. *Journal of Mammalogy* 65(4): 693–94.

———. 1990. Fidelity of female polar bears to winter-den sites. *Journal of Mammalogy* 71(2): 233–36.

Rangel, J. 1987. Boy entered bears' cage on a dare. *New York Times,* May 21.

Rasmussen, K. 1973. *Eskimo Poems from Canada and Greenland.* Translated by Tom Lowenstein. University of Pittsburgh Press.

Raup, D. M. 1991. *Extinction: Bad Genes or Bad Luck?* Norton.

Ray, C. E. 1971. Polar bear and mammoth on the Pribilof Islands. *Arctic* 24(1): 9–18.

Ray, G. C. 1974. Learning the ways of the walrus. *National Geographic* 156(4): 564–80.

Ray, G. C., and M. G. McCormick-Ray. 1981. *Wildlife of the Polar Regions.* Abrams.

Reeves, R. R., B. S. Stewart, P. J. Clapham, and J. A. Powell. 2002. *Guide to the Marine Mammals of the World.* National Audubon Society and Alfred A. Knopf.

Regehr, E. V., N. J. Lunn, S. C. Amstrup, and I. Stirling. 2007. Effects of earlier sea ice breakup on survival and population size of polar bears in western Hudson Bay. *Journal of Wildlife Management* 71(8): 2673–83.

Revelle, R., and H. H. Seuss. 1957. Carbon dioxide exchange between atmosphere and ocean and the question of atmospheric CO_2 during the past decades. *Tellus* 9:18–19.

Revkin, A. C. 1988. Endless summer—Living with the Greenhouse Effect. *Discover* 9(10): 50–61.

———. 2000. Study proposes new strategy to stem global warming. *New York Times,* Aug. 19.

———. 2003a. At the bustling North Pole, here today, gone tomorrow. *New York Times,* Apr. 28.

———. 2003b. Hunt imperils polar bears in Bering Sea, report says. *New York Times,* June 17.

———. 2005a. Bush aide softened greenhouse gas links to global warming. *New York Times,* June 8.

———. 2005b. In melting trend, less ice to go around. *New York Times,* Sept. 29.

———. 2005c. No escape: Thaw gains momentum. *New York Times,* Oct. 25.

———. 2006a. Climate expert says NASA tried to silence him. *New York Times,* Jan. 29.

———. 2006b. Loss of Antarctic ice increases. *New York Times,* Mar. 3.

———. 2006c. Ice retreats in Arctic for 2nd year; some fear most of it will vanish. *New York Times,* Mar. 15.

———. 2006d. Biologists note polar bear cannibalism. *New York Times,* June 13.

———. 2006e. Greenland: Ice cap melting faster. *New York Times,* Aug. 11.

———. 2006f. NASA scientists see new signs of global warming. *New York Times,* Sept. 14.

———. 2006g. By 2040, greenhouse gases could lead to an open Arctic sea in summers. *New York Times,* Dec. 12.

———. 2006h. *The North Pole Was Here.* Kingfisher.

———. 2007a. A team of 2, following the scent of polar bears. *New York Times,* June 5.

———. 2007b. Analysts see "simply incredible" shrinking of floating ice in the Arctic. *New York Times,* Aug. 10.

———. 2007c. Scientists report severe retreat of Arctic ice. *New York Times,* Sept. 21.

———. 2007d. Grim outlook for bears. *New York Times,* Oct. 2.

———. 2007e. Arctic melt unnerves experts. *New York Times,* Oct. 2.

———. 2007f. Arctic update: Resilient bears, shrinking ice. *New York Times,* Dec. 12.

———. 2008a. In Greenland, ice and instability. *New York Times,* Jan. 8.

―――. 2008b. Court forces government to move on polar bear status. *DotEarth,* Apr. 29.

Reynolds, J. N. 1839. *Mocha Dick, or the White Whale of the Pacific.* Scribner's reprint, 1932.

RIA (Russian Information Agency) Novosti. 2008a. WWF says illegal trade in polar bear skins growing in Russia. http://en.rian.ru/russia/20080320/101840778 .html

―――. 2008b. World Wildlife Fund to protect polar bears. http://en.rian.ru/ russia/20080325/102147931.html

Richardson, E., I. Stirling, and D. S. Hik. 2005. Polar bear (*Ursus maritimus*) maternity denning habitat in western Hudson Bay: A bottom-up approach to resource selection functions. *Canadian Journal of Zoology* 83:860–70.

Richardson, E., I. Stirling, and B. Kochtubajda. 2006. The effects of forest fires on maternity denning habitat in western Hudson Bay. *Polar Biology* 30(3): 369–78.

Ridgway, S. H., ed. 1972. *Mammals of the Sea: Biology and Medicine.* Charles C. Thomas.

Ridgway, S. H., and R. J. Harrison, eds. 1981–1999. *Handbook of Marine Mammals.* Six vols. Academic Press.

Ridley, G. 2004. *Clara's Grand Tour: Travels with a Rhinoceros in Eighteenth Century Europe.* Atlantic Books.

Rignot, E., J. L. Bamber, M. R. van den Broeke, C. Davis, Y. Li, W. J. van de Berg, and E. van Meijgaard. 2008. Recent Antarctic ice mass loss from radar interferometry and regional climate modeling. *Nature Geoscience,* 2:106–10.

Roberts, A. M. 2002a. Polar bears suffer at the Suarez Brothers Circus. *Animal Welfare Institute Quarterly* 51(1): 4–6.

―――. 2002b. Saving the Suarez seven. *Animal Welfare Institute Quarterly* 51(2): 3–5.

Roberts, B. 1935. The Cambridge Expedition to Scoresby Sound, East Greenland in 1933. *Geographical Journal* 85(3): 234–51.

Roberts, D. 1982. *Great Exploration Hoaxes.* Sierra Club.

Robinson, A. B., N. E. Robinson, and W. Soon. 2007. Environmental effects of increased atmospheric carbon dioxide. *Journal of American Physicians and Surgeons* 12(3): 79–90.

Rodahl, K., and T. Moore. 1943. The vitamin A content and toxicity of bear and seal liver. *Biochemical Journal* 37:166–68.

Rogers, P. 2006. Polar bear apocalypse. *The Independent,* June 11.

Root, T. L., J. T. Price, K. R. Hall, S. H. Schneider, C. Rosenzweig, and J. A. Pounds. 2003. Fingerprints of global warming on wild animals and plants. *Nature* 421:57–60.

Rosen, Y. 2008. Alaska to sue to block polar bear listing. *Reuters,* May 22.

―――. 2009. Alaska drilling rule vacated, future uncertain. *Reuters,* Mar. 10.

Rosenthal, E. 2007. U.N. report describes risks of inaction on climate change. *New York Times,* Nov. 17.

Rosenthal, E., and A. C. Revkin. 2007. Science panel calls global warming "unequivocal." *New York Times,* Feb. 3.

Rosenzweig, C., D. Karoly, M. Vicarelli, P. Neofotis, Q. Wu, G. Casassa, A. Menzel, T. L. Root, N. Estrella, B. Seguin, P. Tryjanowski, C. Liu, S. Rawlins, and A. Imeson. 2008. Attributing physical and biological impacts to anthropogenic climate change. *Nature* 435:353–57.

Rosing, B. 1998. Issues pertaining to polar bear management in Greenland. Pp. 93–95 in *Proceedings of the Twelfth Working Meeting of the IUCN/SSC Polar Bear Specialist Group, February 3–7, 1977, Oslo, Norway.* IUCN.

Rosing, N. 2000. Bear beginnings: New life on the ice. *National Geographic* 198(6): 30–39.

———. 2006. *The World of the Polar Bear.* Firefly.

Rosing-Arvid, A. 2002. *The Polar Bear Hunt in Greenland.* Technical Report No. 45. Greenland Institute of Natural Resources, Nuuk.

———. 2006. The influence of climate variability on the polar bear (*Ursus maritimus*) and ringed seal (*Pusa hispida*) population dynamics. *Canadian Journal of Zoology* 84(3): 357–64.

Ross, S. R. 2006. Issues of choice and control in the behaviour of a pair of captive polar bears *(Ursus maritimus). Behavioural Processes* 73:117–20.

Rothfels, N. 2002. *Savages and Beasts: The Birth of the Modern Zoo.* Johns Hopkins University Press.

Rothrock, D. A., Y. Yu, and G. A. Maykut. 1999. Thinning of Arctic sea-ice cover. *Geophysical Research Letters* 26(23): 3469–72.

Ruddiman, W. F. 2005. *Plows, Plagues, and Petroleum: How Humans Took Control of Climate.* Princeton University Press.

Russell, R. H. 1975. The food habits of polar bears of James Bay and southwest Hudson Bay in summer and autumn. *Arctic* 28(2): 117–29.

Rynor, B. 2008. Man drives to safety after grizzly bear attack. *National Post* (Canada), May 7.

Ryskin, G. 2003. Methane-driven oceanic eruptions and mass extinctions. *Geology* 31(9): 741–44.

Savours, A. 1984. "A very interesting point in geography": The 1773 Phipps Expedition towards the North Pole. *Arctic* 37(4): 402–28.

Savoury, E. 2004. The shrinking polar bears. *CBC News Online,* July 6.

Schiermeier, Q. 2004. A rising tide. *Nature* 428:114–15.

———. 2008. The long summer begins. *Nature* 454:266–69.

Schliebe, S., and K. Johnson. 2008. *Endangered and Threatened Wildlife and Plants: Determination of Threatened Status for the Polar Bear (Ursus maritimus) Throughout its Range.* U.S. Department of the Interior, Fish and Wildlife Service.

Schrope, M. 2001. Polar bears fuel row over Alaskan oil. *Nature* 414:240.

Schulman, A. 1994. *The Cage.* Avon Books.

Schweinsburg, R. E. 1979. Summer snow dens used by polar bears in the Canadian high Arctic. *Arctic* 32(2): 165–69.

Schweinsburg, R. E., and L. J. Lee. 1982. Movement of four satellite-monitored polar bears in Lancaster Sound, Northwest Territories. *Arctic* 35(4): 505–11.

Schweinsburg, R. E., L. J. Lee, and P. B. Latour. 1982. Distribution, movement and abundance of polar bears in Lancaster Sound, Northwest Territories. *Arctic* 35(1): 159–69.

Scoresby, W. 1820. *An Account of the Arctic Regions with a History and Description of the Northern Whale-Fishery.* Two vols. Archibald Constable. David & Charles reprint, 1969.

Seattle Post-Intelligencer. 2008. Endangered Species Act: Who needs laws? editorial, Aug. 13.

Serreze, M. C., M. Holland, and J. Strove. 2007. Perspectives on Arctic's shrinking ice cover. *Science* 315:1533–66.

Serreze, M. C., J. A. Maslanik, T. A. Scambos, E. Fetterer, J. Stroeve, K. Knowles, C. Fowler, S. Drobot, R. G. Barry, and T. M. Haran. 2003. A record minimum arctic sea ice extent in 2002. *Geophysical Research Letters* 30(3): 1110.

Serreze, M. C., J. E. Walsh, F. S. Chapin, T. Osterkamp, M. Dyurgerov, V. Romanovsky, W. C. Oechel, J. Morrison, T. Zhang, and R. G. Barry. 2000. Observational evidence of recent change in the northern high latitude environment. *Climatic Change* 46:159–207.

Seton, E. T. 1929. *Lives of Game Animals.* Vol. 2, part I: *Bears, Coons, Badgers, Skunks, and Weasels.* Doubleday Page. C. T. Branford reprint, 1953.

Shabecoff, P. 1988. Global warming has begun, expert tells senate. *New York Times,* June 24.

Shipp, E. R. 1982. Polar bear in the Central Park Zoo kills man who climbed into cage. *New York Times,* Sept. 27.

Shirley, R. 2008. Bears are not the only bait for Arctic travel. *Boston Globe,* Jan. 20.

Shnayerson, M. 2008. The edge of extinction. *Vanity Fair* 573 (May): 246–53, 275–78.

Shukman, D. 2007. Vast ice island trapped in Arctic. *BBC News,* Aug. 31.

———. 2008. Vast cracks in Arctic ice. *BBC News,* May 23.

Simon, N., and P. Géroudet. 1970. *Last Survivors.* World.

Skaare, J. U., A. Bernhoft, A. Derocher, G. W. Gabrielsen, A. Goksøyr, E. Henriksen, H. J. Larsen, E. Lie, and Ø. Wiig. 2000. Organochlorines in top predators at Svalbard—occurrence, level, and effects. *Toxicology Letters* 112–113:103–09.

Smith, C. E. 1923. *From the Depths of the Sea: An Epic of the Arctic.* Macmillan.

Smith, J., R. Stone, and J. Fahrenkamp-Uppenbrink. 2002. Trouble in polar paradise. *Science* 297:1489.

Smith, T. G. 1975. Ringed seals in James Bay and Hudson Bay: population estimates and catch statistics. *Arctic* 28:170–82.

Smith, T. G., and F. A. J. Armstrong. 1978. Mercury and selenium in ringed and bearded seal tissues from Arctic Canada. *Arctic* 31(2): 75–84.

Smith, T. G., and B. Sjare. 1990. Predation on belugas and narwhals by polar bears in nearshore areas of the Canadian high Arctic. *Arctic* 43(2): 99–102.

Smith, T. S., S. Herrero, T. D. Debruyn, and J. M. Wilder. 2008. Efficacy of bear deterrent spray in Alaska. *Journal of Wildlife Management* 72(3): 640–45.

Smithwick, M., S. Mabury, K. R. Solomon, C. Sonne, J. W. Martin, E. W. Born, R. Dietz, A. E. Derocher, R. J. Letcher, T. J. Evans, G. W. Gabrielsen, J. Nagy, I. Stirling, M. K. Taylor, and D. C. G. Muir. 2005. Circumpolar study of perfluoroalkyl contaminants in polar bears *(Ursus maritimus)*. *Environmental Science and Technology* 39(15): 5517–23.

Sonne, C., R. Dietz, P. S. Liefsson, G. Asmund, E. W. Born, and M. Kirkegaard. 2007. Are liver and renal lesions in East Greenland polar bears *(Ursus maritimus)* associated with high mercury levels? *Environmental Health,* 2007, 6:11.

Sonne, C., R. Dietz, P. S. Liefsson, E. W. Born, M. Kirkegaard, R. J. Letcher, D. C. Muir, F. E. Riget, and L. Hyldstrup. 2006. Are organohalogen contaminants a cofactor in the development of renal lesions in East Greenland polar bears *(Ursinus maritimus)*? *Environmental Toxicology and Chemistry* 25(6): 1551–57.

Soon, W., and S. Baliunas. 2003. Proxy climatic and environmental changes in the past 1000 years. *Climate Research* 23:89–110.

Sorooshian, R. 2007. Berlin Zoo left with a sore head now Knut has grown. *Sunday Herald* (Scotland), Dec. 8.

Speidel, G. 1949. Milwaukee's polar bears. *Parks & Recreation* 32:235–36.

Stefansson, V. 1906. Icelandic beast and bird lore. *Journal of American Folklore* 19:300–08.

———. 1913. *My Life with the Eskimo.* Macmillan.

———. 1922. *Hunters of the Great North.* Harcourt Brace Jovanovich. Paragon House reprint, 1990.

———. 1939. *Unsolved Mysteries of the Arctic.* Macmillan.

Stempniewicz, l. 1993. The polar bear *Ursus maritimus* feeding in a seabird colony in Frans Josef Land. *Polar Research* 12(1): 33–36.

———. 2008. Polar bear predatory behaviour toward molting barnacle geese and nesting glaucous gulls on Spitsbergen. *Arctic* 59(3): 247–51.

Stenhouse, G. B., L. J. Lee, and K. G. Poole. 1988. Some characteristics of polar bears killed during conflicts with humans in the Northwest Territories, 1976–86. *Arctic* 41(4): 275–78.

Stephan, J. J. 1994. *The Russian Far East: A History.* Stanford University Press.

Stishov, M. S. 1998. Polar bear research in the Wrangel Island State Nature Reserve, Russia. Pp. 147–52 in *Proceedings of the Twelfth Working Meeting of the IUCN/SSC Polar Bear Specialist Group, February 3–7, 1977, Oslo, Norway.* IUCN.

Stirling, I. 1974. Midsummer observations on the behavior of wild polar bears. *Canadian Journal of Zoology* 52:1191–98.

———. 1988. *Polar Bears.* University of Michigan Press.

———. 1989. Sleeping giants. *Natural History* 1/89:35–41.

———. 2002a. Polar bear. Pp. 945–48 in W. Perrin, B. Würsig, and J. G. M. Thewissen, eds., *Encyclopedia of Marine Mammals.* Academic Press.

———. 2002b. Polar bears and seals in the eastern Beaufort Sea and Amundsen Gulf: A synthesis of population trends and ecological relationships over three decades. *Arctic* 55(Suppl. 1): 59–76.

———. 2005. Polar bears, seals, and climate in Hudson Bay and the High Arctic. *Arctic Research Consortium of the U.S. (ARCUS), Fairbanks, AK.*

Stirling, I., and A. E. Derocher. 1993. Possible impacts of climatic warming on polar bears. *Arctic* 46(3): 240–45.

Stirling, I., and C. Jonkel. 1972. The great white bears. *Nature Canada* 1(3): 30–34.

Stirling, I., and C. L. Parkinson. 2006. Possible effects of climate warming on selected populations of polar bears *(Ursus maritimus)* in the Canadian Arctic. *Arctic* (59)3: 261–75.

Stirling, I., N. J. Lunn, and J. Iocazza. 1999. Long-term trends in the population ecology of polar bears in western Hudson Bay in relation to climatic change. *Arctic* 52(3): 294–306.

Stirling, I., A. E. Derocher, W. A. Gough, and K. Rode. 2007. Response to Dyck et al. (2007) on polar bears and climate change in western Hudson Bay. *Ecological Complexity* 5:193–201.

Stirling, I., E. Richardson, G. W. Thiemann, and A. E. Derocher. 2008. Unusual predation attempts of polar bears on ringed seals in the southern Beaufort Sea: Possible significance of changing spring ice conditions. *Arctic* 61(1): 14–22.

Stirling, I., C. Jonkel, P. Smith, R. Robertson, and D. Cross. 1977. Ecology of the polar bear *(Ursus maritimus)* along the western shore of Hudson Bay. *Canadian Wildlife Service Occasional Paper* 33:1–64.

Stirling, I., N. J. Lunn, J. Iacozza, C. Elliott, and M. Obbard. 2004. Polar bear distribution and abundance on the southwestern Hudson Bay coast during open water season, in relation to population trends and annual ice patterns. *Arctic* 57(1): 15–26.

Stone, I. R., and A. E. Derocher. 2007. An incident of polar bear infanticide and cannibalism on Phippsøya, Svalbard. *Polar Record* 43:171–73.

Stonehouse, B. 1971. *Animals of the Arctic: The Ecology of the Far North.* Holt, Rinehart & Winston.

Strehlow, H. 2001. Zoological gardens of Western Europe. Pp. 75–116 in V. N. Kisling, ed., *Zoo and Aquarium History: Ancient Animal Collections to Zoological Gardens.* CRC Press.

Struzik, E. 1999a. Polar pollution, climate change, bode ill for bears. *Edmonton Journal,* Nov. 29.

———. 1999b. Regal looking Peary [caribou] now hard to find in Arctic. *Edmonton Journal,* Nov. 30.

———. 2006. Grizzly bears on ice. *National Wildlife* 44(2): 32–36.

———. 2007. Polar bears on the brink. *Edmonton Journal,* Dec. 2.

———. 2008a. Grizzly found in polar bear country. *Edmonton Journal,* Feb. 3.

———. 2008b. Wayward polar bears surprise town. *Edmonton Journal,* Apr. 4.

Talley, I. 2008. Polar bear to be designated as threatened species. *Wall Street Journal,* May 14.

Tarpy, C. 1993. New zoos: Taking down the bars. *National Geographic* 184(1): 2–37.

Taylor, F. C. 1988. Close-up look at polar bears in Manitoba. *New York Times,* Feb. 28.

Taylor, M., and J. Lee. 1995. Distribution and abundance of Canadian polar bear populations: A management perspective. *Arctic* 48(2): 147–54.

Taylor, M., T. Larsen, and R. E. Schweinsburg. 1985. Observations of intraspecific aggression and cannibalism in polar bears *(Ursus maritimus). Arctic* 38(4): 303–09.

Tesar, C. 2008. Polar bears are the wrong target, say Inuit. *Native American Times,* Feb. 14.

Thadeusz, F. 2008. New baby polar bear sparks German outcry. *BusinessWeek* (Europe), Jan. 15.

Thomas, C. D., A. Cameron, R. E. Green, M. Bakkenes, L. J. Beaumont, Y. C. Collingham, B. F. N. Erasmus, M. F. De Siquera, A. Grainger, L. Hannah, L. Hughes, B. Huntley, A. S. Van Jaarsveld, G. F. Midgley, L. Miles, M. A. Ortega-Huerta, A. T. Peterson, O. L. Phillips, and S. E. Williams. 2004. Extinction risk from climate change. *Nature* 427:145–48.

Thomé, A. 2005. The polar bears' last stand. *Der Spiegel,* Dec. 23.

Thompson, D. N.d. *David Thompson's Narrative of his Explorations in Western America, 1784–1812.* Transcribed by J. B. Tyrell, Champlain Society, 1916.

Thompson, L. G., E. Mosely-Thompson, M. E. Davis, K. A. Henderson, H. H. Brecher, V. S. Zagorodnov, T. A. Mashiotta, P.-N. Lin, V. N. Mikhalenko, D. R. Hardy, and J. Beer. 2002. Kilimanjaro ice core records: Evidence of Holocene climate change in tropical Africa. *Science* 298:589–93.

Uemura, N. 1978. Solo to the North Pole. *National Geographic* 154(3): 298–325.

Umbreit, A. 1991. *Guide to Spitsbergen.* Bradt.

Usborne, D. 2008. Plans to drill for Alaskan oil threaten polar bear numbers. *The Independent,* Jan. 4.

van Meurs, R., and J. F. Splettstoesser. 2003. Farthest north polar bear (*Ursus maritimus*). *Arctic* 56(3): 309.

Vaughan, R. 1994. *The Arctic: A History.* Alan Sutton.

Verreault, J., D. C. G. Muir, R. J. Norstrom, I. Stirling, A. T. Fisk, G. W. Gabrielson, A. E. Derocher, T. J. Evans, R. Dietz, C. Sonne, G. M. Sandala, W. Gebbink, F. R. Riget, E. W. Born, M. K. Taylor, J. Nagy, and R. J. Letcher. 2005. Chlorinated hydrocarbon contaminants and metabolites in polar bears (*Ursus maritimus*) from Alaska, Canada, East Greenland, and Svalbard: 1996–2002. *Science of the Total Environment* 351–352:369–90.

Vonnegut, K. 2008. *Armageddon in Retrospect.* Putnam.

Wagemann, R., W. L. Lockhart, H. Welch, and S. Innes. 2005. Arctic marine mammals as integrators and indicators of mercury in the Arctic. *Water, Air, & Soil Pollution* 80(1–4): 683–93.

Wald, M. L., and A. C. Revkin. 2007. New task for Coast Guard in Arctic's warming seas. *New York Times,* Oct. 19.

Walker, B. 2006. Killing them softly: Health effects in arctic wildlife linked to chemical exposures. *WWF International Arctic Programme and WWF-DetoX.*

Wallis, H. 1984. England's search for the Northern Passages in the sixteenth and early seventeenth centuries. *Arctic* 37(4): 453–72.

Walsh, B. 2008. Polar bears wait-listed as endangered. *Time* 171(3): 34–35.

Ward, P., and S. Kynaston. 1999. *Bears of the World.* Blandford.

Ward, P. D., and D. Brownlee. 2000. *Rare Earth: Why Complex Life is Uncommon in the Universe.* Copernicus.

Weart, S. R. 2003. *The Discovery of Global Warming.* Harvard University Press.

Weaver, A. J., and C. Hillaire-Marcel. 2004. Global warming and the next ice age. *Science* 304:400–02.

Wenzel, G. 1983. Inuit and polar bears: Cultural observations from a hunt near Resolute Bay, N.W.T. *Arctic* 36(1): 90–94.

———. 2005. Nunavut Inuit and polar bear: The cultural politics of the sport hunt. *Senri Ethnological Studies* 67:363–88.

Whitaker, I. 1985. The King's Mirror [*Konung's Skuggsjá*] and northern research. *Polar Record* 22(141): 615–27.

———. 1986. North Atlantic sea creatures in the King's Mirror [*Konung's Skuggsjá*]. *Polar Record* 22(142): 3–13.

Wilford, J. N. 2000. Ages-old icecap at North Pole is now liquid, scientists find. *New York Times,* Aug. 19.

Wilton, K. 2008. Inuit mom who confronted polar bear to get Medal of Bravery. *Montreal Gazette,* Jan. 17.

Wiig, Ø. 2005. Are polar bears threatened? *Science* 309:1814.

Wiig, Ø., and V. Bakken. 1990. Aerial strip surveys of polar bears in the Barents Sea. *Polar Research* 8:309–11.

Wiig, Ø., E. W. Born, and L. T. Pederson. 2003. Movements of female polar bears *(Ursus maritimus)* in the East Greenland pack ice. *Polar Biology* 26(8): 509–16.

Willerroider, M. 2003. Roaming polar bears reveal Arctic route of pollutants. *Nature* 426:5.

Williams, N. 2007a. US signals threat to global warming icon. *Current Biology* 17(2): R37–38.

———. 2007b. Polar bears shift from thinning ice. *Current Biology* 17(15): R571–72.

Wilson, E. O. 2001. Biodiversity: Wildlife in trouble. Pp. 18–20 in M. J. Novacek, ed., *The Biodiversity Crisis: Losing What Counts.* American Museum of Natural History.

———. 2002. *The Future of Life.* Knopf.

Wittmeyer, A. 2007. Rare hybrid bear comes to Idaho—as a trophy. *Santa Fe New Mexican,* Jan. 21.

Witze, A. 2008. Losing Greenland. *Nature* 452:798–802.

Wolffe, A. P., and M. A. Matzke. 1999. Epigenetics: Regulation through repression. *Science* 286:481–86.

Wood, G. L. 1982. *The Guinness Book of Animal Facts and Feats.* Guinness Superlatives Ltd.

Wright, K. 2005. Our preferred poison [mercury]. *Discover* 26(3): 58–65.

Young, S. 2008. Predators and people: How close can we get? *Chicago Tribune,* Mar. 9.

Zimmer, C. 2007. A radical step to preserve a species: Assisted migration. *New York Times,* Jan. 23.

Zwally, H. J., W. Abdalati, T. Herring, K. Larson, J. Saba, and K. Steffen. 2002. Surface melt-induced acceleration of Greenland ice-sheet flow. *Science* 297:218–22.

Zwiers, F., and G. Hegerl. 2008. Attributing cause and effect. *Nature* 453:296–97.

Index

Page numbers in *italics* refer to illustrations and captions

ILLUSTRATION CREDITS

All illustrations not listed here are courtesy of the author.

PAGE 10 James McCarthy

17 Philadelphia Museum of Art, the Collection of Edgar William and
    Bernice Chrysler Garbisch, 1965

19 Gerrit de Veer, 1598

25 From *Marvelous Wonders of the Polar World*, 1885

32 Courtesy of National Maritime Museum, Greenwich

34 Courtesy of Royal Holloway Museum, University of London

38 Courtesy of New Bedford Whaling Museum

43 Norbert Rosing, National Geographic Image Collection

44 Norsk Polarinstitutt

47 From *Marvelous Wonders of the Polar World*, 1885

52 Courtesy the Fram Museum, Oslo

64 National Oceanographic and Atmospheric Administration

66 Fred Bruemmer

71 Jürgen Holfort

73 Jürgen Holfort

78 National Oceanographic and Atmospheric Administration

81 Assiniboine Zoo

83 Nancy Harris

87 Robert Barber, CritterZone

89 From *Lives of Game Animals*, 1929

91 Fred Bruemmer

97 Fred Bruemmer

100 National Oceanographic and Atmospheric Administration

On thin ice